# Amazon CloudFront Developer Guide

A catalogue record for this book is available from the Hong Kong Public Libraries.

Published in Hong Kong by Samurai Media Limited.

Email: info@samuraimedia.org

ISBN 9789888407958

# Contents

# What Is Amazon CloudFront?

Amazon CloudFront is a web service that speeds up distribution of your static and dynamic web content, such as .html, .css, .js, and image files, to your users. CloudFront delivers your content through a worldwide network of data centers called edge locations. When a user requests content that you're serving with CloudFront, the user is routed to the edge location that provides the lowest latency (time delay), so that content is delivered with the best possible performance.

- If the content is already in the edge location with the lowest latency, CloudFront delivers it immediately.
- If the content is not in that edge location, CloudFront retrieves it from an Amazon S3 bucket or an HTTP server (for example, a web server) that you have identified as the source for the definitive version of your content.

This concept is best illustrated by an example. Suppose you're serving an image from a traditional web server, not from CloudFront. For example, you might serve an image, sunsetphoto.png, using the URL `http://example.com/sunsetphoto.png`.

Your users can easily navigate to this URL and see the image. But they probably don't know that their request was routed from one network to another—through the complex collection of interconnected networks that comprise the internet—until the image was found.

Now let's say that the web server that you're serving the image from is in Seattle, Washington, USA, and that a user in Austin, Texas, USA requests the image. The following traceroute list (courtesy of www.WatchMouse.com) shows one way that this request could be routed.

```
1   vrid-225.core-sw.aus.us.siteprotect.com (216.139.225.1) 0.627 ms

2   xe-3-4.brdr-rtr-02.aus.us.siteprotect.com (216.139.253.53) 0.219 ms

3   66.113.197.121 0.452 ms

4   xe-5-2-0.edge3.Dallas1.Level3.net (4.59.112.37) 4.978 ms

5   ae-73-70.ebr3.Dallas1.Level3.net (4.69.145.116) 9.817 ms

6   ae-7-7.ebr3.Atlanta2.Level3.net (4.69.134.22) 30.570 ms

7   ae-2-2.ebr1.Washington1.Level3.net (4.69.132.86) 38.801 ms

8   ae-81-81.csw3.Washington1.Level3.net (4.69.134.138) 41.795 ms

9   ae-3-89.edge2.Washington1.Level3.net (4.68.17.145) 39.193 ms

10  72.21.222.139 35.767 ms
```

Map courtesy of the University of Texas Libraries, The University of Texas at Austin

In this example, the request was routed 10 times within the United States before the image was retrieved, which is not an unusually large number of "hops" (the individual network paths between the person viewing the content and the server the file is served from). If your user were in Europe, the request would be routed through even more networks to reach your server in Seattle. The number of networks and the distance that the request and the image must travel have a significant impact on the performance, reliability, and availability of the image.

CloudFront speeds up the distribution of your content by routing each user request to the edge location that can best serve your content. Typically, this is a CloudFront edge server that provides the fastest delivery to the viewer. This dramatically reduces the number of networks that your users' requests must pass through, which improves performance. Users get lower latency—the time it takes to load the first byte of the file—and higher data transfer rates.

You also get increased reliability and availability because copies of your files (also known as *objects)* are now held (or cached) in multiple edge locations around the world.

For a list of the locations of CloudFront edge servers, see the Amazon CloudFront Product Details page.

**Topics**

- How CloudFront Delivers Content
- Locations and IP Address Ranges of CloudFront Edge Servers
- Accessing CloudFront
- CloudFront Pricing
- CloudFront Compliance

# How CloudFront Delivers Content

After some initial setup, CloudFront works invisibly to speed up delivery of your content. This overview includes both the steps you perform before your first user accesses your application or website, and how CloudFront serves your content when viewers request it.

**Topics**

- Setting up CloudFront to Deliver Your Content
- How CloudFront Delivers Content to Your Users
- How CloudFront Works with Regional Edge Caches

## Setting up CloudFront to Deliver Your Content

You create a CloudFront distribution to tell CloudFront where you want content to be delivered from, and the details about how to track and manage content delivery. Then CloudFront uses computers—edge servers—that are close to your viewers to deliver that content quickly when someone wants to see it or use it.

### How You Configure CloudFront to Deliver Your Content

1. You specify *origin servers*, like an Amazon S3 bucket or your own HTTP server, from which CloudFront gets your files which will then be distributed from CloudFront edge locations all over the world.

   An origin server stores the original, definitive version of your objects. If you're serving content over HTTP, your origin server is either an Amazon S3 bucket or an HTTP server, such as a web server. Your HTTP server can run on an Amazon Elastic Compute Cloud (Amazon EC2) instance or on a server that you manage; these servers are also known as *custom origins*.

   If you use the Adobe Media Server RTMP protocol to distribute media files on demand, your origin server is always an Amazon S3 bucket.

2. You upload your files to your origin servers. Your files, also known as *objects*, typically include web pages, images, and media files, but can be anything that can be served over HTTP or a supported version of Adobe RTMP, the protocol used by Adobe Flash Media Server.

   If you're using an Amazon S3 bucket as an origin server, you can make the objects in your bucket publicly readable, so that anyone who knows the CloudFront URLs for your objects can access them. You also have the option of keeping objects private and controlling who accesses them. See Serving Private Content through CloudFront.

3. You create a CloudFront *distribution*, which tells CloudFront which origin servers to get your files from when users request the files through your web site or application. At the same time, you specify details such as whether you want CloudFront to log all requests and whether you want the distribution to be enabled as soon as it's created.

4. CloudFront assigns a domain name to your new distribution that you can see in the CloudFront console, or that is returned in the response to a programmatic request, for example, an API request.

5. CloudFront sends your distribution's configuration (but not your content) to all of its **edge locations**—collections of servers in geographically dispersed data centers where CloudFront caches copies of your objects.

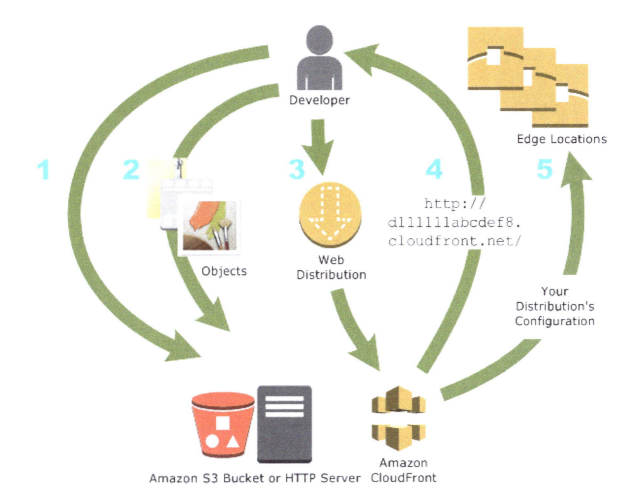

As you develop your website or application, you use the domain name that CloudFront provides for your URLs. For example, if CloudFront returns d111111abcdef8.cloudfront.net as the domain name for your distribution, the URL for logo.jpg in your Amazon S3 bucket (or in the root directory on an HTTP server) will be http://d111111abcdef8.cloudfront.net/logo.jpg.

Or you can configure your CloudFront distribution so you can use your own domain name. In that case, the URL might be http://www.example.com/logo.jpg.

Optionally, you can configure your origin server to add headers to the files, to indicate how long you want the files to stay in the cache in CloudFront edge locations. By default, each object stays in an edge location for 24 hours before it expires. The minimum expiration time is 0 seconds; there isn't a maximum expiration time limit. For more information, see Specifying How Long Objects Stay in a CloudFront Edge Cache (Expiration).

## How CloudFront Delivers Content to Your Users

After you configure CloudFront to deliver your content, here's what happens when users request your objects:

1. A user accesses your website or application and requests one or more objects, such as an image file and an HTML file.

2. DNS routes the request to the CloudFront edge location that can best serve the request—typically the nearest CloudFront edge location in terms of latency—and routes the request to that edge location.

3. In the edge location, CloudFront checks its cache for the requested files. If the files are in the cache, CloudFront returns them to the user. If the files are *not* in the cache, it does the following:

   1. CloudFront compares the request with the specifications in your distribution and forwards the request for the files to the applicable origin server for the corresponding file type—for example, to your Amazon S3 bucket for image files and to your HTTP server for the HTML files.

   2. The origin servers send the files back to the CloudFront edge location.

   3. As soon as the first byte arrives from the origin, CloudFront begins to forward the files to the user. CloudFront also adds the files to the cache in the edge location for the next time someone requests those files.

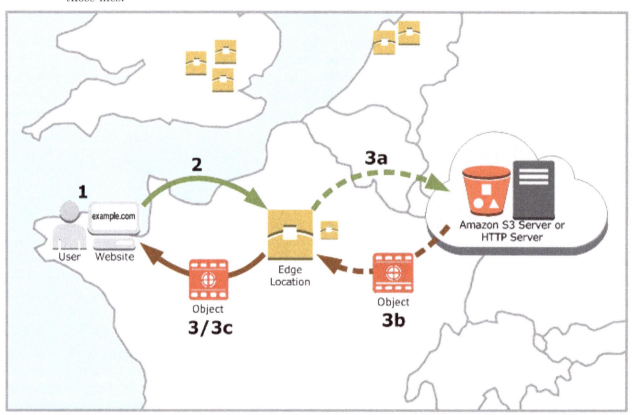

## How CloudFront Works with Regional Edge Caches

CloudFront edge locations make sure that popular content can be served quickly to your viewers. CloudFront also has regional edge caches that bring more of your content closer to your viewers, even when the content is not popular enough to stay at a CloudFront edge location, to help improve performance for that content.

Regional edge caches help with all types of content, particularly content that tends to become less popular over time. Examples include user-generated content, such as video, photos, or artwork; e-commerce assets such as product photos and videos; and news and event-related content that might suddenly find new popularity.

### How Regional Caches Work

Regional edge caches are CloudFront locations that are deployed globally, close to your viewers. They're located between your origin server and the global edge locations that serve content directly to viewers. As objects become less popular, individual edge locations may remove those objects to make room for more popular content. Regional edge caches have a larger cache than an individual edge location, so objects remain in the cache longer at the nearest regional edge cache location. This helps keep more of your content closer to your viewers, reducing the need for CloudFront to go back to your origin server, and improving overall performance for viewers.

When a viewer makes a request on your website or through your application, DNS routes the request to the CloudFront edge location that can best serve the user's request. This location is typically the nearest CloudFront edge location in terms of latency. In the edge location, CloudFront checks its cache for the requested files. If the files are in the cache, CloudFront returns them to the user. If the files are not in the cache, the edge servers go to the nearest regional edge cache to fetch the object.

In the regional edge cache location, CloudFront again checks its cache for the requested files. If the files are in the cache, CloudFront forwards the files to the requested edge location. As soon as the first byte arrives from regional edge cache location, CloudFront begins to forward the files to the user. CloudFront also adds the files to the cache in the requested edge location for the next time someone requests those files.

For files not cached at both the edge location and the regional edge cache location, CloudFront compares the request with the specifications in your distributions and forwards the request for your files to the origin server. After your origin server sends the files back to the regional edge cache location, they are forwarded to the requested edge location, and CloudFront forwards the files to the user. In this case, CloudFront also adds the files to the cache in the regional edge cache location in addition to the edge location for the next time a viewer requests those files. This makes sure that all of the edge locations in a region share a local cache, eliminating multiple requests to origin servers. CloudFront also keeps persistent connections with origin servers so files are fetched from the origins as quickly as possible.

**Note**
Regional edge caches have feature parity with edge locations. For example, a cache invalidation request removes an object from both edge caches and regional edge caches before it expires. The next time a viewer requests the object, CloudFront returns to the origin to fetch the latest version of the object. Proxy methods PUT/POST/PATCH/OPTIONS/DELETE go directly to the origin from the edge locations and do not proxy through the Regional Edge Caches. Regional edge caches are used for custom origins, but not Amazon S3 origins. Dynamic content, as determined at request time (cache-behavior configured to forward all headers), does not flow through regional edge caches, but goes directly to the origin.

# Locations and IP Address Ranges of CloudFront Edge Servers

For a list of the locations of CloudFront edge servers, see the Amazon CloudFront Product Details page.

Amazon Web Services (AWS) publishes its current IP address ranges in JSON format. To view the current ranges, download ip-ranges.json. For more information, see AWS IP Address Ranges in the *Amazon Web Services General Reference*.

To find the IP address ranges that are associated with CloudFront edge servers, search ip-ranges.json for the following string:

```
"service": "CLOUDFRONT"
```

Alternatively, you can view only the CloudFront IP ranges here.

# Accessing CloudFront

You can access Amazon CloudFront in the following ways:

- **AWS Management Console** – The procedures throughout this guide explain how to use the AWS Management Console to perform tasks.
- **AWS SDKs** – If you're using a programming language that AWS provides an SDK for, you can use an SDK to access CloudFront. SDKs simplify authentication, integrate easily with your development environment, and provide access to CloudFront commands. For more information, see Tools for Amazon Web Services.
- **CloudFront API** – If you're using a programming language that an SDK isn't available for, see the Amazon CloudFront API Reference for information about API actions and about how to make API requests.
- **AWS Command Line Interface** – For more information, see Getting Set Up with the AWS Command Line Interface in the *AWS Command Line Interface User Guide.*
- **AWS Tools for Windows PowerShell** – For more information, see Setting up the AWS Tools for Windows PowerShell in the *AWS Tools for Windows PowerShell User Guide.*

# CloudFront Pricing

Amazon CloudFront is designed so you don't have to pay any up-front fees or commit to how much content you'll have. As with the other AWS services, you pay as you go and pay only for what you use.

AWS provides two usage reports for CloudFront: a billing report and a report that summarizes usage activity. To learn more about these reports, see AWS Billing and Usage Reports for CloudFront.

The following diagram and list summarize the charges to use CloudFront.

Your monthly bill from AWS allocates your usage and dollar amounts by AWS service and function. The following explains the charges that are illustrated in the previous graphic. For more information, see Amazon CloudFront Pricing.

1. **Charge for storage in an Amazon S3 bucket.** You pay normal Amazon S3 storage charges to store objects in your bucket. The charges appear in the Amazon S3 portion of your AWS statement.

2. **Charge for serving objects from edge locations.** You incur CloudFront charges when CloudFront responds to requests for your objects. These charges are lower than the corresponding Amazon S3 charges. The CloudFront charges appear in the CloudFront portion of your AWS statement.

3. **Charge for submitting data to your origin.** You incur CloudFront charges when users transfer data to your origin, which includes `DELETE`, `OPTIONS`, `PATCH`, `POST`, and `PUT` requests. The CloudFront charges appear in the CloudFront portion of your AWS statement.

**Note**
You also incur a surcharge for HTTPS requests, and an additional surcharge for requests that also have field-level encryption enabled. For more information, see Amazon CloudFront Pricing.

# CloudFront Compliance

For information about CloudFront compliance with various security compliance regulations and audits standards, see the following pages:

- AWS Cloud Compliance
- AWS Services in Scope by Compliance Program

If you run PCI or HIPAA-compliant workloads, based on the AWS Shared Responsibility Model, we recommend that you log your CloudFront usage data for the last 365 days for future auditing purposes. To log usage data, you can do the following:

- Enable CloudFront access logs. For more information, see Access Logs.
- Capture requests that are sent to the CloudFront API. For more information, see Using AWS CloudTrail to Capture Requests Sent to the CloudFront API.

In addition, see the following for details about how CloudFront is compliant with the PCI DSS, HIPAA, and SOC standards.

## PCI DSS

CloudFront supports the processing, storage, and transmission of credit card data by a merchant or service provider, and has been validated as being compliant with Payment Card Industry (PCI) Data Security Standard (DSS). For more information about PCI DSS, including how to request a copy of the AWS PCI Compliance Package, see PCI DSS Level 1.

As a security best practice, we recommend that you don't cache credit card information in CloudFront edge caches. For example, you can configure your origin to include a `Cache-Control:no-cache="`*field-name*`"` header in responses that contain credit card information, such as the last four digits of a credit card number and the card owner's contact information.

## HIPAA

The AWS HIPAA compliance program includes CloudFront as a HIPAA Eligible Service. If you have an executed Business Associate Agreement (BAA) with AWS, you can use CloudFront to deliver content containing protected health information (PHI). For more information, see HIPAA Compliance.

## SOC 1, SOC 2, and SOC 3

Amazon CloudFront is compliant with SOC (System and Organization Control) measures. SOC Reports are independent third-party examination reports that demonstrate how AWS achieves key compliance controls and objectives. These audits ensure that the appropriate safeguards and procedures are in place to protect against risks that may affect the security, confidentiality, and availability of customer and company data. The results of these third-party audits are available on the AWS SOC Compliance website, where customers can view the published reports to get more information about the controls established to support AWS operations and compliance.

# AWS Billing and Usage Reports for CloudFront

AWS provides two usage reports for CloudFront:

- The billing report is a high-level view of all of the activity for the AWS services that you're using, including CloudFront. For more information, see AWS Billing Report for CloudFront.
- The usage report is a summary of activity for a specific service, aggregated by hour, day, or month. It also includes usage charts the provide a graphical representation of your CloudFront usage. For more information, see AWS Usage Report for CloudFront.

To help you understand these reports, see the detailed information in Interpreting Your AWS Bill and the AWS Usage Report for CloudFront.

**Note**
Like other AWS services, CloudFront charges you for only what you use. For more information, see CloudFront Pricing.

# AWS Billing Report for CloudFront

You can view a summary of your AWS usage and charges, listed by service, on the Bills page in the AWS Management Console.

You can also download a more detailed version of the report in CSV format. The detailed billing report includes the following values that are applicable to CloudFront:

- **ProductCode** — `AmazonCloudFront`
- **UsageType** — One of the following values
    - A code that identifies the type of data transfer
    - `Invalidations`
    - `SSL-Cert-Custom`

    For more information, see Interpreting Your AWS Bill and the AWS Usage Report for CloudFront.

- **ItemDescription** — A description of the billing rate for the **UsageType**.
- **Usage Start Date/Usage End Date** — The day that the usage applies to, in Coordinated Universal Time (UTC).
- **Usage Quantity** — One of the following values:
    - The number of requests during the specified time period
    - The amount of data transferred in gigabytes
    - The number of objects invalidated
    - The sum of the prorated months that you had SSL certificates associated with enabled CloudFront distributions. For example, if you have one certificate associated with an enabled distribution for an entire month and another certificate associated with an enabled distribution for half of the month, this value will be 1.5.

**To display summary billing information and download the detailed billing report**

1. Sign in to the AWS Management Console at https://console.aws.amazon.com/console/home.
2. In the title bar, click your IAM user name, and click **Billing & Cost Management**.
3. In the navigation pane, click **Bills**.
4. To view summary information for CloudFront, under **Details**, click **CloudFront**.
5. To download a detailed billing report in CSV format, click **Download CSV**, and follow the on-screen prompts to save the report.

# AWS Usage Report for CloudFront

AWS provides a CloudFront usage report that is more detailed than the billing report but less detailed than CloudFront access logs. The usage report provides aggregate usage data by hour, day, or month; and it lists operations by region and usage type, such as data transferred out of the Australia region.

The CloudFront usage report includes the following values:

- **Service** — `AmazonCloudFront`

- **Operation** — HTTP method. Values include `DELETE`, `GET`, `HEAD`, `OPTIONS`, `PATCH`, `POST`, and `PUT`.

- **UsageType** — One of the following values

  - A code that identifies the type of data transfer
  - `Invalidations`
  - `SSL-Cert-Custom`

  For more information, see Interpreting Your AWS Bill and the AWS Usage Report for CloudFront.

- **Resource** — Either the ID of the CloudFront distribution associated with the usage or the certificate ID of an SSL certificate that you have associated with a CloudFront distribution.

- **StartTime/EndTime** — The day that the usage applies to, in Coordinated Universal Time (UTC).

- **UsageValue** — (1) The number of requests during the specified time period or (2) the amount of data transferred in bytes.

If you're using Amazon S3 as the origin for CloudFront, consider running the usage report for Amazon S3, too. However, if you use Amazon S3 for purposes other than as an origin for your CloudFront distributions, it might not be clear what portion applies to your CloudFront usage.

**Tip**
For detailed information about every request that CloudFront receives for your objects, turn on CloudFront access logs for your distribution. For more information, see Access Logs.

**To download the usage report for CloudFront or Amazon S3**

1. Sign in to the AWS Management Console at https://console.aws.amazon.com/console/home.

2. In the title bar, click your IAM user name, and click **Billing & Cost Management**.

3. In the navigation pane, click **Reports**.

4. Under **AWS Usage Report**, click **AWS Usage Report**.

5. In the **Service** list, click **CloudFront** or **Amazon Simple Storage Service**.

6. Select the applicable settings:

   - **Usage Types** — For a detailed explanation of CloudFront usage types, see Interpreting Your AWS Bill and the AWS Usage Report for CloudFront.

     For Amazon S3, select **All Usage Types**.

   - **Operation** — Select **All Operations**.

   - **Time Period** — Select the time period that you want the report to cover.

   - **Report Granularity** — Select whether you want the report to include subtotals by the hour, by the day, or by the month.

7. Click the download button for the desired format.

8. Follow the on-screen prompts to view or save the report.

# Interpreting Your AWS Bill and the AWS Usage Report for Cloud-Front

Your AWS bill for CloudFront service includes codes and abbreviations that might not be immediately obvious. The first column in the following table lists items that appear in your bill and explains what each means.

In addition, you can get an AWS usage report for CloudFront that contains more detail than the AWS bill for CloudFront. The second column in the table lists items that appear in the usage report and shows the correlation between bill items and usage report items.

Most codes in both columns include a two-letter abbreviation that indicates the location of the activity. In the following table, *region* in a code is replaced in your AWS bill and in the usage report by one of the following two-letter abbreviations :

- **AP:** Hong Kong, Philippines, South Korea, Singapore, and Taiwan (Asia Pacific)
- **AU:** Australia
- **CA:** Canada
- **EU:** Europe
- **IN:** India
- **JP:** Japan
- **SA:** South America
- **US:** United States

For more information about pricing by region, see Amazon CloudFront Pricing.

**Note**
This table doesn't include charges for transferring your objects from an Amazon S3 bucket to CloudFront edge locations. These charges, if any, appear in the **AWS Data Transfer** portion of your AWS bill.

| Items in Your CloudFront Bill | Values in the Usage Type Column in the CloudFront Usage Report |
|---|---|
| *region***-DataTransfer-Out-Bytes** Sum of bytes that CloudFront served for web and RTMP distributions: [See the AWS documentation website for more details] *region***-DataTransfer-Out-OBytes** **Web distributions only:** Total bytes transferred from CloudFront edge locations to your origin in response to `DELETE`, `OPTIONS`, `PATCH`, `POST`, and `PUT` requests. | **Web distributions:** [See the AWS documentation website for more details] **RTMP distributions:** [See the AWS documentation website for more details] *region***-Out-OBytes-HTTP-Proxy** Total bytes transferred via HTTP from CloudFront edge locations to your origin in response to `DELETE`, `OPTIONS`, `PATCH`, `POST`, and `PUT` requests. *region***-Out-OBytes-HTTPS-Proxy** Total bytes transferred via HTTPS from CloudFront edge locations to your origin in response to `DELETE`, `OPTIONS`, `PATCH`, `POST`, and `PUT` requests. |
| *region***-Requests-Tier1** **Web distributions only:** Number of HTTP `GET` and `HEAD` requests | *region***-Requests-HTTP-Static** Number of HTTP `GET` and `HEAD` requests served for objects with TTL 3600 seconds *region***-Requests-HTTP-Dynamic** Number of HTTP `GET` and `HEAD` requests served for objects with TTL < 3600 seconds |

| Items in Your CloudFront Bill | Values in the Usage Type Column in the CloudFront Usage Report |
|---|---|
| *region*\*\*-Requests-Tier2-HTTPS\*\* **Web distributions only:** Number of HTTPS `GET` and `HEAD` requests | *region*\*\*-Requests-HTTPS-Static\*\* Number of HTTPS `GET` and `HEAD` requests served for objects with TTL 3600 seconds *region*\*\*-Requests-HTTPS-Dynamic\*\* Number of HTTPS `GET` and `HEAD` requests served for objects with TTL < 3600 seconds |
| *region*\*\*-Requests-HTTP-Proxy\*\* **Web distributions only:** Number of HTTP `DELETE`, `OPTIONS`, `PATCH`, `POST`, and `PUT` requests that CloudFront forwards to your origin | *region*\*\*-Requests-HTTP-Proxy\*\* Same as the corresponding item in your CloudFront bill |
| *region*\*\*-Requests-HTTPS-Proxy\*\* **Web distributions only:** Number of HTTPS `DELETE`, `OPTIONS`, `PATCH`, `POST`, and `PUT` requests that CloudFront forwards to your origin | *region*\*\*-Requests-HTTPS-Proxy\*\* Same as the corresponding item in your CloudFront bill |
| *region*\*\*-Requests-HTTPS-Proxy-FLE\*\* **Web distributions only:** Number of HTTPS `DELETE`, `OPTIONS`, `PATCH`, and `POST` requests that CloudFront forwards to your origin which were processed with field-level encryption. | *region*\*\*-Requests-HTTPS-Proxy-FLE\*\* Same as the corresponding item in your CloudFront bill |
| **Invalidations Web distributions only:** The charge for invalidating objects (removing the objects from CloudFront edge locations); for more information, see Paying for Object Invalidation. | **Invalidations** Same as the corresponding item in your CloudFront bill |
| **SSL-Cert-Custom Web distributions only:** The charge for using an SSL certificate with a CloudFront alternate domain name such as example.com instead of using the default CloudFront SSL certificate and the domain name that CloudFront assigned to your distribution. | **SSL-Cert-Custom** Same as the corresponding item in your CloudFront bill |

# CloudFront Reports

The CloudFront console includes a variety of reports:

- CloudFront Cache Statistics Reports
- CloudFront Popular Objects Report
- CloudFront Top Referrers Report
- CloudFront Usage Reports
- CloudFront Viewers Reports

Most of these reports are based on the data in CloudFront access logs, which contain detailed information about every user request that CloudFront receives. You don't need to enable access logs to view the reports. For more information, see Access Logs. The CloudFront usage report is based on the AWS usage report for CloudFront, which also doesn't require any special configuration. For more information, see AWS Usage Report for CloudFront.

## CloudFront Cache Statistics Reports

The CloudFront cache statistics report includes the following information:

- **Total Requests** – Shows the total number of requests for all HTTP status codes (for example, 200 or 404) and all methods (for example, GET, HEAD, or POST)
- **Percentage of Viewer Requests by Result Type** – Shows hits, misses, and errors as a percentage of total viewer requests for the selected CloudFront distribution
- **Bytes Transferred to Viewers** – Shows total bytes and bytes from misses
- **HTTP Status Codes** – Shows viewer requests by HTTP status code
- **Percentage of GET Requests that Didn't Finish Downloading**– Shows viewer GET requests that didn't finish downloading the requested object as a percentage of total requests

For more information, see CloudFront Cache Statistics Reports.

## CloudFront Popular Objects Report

The CloudFront popular objects report lists the 50 most popular objects and statistics about those objects, including the number of requests for the object, the number of hits and misses, the hit ratio, the number of bytes served for misses, the total bytes served, the number of incomplete downloads, and the number of requests by HTTP status code (2xx, 3xx, 4xx, and 5xx).

For more information, see CloudFront Popular Objects Report.

## CloudFront Top Referrers Report

The CloudFront top referrers report includes the top 25 referrers, the number of requests from a referrer, and the number of requests from a referrer as a percentage of the total number of requests during the specified period.

For more information, see CloudFront Top Referrers Report.

## CloudFront Usage Reports

The CloudFront usage reports include the following information:

- **Number of Requests** – Shows the number of HTTP and HTTPS requests that CloudFront responds to from edge locations in the selected region during each time interval for the specified CloudFront distribution
- **Data Transferred by Protocol** – Shows the total amount of data transferred over HTTP and HTTPS from CloudFront edge locations in the selected region during each time interval for the specified CloudFront distribution
- **Data Transferred by Destination**– Shows the total amount of data transferred over HTTP and HTTPS from CloudFront edge locations in the selected region during each time interval for the specified CloudFront distribution

For more information, see CloudFront Usage Reports.

**CloudFront Viewers Reports**

The CloudFront viewers reports include the following information:

- **Devices** – Shows the types of devices (for example, Desktop or Mobile) that your users use to access your content
- **Browsers** – Shows the name (or the name and version) of the browsers that your users use most frequently to access your content, for example, Chrome or Firefox
- **Operating Systems** – Shows the name (or the name and version) of the operating system that viewers run on most frequently when accessing your content, for example, Linux, Mac OS X, or Windows
- **Locations** – Shows the locations, by country or by U.S. state/territory, of the viewers that access your content most frequently

For more information, see CloudFront Viewers Reports.

# CloudFront Cache Statistics Reports

You can use the Amazon CloudFront console to display a graphical representation of statistics related to CloudFront edge locations. Data for these statistics are drawn from the same source as CloudFront access logs. You can display charts for a specified date range in the last 60 days, with data points every hour or every day. You can usually view data about requests that CloudFront received as recently as an hour ago, but data can occasionally be delayed by as much as 24 hours.

**Note**
You don't need to enable access logging to view cache statistics.

**To display CloudFront cache statistics**

1. Sign in to the AWS Management Console and open the CloudFront console at https://console.aws.amazon.com/cloudfront/.

2. In the navigation pane, click **Cache Statistics**.

3. In the **CloudFront Cache Statistics Reports** pane, for **Start Date** and **End Date**, select the date range for which you want to display cache statistics charts. Available ranges depend on the value that you select for **Granularity**:

   - **Daily** – To display charts with one data point per day, select any date range in the previous 60 days.
   - **Hourly** – To display charts with one data point every hour, select any date range of up to 14 days within the previous 60 days.

   Dates and times are in Coordinated Universal Time (UTC).

4. For **Granularity**, specify whether to display one data point per day or one data point per hour in the charts. If you specify a date range greater than 14 days, the option to specify one data point per hour is not available.

5. For **Viewer Location**, choose the continent from which viewer requests originated, or choose **All Locations**. Cache statistics charts include data for requests that CloudFront received from the specified location.

6. In the **Distribution** list, select the distributions for which you want to display data in the usage charts:

   - **An individual web distribution** – The charts display data for the selected CloudFront web distribution. The **Distribution** list displays the distribution ID and alternate domain names (CNAMEs) for the distribution, if any. If a distribution has no alternate domain names, the list includes origin domain names for the distribution.
   - **All Web Distributions** – The charts display summed data for all web distributions that are associated with the current AWS account, excluding web distributions that you have deleted.

7. Click **Update**.

8. To view data for a daily or hourly data point within a chart, move your mouse pointer over the data point.

9. For charts that show data transferred, note that you can change the vertical scale to gigabytes, megabytes, or kilobytes for each chart.

**Topics**
- Downloading Data in CSV Format
- How Cache Statistics Charts Are Related to Data in the CloudFront Access Logs

## Downloading Data in CSV Format

You can download the Cache Statistics report in CSV format. This section explains how to download the report and describes the values in the report.

### To download the Cache Statistics report in CSV format

1. While viewing the Cache Statistics report, click **CSV**.

2. In the **Opening** *file name* dialog box, choose whether to open or save the file.

## Information About the Report

The first few rows of the report include the following information:

**Version**
The version of the format for this CSV file.

**Report**
The name of the report.

**DistributionID**
The ID of the distribution that you ran the report for, or `ALL` if you ran the report for all distributions.

**StartDateUTC**
The beginning of the date range for which you ran the report, in Coordinated Universal Time (UTC).

**EndDateUTC**
The end of the date range for which you ran the report, in Coordinated Universal Time (UTC).

**GeneratedTimeUTC**
The date and time on which you ran the report, in Coordinated Universal Time (UTC).

**Granularity**
Whether each row in the report represents one hour or one day.

**ViewerLocation**
The continent that viewer requests originated from, or `ALL`, if you chose to download the report for all locations.

## Data in the Cache Statistics Report

The report includes the following values:

**DistributionID**
The ID of the distribution that you ran the report for, or `ALL` if you ran the report for all distributions.

**FriendlyName**
An alternate domain name (CNAME) for the distribution, if any. If a distribution has no alternate domain names, the list includes an origin domain name for the distribution.

**ViewerLocation**
The continent that viewer requests originated from, or `ALL`, if you chose to download the report for all locations.

**TimeBucket**
The hour or the day that data applies to, in Coordinated Universal Time (UTC).

**RequestCount**
The total number of requests for all HTTP status codes (for example, 200 or 404) and all methods (for example, GET, HEAD, or POST).

**HitCount**
The number of viewer requests for which the object is served from a CloudFront edge cache.

**MissCount**
The number of viewer requests for which the object isn't currently in an edge cache, so CloudFront must get the object from your origin.

**ErrorCount**

The number of viewer requests that resulted in an error, so CloudFront didn't serve the object.

**IncompleteDownloadCount**

The number of viewer requests for which the viewer started but didn't finish downloading the object.

**HTTP2xx**

The number of viewer requests for which the HTTP status code was a 2xx value (succeeded).

**HTTP3xx**

The number of viewer requests for which the HTTP status code was a 3xx value (additional action is required).

**HTTP4xx**

The number of viewer requests for which the HTTP status code was a 4xx value (client error).

**HTTP5xx**

The number of viewer requests for which the HTTP status code was a 5xx value (server error).

**TotalBytes**

The total number of bytes served to viewers by CloudFront in response to all requests for all HTTP methods.

**BytesFromMisses**

The number of bytes served to viewers for objects that were not in the applicable edge cache at the time of the request. This value is a good approximation of bytes transferred from your origin to CloudFront edge caches. However, it excludes requests for objects that are already in the edge cache but that have expired.

## How Cache Statistics Charts Are Related to Data in the CloudFront Access Logs

The following table shows how cache statistics charts in the CloudFront console correspond with values in CloudFront access logs. For more information about CloudFront access logs, see Access Logs.

**Total Requests**

This chart shows the total number of requests for all HTTP status codes (for example, 200 or 404) and all methods (for example, `GET`, `HEAD`, or `POST`). Total requests shown in this chart equal the total number of requests in the access log files for the same time period.

**Percentage of Viewer Requests by Result Type**

This chart shows hits, misses, and errors as a percentage of total viewer requests for the selected CloudFront distribution:

- **Hit** – A viewer request for which the object is served from a CloudFront edge cache. In access logs, these are requests for which the value of `x-edge-response-result-type` is `Hit`.
- **Miss** – A viewer request for which the object isn't currently in an edge cache, so CloudFront must get the object from your origin. In access logs, these are requests for which the value of `x-edge-response-result-type` is `Miss`.
- **Error** – A viewer request that resulted in an error, so CloudFront didn't serve the object. In access logs, these are requests for which the value of `x-edge-response-result-type` is `Error`, `LimitExceeded`, or `CapacityExceeded`. The chart does not include refresh hits—requests for objects that are in the edge cache but that have expired. In access logs, refresh hits are requests for which the value of `x-edge-response-result-type` is `RefreshHit`.

**Bytes Transferred to Viewers**

This chart shows two values:

- **Total Bytes** – The total number of bytes served to viewers by CloudFront in response to all requests for all HTTP methods. In CloudFront access logs, **Total Bytes** is the sum of the values in the `sc-bytes` column for all of the requests during the same time period.
- **Bytes from Misses** – The number of bytes served to viewers for objects that were not in the applicable edge cache at the time of the request. In CloudFront access logs, **Bytes from Misses** is the sum of the values in the `sc-bytes` column for requests for which the value of `x-edge-result-type` is `Miss`. This

value is a good approximation of bytes transferred from your origin to CloudFront edge caches. However, it excludes requests for objects that are already in the edge cache but that have expired.

**HTTP Status Codes**

This chart shows viewer requests by HTTP status code. In CloudFront access logs, status codes appear in the `sc-status` column:

- **2xx** – The request succeeded.
- **3xx** – Additional action is required. For example, 301 (Moved Permanently) means that the requested object has moved to a different location.
- **4xx** – The client apparently made an error. For example, 404 (Not Found) means that the client requested an object that could not be found.
- **5xx** – The origin server didn't fill the request. For example, 503 (Service Unavailable) means that the origin server is currently unavailable.

**Percentage of GET Requests that Didn't Finish Downloading**

This chart shows viewer `GET` requests that didn't finish downloading the requested object as a percentage of total requests. Typically, downloading an object doesn't complete because the viewer canceled the download, for example, by clicking a different link or by closing the browser. In CloudFront access logs, these requests have a value of 200 in the `sc-status` column and a value of `Error` in the `x-edge-result-type` column.

# CloudFront Popular Objects Report

The Amazon CloudFront console can display a list of the 50 most popular objects for a distribution during a specified date range in the previous 60 days.

Data for the Popular Objects report is drawn from the same source as CloudFront access logs. To get an accurate count of the top 50 objects, CloudFront counts the requests for all of your objects in 10-minute intervals beginning at midnight and keeps a running total of the top 150 objects for the next 24 hours. (CloudFront also retains daily totals for the top 150 objects for 60 days.) Near the bottom of the list, objects constantly rise onto or drop off of the list, so the totals for those objects are approximations. The fifty objects at the top of the list of 150 objects may rise and fall within the list, but they rarely drop off of the list altogether, so the totals for those objects typically are more reliable.

When an object drops off of the list of the top 150 objects and then rises onto the list again over the course of a day, CloudFront adds an estimated number of requests for the period that the object was missing from the list. The estimate is based on the number of requests received by whichever object was at the bottom of the list during that time period. If the object rises into the top 50 objects later in the day, the estimates of the number of requests that CloudFront received while the object was out of the top 150 objects usually causes the number of requests in the Popular Objects report to exceed the number of requests that appear in the access logs for that object.

**Note**
You don't need to enable access logging to view a list of popular objects.

**To display popular objects for a distribution**

1. Sign in to the AWS Management Console and open the CloudFront console at https://console.aws.amazon.com/cloudfront/.

2. In the navigation pane, click **Popular Objects**.

3. In the **CloudFront Popular Objects Report** pane, for **Start Date** and **End Date**, select the date range for which you want to display a list of popular objects. You can choose any date range in the previous 60 days.

   Dates and times are in Coordinated Universal Time (UTC).

4. In the **Distribution** list, select the distribution for which you want to display a list of popular objects.

5. Click **Update**.

**Topics**

- Downloading Data in CSV Format
- How Data in the Popular Objects Report Is Related to Data in the CloudFront Access Logs

## Downloading Data in CSV Format

You can download the Popular Objects report in CSV format. This section explains how to download the report and describes the values in the report.

**To download the Popular Objects report in CSV format**

1. While viewing the Popular Objects report, click **CSV**.

2. In the **Opening** *file name* dialog box, choose whether to open or save the file.

## Information About the Report

The first few rows of the report include the following information:

**Version**
The version of the format for this CSV file.

**Report**
The name of the report.

**DistributionID**
The ID of the distribution that you ran the report for.

**StartDateUTC**
The beginning of the date range for which you ran the report, in Coordinated Universal Time (UTC).

**EndDateUTC**
The end of the date range for which you ran the report, in Coordinated Universal Time (UTC).

**GeneratedTimeUTC**
The date and time on which you ran the report, in Coordinated Universal Time (UTC).


## Data in the Popular Objects Report

The report includes the following values:

**DistributionID**
The ID of the distribution that you ran the report for.

**FriendlyName**
An alternate domain name (CNAME) for the distribution, if any. If a distribution has no alternate domain names, the list includes an origin domain name for the distribution.

**Object**
The last 500 characters of the URL for the object.

**RequestCount**
The total number of requests for this object.

**HitCount**
The number of viewer requests for which the object is served from a CloudFront edge cache.

**MissCount**
The number of viewer requests for which the object isn't currently in an edge cache, so CloudFront must get the object from your origin.

**HitCountPct**
The value of `HitCount` as a percentage of the value of `RequestCount`.

**BytesFromMisses**
The number of bytes served to viewers for this object when the object was not in the applicable edge cache at the time of the request.

**TotalBytes**
The total number of bytes served to viewers by CloudFront for this object in response to all requests for all HTTP methods.

**IncompleteDownloadCount**
The number of viewer requests for this object for which the viewer started but didn't finish downloading the object.

### HTTP2xx

The number of viewer requests for which the HTTP status code was a 2xx value (succeeded).

### HTTP3xx

The number of viewer requests for which the HTTP status code was a 3xx value (additional action is required).

### HTTP4xx

The number of viewer requests for which the HTTP status code was a 4xx value (client error).

### HTTP5xx

The number of viewer requests for which the HTTP status code was a 5xx value (server error).

## How Data in the Popular Objects Report Is Related to Data in the CloudFront Access Logs

The following list shows how values in the Popular Objects report in the CloudFront console correspond with values in CloudFront access logs. For more information about CloudFront access logs, see Access Logs.

### URL

The last 500 characters of the URL that viewers use to access the object.

### Requests

The total number of requests for the object. This value generally corresponds closely with the number of `GET` requests for the object in CloudFront access logs.

### Hits

The number of viewer requests for which the object was served from a CloudFront edge cache. In access logs, these are requests for which the value of `x-edge-response-result-type` is `Hit`.

### Misses

The number of viewer requests for which the object wasn't in an edge cache, so CloudFront retrieved the object from your origin. In access logs, these are requests for which the value of `x-edge-response-result-type` is `Miss`.

### Hit Ratio

The value of the **Hits** column as a percentage of the value of the **Requests** column.

### Bytes from Misses

The number of bytes served to viewers for objects that were not in the applicable edge cache at the time of the request. In CloudFront access logs, **Bytes from Misses** is the sum of the values in the `sc-bytes` column for requests for which the value of `x-edge-result-type` is `Miss`.

### Total Bytes

The total number of bytes that CloudFront served to viewers in response to all requests for the object for all HTTP methods. In CloudFront access logs, **Total Bytes** is the sum of the values in the `sc-bytes` column for all of the requests during the same time period.

### Incomplete Downloads

The number of viewer requests that did not finish downloading the requested object. Typically, the reason that a download doesn't complete is that the viewer canceled it, for example, by clicking a different link or by closing the browser. In CloudFront access logs, these requests have a value of 200 in the `sc-status` column and a value of `Error` in the `x-edge-result-type` column.

### 2xx

The number of requests for which the HTTP status code is 2xx, `Successful`. In CloudFront access logs, status codes appear in the `sc-status` column.

### 3xx

The number of requests for which the HTTP status code is 3xx, `Redirection`. 3xx status codes indicate that

41

additional action is required. For example, 301 (Moved Permanently) means that the requested object has moved to a different location.

**4xx**

The number of requests for which the HTTP status code is `4xx`, `Client Error`. `4xx` status codes indicate that the client apparently made an error. For example, 404 (Not Found) means that the client requested an object that could not be found.

**5xx**

The number of requests for which the HTTP status code is `5xx`, `Server Error`. `5xx` status codes indicate that the origin server didn't fill the request. For example, 503 (Service Unavailable) means that the origin server is currently unavailable.

# CloudFront Top Referrers Report

The CloudFront console can display a list of the 25 domains of the websites that originated the most HTTP and HTTPS requests for objects that CloudFront is distributing for a specified distribution. These top referrers can be search engines, other websites that link directly to your objects, or your own website. For example, if http://example/.com/index/.html links to 10 graphics, example.com is the referrer for all 10 graphics. You can display the Top Referrers report for any date range in the previous 60 days.

**Note**
If a user enters a URL directly into the address line of a browser, there is no referrer for the requested object.

Data for the Top Referrers report is drawn from the same source as CloudFront access logs. To get an accurate count of the top 25 referrers, CloudFront counts the requests for all of your objects in 10-minute intervals and keeps a running total of the top 75 referrers. Near the bottom of the list, referrers constantly rise onto or drop off of the list, so the totals for those referrers are approximations. The 25 referrers at the top of the list of 75 referrers may rise and fall within the list, but they rarely drop off of the list altogether, so the totals for those referrers typically are more reliable.

**Note**
You don't need to enable access logging to view a list of top referrers.

**To display top referrers for a distribution**

1. Sign in to the AWS Management Console and open the CloudFront console at https://console.aws.amazon.com/cloudfront/.

2. In the navigation pane, click **Top Referrers**.

3. In the **CloudFront Top Referrers Report** pane, for **Start Date** and **End Date**, select the date range for which you want to display a list of top referrers.

   Dates and times are in Coordinated Universal Time (UTC).

4. In the **Distribution** list, select the distribution for which you want to display a list of top referrers.

5. Click **Update**.

**Topics**

- Downloading Data in CSV Format
- How Data in the Top Referrers Report Is Related to Data in the CloudFront Access Logs

## Downloading Data in CSV Format

You can download the Top Referrers report in CSV format. This section explains how to download the report and describes the values in the report.

**To download the Top Referrers report in CSV format**

1. While viewing the Top Referrers report, click **CSV**.

2. In the **Opening** *file name* dialog box, choose whether to open or save the file.

**Information About the Report**

The first few rows of the report include the following information:

**Version**
The version of the format for this CSV file.

**Report**

The name of the report.

**DistributionID**

The ID of the distribution that you ran the report for, or `ALL` if you ran the report for all distributions.

**StartDateUTC**

The beginning of the date range for which you ran the report, in Coordinated Universal Time (UTC).

**EndDateUTC**

The end of the date range for which you ran the report, in Coordinated Universal Time (UTC).

**GeneratedTimeUTC**

The date and time on which you ran the report, in Coordinated Universal Time (UTC).

**Data in the Top Referrers Report**

The report includes the following values:

**DistributionID**

The ID of the distribution that you ran the report for, or `ALL` if you ran the report for all distributions.

**FriendlyName**

An alternate domain name (CNAME) for the distribution, if any. If a distribution has no alternate domain names, the list includes an origin domain name for the distribution.

**Referrer**

The domain name of the referrer.

---

The total number of requests from the domain name in the `Referrer` column.

**RequestsPct**

The number of requests submitted by the referrer as a percentage of the total number of requests during the specified period.

## How Data in the Top Referrers Report Is Related to Data in the CloudFront Access Logs

The following list shows how values in the Top Referrers report in the CloudFront console correspond with values in CloudFront access logs. For more information about CloudFront access logs, see Access Logs.

**Referrer**

The domain name of the referrer. In access logs, referrers are listed in the `cs(Referer)` column.

**Request Count**

The total number of requests from the domain name in the **Referrer** column. This value generally corresponds closely with the number of `GET` requests from the referrer in CloudFront access logs.

**Request %**

The number of requests submitted by the referrer as a percentage of the total number of requests during the specified period. If you have more than 25 referrers, then you can't calculate **Request %** based on the data in this table because the **Request Count** column doesn't include all of the requests during the specified period.

# CloudFront Usage Reports

The Amazon CloudFront console can display a graphical representation of your CloudFront usage that is based on a subset of the usage report data. You can display charts for a specified date range in the last 60 days, with data points every hour or every day. You can usually view data about requests that CloudFront received as recently as four hours ago, but data can occasionally be delayed by as much as 24 hours.

For more information, see How the Usage Charts Are Related to Data in the CloudFront Usage Report.

**To display CloudFront usage charts**

1. Sign in to the AWS Management Console and open the CloudFront console at https://console.aws.amazon.com/cloudfront/.

2. In **navigation** pane, click **Usage Reports**.

3. In the **CloudFront Usage Reports** pane, for **Start Date** and **End Date**, select the date range for which you want to display usage charts. Available ranges depend on the value that you select for **Granularity**:

   - **Daily** — To display charts with one data point per day, select any date range in the previous 60 days.
   - **Hourly** — To display charts with one data point every hour, select any date range of up to 14 days within the previous 60 days.

   Dates and times are in Coordinated Universal Time (UTC).

4. For **Granularity**, specify whether to display one data point per day or one data point per hour in the charts. If you specify a date range greater than 14 days, the option to specify one data point per hour is not available.

5. For **Billing Region**, choose the CloudFront billing region that has the data you want to view, or choose **All Regions**. Usage charts include data for requests that CloudFront processes in edge locations in the specified region. The region where CloudFront processes requests might or might not correspond with the location of your users.

   Select only regions that are included in the price class for your distribution; otherwise, the usage charts probably won't contain any data. For example, if you chose Price Class 200 for your distribution, the South America and Australia billing regions are not included, so CloudFront generally won't process your requests from those regions. For more information about price classes, see Choosing the Price Class for a CloudFront Distribution.

6. In the **Distribution** list, select the distributions for which you want to display data in the usage charts:

   - **An individual web distribution** — The charts display data for the selected CloudFront distribution. The **Distribution** list displays the distribution ID and alternate domain names (CNAMEs) for the distribution, if any. If a distribution has no alternate domain names, the list includes origin domain names for the distribution.
   - **All Web Distributions (excludes deleted)** — The charts display summed data for all web distributions that are associated with the current AWS account, excluding web distributions that you have deleted.
   - **All Deleted Distributions** — The charts display summed data for all web distributions that are associated with the current AWS account and that were deleted in the last 60 days.

7. Click **Update Graphs**.

8. To view data for a daily or hourly data point within a chart, move your mouse pointer over the data point.

9. For charts that show data transferred, note that you can change the vertical scale to gigabytes, megabytes, or kilobytes for each chart.

**Topics**

- Downloading Data in CSV Format

- How the Usage Charts Are Related to Data in the CloudFront Usage Report

## Downloading Data in CSV Format

You can download the Usage report in CSV format. This section explains how to download the report and describes the values in the report.

**To download the Usage report in CSV format**

1. While viewing the Usage report, click **CSV**.

2. In the **Opening** *file name* dialog box, choose whether to open or save the file.

### Information About the Report

The first few rows of the report include the following information:

**Version**
The version of the format for this CSV file.

**Report**
The name of the report.

**DistributionID**
The ID of the distribution that you ran the report for, `ALL` if you ran the report for all distributions, or `ALL_DELETED` if you ran the report for all deleted distributions.

**StartDateUTC**
The beginning of the date range for which you ran the report, in Coordinated Universal Time (UTC).

**EndDateUTC**
The end of the date range for which you ran the report, in Coordinated Universal Time (UTC).

**GeneratedTimeUTC**
The date and time on which you ran the report, in Coordinated Universal Time (UTC).

**Granularity**
Whether each row in the report represents one hour or one day.

**BillingRegion**
The continent that viewer requests originated from, or `ALL`, if you chose to download the report for all billing regions.

### Data in the Usage Report

The report includes the following values:

**DistributionID**
The ID of the distribution that you ran the report for, `ALL` if you ran the report for all distributions, or `ALL_DELETED` if you ran the report for all deleted distributions.

**FriendlyName**
An alternate domain name (CNAME) for the distribution, if any. If a distribution has no alternate domain names, the list includes an origin domain name for the distribution.

**BillingRegion**
The CloudFront billing region that you ran the report for, or `ALL`.

**TimeBucket**
The hour or the day that data applies to, in Coordinated Universal Time (UTC).

## HTTP

The number of HTTP requests that CloudFront responded to from edge locations in the selected region during each time interval for the specified CloudFront distribution. Values include:

- The number of `GET` and `HEAD` requests, which cause CloudFront to transfer data to your users
- The number of `DELETE`, `OPTIONS`, `PATCH`, `POST`, and `PUT` requests, which cause CloudFront to transfer data to your origin

## HTTPS

The number of HTTPS requests that CloudFront responded to from edge locations in the selected region during each time interval for the specified CloudFront distribution. Values include:

- The number of `GET` and `HEAD` requests, which cause CloudFront to transfer data to your users
- The number of `DELETE`, `OPTIONS`, `PATCH`, `POST`, and `PUT` requests, which cause CloudFront to transfer data to your origin

## HTTPBytes

The total amount of data transferred over HTTP from CloudFront edge locations in the selected billing region during the time period for the specified CloudFront distribution. Values include:

- Data transferred from CloudFront to your users in response to `GET` and `HEAD` requests
- Data transferred from CloudFront to your origin for `DELETE`, `OPTIONS`, `PATCH`, `POST`, and `PUT` requests
- Data transferred from CloudFront to your users in response to DELETE, OPTIONS, PATCH, POST, and PUT requests

## HTTPSBytes

The total amount of data transferred over HTTPS from CloudFront edge locations in the selected billing region during the time period for the specified CloudFront distribution. Values include:

- Data transferred from CloudFront to your users in response to `GET` and `HEAD` requests
- Data transferred from CloudFront to your origin for `DELETE`, `OPTIONS`, `PATCH`, `POST`, and `PUT` requests
- Data transferred from CloudFront to your users in response to DELETE, OPTIONS, PATCH, POST, and PUT requests

## BytesIn

The total amount of data transferred from CloudFront to your origin for `DELETE`, `OPTIONS`, `PATCH`, `POST`, and `PUT` requests in the selected region during each time interval for the specified CloudFront distribution.

## BytesOut

The total amount of data transferred over HTTP and HTTPS from CloudFront to your users in the selected region during each time interval for the specified CloudFront distribution. Values include:

- Data transferred from CloudFront to your users in response to `GET` and `HEAD` requests
- Data transferred from CloudFront to your users in response to `DELETE`, `OPTIONS`, `PATCH`, `POST`, and `PUT` requests

## How the Usage Charts Are Related to Data in the CloudFront Usage Report

The following list shows how the usage charts in the CloudFront console correspond with values in the **Usage Type** column in the CloudFront usage report.

### Topics

- Number of Requests
- Data Transferred by Protocol
- Data Transferred by Destination

**Number of Requests**

This chart shows the number of HTTP and HTTPS requests that CloudFront responds to from edge locations in the selected region during each time interval for the specified CloudFront distribution.

**Number of HTTP Requests**

- *region***-Requests-HTTP-Static:** Number of HTTP `GET` and `HEAD` requests served for objects with TTL 3600 seconds
- *region***-Requests-HTTP-Dynamic:** Number of HTTP `GET` and `HEAD` requests served for objects with TTL < 3600 seconds
- *region***-Requests-HTTP-Proxy:** Number of HTTP `DELETE`, `OPTIONS`, `PATCH`, `POST`, and `PUT` requests that CloudFront forwards to your origin

**Number of HTTPS Requests**

- *region***-Requests-HTTPS-Static:** Number of HTTPS `GET` and `HEAD` requests served for objects with TTL 3600 seconds
- *region***-Requests-HTTPS-Dynamic:** Number of HTTPS `GET` and `HEAD` requests served for objects with TTL < 3600 seconds
- *region***-Requests-HTTPS-Proxy:** Number of HTTPS `DELETE`, `OPTIONS`, `PATCH`, `POST`, and `PUT` requests that CloudFront forwards to your origin

**Data Transferred by Protocol**

This chart shows the total amount of data transferred over HTTP and HTTPS from CloudFront edge locations in the selected region during each time interval for the specified CloudFront distribution.

**Data Transferred over HTTP**

- *region***-Out-Bytes-HTTP-Static:** Bytes served via HTTP for objects with TTL 3600 seconds
- *region***-Out-Bytes-HTTP-Dynamic:** Bytes served via HTTP for objects with TTL < 3600 seconds
- *region***-Out-Bytes-HTTP-Proxy:** Bytes returned from CloudFront to viewers via HTTP in response to `DELETE`, `OPTIONS`, `PATCH`, `POST`, and `PUT` requests
- *region***-Out-OBytes-HTTP-Proxy:** Total bytes transferred via HTTP from CloudFront edge locations to your origin in response to `DELETE`, `OPTIONS`, `PATCH`, `POST`, and `PUT` requests

**Data Transferred over HTTPS**

- *region***-Out-Bytes-HTTPS-Static:** Bytes served via HTTPS for objects with TTL 3600 seconds
- *region***-Out-Bytes-HTTPS-Dynamic:** Bytes served via HTTPS for objects with TTL < 3600 seconds
- *region***-Out-Bytes-HTTPS-Proxy:** Bytes returned from CloudFront to viewers via HTTPS in response to `DELETE`, `OPTIONS`, `PATCH`, `POST`, and `PUT` requests
- *region***-Out-OBytes-HTTPS-Proxy:** Total bytes transferred via HTTPS from CloudFront edge locations to your origin in response to `DELETE`, `OPTIONS`, `PATCH`, `POST`, and `PUT` requests

**Data Transferred by Destination**

This chart shows the total amount of data transferred over HTTP and HTTPS from CloudFront edge locations in the selected region during each time interval for the specified CloudFront distribution.

**Data Transferred from CloudFront to Your Users**

- *region***-Out-Bytes-HTTP-Static:** Bytes served via HTTP for objects with TTL 3600 seconds
- *region***-Out-Bytes-HTTPS-Static:** Bytes served via HTTPS for objects with TTL 3600 seconds
- *region***-Out-Bytes-HTTP-Dynamic:** Bytes served via HTTP for objects with TTL < 3600 seconds
- *region***-Out-Bytes-HTTPS-Dynamic:** Bytes served via HTTPS for objects with TTL < 3600 seconds

- *region***-Out-Bytes-HTTP-Proxy:** Bytes returned from CloudFront to viewers via HTTP in response to `DELETE`, `OPTIONS`, `PATCH`, `POST`, and `PUT` requests
- *region***-Out-Bytes-HTTPS-Proxy:** Bytes returned from CloudFront to viewers via HTTPS in response to `DELETE`, `OPTIONS`, `PATCH`, `POST`, and `PUT` requests

**Data Transferred from CloudFront to Your Origin**

- *region***-Out-OBytes-HTTP-Proxy:** Total bytes transferred via HTTP from CloudFront edge locations to your origin in response to `DELETE`, `OPTIONS`, `PATCH`, `POST`, and `PUT` requests
- *region***-Out-OBytes-HTTPS-Proxy:** Total bytes transferred via HTTPS from CloudFront edge locations to your origin in response to `DELETE`, `OPTIONS`, `PATCH`, `POST`, and `PUT` requests

# CloudFront Viewers Reports

The CloudFront console can display four reports about the physical devices (desktop computers, mobile devices) and about the viewers (typically web browsers) that are accessing your content:

- **Devices** – The type of the devices that your users use most frequently to access your content, for example, Desktop or Mobile.
- **Browsers** – The name (or the name and version) of the browsers that your users use most frequently to access your content, for example, Chrome or Firefox. The report lists the top 10 browsers.
- **Operating Systems** – The name (or the name and version) of the operating system that viewers run on most frequently when accessing your content, for example, Linux, Mac OS X, or Windows. The report lists the top 10 operating systems.
- **Locations** – The locations, by country or by U.S. state/territory, of the viewers that access your content most frequently. The report lists the top 50 countries or U.S. states/territories.

You can display all four Viewers reports for any date range in the previous 60 days. For the Locations report, you can also display the report with data points every hour for any date range of up to 14 days in the previous 60 days.

**Note**
You don't need to enable access logging to view Viewers charts and reports.

**Topics**

- Displaying Viewers Charts and Reports
- Downloading Data in CSV Format
- How Data in the Locations Report Is Related to Data in the CloudFront Access Logs

## Displaying Viewers Charts and Reports

To display CloudFront Viewers charts and reports, perform the following procedure.

**To display CloudFront Viewers charts and reports**

1. Sign in to the AWS Management Console and open the CloudFront console at https://console.aws.amazon.com/cloudfront/.

2. In the navigation pane, click **Viewers**.

3. In the **CloudFront Viewers** pane, for **Start Date** and **End Date**, select the date range for which you want to display viewer charts and reports.

   For the Locations chart, available ranges depend on the value that you select for **Granularity**:

   - **Daily** – To display charts with one data point per day, select any date range in the previous 60 days.
   - **Hourly** – To display charts with one data point every hour, select any date range of up to 14 days within the previous 60 days.

   Dates and times are in Coordinated Universal Time (UTC).

4. (Browsers and Operating Systems charts only) For **Grouping**, specify whether you want to group browsers and operating systems by name (Chrome, Firefox) or by name and version (Chrome 40.0, Firefox 35.0).

5. (Locations chart only) For **Granularity**, specify whether to display one data point per day or one data point per hour in the charts. If you specify a date range greater than 14 days, the option to specify one data point per hour is not available.

6. (Locations chart only) For **Details**, specify whether to display the top locations by countries or by U.S. states.

7. In the **Distribution** list, select the distribution for which you want to display data in the usage charts:

- **An individual web distribution** – The charts display data for the selected CloudFront web distribution. The **Distribution** list displays the distribution ID and an alternate domain name (CNAME) for the distribution, if any. If a distribution has no alternate domain names, the list includes an origin domain name for the distribution.
- **All Web Distributions (excludes deleted)** – The charts display summed data for all web distributions that are associated with the current AWS account, excluding web distributions that you have deleted.

8. Click **Update**.

9. To view data for a daily or hourly data point within a chart, move your mouse pointer over the data point.

## Downloading Data in CSV Format

You can download each of the Viewer reports in CSV format. This section explains how to download the reports and describes the values in the report.

**To download the Viewer reports in CSV format**

1. While viewing the applicable Viewer report, click **CSV**.

2. Choose the data that you want to download, for example, **Devices** or **Devices Trends**.

3. In the **Opening** *file name* dialog box, choose whether to open or save the file.

**Topics**

- Information About the Reports
- Devices Report
- Device Trends Report
- Browsers Report
- Browser Trends Report
- Operating Systems Report
- Operating System Trends Report
- Locations Report
- Location Trends Report

**Information About the Reports**

The first few rows of each report includes the following information:

**Version**
The version of the format for this CSV file.

**Report**
The name of the report.

**DistributionID**
The ID of the distribution that you ran the report for, or `ALL` if you ran the report for all web distributions.

**StartDateUTC**
The beginning of the date range for which you ran the report, in Coordinated Universal Time (UTC).

**EndDateUTC**
The end of the date range for which you ran the report, in Coordinated Universal Time (UTC).

**GeneratedTimeUTC**
The date and time on which you ran the report, in Coordinated Universal Time (UTC).

### Grouping (Browsers and Operating Systems Reports Only)
Whether the data is grouped by the name or by the name and version of the browser or operating system.

### Granularity
Whether each row in the report represents one hour or one day.

### Details (Locations Report Only)
Whether requests are listed by country or by U.S. state.


### Devices Report

The report includes the following values:

### DistributionID
The ID of the distribution that you ran the report for, or ALL if you ran the report for all distributions.

### FriendlyName
An alternate domain name (CNAME) for the distribution, if any. If a distribution has no alternate domain names, the list includes an origin domain name for the distribution.

### Requests
The number of requests that CloudFront received from each type of device.

### RequestsPct
The number of requests that CloudFront received from each type of device as a percentage of the total number of requests that CloudFront received from all devices.


### Device Trends Report

The report includes the following values:

### DistributionID
The ID of the distribution that you ran the report for, or ALL if you ran the report for all distributions.

### FriendlyName
An alternate domain name (CNAME) for the distribution, if any. If a distribution has no alternate domain names, the list includes an origin domain name for the distribution.

### TimeBucket
The hour or the day that the data applies to, in Coordinated Universal Time (UTC).

### Desktop
The number of requests that CloudFront received from desktop computers during the period.

### Mobile
The number of requests that CloudFront received from mobile devices during the period. Mobile devices can include both tablets and mobile phones. If CloudFront can't determine whether a request originated from a mobile device or a tablet, it's counted in the Mobile column.

### Smart-TV
The number of requests that CloudFront received from smart TVs during the period.

### Tablet
The number of requests that CloudFront received from tablets during the period. If CloudFront can't determine whether a request originated from a mobile device or a tablet, it's counted in the Mobile column.

### Unknown
Requests for which the value of the User-Agent HTTP header was not associated with one of the standard device types, for example, Desktop or Mobile.

**Empty**

The number of requests that CloudFront received that didn't include a value in the HTTP `User-Agent` header during the period.

## Browsers Report

The report includes the following values:

**DistributionID**

The ID of the distribution that you ran the report for, or `ALL` if you ran the report for all distributions.

**FriendlyName**

An alternate domain name (CNAME) for the distribution, if any. If a distribution has no alternate domain names, the list includes an origin domain name for the distribution.

**Group**

The browser or the browser and version that CloudFront received requests from, depending on the value of `Grouping`. In addition to browser names, possible values include the following:

- **Bot/Crawler** – primarily requests from search engines that are indexing your content.
- **Empty** – requests for which the value of the `User-Agent` HTTP header was empty.
- **Other** – browsers that CloudFront identified but that aren't among the most popular. If `Bot/Crawler`, `Empty`, and/or `Unknown` don't appear among the first nine values, then they're also included in `Other`.
- **Unknown** – requests for which the value of the `User-Agent` HTTP header was not associated with a standard browser. Most requests in this category come from custom applications or scripts.

**Requests**

The number of requests that CloudFront received from each type of browser.

**RequestsPct**

The number of requests that CloudFront received from each type of browser as a percentage of the total number of requests that CloudFront received during the time period.

## Browser Trends Report

The report includes the following values:

**DistributionID**

The ID of the distribution that you ran the report for, or `ALL` if you ran the report for all distributions.

**FriendlyName**

An alternate domain name (CNAME) for the distribution, if any. If a distribution has no alternate domain names, the list includes an origin domain name for the distribution.

**TimeBucket**

The hour or the day that the data applies to, in Coordinated Universal Time (UTC).

**(Browsers)**

The remaining columns in the report list the browsers or the browsers and their versions, depending on the value of `Grouping`. In addition to browser names, possible values include the following:

- **Bot/Crawler** – primarily requests from search engines that are indexing your content.
- **Empty** – requests for which the value of the `User-Agent` HTTP header was empty.
- **Other** – browsers that CloudFront identified but that aren't among the most popular. If `Bot/Crawler`, `Empty`, and/or `Unknown` don't appear among the first nine values, then they're also included in `Other`.
- **Unknown** – requests for which the value of the `User-Agent` HTTP header was not associated with a standard browser. Most requests in this category come from custom applications or scripts.

## Operating Systems Report

The report includes the following values:

### DistributionID
The ID of the distribution that you ran the report for, or `ALL` if you ran the report for all distributions.

### FriendlyName
An alternate domain name (CNAME) for the distribution, if any. If a distribution has no alternate domain names, the list includes an origin domain name for the distribution.

### Group
The operating system or the operating system and version that CloudFront received requests from, depending on the value of `Grouping`. In addition to operating system names, possible values include the following:

- **Bot/Crawler** – primarily requests from search engines that are indexing your content.
- **Empty** – requests for which the value of the `User-Agent` HTTP header was empty.
- **Other** – operating systems that CloudFront identified but that aren't among the most popular. If `Bot/Crawler`, `Empty`, and/or `Unknown` don't appear among the first nine values, then they're also included in `Other`.
- **Unknown** – requests for which the value of the `User-Agent` HTTP header was not associated with a standard browser. Most requests in this category come from custom applications or scripts.

### Requests
The number of requests that CloudFront received from each type of operating system.

### RequestsPct
The number of requests that CloudFront received from each type of operating system as a percentage of the total number of requests that CloudFront received during the time period.

## Operating System Trends Report

The report includes the following values:

### DistributionID
The ID of the distribution that you ran the report for, or `ALL` if you ran the report for all distributions.

### FriendlyName
An alternate domain name (CNAME) for the distribution, if any. If a distribution has no alternate domain names, the list includes an origin domain name for the distribution.

### TimeBucket
The hour or the day that the data applies to, in Coordinated Universal Time (UTC).

### (Operating systems)
The remaining columns in the report list the operating systems or the operating systems and their versions, depending on the value of `Grouping`. In addition to operating system names, possible values include the following:

- **Bot/Crawler** – primarily requests from search engines that are indexing your content.
- **Empty** – requests for which the value of the `User-Agent` HTTP header was empty.
- **Other** – operating systems that CloudFront identified but that aren't among the most popular. If `Bot/Crawler`, `Empty`, and/or `Unknown` don't appear among the first nine values, then they're also included in `Other`.
- **Unknown** – requests for which the operating system isn't specified in the `User-Agent` HTTP header.

## Locations Report

The report includes the following values:

**DistributionID**

The ID of the distribution that you ran the report for, or `ALL` if you ran the report for all distributions.

**FriendlyName**

An alternate domain name (CNAME) for the distribution, if any. If a distribution has no alternate domain names, the list includes an origin domain name for the distribution.

**LocationCode**

The abbreviation for the location that CloudFront received requests from. For more information about possible values, see the description of Location in How Data in the Locations Report Is Related to Data in the CloudFront Access Logs.

**LocationName**

The name of the location that CloudFront received requests from.

**Requests**

The number of requests that CloudFront received from each location.

**RequestsPct**

The number of requests that CloudFront received from each location as a percentage of the total number of requests that CloudFront received from all locations during the time period.

**TotalBytes**

The number of bytes that CloudFront served to viewers in this country or state, for the specified distribution and period.


**Location Trends Report**

The report includes the following values:

**DistributionID**

The ID of the distribution that you ran the report for, or `ALL` if you ran the report for all distributions.

**FriendlyName**

An alternate domain name (CNAME) for the distribution, if any. If a distribution has no alternate domain names, the list includes an origin domain name for the distribution.

**TimeBucket**

The hour or the day that the data applies to, in Coordinated Universal Time (UTC).

**(Locations)**

The remaining columns in the report list the locations that CloudFront received requests from. For more information about possible values, see the description of Location in How Data in the Locations Report Is Related to Data in the CloudFront Access Logs.


## How Data in the Locations Report Is Related to Data in the CloudFront Access Logs

The following list shows how data in the Locations report in the CloudFront console corresponds with values in CloudFront access logs. For more information about CloudFront access logs, see Access Logs.

**Location**

The country or U.S. state that the viewer is in. In access logs, the `c-ip` column contains the IP address of the device that the viewer is running on. We use geolocation data to identify the geographic location of the device based on the IP address.

If you're displaying the **Locations** report by country, note that the country list is based on ISO 3166-2, *Codes for the representation of names of countries and their subdivisions – Part 2: Country subdivision code*. The country list includes the following additional values:

- **Anonymous Proxy** – The request originated from an anonymous proxy.
- **Satellite Provider** – The request originated from a satellite provider that provides internet service to multiple countries. Users might be in countries with a high risk of fraud.
- **Europe (Unknown)** – The request originated from an IP in a block that is used by multiple European countries. The country that the request originated from cannot be determined. CloudFront uses **Europe (Unknown)** as the default.
- **Asia/Pacific (Unknown)** – The request originated from an IP in a block that is used by multiple countries in the Asia/Pacific region. The country that the request originated from cannot be determined. CloudFront uses **Asia/Pacific (Unknown)** as the default. If you display the **Locations** report by U.S. state, note that the report can include U.S. territories and U.S. Armed Forces regions.
  
  If CloudFront can't determine a user's location, the location will appear as Unknown in viewer reports.

### Request Count
The total number of requests from the country or U.S. state that the viewer is in, for the specified distribution and period. This value generally corresponds closely with the number of GET requests from IP addresses in that country or state in CloudFront access logs.

### Request %
One of the following, depending on the value that you selected for **Details**:

- **Countries** – The requests from this country as a percentage of the total number of requests.
- **U.S. States** – The requests from this state as a percentage of the total number of requests from the United States. If requests came from more than 50 countries, then you can't calculate **Request %** based on the data in this table because the **Request Count** column doesn't include all of the requests during the specified period.

### Bytes
The number of bytes that CloudFront served to viewers in this country or state, for the specified distribution and period. To change the display of data in this column to KB, MB, or GB, click the link in the column heading.

# Getting Started with CloudFront

The example in this topic gives you a quick overview of how to use CloudFront to:

- Store the original versions of your objects in one Amazon Simple Storage Service (Amazon S3) bucket.
- Distribute download content such as text or graphics.
- Make your objects accessible to everyone.
- Use the CloudFront domain name in URLs for your objects (for example, `http://d111111abcdef8.cloudfront.net/image.jpg`) instead of your own domain name (for example, `http://www.example.com/image.jpg`).
- Keep your objects in CloudFront edge locations for the default duration of 24 hours. (The minimum duration is 0 seconds.)

For information about how to use CloudFront when you want to use other options, see Task List for Creating a Web Distribution or Task List for Streaming Media Files Using RTMP.

You only need to perform a few basic steps to start delivering your content using CloudFront. The first step is signing up. After that, you create a CloudFront distribution, and then use the CloudFront domain name to reference content in your web pages or applications.

**Topics**

- Step 1: Sign up for Amazon Web Services
- Step 2: Upload your content to Amazon S3 and grant object permissions
- Step 3: Create a CloudFront Web Distribution
- Step 4: Test your links

## Step 1: Sign up for Amazon Web Services

If you haven't already done so, sign up for Amazon Web Services at http://aws.amazon.com. Just choose **Sign Up Now** and enter any required information.

## Step 2: Upload your content to Amazon S3 and grant object permissions

An Amazon S3 bucket is a container that can contain objects or folders. CloudFront can distribute almost any type of object for you using an Amazon S3 bucket as the source, for example, text, images, and videos. You can create multiple buckets, and there is no limit to the amount of data that you can store on Amazon S3.

By default, your Amazon S3 bucket and all of the objects in it are private—only the AWS account that created the bucket has permission to read or write the objects in it. If you want to allow anyone to access the objects in your Amazon S3 bucket using CloudFront URLs, you must grant public read permissions to the objects. (This is one of the most common mistakes when working with CloudFront and Amazon S3. You must explicitly grant privileges to each object in an Amazon S3 bucket.)

**Note**
If you want to restrict who can download your content, you can use the CloudFront private content feature. For more information about distributing private content, see Serving Private Content through CloudFront.

**To upload your content to Amazon S3 and grant read permission to everyone**

1. Sign in to the AWS Management Console and open the Amazon S3 console at https://console.aws.amazon.com/s3/.

2. In the Amazon S3 console, choose **Create Bucket**.

3. In the **Create Bucket** dialog, enter a bucket name. **Important**
   For your bucket to work with CloudFront, the name must conform to DNS naming requirements. For more

information, go to Bucket Restrictions and Limitations in the *Amazon Simple Storage Service Developer Guide*.

4. Select a region for your bucket. By default, Amazon S3 creates buckets in the US East (N. Virginia) region. We recommend that you choose a region close to you to optimize latency, minimize costs, or to address regulatory requirements.

5. Choose **Create**.

6. Select your bucket in the **Buckets** pane, and choose **Upload**.

7. On the **Upload - Select Files** page, choose **Add Files**, and choose the files that you want to upload.

8. Enable public read privileges for each object that you upload to your Amazon S3 bucket.

   1. Choose **Next** to set permissions.

   2. In the **Manage public permissions** drop-down list, choose **Grant public read access to this object(s)**.

   3. Choose **Next**.

9. Set any properties that you want for the object, such as encryption or tagging, and then Choose **Next**.

10. Choose **Upload**.

    After the upload completes, you can navigate to the item by using its URL. In the case of the previous example, the URL would be:

    `http://s3.amazonaws.com/example-myawsbucket/filename`

    Use your Amazon S3 URL to verify that your content is publicly accessible, but remember that this is not the URL you will use when you are ready to distribute your content.

## Step 3: Create a CloudFront Web Distribution

**To create a CloudFront web distribution**

1. Open the CloudFront console at https://console.aws.amazon.com/cloudfront/.

2. Choose **Create Distribution**.

3. On the **Select a delivery method for your content** page, in the **Web** section, choose **Get Started**.

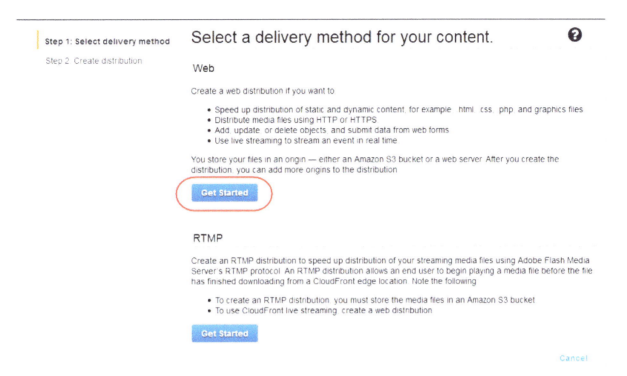

## Select a delivery method for your content.

### Web

Create a web distribution if you want to

- Speed up distribution of static and dynamic content, for example, html, css, php, and graphics files
- Distribute media files using HTTP or HTTPS
- Add, update, or delete objects, and submit data from web forms
- Use live streaming to stream an event in real time

You store your files in an origin — either an Amazon S3 bucket or a web server. After you create the distribution, you can add more origins to the distribution

Get Started

### RTMP

Create an RTMP distribution to speed up distribution of your streaming media files using Adobe Flash Media Server's RTMP protocol. An RTMP distribution allows an end user to begin playing a media file before the file has finished downloading from a CloudFront edge location. Note the following

- To create an RTMP distribution, you must store the media files in an Amazon S3 bucket
- To use CloudFront live streaming, create a web distribution

Get Started

Cancel

4. On the **Create Distribution** page, under **Origin Settings**, choose the Amazon S3 bucket that you created earlier. For **Origin ID**, **Origin Path**, **Restrict Bucket Access**, and **Origin Custom Headers**, accept the default values.

## Create Distribution

## Origin Settings

| | |
|---|---|
| Origin Domain Name | myawsbucket100.com.s3.amazonaws.co |
| Origin Path | |
| Origin ID | S3-myawsbucket100.com |
| Restrict Bucket Access | ○ Yes  ● No |
| Origin Custom Headers | Header Name        Value |

5. Under **Default Cache Behavior Settings**, accept the default values, and CloudFront will:

- Forward all requests that use the CloudFront URL for your distribution (for example, `http://d111111abcdef8.cloudfront.net/image.jpg`) to the Amazon S3 bucket that you specified in Step 4.
- Allow end users to use either HTTP or HTTPS to access your objects.
- Respond to requests for your objects.
- Cache your objects at CloudFront edge locations for 24 hours.
- Forward only the default request headers to your origin and not cache your objects based on the values in the headers.
- Exclude cookies and query string parameters, if any, when forwarding requests for objects to your origin. (Amazon S3 doesn't process cookies and processes only a limited set of query string parameters.)

59

- Not be configured to distribute media files in the Microsoft Smooth Streaming format.
- Allow everyone to view your content.
- Not automatically compress your content.

For more information about cache behavior options, see Cache Behavior Settings.

# Default Cache Behavior Settings

| | |
|---|---|
| **Path Pattern** | Default (*) ⓘ |
| **Viewer Protocol Policy** | ◉ HTTP and HTTPS ⓘ <br> ○ Redirect HTTP to HTTPS <br> ○ HTTPS Only |
| **Allowed HTTP Methods** | ◉ GET, HEAD ⓘ <br> ○ GET, HEAD, OPTIONS <br> ○ GET, HEAD, OPTIONS, PUT, POST, PATCH, DELETE |
| **Cached HTTP Methods** | GET, HEAD (Cached by default) ⓘ |
| **Forward Headers** | None (Improves Caching) ▾ ⓘ |
| **Object Caching** | ◉ Use Origin Cache Headers ⓘ <br> ○ Customize <br> Learn More |
| **Minimum TTL** | 0 ⓘ |
| **Maximum TTL** | 31536000 ⓘ |
| **Default TTL** | 86400 ⓘ |
| **Forward Cookies** | None (Improves Caching) ▾ ⓘ |
| **Forward Query Strings** | ○ Yes ⓘ <br> ◉ No (Improves Caching) |
| **Smooth Streaming** | ○ Yes ⓘ <br> ◉ No |
| **Restrict Viewer Access (Use Signed URLs or Signed Cookies)** | ○ Yes ⓘ <br> ◉ No |
| **Compress Objects Automatically** | ○ Yes ⓘ <br> ◉ No <br> Learn More |

6. Under **Distribution Settings**, enter the applicable values:

**Price Class**

Select the price class that corresponds with the maximum price that you want to pay for CloudFront service. By default, CloudFront serves your objects from edge locations in all CloudFront regions.

For more information about price classes and about how your choice of price class affects CloudFront performance for your distribution, go to Choosing the Price Class for a CloudFront Distribution. For information about CloudFront pricing, including how price classes map to CloudFront regions, go to Amazon CloudFront Pricing.

**AWS WAF Web ACL**

If you want to use AWS WAF to allow or block HTTP and HTTPS requests based on criteria that you specify, choose the web ACL to associate with this distribution. For more information about AWS WAF, see the AWS WAF Developer Guide.

**Alternate Domain Names (CNAMEs) (Optional)**

Specify one or more domain names that you want to use for URLs for your objects instead of the domain name that CloudFront assigns when you create your distribution. For example, if you want the URL for the object:

`/images/image.jpg`

to look like this:

`http://www.example.com/images/image.jpg`

instead of like this:

`http://d111111abcdef8.cloudfront.net/images/image.jpg`

you would create a CNAME for `www.example.com`.

If you add a CNAME for `www.example.com` to your distribution, you also need to create (or update) a CNAME record with your DNS service to route queries for `www.example.com` to `d111111abcdef8.cloudfront.net`. You must have permission to create a CNAME record with the DNS service provider for the domain. Typically, this means that you own the domain, but you may also be developing an application for the domain owner. For more information about CNAMEs, see Adding and Moving Alternate Domain Names (CNAMEs). For the current limit on the number of alternate domain names that you can add to a distribution or request a higher limit, see General Limits on Web Distributions.

**SSL Certificate**

Accept the default value, **Default CloudFront Certificate**.

**Default Root Object (Optional)**

The object that you want CloudFront to request from your origin (for example, `index.html`) when a viewer requests the root URL of your distribution (`http://www.example.com/`) instead of an object in your distribution (`http://www.example.com/product-description.html`). Specifying a default root object avoids exposing the contents of your distribution.

**Logging (Optional)**

If you want CloudFront to log information about each request for an object and store the log files in an Amazon S3 bucket, select **On**, and specify the bucket and an optional prefix for the names of the log files. There is no extra charge to enable logging, but you accrue the usual Amazon S3 charges for storing and accessing the files. CloudFront doesn't delete the logs automatically, but you can delete them at any time.

**Cookie Logging**

In this example, we're using Amazon S3 as the origin for your objects, and Amazon S3 doesn't process cookies, so we recommend that you select **Off** for the value of **Cookie Logging**.

**Comment (Optional)**

Enter any comments that you want to save with the distribution.

**Distribution State**

Select **Enabled** if you want CloudFront to begin processing requests as soon as the distribution is created, or select **Disabled** if you do not want CloudFront to begin processing requests after the distribution is created.

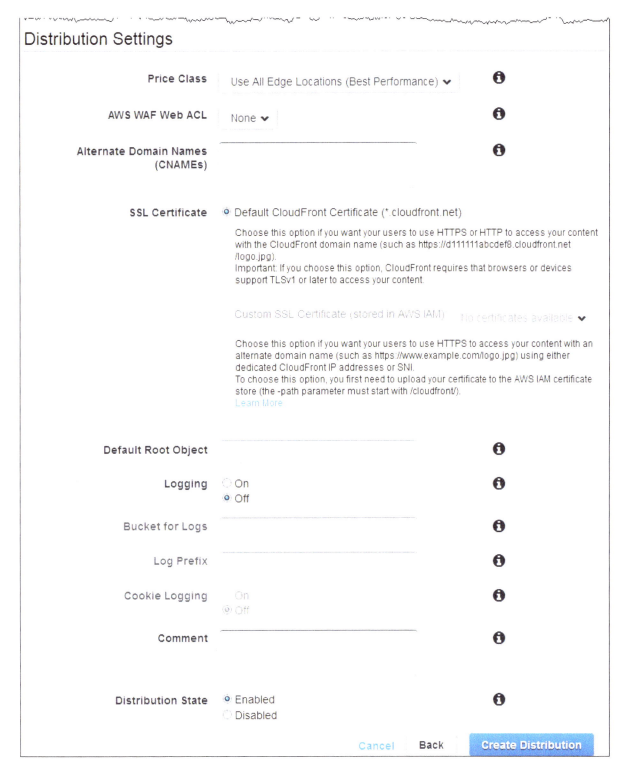

## Distribution Settings

| | |
|---|---|
| **Price Class** | Use All Edge Locations (Best Performance) ▾ ❶ |
| **AWS WAF Web ACL** | None ▾ ❶ |
| **Alternate Domain Names (CNAMEs)** | ❶ |
| **SSL Certificate** | ⦿ Default CloudFront Certificate (*.cloudfront.net) |

Choose this option if you want your users to use HTTPS or HTTP to access your content with the CloudFront domain name (such as https://d111111abcdef8.cloudfront.net /logo.jpg).
Important: If you choose this option, CloudFront requires that browsers or devices support TLSv1 or later to access your content.

○ Custom SSL Certificate (stored in AWS IAM)　No certificates available ▾

Choose this option if you want your users to use HTTPS to access your content with an alternate domain name (such as https://www.example.com/logo.jpg) using either dedicated CloudFront IP addresses or SNI.
To choose this option, you first need to upload your certificate to the AWS IAM certificate store (the -path parameter must start with /cloudfront/).
Learn More

| | |
|---|---|
| **Default Root Object** | ❶ |
| **Logging** | ○ On <br> ⦿ Off ❶ |
| **Bucket for Logs** | ❶ |
| **Log Prefix** | ❶ |
| **Cookie Logging** | ○ On <br> ⦿ Off ❶ |
| **Comment** | ❶ |
| **Distribution State** | ⦿ Enabled <br> ○ Disabled ❶ |

Cancel   **Back**   **Create Distribution**

7. Choose **Create Distribution**.

8. After CloudFront has created your distribution, the value of the **Status** column for your distribution will change from **InProgress** to **Deployed**. If you chose to enable the distribution, it will then be ready to process requests. This typically takes between 20 and 40 minutes.

   The domain name that CloudFront assigns to your distribution appears in the list of distributions. (It also appears on the **General** tab for a selected distribution.)

63

## Step 4: Test your links

After you've created your distribution, CloudFront knows where your Amazon S3 origin server is, and you know the domain name associated with the distribution. You can create a link to your Amazon S3 bucket content with that domain name, and have CloudFront serve it.

**Note**
You must wait until the status of your distribution changes to **Deployed** before testing your links.

\*\*\*\*

**To link to your objects**

1. Copy the following HTML into a new file:

   - Replace with the domain name that CloudFront assigned to your distribution.
   - Replace with the name of a file in your Amazon S3 bucket.

```
1  1. <html>
2  2. <head>My CloudFront Test</head>
3  3. <body>
4  4. <p>My text content goes here.</p>
5  5. <p><img src="http://domain name/object name" alt="my test image"/>
6  6. </body>
7  7. </html>
```

   For example, if your domain name was `d111111abcdef8.cloudfront.net` and your object was `image.jpg`, the URL for the link would be:

   `http://d111111abcdef8.cloudfront.net/image.jpg`.

   If your object is in a folder within your bucket, include the folder in the URL. For example, if image.jpg is located in an images folder, then the URL would be:

   http://d111111abcdef8/.cloudfront/.net/images/image/.jpg

2. Save the text in a file that has a .html filename extension.

3. Open your web page in a browser to ensure that you can see your content. If you cannot see the content, confirm that you have performed all of the steps correctly. You can also see the tips in Troubleshooting.

The browser returns your page with the embedded image file, served from the edge location that CloudFront determined was appropriate to serve the object.

For more information on using CloudFront, go to Amazon CloudFront Resources.

# Working with Distributions

**Topics**

- Overview of Web and RTMP Distributions
- Creating Web and RTMP Distributions
- Viewing and Updating CloudFront Distributions
- Deleting a Distribution
- Adding and Moving Alternate Domain Names (CNAMEs)
- Choosing the Price Class for a CloudFront Distribution
- Using CloudFront with Amazon S3
- Tracking Configuration Changes with AWS Config
- Changes to the CloudFront API

The following table lists the CloudFront actions that you can take to work with distributions and provides links to the corresponding documentation on how to do the actions with the CloudFront console and the CloudFront API.

| Action | Using the CloudFront Console | Using the CloudFront API: Web Distributions | Using the CloudFront API: RTMP Distributions |
|---|---|---|---|
| Create a distribution | **Web Distributions:** See Task List for Creating a Web Distribution **RTMP Distributions:** See Task List for Streaming Media Files Using RTMP | Go to CreateDistribution | Go to CreateStreamingDistribution |
| List your distributions | See Viewing and Updating CloudFront Distributions | Go to ListDistributions | Go to ListStreamingDistributions |
| Get all information about a distribution | See Viewing and Updating CloudFront Distributions | Go to GetDistribution | Go to GetStreamingDistribution |
| Get the distribution configuration | See Viewing and Updating CloudFront Distributions | Go to GetDistributionConfig | Go to GetStreamingDistributionConfig |
| Update a distribution | See Viewing and Updating CloudFront Distributions | Go to UpdateDistributionConfig | Go to UpdateStreamingDistributionConfig |
| Delete a distribution | See Deleting a Distribution | Go to Delete Distribution | Go to Delete Streaming Distribution |

# Overview of Web and RTMP Distributions

When you want to use CloudFront to distribute your content, you create a distribution and specify configuration settings such as:

- Your origin, which is the Amazon S3 bucket or HTTP server from which CloudFront gets the files that it distributes. You can specify any combination of up to 25 Amazon S3 buckets and/or HTTP servers as your origins.
- Whether you want the files to be available to everyone or you want to restrict access to selected users.
- Whether you want CloudFront to require users to use HTTPS to access your content.
- Whether you want CloudFront to forward cookies and/or query strings to your origin.
- Whether you want CloudFront to prevent users in selected countries from accessing your content.
- Whether you want CloudFront to create access logs.

For the current limit on the number of distributions that you can create for each AWS account, see General Limits on Web Distributions and Limits on RTMP Distributions.

The number of files that you can serve per distribution is unlimited.

## Web Distributions

You can use web distributions to serve the following content over HTTP or HTTPS:

- Static and dynamic download content, for example, .html, .css, .js, and image files, using HTTP or HTTPS.

- Multimedia content on demand using progressive download and Apple HTTP Live Streaming (HLS). For more information, see the applicable topic in Working with Web Distributions.

  You can't serve Adobe Flash multimedia content over HTTP or HTTPS, but you can serve it using a CloudFront RTMP distribution. See RTMP Distributions below.

- A live event, such as a meeting, conference, or concert, in real time. For live streaming, you create the distribution automatically by using an AWS CloudFormation stack. For more information, see the applicable live-streaming tutorial in CloudFront Streaming Tutorials.

For web distributions, your origin can be either an Amazon S3 bucket or an HTTP server, for example, a web server. For more information about how web distributions work, including the values that you specify when you create a web distribution, see Working with Web Distributions. For information about creating a web distribution, see Task List for Creating a Web Distribution.

## RTMP Distributions

RTMP distributions stream media files using Adobe Media Server and the Adobe Real-Time Messaging Protocol (RTMP). An RTMP distribution must use an Amazon S3 bucket as the origin.

For information about the values you specify when you create an RTMP distribution, see Working with RTMP Distributions. For information about creating an RTMP distribution, see Task List for Streaming Media Files Using RTMP.

# Creating Web and RTMP Distributions

**Web distributions:** For information about creating web distributions using the CloudFront console, see Task List for Creating a Web Distribution. For information about creating web distributions using the CloudFront API, see CreateDistribution in the *Amazon CloudFront API Reference.*

**RTMP distributions:** For information about creating RTMP distributions using the CloudFront console, see Task List for Streaming Media Files Using RTMP. For information about creating RTMP distributions using the CloudFront API, see CreateStreamingDistribution in the *Amazon CloudFront API Reference.*

# Viewing and Updating CloudFront Distributions

In the CloudFront console, you can see the CloudFront distributions that are associated with your AWS account, view the settings for a distribution, and update most settings. Be aware that settings changes that you make won't take effect until the distribution has propagated to the AWS edge locations.

**To Update CloudFront Distributions Using the CloudFront Console**

1. Sign in to the AWS Management Console and open the CloudFront console at https://console.aws.amazon.com/cloudfront/.

2. Select the ID of a distribution. The list includes all of the distributions associated with the AWS account that you used to sign in to the CloudFront console.

3. To view or edit settings for a distribution, choose the **Distribution Settings** tab.

4. To make updates, do one of the following:

    1. For RTMP distribution settings, choose **Edit**, and then update values.

       For information about the fields, see Values that You Specify When You Create or Update an RTMP Distribution.

    2. For web distribution settings, to update general settings, choose **Edit**. Otherwise, choose the tab for the settings that you want to view or update: **Origins** or **Behaviors**.

5. Make the updates, and then, to save your changes, choose **Yes, Edit**. For information about the fields, see the following topics:

    - **General settings:** Distribution Details
    - **Origin settings:** Origin Settings
    - **Cache behavior settings:** Cache Behavior Settings

6. If you want to delete an origin in your distribution, do the following:

    1. Choose **Behaviors**, and make sure you have moved any default cache behaviors associated with the origin to another origin.

    2. Choose **Origins**, and then select an origin.

    3. Choose **Delete**.

When you save changes to your distribution configuration, CloudFront starts to propagate the changes to all edge locations. Until your configuration is updated in an edge location, CloudFront continues to serve your content from that location based on the previous configuration. After your configuration is updated in an edge location, CloudFront immediately starts to serve your content from that location based on the new configuration.

Your changes don't propagate to every edge location instantaneously. When propagation is complete, the status of your distribution changes from **InProgress** to **Deployed**. While CloudFront is propagating your changes, we unfortunately can't determine whether a given edge location is serving your content based on the previous configuration or the new configuration.

# Deleting a Distribution

If you no longer want to use a distribution, use the following procedure to delete it using the CloudFront console.

You can also delete a distribution using the CloudFront API:

- To delete a web distribution, use the `DeleteDistribution` API action. For more information, go to DeleteDistribution in the *Amazon CloudFront API Reference.*
- To delete an RTMP distribution, use the `DeleteStreamingDistribution` API action. For more information, go to DeleteStreamingDistribution in the *Amazon CloudFront API Reference.*

**Note**
CloudFront lets you create a total of up to 200 web distributions and 100 RTMP distributions for an AWS account.

**To Delete a CloudFront Distribution Using the CloudFront Console**

1. Sign in to the AWS Management Console and open the CloudFront console at https://console.aws.amazon.com/cloudfront/.

2. In the right pane of the CloudFront console, find the distribution that you want to delete.

3. If the value of the **State** column is **Disabled**, skip to Step 7.

   If the value of **State** is **Enabled** and the value of **Status** is **Deployed**, continue with Step 4 to disable the distribution before deleting it.

   If the value of **State** is **Enabled** and the value of **Status** is **InProgress**, wait until **Status** changes to **Deployed**. Then continue with Step 4 to disable the distribution before deleting it.

4. In the right pane of the CloudFront console, check the check box for the distribution that you want to delete.

5. Click **Disabled** to disable the distribution, and click **Yes, Disable** to confirm. Then click **Close**.

6. The value of the **State** column immediately changes to **Disabled**. Wait until the value of the **Status** column changes to **Deployed**.

7. Check the check box for the distribution that you want to delete.

8. Click **Delete**, and click **Yes, Delete** to confirm. Then click **Close**.

# Adding and Moving Alternate Domain Names (CNAMEs)

In CloudFront, an alternate domain name, also known as a CNAME, lets you use your own domain name (for example, `www.example.com`) for links to your objects instead of using the domain name that CloudFront assigns to your distribution. Both web and RTMP distributions support alternate domain names.

When you create a distribution, CloudFront returns a domain name for the distribution, for example:

`d111111abcdef8.cloudfront.net`

When you use the CloudFront domain name for your objects, the URL for an object called `/images/image.jpg` is:

`http://d111111abcdef8.cloudfront.net/images/image.jpg`

If you want to use your own domain name, such as `www.example.com`, instead of the `cloudfront.net` domain name that CloudFront assigned to your distribution, you can add an alternate domain name to your distribution for `www.example.com`. You can then use the following URL for `/images/image.jpg`:

`http://www.example.com/images/image.jpg`

**Topics**

- Adding an Alternate Domain Name
- Moving an Alternate Domain Name to a Different CloudFront Distribution
- Removing an Alternate Domain Name
- Using the * Wildcard in Alternate Domain Names
- Restrictions on Using Alternate Domain Names

## Adding an Alternate Domain Name

The following task list describes the process for using the CloudFront console to add an alternate domain name to your distribution so you can use your own domain name in your links instead of the CloudFront domain name that is automatically associated with your distribution. For information about updating your distribution using the CloudFront API, see Working with Distributions.

**Note**
If you want viewers to use HTTPS with your alternate domain name, see Using Alternate Domain Names and HTTPS.

**Adding an Alternate Domain Name (Console)**

1. Sign in to the AWS Management Console and open the CloudFront console at https://console.aws.amazon.com/cloudfront/.

2. Choose the ID for the distribution that you want to update.

3. On the **General** tab, choose **Edit**.

4. Update the following values:
   **Alternate Domain Names (CNAMEs)**
   Add your alternate domain names. Separate domain names with commas, or type each domain name on a new line.
   **SSL Certificate (Web Distributions Only)**
   Choose an option, depending on whether you want viewers to use HTTPS to access your content:

   - **Don't use HTTPS** – Choose **Default CloudFront Certificate**.

   - **Use HTTPS** – Choose **Custom SSL Certificate**, and choose a certificate from the list. The list can include certificates provisioned by AWS Certificate Manager (ACM), certificates that you purchased from another certificate authority and uploaded to ACM, and certificates that you purchased from another certificate authority and uploaded to the IAM certificate store.

If you uploaded a certificate to the IAM certificate store but it doesn't appear in the list, review the procedure Importing an SSL/TLS Certificate to confirm that you correctly uploaded the certificate.

If you choose this setting, we recommend that you use only an alternate domain name in your object URLs (https://example/.com/logo/.jpg/)/. If you use your CloudFront distribution domain name (https://d111111abcdef8/.cloudfront/.net/logo/.jpg/) and the viewer supports SNI, then CloudFront behaves normally. However, a viewer that does not support SNI exhibits one of the following behaviors, depending on the value of **Clients Supported**:

- **All Clients**: If the viewer doesn't support SNI, it displays a warning because the CloudFront domain name doesn't match the domain name in your SSL/TLS certificate.
- **Only Clients that Support Server Name Indication (SNI)**: CloudFront drops the connection with the viewer without returning the object.
  **Clients Supported (Web Distributions Only)**
  Choose the applicable options:

- **All Clients**: CloudFront serves your HTTPS content using dedicated IP addresses. If you select this option, you incur additional charges when you associate your SSL/TLS certificate with a distribution that is enabled. For more information, see http://aws.amazon.com/cloudfront/pricing.

- **Only Clients that Support Server Name Indication (SNI)**: Older browsers or other clients that don't support SNI must use another method to access your content. For more information, see Choosing How CloudFront Serves HTTPS Requests.

5. Choose **Yes, Edit**.

6. On the **General** tab for the distribution, confirm that **Distribution Status** has changed to **Deployed**. If you try to use an alternate domain name before the updates to your distribution have been deployed, the links that you create in the following steps might not work.

7. Configure the DNS service for the domain to route traffic for the domain, such as example.com, to the CloudFront domain name for your distribution, such as d111111abcdef8.cloudfront.net. The method that you use depends on whether you're using Route 53 as the DNS service provider for the domain. **Note** If your DNS record already points to a distribution that is not the distribution that you are creating, then you can't add the alternate domain name to your distribution without updating your DNS. For more information, see Restrictions on Using Alternate Domain Names.
   **Route 53**
   Create an alias resource record set. With an alias resource record set, you don't pay for Route 53 queries. In addition, you can create an alias resource record set for the root domain name (example.com), which DNS doesn't allow for CNAMEs. For more information, see Routing Queries to an Amazon CloudFront Distribution in the *Amazon Route 53 Developer Guide.*
   **Another DNS service provider**
   Use the method provided by your DNS service provider to add a CNAME resource record set to the hosted zone for your domain. This new CNAME resource record set will redirect DNS queries from your domain (for example, www.example.com) to the CloudFront domain name for your distribution (for example, d111111abcdef8.cloudfront.net). For more information, see the documentation provided by your DNS service provider.
   If you already have an existing CNAME record for your domain name, update that resource record set or replace it with a new one that points to the CloudFront domain name for your distribution.
   In addition, confirm that your CNAME resource record set points to your distribution's domain name and not to one of your origin servers.

8. Using dig or a similar tool, confirm that the resource record set that you created in step 7 points to the domain name for your distribution. For more information about dig, go to http://www.kloth.net/services/dig.php.

The following example shows a dig request on the images.example.com domain, as well as the relevant part of the response.

```
 1 [prompt]--> dig images.example.com
 2
 3 ; <<>> DiG 9.3.3rc2 <<>> images.example.com
 4 ;; global options:   printcmd
 5 ;; Got answer:
 6 ;; ->>HEADER<<- opcode: QUERY, status: NOERROR, id: 15917
 7 ;; flags: qr rd ra; QUERY: 1, ANSWER: 9, AUTHORITY: 2, ADDITIONAL: 0
 8
 9 ;; QUESTION SECTION:
10 ;images.example.com.       IN    A
11
12 ;; ANSWER SECTION:
13 images.example.com. 10800 IN CNAME    d111111abcdef8.cloudfront.net.
14 ...
15 ...
```

The line in the Answer Section shows a CNAME resource record set that routes queries for images.example.com to the CloudFront distribution domain name d111111abcdef8.cloudfront.net. The CNAME resource record set is configured correctly if the name on the right side of `CNAME` is the domain name for your CloudFront distribution. If that is any other value, for example, the domain name for your Amazon S3 bucket, then the CNAME resource record set is configured incorrectly. In that case, go back to Step 4 and correct the CNAME record to point to the domain name for your distribution.

9. Test the alternate domain name by creating some test links that use your domain name in the URL instead of the CloudFront domain name for your distribution.

10. In your application, change the links for your objects to use your alternate domain name instead of the domain name of your CloudFront distribution.

## Moving an Alternate Domain Name to a Different CloudFront Distribution

If you want to move an alternate domain name from one CloudFront distribution to another distribution, the steps you must take depend on the domain name that you want to move:

- For a subdomain like `marketing.example.com`, you can move the domain yourself. For detailed steps, see Move a subdomain name, like marketing.example.com, to another distribution.
- For a domain like `example.com` (a second-level domain), you must work with AWS support to move the domain to another distribution  Move a domain name, like example.com, to another distribution.

### Move a subdomain name, like marketing.example.com, to another distribution

Follow these steps to move the subdomain name.

**To move a subdomain name to a new distribution**

1. Sign in to the AWS Management Console and open the CloudFront console at https://console.aws.amazon.com/cloudfront/.

2. If you don't have a new distribution to move the domain name to, create one. For more information, see Creating a Web Distribution.

3. Add to the distribution an alternate domain name that includes a wildcard for the alias record set or CNAME record. For example, if the subdomain name that you want to move to the new distribution is `marketing.example.com`, add the alternate domain name `*.example.com`. For more information, see Using the * Wildcard in Alternate Domain Names. **Note**

You can't add a wildcard to a top level domain name, such as `*.com`, so if you want to move a domain name like `example.com` to a new distribution, see Move a domain name, like example.com, to another distribution.

4. Update the DNS configuration for your subdomain to point to the new distribution. For example, you would update the DNS service for the subdomain `marketing.example.com` to route traffic to the CloudFront domain name for your distribution, `d111111abcdef8.cloudfront.net`.

   To update the configuration, do one of the following:

   - **If you're using Route 53,** update alias records or CNAME records, depending how you set up the alternate domain name originally. For more information, see Editing Records in the *Amazon Route 53 Developer Guide.*
   - **If you're using another DNS service provider,** use the method provided by the DNS service provider to update the CNAME record that directs traffic to CloudFront. For more information, see the documentation provided by your DNS service provider.

5. Using dig or a similar tool, confirm that the resource record set that you created in step 4 points to the domain name for your distribution. For more information about dig, go to http://www.kloth.net/services/dig.php.

   The following example shows a dig request on the images.example.com domain, as well as the relevant part of the response.

```
1  [prompt]--> dig images.example.com
2
3  ; <<>> DiG 9.3.3rc2 <<>> images.example.com
4  ;; global options:   printcmd
5  ;; Got answer:
6  ;; ->>HEADER<<- opcode: QUERY, status: NOERROR, id: 15917
7  ;; flags: qr rd ra; QUERY: 1, ANSWER: 9, AUTHORITY: 2, ADDITIONAL: 0
8
9  ;; QUESTION SECTION:
10 ;images.example.com.      IN    A
11
12 ;; ANSWER SECTION:
13 images.example.com. 10800 IN CNAME    d111111abcdef8.cloudfront.net.
14 ...
15 ...
```

   The line in the Answer Section shows a CNAME resource record set that routes queries for images.example.com to the CloudFront distribution domain name d111111abcdef8.cloudfront.net. The CNAME resource record set is configured correctly if the name on the right side of `CNAME` is the domain name for your CloudFront distribution. If that is any other value, for example, the domain name for your Amazon S3 bucket, then the CNAME resource record set is configured incorrectly. In that case, go back to Step 4 and correct the CNAME record to point to the domain name for your distribution.

6. Remove the CNAME from the existing distribution and move it to the new CloudFront distribution. For example, move `marketing.example.com` to a new distribution that by default is pointed to by something like `d111111abcdef8.cloudfront.net`.

7. Test the alternate domain name by creating some test links that use your domain name in the URL instead of the CloudFront domain name for your distribution.

8. If you're no longer using the original distribution, delete it. For more information, see Deleting a Distribution.

**Move a domain name, like example.com, to another distribution**

For second-level domain names, like example.com, you must contact AWS Support to move the domain name to another CloudFront distribution. The extra steps are required because moving a domain yourself, as described in the previous procedure, requires setting up domain routing using a wildcard for part of the domain name. For second-level domains, for this step, you would have to set up routing as *.com, which isn't allowed.

Before you get started, if you don't have a new distribution to move the domain name to, create one. For more, information see Creating a Web Distribution.

Moving a domain name like example.com to a new distribution takes two steps:

Step 1: Provide proof to AWS Support that you own the domain name by creating a TXT record for your domain at your DNS service provider. This helps prevent someone else from making changes to your distribution configuration.

Step 2: Request that AWS Support move your domain to the new CloudFront distribution.

Here are the specific steps to take.

**Step 1: Create a TXT record for your domain**

1.  Sign in to your DNS service provider website.

    If your service provider is Route 53, sign in to the Route 53 console.

2.  Create a TXT record for your domain like the following:

    TXT

    For example: `example.com TXT d123.cloudfront.net`

    - If your DNS service provider is Route 53, go to Step 3 for detailed steps.
    - If your domain is hosted by another DNS service provider, see the documentation at the DNS service provider. You may need to request that your service provider create the TXT record for you. **Tip** If your service provider does not allow a TXT name for a domain to have the same information as a CNAME record, consider creating a TXT record that uses your domain name with an underscore (_) prepended to it. For an example, see the following Knowledge Center article: Resolve CNAME Already Exists Error.

3.  If your DNS service provider is Route 53, use the following steps to create a TXT record to prove domain ownership:

    1.  On the **Hosted Zones** page, double-click the row for the hosted zone in which you want to edit records.

    2.  Choose **Create Record Set**.

    3.  Enter the following values:

        - **Name**: The domain name you want to move to a new CloudFront distribution.
        - **Type**: TXT
        - **Alias**: No
        - **TTL**: 60 seconds
        - **Value**: The name of the CloudFront distribution that you want to add this domain name to, such as d123.cloudfront.net.
        - **Routing policy**: Simple

    4.  Choose **Create**.

**Step 2: Request that AWS Support move your domain to the new CloudFront distribution**

- Sign in to AWS and contact AWS support to request that they verify that you own the domain, and move the domain to the new CloudFront distribution. **Note**

AWS Support can't verify your domain ownership until they can view the TXT record that you created for your domain. Be aware that records that you create at your DNS provider can take a while (up to several days) to propagate through the DNS system.

## Removing an Alternate Domain Name

If you want to stop routing traffic for a domain or subdomain to a CloudFront distribution, follow the steps in this section to update both the DNS configuration and the CloudFront distribution.

It's important that you remove the alternate domain names from the distribution as well as update your DNS configuration. This helps prevent issues later if you want to associate the domain name with another CloudFront distribution. If an alternate domain name is already associated with one distribution, it can't be set up with another.

**Note**
If you want to remove the alternate domain name from this distribution so you can add it to another one, follow the steps in Moving an Alternate Domain Name to a Different CloudFront Distribution. If you follow the steps here instead (to remove a domain) and then add the domain to another distribution, there will be a period of time during which the domain won't link to the new distribution because CloudFront is propagating to the updates to edge locations.

**To remove an alternate domain name from a distribution**

1. To start, route internet traffic for your domain to another resource that isn't your CloudFront distribution, such as an Elastic Load Balancing load balancer. Or you can delete the DNS record that's routing traffic to CloudFront.

   Do one of the following, depending on the DNS service for your domain:

   - **If you're using Route 53**, update or delete alias records or CNAME records. For more information, see Editing Records or Deleting Records.
   - **If you're using another DNS service provider**, use the method provided by the DNS service provider to update or delete the CNAME record that directs traffic to CloudFront. For more information, see the documentation provided by your DNS service provider.

2. After you update your domain's DNS records, wait until the changes have propagated and DNS resolvers are routing traffic to the new resource. You can check to see when this is complete by creating some test links that use your domain in the URL.

3. Now, sign in to the AWS Management Console and open the CloudFront console at https://console.aws.amazon.com/cloudfront/, and then update your CloudFront distribution to remove the domain name by doing the following:

   1. Choose the ID for the distribution that you want to update.

   2. On the **General** tab, choose **Edit**.

   3. In **Alternate Domain Names (CNAMEs)**, remove the alternate domain name (or domain names) that you no longer want to use for your distribution.

   4. Choose **Yes, Edit**.

## Using the * Wildcard in Alternate Domain Names

When you add alternate domain names, you can use the * wildcard at the beginning of a domain name instead of adding subdomains individually. For example, with an alternate domain name of `*.example.com`, you can use any domain name that ends with example.com in your object URLs, such as `www.example.com`, `product-name.example.com`, and `marketing.product-name.example.com`. The name of an object is the same regardless of the domain name, for example:

```
www.example.com/images/image.jpg
```

```
product-name.example.com/images/image.jpg
```

```
marketing.product-name.example.com/images/image.jpg
```

The alternate domain name must begin with an asterisk and a dot ( `*.` ). You *cannot* use a wildcard to replace part of a subdomain name, like this: `*domain.example.com`, and you cannot replace a subdomain in the middle of a domain name, like this: `subdomain.*.example.com`.

A wildcard alternate domain name, such as `*.example.com`, can include another alternate domain name, such as `example.com`, as long as they're both in the same CloudFront distribution or they're in distributions that were created by using the same AWS account.

## Restrictions on Using Alternate Domain Names

Note the following restrictions on using alternate domain names:

**CNAMEs Must be Lowercase**
All CNAMES must be lowercase to be valid.

**Maximum Number of Alternate Domain Names**
For the current limit on the number of alternate domain names that you can add to a distribution or to request a higher limit, see General Limits on Web Distributions.

**Permission to Change DNS Configuration**
If you're adding alternate domain names to your distribution, you must create CNAME records to route DNS queries for the domain names to your CloudFront distribution. So you must have permission to create CNAME records with the DNS service provider for the domains you're using. Typically, this means that you own the domains, but you might be developing an application for the domain owner.

**Duplicate and Overlapping Alternate Domain Names**
You cannot add an alternate domain name to a CloudFront distribution if the alternate domain name already exists in another CloudFront distribution, even if your AWS account owns the other distribution.
However, you can add a wildcard alternate domain name, such as `*.example.com`, that includes (that overlaps with) a non-wildcard alternate domain name, such as `www.example.com`. Overlapping domain names can be in the same distribution or in separate distributions as long as both distributions were created by using the same AWS account.

**Alternate Domain Names that Already Point to a Distribution**
If your DNS record points to a distribution that is not the distribution that you are creating or modifying, then you can't add the alternate domain name to your distribution. In this scenario, you must update your DNS at your DNS provider before you can add the domain name for your CloudFront distribution.
To correct this, sign in to your DNS provider and remove the existing DNS record, or contact your DNS provider to remove it for you. Then create the correct DNS record for your distribution, following the steps for adding or changing the alternate domain name for a distribution. For more information, see Adding an Alternate Domain Name (Console) or Moving an Alternate Domain Name to a Different CloudFront Distribution.

**Adding an Alternate Domain Name at the Top Node (Zone Apex) for a Domain**
When you add an alternate domain name to a distribution, you typically create a CNAME record in your DNS configuration to route DNS queries for the domain name to your CloudFront distribution. However, you can't create a CNAME record for the top node of a DNS namespace, also known as the zone apex; the DNS protocol doesn't allow it. For example, if you register the DNS name `example.com`, the zone apex is `example.com`. You can't create a CNAME record for `example.com`, but you can create CNAME records for `www.example.com`, `newproduct.example.com`, and so on.
If you're using Route 53 as your DNS service, you can create an alias resource record set, which has two advantages over CNAME records. You can create an alias resource record set for a domain name at the top node (example.com). In addition, when you use an alias resource record set, you don't pay for Route 53 queries. If you enable IPv6, you must create two alias resource record sets: one to route IPv4 traffic (an A record) and

one to route IPv6 traffic (an AAAA record). For more information, see Enable IPv6 in the topic Values That You Specify When You Create or Update a Web Distribution. For more information, see Routing Queries to an Amazon CloudFront Distribution in the *Amazon Route 53 Developer Guide*.

**Alternate Domain Names and HTTPS**

If you want viewers to use HTTPS with an alternate domain names, additional configuration is required. For more information, see Using Alternate Domain Names and HTTPS.

# Choosing the Price Class for a CloudFront Distribution

CloudFront has edge locations all over the world. Our cost for each edge location varies and, as a result, the price that we charge you varies depending on the edge location from which CloudFront serves your requests.

CloudFront edge locations are grouped into geographic regions, and we've grouped regions into price classes. The default price class includes all regions. Another price class includes most regions (the United States; Europe; Hong Kong, Korea, and Singapore; Japan; and India regions) but excludes the most-expensive regions. A third price class includes only the least-expensive regions (the United States and Europe regions).

By default, CloudFront responds to requests for your objects based only on performance: objects are served from the edge location for which latency is lowest for that viewer. If you're willing to accept higher latency for your viewers in some geographic regions in return for lower cost, you can choose a price class that doesn't include all CloudFront regions. Although CloudFront will serve your objects only from the edge locations in that price class, it still serves content from the edge location that has the lowest latency among the edge locations in your selected price class. However, some of your viewers, especially those in geographic regions that are not in your price class, may see higher latency than if your content were being served from all CloudFront edge locations. For example, if you choose the price class that includes only the United States and Europe, viewers in Australia and in Asia may experience higher latency than if you choose the price class that includes Australia and Asia.

If you choose a price class that does not include all edge locations, CloudFront may still occasionally serve requests for your content from an edge location in a region that is not included in your price class. When this happens, you are not charged the rate for the more expensive region from which your objects were served. Instead, you're charged the rate for the least-expensive region in your selected price class.

You can choose a price class when you create or update a CloudFront web distribution or RTMP distribution. To find the applicable topic about creating or updating a web or an RTMP distribution using the CloudFront console or API, see Working with Distributions.

If you're creating or updating a distribution by using the CloudFront API, one of the AWS SDKs, or AWS CloudFormation, see the applicable topic for a list of valid values (search for `PriceClass`):

- **Web distributions** – DistributionConfig Complex Type
- **RTMP distributions** – StreamingDistributionConfig Complex Type

For more information about CloudFront pricing and price classes, go to Amazon CloudFront Pricing.

# Using CloudFront with Amazon S3

You can store your content in an Amazon S3 bucket and use CloudFront to distribute the content. This topic explains how to use CloudFront with your S3 bucket, and how to update your CloudFront distribution if you move the S3 bucket to a different region.

**Topics**

- Adding CloudFront When You're Distributing Content from Amazon S3
- Moving an Amazon S3 Bucket to a Different Region

## Adding CloudFront When You're Distributing Content from Amazon S3

If you store your objects in an Amazon S3 bucket, you can either have your users get your objects directly from S3, or you can configure CloudFront to get your objects from S3 and distribute them to your users.

**Note**
To learn more about using Amazon S3 buckets for your origin with CloudFront, including when you have an Amazon S3 bucket configured as a website endpoint, see Using Amazon S3 Origins and Custom Origins for Web Distributions.

Using CloudFront can be more cost effective if your users access your objects frequently because, at higher usage, the price for CloudFront data transfer is lower than the price for Amazon S3 data transfer. In addition, downloads are faster with CloudFront than with Amazon S3 alone because your objects are stored closer to your users.

**Note**
If you want CloudFront to respect Amazon S3 cross-origin resource sharing settings, configure CloudFront to forward the `Origin` header to Amazon S3. For more information, see Configuring CloudFront to Cache Objects Based on Request Headers.

If you currently distribute content directly from your Amazon S3 bucket using your own domain name (such as example.com) instead of the domain name of your Amazon S3 bucket (such as MyAWSBucket.s3.amazonaws.com), you can add CloudFront with no disruption by using the following procedure.

**To add CloudFront when you're already distributing your content from Amazon S3**

1. Create a CloudFront distribution using the procedure described in the applicable topic:

   - Task List for Creating a Web Distribution
   - Task List for Streaming Media Files Using RTMP

   When you create the distribution, specify the name of your Amazon S3 bucket as the origin server.
   **Important**
   For your bucket to work with CloudFront, the name must conform to DNS naming requirements. For more information, see Bucket Restrictions and Limitations in the *Amazon Simple Storage Service Developer Guide*.

   If you're using a CNAME with Amazon S3, specify the CNAME for your distribution, too.

2. Create a test web page that contains links to publicly readable objects in your Amazon S3 bucket, and test the links. For this initial test, use the CloudFront domain name of your distribution in the object URLs, for example, `http://d111111abcdef8.cloudfront.net/images/image.jpg`.

   For more information about the format of CloudFront URLs, see Format of URLs for Objects.

3. If you're using Amazon S3 CNAMEs, your application uses your domain name (for example, example.com) to reference the objects in your Amazon S3 bucket instead of using the name of your bucket (for example, myawsbucket.s3.amazonaws.com). To continue using your domain name to reference objects instead of

using the CloudFront domain name for your distribution (for example, d111111abcdef8.cloudfront.net), you need to update your settings with your DNS service provider.

For Amazon S3 CNAMEs to work, your DNS service provider must have a CNAME resource record set for your domain that currently routes queries for the domain to your Amazon S3 bucket. For example, if a user requests this object:

```
http://example.com/images/image.jpg
```

the request is automatically rerouted, and the user sees this object:

```
http://myawsbucket.s3.amazonaws.com/images/image.jpg
```

To route queries to your CloudFront distribution instead of your Amazon S3 bucket, you need to use the method provided by your DNS service provider to update the CNAME resource record set for your domain. This updated CNAME record will start to redirect DNS queries from your domain to the CloudFront domain name for your distribution. For more information, see the documentation provided by your DNS service provider. **Note**
If you're using Route 53 as your DNS service, you can use either a CNAME resource record set or an alias resource record set. For information about editing resource record sets, see Editing Resource Record Sets. For information about alias resource record sets, see Choosing Between Alias and Non-Alias Resource Record Sets. Both topics are in the *Amazon Route 53 Developer Guide*.

For more information about using CNAMEs with CloudFront, see Adding and Moving Alternate Domain Names (CNAMEs).

After you update the CNAME resource record set, it can take up to 72 hours for the change to propagate throughout the DNS system, although it usually happens faster. During this time, some requests for your content will continue to be routed to your Amazon S3 bucket, and others will be routed to CloudFront.

## Moving an Amazon S3 Bucket to a Different Region

If you're using Amazon S3 as the origin for a CloudFront distribution and you move the bucket to a different region, CloudFront can take up to an hour to update its records to include the change of region when both of the following are true:

- You're using a CloudFront origin access identity (OAI) to restrict access to the bucket
- You move the bucket to an Amazon S3 region that requires Signature Version 4 for authentication

When you're using OAIs, CloudFront uses the region (among other values) to calculate the signature that it uses to request objects from your bucket. For more information about OAIs, see Using an Origin Access Identity to Restrict Access to Your Amazon S3 Content. For a list of Amazon S3 regions and the signature versions that they support, see Amazon Simple Storage Service (Amazon S3) in the "Regions and Endpoints" chapter of the *Amazon Web Services General Reference*.

To force a faster update to CloudFront's records, you can update your CloudFront distribution, for example, by updating the **Comment** field on the **General** tab in the CloudFront console. When you update a distribution, CloudFront immediately checks on the region that your bucket is in; propagation of the change to all edge locations should take less than 15 minutes.

# Tracking Configuration Changes with AWS Config

You can use AWS Config to record configuration changes for CloudFront distribution settings changes. For example, you can capture changes to distribution states, price classes, origins, geo restriction settings, and Lambda@Edge configurations.

## Set Up AWS Config with CloudFront

When you set up AWS Config, you can choose to record all supported AWS resources, or you can specify only certain resources to record configuration changes for, such as just recording changes for CloudFront. To see the specific resources supported for CloudFront, see the list of  Supported AWS Resource Types in the *AWS Config Developer Guide.*

To track configuration changes to your CloudFront distribution, you must log in to the AWS Management Console in the US East (N. Virginia) Region.

**Note**
There might be a delay in recording resources with AWS Config. AWS Config records resources only after it discovers the resources.

**Set up AWS Config with CloudFront (console)**

1. Sign in to the AWS Management Console and open the AWS Config console at https://console.aws.amazon. com/config/.

2. Choose **Get Started Now**.

3. On the **Settings** page, for **Resource types to record**, specify the AWS resource types that you want AWS Config to record. If you want to record only CloudFront changes, choose **Specific types**, and then, under **CloudFront**, choose the distribution or streaming distribution that you want to track changes for.

   To add or change which distributions to track, choose **Settings** on the left, after completing your initial setup.

4. Specify additional required options for AWS Config: set up a notification, specify a location for the configuration information, and add rules for evaluating resource types.

For more information, see Setting up AWS Config with the Console in the *AWS Config Developer Guide.*

To set up AWS Config with CloudFront by using the AWS CLI or by using an API, see one of the following:

- **Use the AWS CLI:** Setting up AWS Config with the AWS CLI in the *AWS Config Developer Guide*
- **Use an API:** The  StartConfigurationRecorder operation and other information in the *AWS Config API Reference*

## View CloudFront Configuration History

After AWS Config starts recording configuration changes to your distributions, you can get the configuration history of any distribution that you have configured for CloudFront.

You can view configuration histories in any of the following ways:

- **Use the AWS Config console.** For each recorded resource, you can view a timeline page, which provides a history of configuration details. To view this page, choose the gray icon in the **Config Timeline** column of the **Dedicated Hosts** page. For more information, see Viewing Configuration Details in the AWS Config Console in the *AWS Config Developer Guide.*

- **Run AWS CLI commands.** To get a list of all of your distributions, use the list-discovered-resources command. To get the configuration details of a distribution for a specific time interval, use the get-resource-config-history command. For more information, see View Configuration Details Using the CLI in the *AWS Config Developer Guide.*
- \*\*Use the AWS Config API in your applications. \*\* To get a list of all of your distributions use the ListDiscoveredResources operation. To get the configuration details of a distribution for a specific time interval, use the GetResourceConfigHistory action. For more information, see the AWS Config API Reference.

For example, to get a list of all of your distributions from AWS Config, you could run a CLI command such as the following:

```
aws configservice list-discovered-resources --resource-type AWS::CloudFront::Distribution
```

Or, to get a list of all of your RTMP streaming distributions from AWS Config, run a CLI command such as the following:

```
aws configservice list-discovered-resources --resource-type AWS::CloudFront::
StreamingDistribution
```

# Changes to the CloudFront API

Beginning with the 2012-05-05 version of the CloudFront API, we made substantial changes to the format of the XML document that you include in the request body when you create or update a web distribution or an RTMP distribution, and when you invalidate objects. With previous versions of the API, we discovered that it was too easy to accidentally delete one or more values for an element that accepts multiple values, for example, CNAMEs and trusted signers. Our changes for the 2012-05-05 release are intended to prevent these accidental deletions and to notify you when there's a mismatch between the number of values you say you're specifying in the `Quantity` element and the number of values you're actually specifying.

Note the following about using the 2012-05-05 API version or later with web and RTMP distributions that were created using earlier API versions:

- You cannot use versions of the API earlier than 2012-05-05 to update a web distribution that was created or updated using the 2012-05-05 or later CloudFront API.
- You can use the new API version to get a list of distributions, get information about a distribution, or get distribution configuration. CloudFront returns an XML document in the new XML format.
- To update a distribution that was created using an earlier API version, use the 2012-05-05 or later version of GET Distribution or GET Streaming Distribution to get an XML document in the new XML format, change the data as applicable, and use the 2012-05-05 or later version of PUT Distribution Config or PUT Streaming Distribution Config to submit the changes to CloudFront.
- You can use the new API to delete a distribution that was created using an earlier API version. The distribution must already be disabled.

# Working with Web Distributions

This section describes how you configure and manage CloudFront web distributions. For a basic explanation of distributions, see Working with Distributions. For information about CloudFront RTMP distributions, see Working with RTMP Distributions.

**Topics**

- Task List for Creating a Web Distribution
- Creating a Web Distribution
- Testing a Web Distribution
- Using Amazon S3 Origins and Custom Origins for Web Distributions
- Values That You Specify When You Create or Update a Web Distribution
- Values that CloudFront Displays in the Console When You Create or Update a Web Distribution
- Using Field-Level Encryption to Help Protect Sensitive Data
- Using AWS WAF to Control Access to Your Content
- Restricting the Geographic Distribution of Your Content
- Configuring Video Streaming Web Distributions

# Task List for Creating a Web Distribution

The following task list summarizes the process for creating a web distribution.

**To Create a Web Distribution**

1. Create one or more Amazon S3 buckets or configure HTTP servers as your origin servers. An origin is the location where you store the original version of your web content. When CloudFront gets a request for your files, it goes to the origin to get the files that it distributes at edge locations. You can use any combination of Amazon S3 buckets and HTTP servers as your origin servers.

   If you're using Amazon S3, note that the name of your bucket must be all lowercase and cannot contain spaces.

   If you're using an Amazon EC2 server or another custom origin, review Using Amazon EC2 or Other Custom Origins.

   For the current limit on the number of origins that you can create for a distribution or to request a higher limit, see General Limits on Web Distributions.

2. Upload your content to your origin servers. If you don't want to restrict access to your content using CloudFront signed URLs, make the objects publicly readable. **Important**
   You are responsible for ensuring the security of your origin server. You must ensure that CloudFront has permission to access the server and that the security settings are appropriate to safeguard your content.

3. Create your CloudFront web distribution:

   - For more information about creating a web distribution using the CloudFront console, see Creating a Web Distribution.
   - For information about creating a web distribution using the CloudFront API, go to CreateDistribution in the *Amazon CloudFront API Reference.*

4. Optional: If you created your distribution using the CloudFront console, create more cache behaviors or origins for your distribution. For more information, see To Update CloudFront Distributions Using the CloudFront Console.

5. Test your web distribution. For more information, see Testing a Web Distribution.

6. Develop your website or application to access your content using the domain name that CloudFront returned after you created your distribution in Step 3. For example, if CloudFront returns d111111abcdef8.cloudfront.net as the domain name for your distribution, the URL for the file `image.jpg` in an Amazon S3 bucket or in the root directory on an HTTP server will be `http://d111111abcdef8.cloudfront.net/image.jpg`.

   If you specified one or more alternate domain names (CNAMEs) when you created your distribution, you can use your own domain name. In that case, the URL for `image.jpg` might be `http://www.example.com/image.jpg`.

   Note the following:

   - If you want to use signed URLs to restrict access to your content, see Serving Private Content through CloudFront.
   - If you want to serve compressed content, see Serving Compressed Files.
   - For information about CloudFront request and response behavior for Amazon S3 and custom origins, see Request and Response Behavior.

# Creating a Web Distribution

You can create or update a web distribution by using the CloudFront console or programmatically. This topic is about working with web distributions by using the console.

If you want to create or update a web distribution by using the CloudFront API, see CreateDistribution or UpdateDistribution in the *Amazon CloudFront API Reference.*

**Note**
To see the current limit on the number of web distributions that you can create for each AWS account, or to request a higher limit, General Limits on Web Distributions.

**To create a CloudFront web distribution using the CloudFront console**

1. Sign in to the AWS Management Console and open the CloudFront console at https://console.aws.amazon. com/cloudfront/.

2. Choose **Create Distribution**.

3. On the first page of the **Create Distribution Wizard**, in the **Web** section, choose **Get Started**.

4. Specify settings for the distribution. For more information, see Values That You Specify When You Create or Update a Web Distribution.

5. Save changes.

6. After CloudFront creates your distribution, the value of the **Status** column for your distribution will change from **InProgress** to **Deployed**. If you chose to enable the distribution, it will be ready to process requests after the status switches to **Deployed**.

   The domain name that CloudFront assigns to your distribution appears in the list of distributions. (It also appears on the **General** tab for a selected distribution.) **Tip**
   You can use an alternate domain name, instead of the name assigned to you by CloudFront; by following the steps in Adding and Moving Alternate Domain Names (CNAMEs).

7. When your distribution is deployed, confirm that you can access your content using your new CloudFront URL or CNAME. For more information, see Testing a Web Distribution.

To update a web distribution (for example, to add or change cache behaviors), see Viewing and Updating CloudFront Distributions.

# Testing a Web Distribution

After you've created your distribution, CloudFront knows where your origin server is, and you know the domain name associated with the distribution. You can create links to your objects using the CloudFront domain name, and CloudFront will serve the objects to your web page or application.

**Note**
You must wait until the status of the distribution changes to **Deployed** before you can test your links.

**To create links to objects in a web distribution**

1. Copy the following HTML code into a new file, replace *domain-name* with your distribution's domain name, and replace *object-name* with the name of your object.

```
1 <html>
2 <head>My CloudFront Test</head>
3 <body>
4 <p>My text content goes here.</p>
5 <p><img src="http://domain-name/object-name" alt="my test image"
6 </body>
7 </html>
```

   For example, if your domain name were `d111111abcdef8.cloudfront.net` and your object were `image.jpg`, the URL for the link would be:

   `http://d111111abcdef8.cloudfront.net/image.jpg`.

   If your object is in a folder on your origin server, then the folder must also be included in the URL. For example, if image.jpg were located in the images folder on your origin server, then the URL would be:

   `http://d111111abcdef8.cloudfront.net/images/image.jpg`

2. Save the HTML code in a file that has a .html filename extension.

3. Open your web page in a browser to ensure that you can see your object.

The browser returns your page with the embedded image file, served from the edge location that CloudFront determined was appropriate to serve the object.

# Using Amazon S3 Origins and Custom Origins for Web Distributions

When you create a web distribution, you specify where CloudFront sends requests for the files. CloudFront supports using several AWS resources as origins. For example, you can specify an Amazon S3 buckets or an AWS Elemental MediaStore container, as well as custom origins, such as an Amazon EC2 instance or your own HTTP web server.

**Topics**

- Using Amazon S3 Buckets for Your Origin
- Using Amazon S3 Buckets Configured as Website Endpoints for Your Origin
- Using an AWS Elemental MediaStore container or an AWS Elemental MediaPackage Channel for Your Origin
- Using Amazon EC2 or Other Custom Origins

## Using Amazon S3 Buckets for Your Origin

When you use Amazon S3 as an origin for your distribution, you place any objects that you want CloudFront to deliver in an Amazon S3 bucket. You can use any method that is supported by Amazon S3 to get your objects into Amazon S3, for example, the Amazon S3 console or API, or a third-party tool. You can create a hierarchy in your bucket to store the objects, just as you would with any other Amazon S3 bucket.

Using an existing Amazon S3 bucket as your CloudFront origin server doesn't change the bucket in any way; you can still use it as you normally would to store and access Amazon S3 objects at the standard Amazon S3 price. You incur regular Amazon S3 charges for storing the objects in the bucket. For more information about the charges to use CloudFront, see CloudFront Reports.

**Important**
For your bucket to work with CloudFront, the name must conform to DNS naming requirements. For more information, go to Bucket Restrictions and Limitations in the *Amazon Simple Storage Service Developer Guide*.

When you specify the Amazon S3 bucket that you want CloudFront to get objects from, in general, use the following format:

```
bucket-name.s3.amazonaws.com
```

If your bucket is in the US Standard region and you want Amazon S3 to route requests to a facility in Northern Virginia, use the following format:

```
bucket-name.s3-external-1.amazonaws.com
```

When you specify the bucket name in this format, you can use the following CloudFront features:

- Configure CloudFront to communicate with your Amazon S3 bucket using SSL. For more information, see Using HTTPS with CloudFront.
- Use an origin access identity to require that your users access your content using CloudFront URLs, not by using Amazon S3 URLs. For more information, see Using an Origin Access Identity to Restrict Access to Your Amazon S3 Content.
- Update the content of your bucket by submitting POST and PUT requests to CloudFront. For more information, see HTTP Methods in the topic How CloudFront Processes and Forwards Requests to Your Amazon S3 Origin Server.

Do not specify the bucket using the following formats:

- The Amazon S3 path style, s3.amazonaws.com/bucket-name
- The Amazon S3 CNAME, if any

# Using Amazon S3 Buckets Configured as Website Endpoints for Your Origin

You can set up an Amazon S3 bucket that is configured as a website endpoint as custom origin with CloudFront.

- When you configure your CloudFront distribution, for the origin, enter the Amazon S3 static website hosting endpoint for your bucket. This value appears in the Amazon S3 console, on the **Properties** page under **Static Website Hosting**. For example:

  `http://bucket-name.s3-website-us-west-2.amazonaws.com`

For more information about specifying Amazon S3 static website endpoints, see Website Endpoints in the Amazon S3 documentation.

When you specify the bucket name in this format as your origin, you can use Amazon S3 redirects and Amazon S3 custom error documents. For more information about Amazon S3 features, see the Amazon S3 documentation. (CloudFront also provides custom error pages. For more information, see Customizing Error Responses.)

Using an Amazon S3 bucket as your CloudFront origin server doesn't change it in any way. You can still use it as you normally would and you incur regular Amazon S3 charges. For more information about the charges to use CloudFront, see CloudFront Reports.

**Note**
If you use the CloudFront API to create your distribution with an Amazon S3 bucket that is configured as a website endpoint, you must configure it by using `CustomOriginConfig`, even though the website is hosted in an Amazon S3 bucket. For more information about creating distributions by using the CloudFront API, see CreateDistribution in the *Amazon CloudFront API Reference*.

# Using an AWS Elemental MediaStore container or an AWS Elemental MediaPackage Channel for Your Origin

To stream on-demand or live video in CloudFront, you can set up an Amazon S3 bucket that is configured as an AWS Elemental MediaStore container, or create a channel and endpoints with AWS Elemental MediaPackage. Then you create and configure a distribution in CloudFront to stream the video.

For more information and step-by-step instructions, see the following topics:

- Configuring On-Demand Video with AWS Elemental MediaStore
- Serving Live Video Formatted with AWS Elemental MediaPackage

# Using Amazon EC2 or Other Custom Origins

A custom origin is an HTTP server, for example, a web server. The HTTP server can be an Amazon EC2 instance or an HTTP server that you manage privately. An Amazon S3 origin configured as a website endpoint is also considered a custom origin.

When you use a custom origin that is your own HTTP server, you specify the DNS name of the server, along with the HTTP and HTTPS ports and the protocol that you want CloudFront to use when fetching objects from your origin.

Most CloudFront features are supported when you use a custom origin with the following exceptions:

- **RTMP distributions**—Not supported.
- **Private content**—Although you can use a signed URL to distribute content from a custom origin, for CloudFront to access the custom origin, the origin must remain publicly accessible. For more information, see Serving Private Content through CloudFront.

Follow these guidelines for using Amazon EC2 instances and other custom origins with CloudFront.

- Host and serve the same content on all servers that are serving content for the same CloudFront origin. For more information, see Origin Settings in the Values That You Specify When You Create or Update a Web Distribution topic.
- Log the `X-Amz-Cf-Id` header entries on all servers; CloudFront requires this information for debugging.
- Restrict access requests to the HTTP and HTTPS ports that your custom origin listens on.
- Synchronize the clocks of all servers in your implementation. Note that CloudFront uses Coordinated Universal Time (UTC) for signed URLs and signed cookies, for access logs, and reports. In addition, if you monitor CloudFront activity using CloudWatch metrics, note that CloudWatch also uses UTC.
- Use redundant servers to handle failures.
- For information about using a custom origin to serve private content, see Using an HTTP Server for Private Content.
- For information about request and response behavior and about supported HTTP status codes, see Request and Response Behavior.

If you use Amazon Elastic Compute Cloud for your custom origins, we recommend that you do the following:

1. Use an Amazon Machine Image that automatically installs the software for a web server. For more information, see the Amazon EC2 documentation.

2. Use an Elastic Load Balancing load balancer to handle traffic across multiple Amazon EC2 instances and to isolate your application from changes to Amazon EC2 instances. For example, if you use a load balancer, you can add and delete Amazon EC2 instances without changing your application. For more information, see the Elastic Load Balancing documentation.

3. When you create your CloudFront distribution, specify the URL of the load balancer for the domain name of your origin server. For more information, see Working with Web Distributions.

# Values That You Specify When You Create or Update a Web Distribution

When you create a new web distribution or update an existing distribution, you specify the following values. For information about creating or updating a web distribution using the CloudFront console, see the applicable topic:

- Working with Web Distributions
- Viewing and Updating CloudFront Distributions

**Delivery Method**

**Origin Settings**

- Origin Domain Name
- Origin Path
- Origin ID
- Restrict Bucket Access (Amazon S3 Only)
- Origin Access Identity (Amazon S3 Only)
- Comment for New Identity (Amazon S3 Only)
- Your Identities (Amazon S3 Only)
- Grant Read Permissions on Bucket (Amazon S3 Only)
- Origin SSL Protocols (Amazon EC2, Elastic Load Balancing, and Other Custom Origins Only)
- Origin Protocol Policy (Amazon EC2, Elastic Load Balancing, and Other Custom Origins Only)
- Origin Response Timeout (Amazon EC2, Elastic Load Balancing, and Other Custom Origins Only)
- Origin Keep-alive Timeout (Amazon EC2, Elastic Load Balancing, and Other Custom Origins Only)
- HTTP Port (Amazon EC2, Elastic Load Balancing, and Other Custom Origins Only)
- HTTPS Port (Amazon EC2, Elastic Load Balancing, and Other Custom Origins Only)
- Origin Custom Headers

**Cache Behavior Settings**

- Path Pattern
- Origin (Existing Distributions Only)
- Viewer Protocol Policy
- Allowed HTTP Methods
- Field Level Encryption
- Cached HTTP Methods
- Cache Based on Selected Request Headers
- Whitelist Headers
- Object Caching
- Minimum TTL
- Maximum TTL
- Default TTL
- Forward Cookies (Amazon EC2 and Other Custom Origins Only)
- Whitelist Cookies (Amazon EC2 and Other Custom Origins Only)
- Query String Forwarding and Caching
- Query String Whitelist
- Smooth Streaming
- Restrict Viewer Access (Use Signed URLs)
- Trusted Signers
- AWS Account Numbers
- Compress Objects Automatically
- Event Type
- Lambda Function ARN

**Distribution Details**

- Price Class
- AWS WAF Web ACL
- Alternate Domain Names (CNAMEs)
- SSL Certificate
- Clients Supported
- Security Policy
- Minimum SSL Security Protocol – See Security Policy
- Supported HTTP Versions
- Default Root Object
- Logging
- Bucket for Logs
- Log Prefix
- Cookie Logging
- Enable IPv6
- Comment
- Distribution State

### Custom Error Pages and Error Caching

- Error Code
- Response Page Path
- Response Code
- Error Caching Minimum TTL

### Restrictions

- Enable Geo Restriction
- Restriction Type
- Countries

## Delivery Method

You specify the delivery method when you create a distribution. For a web distribution, this value is always **Web**. You can't change the delivery method for an existing distribution.

## Origin Settings

When you create or update a distribution, you provide information about one or more locations—known as origins—where you store the original versions of your web content. CloudFront gets your web content from your origins and serves it to viewers via a world-wide network of edge servers. Each origin is either an Amazon S3 bucket or an HTTP server, for example, a web server.

For the current limit on the number of origins that you can create for a distribution or to request a higher limit, see General Limits on Web Distributions.

If you want to delete an origin, you must first edit or delete the cache behaviors that are associated with that origin.

**Important**
If you delete an origin, confirm that files that were previously served by that origin are available in another origin and that your cache behaviors are now routing requests for those files to the new origin.

When you create or update a distribution, you specify the following values for each origin.

## Origin Domain Name

The DNS domain name of the Amazon S3 bucket or HTTP server from which you want CloudFront to get objects for this origin, for example:

- **Amazon S3 bucket** – `myawsbucket.s3.amazonaws.com`
- **Amazon S3 bucket configured as a website** – `http://bucket-name.s3-website-us-west-2.amazonaws.com`
- **AWS Elemental MediaStore container** – `mymediastore.data.mediastore.us-west-1.amazonaws.com`
- **AWS Elemental MediaPackage endpoint** – `mymediapackage.mediapackage.us-west-1.amazon.com`
- **Amazon EC2 instance** – `ec2-203-0-113-25.compute-1.amazonaws.com`
- **Elastic Load Balancing load balancer** – `my-load-balancer-1234567890.us-west-2.elb.amazonaws.com`
- **Your own web server** – `https://example.com`

If your origin is an HTTP server, type the domain name of the resource. The files must be publicly readable.

If your origin is an Amazon S3 bucket, in the CloudFront console, choose in the **Origin Domain Name** field, and a list enumerates the Amazon S3 buckets that are associated with the current AWS account. Note the following:

- If the bucket is configured as a website, enter the Amazon S3 static website hosting endpoint for your bucket; do not select the bucket name from the list in the **Origin Domain Name** field. The static website hosting endpoint appears in the Amazon S3 console, on the **Properties** page under **Static Website Hosting**. For more information, see Using Amazon S3 Buckets Configured as Website Endpoints for Your Origin.

- If you configured Amazon S3 Transfer Acceleration for your bucket, do not specify the `s3-accelerate` endpoint for **Origin Domain Name**.

- If you're using a bucket from a different AWS account and if the bucket is not configured as a website, type the name in the following format:

  `bucket-name.s3.amazonaws.com`

  If your bucket is in the US Standard region and you want Amazon S3 to route requests to a facility in Northern Virginia, use the following format:

  `bucket-name.s3-external-1.amazonaws.com`

  If your bucket is in the EU (Frankfurt) region, you can also use the following format:

  `bucket-name.s3.eu-central-1.amazonaws.com`

- The files must be publicly readable unless you secure your content in Amazon S3 by using a CloudFront origin access identity. For more information, see Using an Origin Access Identity to Restrict Access to Your Amazon S3 Content.

### Important
If the origin is an Amazon S3 bucket, the bucket name must conform to DNS naming requirements. For more information, go to Bucket Restrictions and Limitations in the *Amazon Simple Storage Service Developer Guide*.

When you change the value of **Origin Domain Name** for an origin, CloudFront immediately begins replicating the change to CloudFront edge locations. Until the distribution configuration is updated in a given edge location, CloudFront will continue to forward requests to the previous HTTP server or Amazon S3 bucket. As soon as the distribution configuration is updated in that edge location, CloudFront begins to forward requests to the new HTTP server or Amazon S3 bucket.

Changing the origin does not require CloudFront to repopulate edge caches with objects from the new origin. As long as the viewer requests in your application have not changed, CloudFront will continue to serve objects that are already in an edge cache until the TTL on each object expires or until seldom-requested objects are evicted.

## Origin Path

If you want CloudFront to request your content from a directory in your AWS resource or your custom origin, enter the directory path, beginning with a slash (/). CloudFront appends the directory path to the value of **Origin Domain Name**, for example, **cf-origin.example.com/production/images**. Do not add a slash (/) at the end of the path.

For example, suppose you've specified the following values for your distribution:

- **Origin Domain Name** – An Amazon S3 bucket named **myawsbucket**
- **Origin Path** – /production
- **Alternate Domain Names (CNAMEs)** – example.com

When a user enters **example.com/index.html** in a browser, CloudFront sends a request to Amazon S3 for **myawsbucket/production/index.html**.

When a user enters **example.com/acme/index.html** in a browser, CloudFront sends a request to Amazon S3 for **myawsbucket/production/acme/index.html**.

## Origin ID

A string that uniquely distinguishes this origin from other origins in this distribution. If you create cache behaviors in addition to the default cache behavior, you use the origin ID that you specify here to identify the origin to which you want CloudFront to route a request when the request matches the path pattern for that cache behavior. For more information, see Cache Behavior Settings.

## Restrict Bucket Access (Amazon S3 Only)

Choose **Yes** if you want to require users to access objects in an Amazon S3 bucket by using only CloudFront URLs, not by using Amazon S3 URLs. Then specify the applicable values.

Choose **No** if you want users to be able to access objects using either CloudFront URLs or Amazon S3 URLs.

For more information, see Using an Origin Access Identity to Restrict Access to Your Amazon S3 Content.

For information about how to require users to access objects on a custom origin by using only CloudFront URLs, see Using Custom Headers to Restrict Access to Your Content on a Custom Origin.

## Origin Access Identity (Amazon S3 Only)

If you chose **Yes** for **Restrict Bucket Access**, choose whether to create a new origin access identity or use an existing one that is associated with your AWS account. If you already have an origin access identity, we recommend that you reuse it to simplify maintenance. For more information about origin access identities, see Using an Origin Access Identity to Restrict Access to Your Amazon S3 Content.

## Comment for New Identity (Amazon S3 Only)

If you chose **Create a New Identity** for **Origin Access Identity**, enter a comment that identifies the new origin access identity. CloudFront will create the origin access identity when you create this distribution.

## Your Identities (Amazon S3 Only)

If you chose **Use an Existing Identity** for **Origin Access Identity**, choose the origin access identity that you want to use. You cannot use an origin access identity that is associated with another AWS account.

## Grant Read Permissions on Bucket (Amazon S3 Only)

If you want CloudFront to automatically grant the origin access identity the permission to read objects in your Amazon S3 bucket, choose **Yes, Update Bucket Policy**.

**Important**
If you choose **Yes, Update Bucket Policy**, CloudFront updates the bucket policy to grant the specified origin access identity the permission to read objects in your bucket. However, CloudFront does not remove existing permissions in the bucket policy or permissions on individual objects. If users currently have permission to access the objects in your bucket using Amazon S3 URLs, they will still have that permission after CloudFront updates your bucket policy. To view or change the existing bucket policy and the existing permissions on the objects in your bucket, use a method provided by Amazon S3. For more information, see Granting the Origin Access Identity Permission to Read Objects in Your Amazon S3 Bucket.

If you want to update permissions manually, for example, if you want to update ACLs on your objects instead of updating bucket permissions, choose **No, I will Update Permissions**.

## Origin SSL Protocols (Amazon EC2, Elastic Load Balancing, and Other Custom Origins Only)

Choose the SSL protocols that CloudFront can use when establishing an HTTPS connection with your origin. The SSLv3 protocol is less secure, so we recommend that you choose SSLv3 only if your origin doesn't support TLSv1 or later.

**Note**
If you select SSLv3, CloudFront does not attempt to make a connection to the Origin using TLS.

If the origin is an Amazon S3 bucket, CloudFront always uses TLSv1.2.

## Origin Protocol Policy (Amazon EC2, Elastic Load Balancing, and Other Custom Origins Only)

The protocol policy that you want CloudFront to use when fetching objects from your origin server.

**Important**
If your Amazon S3 bucket is configured as a website endpoint, you must specify HTTP Only. Amazon S3 doesn't support HTTPS connections in that configuration.

Choose the applicable value:

- **HTTP Only:** CloudFront uses only HTTP to access the origin.
- **HTTPS Only:** CloudFront uses only HTTPS to access the origin.
- **Match Viewer:** CloudFront communicates with your origin using HTTP or HTTPS, depending on the protocol of the viewer request. CloudFront caches the object only once even if viewers make requests using both HTTP and HTTPS protocols. **Important**
  For HTTPS viewer requests that CloudFront forwards to this origin, one of the domain names in the SSL certificate on your origin server must match the domain name that you specify for **Origin Domain Name**. Otherwise, CloudFront responds to the viewer requests with an HTTP status code 502 (Bad Gateway) instead of the requested object. For more information, see Requirements for Using SSL/TLS Certificates with CloudFront.

**Origin Response Timeout (Amazon EC2, Elastic Load Balancing, and Other Custom Origins Only)**

The origin response timeout , also known as the origin read timeout or origin request timeout, applies to both of the following values:

- The amount of time, in seconds, that CloudFront waits for a response after forwarding a request to a custom origin
- The amount of time, in seconds, that CloudFront waits after receiving a packet of a response from the origin and before receiving the next packet

The default timeout is 30 seconds. You can change the value to between 4 and 60 seconds. If you need a timeout value outside that range, request a change to the limit.

**Tip**
If you want to increase the origin response timeout value because viewers are experiencing HTTP 504 status code errors, consider exploring other ways to eliminate those errors before changing the timeout value. See the troubleshooting suggestions in HTTP 504 Status Code (Gateway Timeout).

CloudFront behavior depends on the HTTP method in the viewer request:

- GET and HEAD requests – If the origin doesn't respond before the read timeout elapses or if the origin stops responding for the configured timeout, CloudFront drops the connection and tries two more times to contact the origin. After the third try, if the origin doesn't respond before the read timeout elapses, CloudFront doesn't try again until it receives another request for content on the same origin.
- DELETE, OPTIONS, PATCH, PUT, and POST requests – If the origin doesn't respond before the read timeout elapses, CloudFront drops the connection and doesn't try again to contact the origin. The client can resubmit the request if necessary.

**Origin Keep-alive Timeout (Amazon EC2, Elastic Load Balancing, and Other Custom Origins Only)**

The amount of time, in seconds, that CloudFront tries to maintain a connection to your custom origin after it gets the last packet of a response. Maintaining a persistent connection saves the time that is required to re-establish the TCP connection and perform another TLS handshake for subsequent requests. Increasing the keep-alive timeout helps improve the request-per-connection metric for distributions.

**Note**
For the **Origin Keep-alive Timeout** value to have an effect, your origin must be configured to allow persistent connections.

The default timeout is 5 seconds. You can change the value to between 1 and 60 seconds. If you need a keep-alive timeout longer than 60 seconds, request a change to the limit.

**HTTP Port (Amazon EC2, Elastic Load Balancing, and Other Custom Origins Only)**

Optional. The HTTP port that the custom origin listens on. Valid values include ports 80, 443, and 1024 to 65535. The default value is port 80.

**HTTPS Port (Amazon EC2, Elastic Load Balancing, and Other Custom Origins Only)**

Optional. The HTTPS port that the custom origin listens on. Valid values include ports 80, 443, and 1024 to 65535. The default value is port 443.

**Origin Custom Headers**

If you want CloudFront to include custom headers whenever it forwards a request to your origin, specify the following values:

**Header Name**
The name of a header that you want CloudFront to forward to your origin.

**Value**
The value for the header that you specified in the **Custom Header** field.

For more information, see Forwarding Custom Headers to Your Origin (Web Distributions Only).

For the current limit on the maximum number of custom headers that you can forward to the origin, the maximum length of a custom header name and value, and the total length of all header names and values, see Limits.

## Cache Behavior Settings

A cache behavior lets you configure a variety of CloudFront functionality for a given URL path pattern for files on your website. For example, one cache behavior might apply to all `.jpg` files in the `images` directory on a web server that you're using as an origin server for CloudFront. The functionality you can configure for each cache behavior includes:

- The path pattern.
- If you have configured multiple origins for your CloudFront distribution, which origin you want CloudFront to forward your requests to.
- Whether to forward query strings to your origin.
- Whether accessing the specified files requires signed URLs.
- Whether to require users to use HTTPS to access those files.
- The minimum amount of time that those files stay in the CloudFront cache regardless of the value of any `Cache-Control` headers that your origin adds to the files.

When you create a new distribution, you specify settings for the default cache behavior, which automatically forwards all requests to the origin that you specify when you create the distribution. After you create a distribution, you can create additional cache behaviors that define how CloudFront responds when it receives a request for objects that match a path pattern, for example, `*.jpg`. If you create additional cache behaviors, the default cache behavior is always the last to be processed. Other cache behaviors are processed in the order in which they're listed in the CloudFront console or, if you're using the CloudFront API, the order in which they're listed in the `DistributionConfig` element for the distribution. For more information, see Path Pattern.

When you create a cache behavior, you specify the one origin from which you want CloudFront to get objects. As a result, if you want CloudFront to distribute objects from all of your origins, you must have at least as many cache behaviors (including the default cache behavior) as you have origins. For example, if you have two origins and only the default cache behavior, the default cache behavior will cause CloudFront to get objects from one of the origins, but the other origin will never be used.

For the current limit on the number of cache behaviors that you can add to a distribution or to request a higher limit, see General Limits on Web Distributions.

### Path Pattern

A path pattern (for example, `images/*.jpg`) specifies which requests you want this cache behavior to apply to. When CloudFront receives an end-user request, the requested path is compared with path patterns in the order in which cache behaviors are listed in the distribution. The first match determines which cache behavior is applied to that request. For example, suppose you have three cache behaviors with the following three path patterns, in this order:

- images/*.jpg
- images/*
- *.gif

**Note**

You can optionally include a slash (/) at the beginning of the path pattern, for example, /images/*.jpg. CloudFront behavior is the same with or without the leading /.

A request for the file images/sample.gif doesn't satisfy the first path pattern, so the associated cache behaviors are not be applied to the request. The file does satisfy the second path pattern, so the cache behaviors associated with the second path pattern are applied even though the request also matches the third path pattern.

**Note**

When you create a new distribution, the value of **Path Pattern** for the default cache behavior is set to * (all files) and cannot be changed. This value causes CloudFront to forward all requests for your objects to the origin that you specified in the Origin Domain Name field. If the request for an object does not match the path pattern for any of the other cache behaviors, CloudFront applies the behavior that you specify in the default cache behavior.

**Important**

Define path patterns and their sequence carefully or you may give users undesired access to your content. For example, suppose a request matches the path pattern for two cache behaviors. The first cache behavior does not require signed URLs and the second cache behavior does require signed URLs. Users will be able to access the objects without using a signed URL because CloudFront processes the cache behavior associated with the first match.

If you're working with an AWS Elemental MediaPackage channel, you must include specific path patterns for the cache behavior that you define for the endpoint type for your origin. For example, for a DASH endpoint, you type *.mpd for **Path Pattern**. For more information and specific instructions, see Serving Live Video Formatted with AWS Elemental MediaPackage.

The path you specify applies to requests for all files in the specified directory and in subdirectories below the specified directory. CloudFront does not consider query strings or cookies when evaluating the path pattern. For example, if an images directory contains product1 and product2 subdirectories, the path pattern images/*.jpg applies to requests for any .jpg file in the images, images/product1, and images/product2 directories. If you want to apply a different cache behavior to the files in the images/product1 directory than the files in the images and images/product2 directories, create a separate cache behavior for images/product1 and move that cache behavior to a position above (before) the cache behavior for the images directory.

You can use the following wildcard characters in your path pattern:

- * matches 0 or more characters.
- ? matches exactly 1 character.

The following examples show how the wildcard characters work:

| Path pattern | Files that match the path pattern |
| --- | --- |
| *.jpg | All .jpg files |
| images/*.jpg | All .jpg files in the images directory and in subdirectories under the images directory |
| a*.jpg | [See the AWS documentation website for more details] |
| a??.jpg | All .jpg files for which the filename begins with a and is followed by exactly two other characters, for example, ant.jpg and abe.jpg |

| Path pattern | Files that match the path pattern |
|---|---|
| `*.doc*` | All files for which the filename extension begins with .doc, for example, .doc, .docx, and .docm files. You can't use the path pattern `*.doc?` in this case, because that path pattern wouldn't apply to requests for .doc files; the ? wildcard character replaces exactly one character. |

The maximum length of a path pattern is 255 characters. The value can contain any of the following characters:

- A-Z, a-z

  Path patterns are case sensitive, so the path pattern `*.jpg` doesn't apply to the file `LOGO.JPG`.

- 0-9

- _ - . * $ / ~ " ' @ : +

- &, passed and returned as `&amp;`

## Origin (Existing Distributions Only)

Enter the value of **Origin ID** for an existing origin. This identifies the origin that you want CloudFront to route requests to when a request (such as http://example/.com/logo/.jpg/) matches the path pattern for a cache behavior (such as *.jpg) or for the default cache behavior (*).

## Viewer Protocol Policy

Choose the protocol policy that you want viewers to use to access your content in CloudFront edge locations:

- **HTTP and HTTPS**: Viewers can use both protocols.
- **Redirect HTTP to HTTPS**: Viewers can use both protocols, but HTTP requests are automatically redirected to HTTPS requests.
- **HTTPS Only**: Viewers can only access your content if they're using HTTPS.

For more information, see Requiring HTTPS for Communication Between Viewers and CloudFront.

## Field Level Encryption

If you want to enforce field-level encryption on specific data fields, in the drop-down list, choose a field-level encryption configuration.

For more information, see Using Field-Level Encryption to Help Protect Sensitive Data.

## Allowed HTTP Methods

Specify the HTTP methods that you want CloudFront to process and forward to your origin:

- **GET, HEAD:** You can use CloudFront only to get objects from your origin or to get object headers.
- **GET, HEAD, OPTIONS:** You can use CloudFront only to get objects from your origin, get object headers, or retrieve a list of the options that your origin server supports.

- **GET, HEAD, OPTIONS, PUT, POST, PATCH, DELETE:** You can use CloudFront to get, add, update, and delete objects, and to get object headers. In addition, you can perform other POST operations such as submitting data from a web form. **Note**
  CloudFront caches responses to `GET` and `HEAD` requests and, optionally, `OPTIONS` requests. CloudFront does not cache responses to requests that use the other methods.

If you use an Amazon S3 bucket as the origin for your distribution and if you use CloudFront origin access identities, `POST` requests aren't supported in some Amazon S3 regions and `PUT` requests in those regions require an additional header. For more information, see Using an Origin Access Identity in Amazon S3 Regions that Support Only Signature Version 4 Authentication.

**Important**
If you choose **GET, HEAD, OPTIONS** or **GET, HEAD, OPTIONS, PUT, POST, PATCH, DELETE**, you might need to restrict access to your Amazon S3 bucket or to your custom origin to prevent users from performing operations that you don't want them to perform. The following examples explain how to restrict access:
**If you're using Amazon S3 as an origin for your distribution:** Create a CloudFront origin access identity to restrict access to your Amazon S3 content, and grant the origin access identity the applicable permissions. For example, if you configure CloudFront to accept and forward these methods *only* because you want to use `PUT`, you must still configure Amazon S3 bucket policies or ACLs to handle `DELETE` requests appropriately. For more information, see Using an Origin Access Identity to Restrict Access to Your Amazon S3 Content. **If you're using a custom origin:** Configure your origin server to handle all methods. For example, if you configure CloudFront to accept and forward these methods *only* because you want to use `POST`, you must still configure your origin server to handle `DELETE` requests appropriately.

### Cached HTTP Methods

Specify whether you want CloudFront to cache the response from your origin when a viewer submits an `OPTIONS` request. CloudFront always caches the response to `GET` and `HEAD` requests.

### Cache Based on Selected Request Headers

Specify whether you want CloudFront to cache objects based on the values of specified headers:

- **None (improves caching)** – CloudFront doesn't cache your objects based on header values.
- **Whitelist** – CloudFront caches your objects based only on the values of the specified headers. Use **Whitelist Headers** to choose the headers that you want CloudFront to base caching on.
- **All** – CloudFront doesn't cache the objects that are associated with this cache behavior. Instead, CloudFront sends every request to the origin. (Not recommended for Amazon S3 origins.)

Regardless of the option that you choose, CloudFront forwards certain headers to your origin and takes specific actions based on the headers that you forward. For more information about how CloudFront handles header forwarding, see HTTP Request Headers and CloudFront Behavior (Custom and S3 Origins).

For more information about how to configure caching in CloudFront by using request headers, see Configuring CloudFront to Cache Objects Based on Request Headers.

### Whitelist Headers

Specify the headers that you want CloudFront to consider when caching your objects. Select headers from the list of available headers and choose **Add**. To forward a custom header, enter the name of the header in the field, and choose **Add Custom**.

For the current limit on the number of headers that you can whitelist for each cache behavior or to request a higher limit, see Limits on Custom Headers (Web Distributions Only).

## Object Caching

If your origin server is adding a `Cache-Control` header to your objects to control how long the objects stay in the CloudFront cache and if you don't want to change the `Cache-Control` value, choose **Use Origin Cache Headers**.

To specify a minimum and maximum time that your objects stay in the CloudFront cache regardless of `Cache-Control` headers, and a default time that your objects stay in the CloudFront cache when the `Cache-Control` header is missing from an object, choose **Customize**. Then, in the **Minimum TTL**, **Default TTL**, and **Maximum TTL** fields, specify the applicable value.

For more information, see Specifying How Long Objects Stay in a CloudFront Edge Cache (Expiration).

## Minimum TTL

Specify the minimum amount of time, in seconds, that you want objects to stay in CloudFront caches before CloudFront forwards another request to your origin to determine whether the object has been updated. The default value for **Minimum TTL** is 0 seconds.

### Important

If you configure CloudFront to forward all headers to your origin for a cache behavior, CloudFront never caches the associated objects. Instead, CloudFront forwards all requests for those objects to the origin. In that configuration, the value of **Minimum TTL** must be 0.

To specify a value for **Minimum TTL**, you must choose the **Customize** option for the **Object Caching** setting.

For more information, see Specifying How Long Objects Stay in a CloudFront Edge Cache (Expiration).

## Maximum TTL

Specify the maximum amount of time, in seconds, that you want objects to stay in CloudFront caches before CloudFront queries your origin to see whether the object has been updated. The value that you specify for **Maximum TTL** applies only when your origin adds HTTP headers such as `Cache-Control max-age`, `Cache-Control s-maxage`, or `Expires` to objects. For more information, see Specifying How Long Objects Stay in a CloudFront Edge Cache (Expiration).

To specify a value for **Maximum TTL**, you must choose the **Customize** option for the **Object Caching** setting.

The default value for **Maximum TTL** is 31536000 seconds (one year). If you change the value of **Minimum TTL** or **Default TTL** to more than 31536000 seconds, then the default value of **Maximum TTL** changes to the value of **Default TTL**.

## Default TTL

Specify the default amount of time, in seconds, that you want objects to stay in CloudFront caches before CloudFront forwards another request to your origin to determine whether the object has been updated. The value that you specify for **Default TTL** applies only when your origin does *not* add HTTP headers such as `Cache-Control max-age`, `Cache-Control s-maxage`, or `Expires` to objects. For more information, see Specifying How Long Objects Stay in a CloudFront Edge Cache (Expiration).

To specify a value for **Default TTL**, you must choose the **Customize** option for the **Object Caching** setting.

The default value for **Default TTL** is 86400 seconds (one day). If you change the value of **Minimum TTL** to more than 86400 seconds, then the default value of **Default TTL** changes to the value of **Minimum TTL**.

### Forward Cookies (Amazon EC2 and Other Custom Origins Only)

Specify whether you want CloudFront to forward cookies to your origin server and, if so, which ones. If you choose to forward only selected cookies (a whitelist of cookies), enter the cookie names in the **Whitelist Cookies** field. If you choose **All**, CloudFront forwards all cookies regardless of how many your application uses.

Amazon S3 doesn't process cookies, and forwarding cookies to the origin reduces cacheability. For cache behaviors that are forwarding requests to an Amazon S3 origin, choose **None** for **Forward Cookies**.

For more information about forwarding cookies to the origin, go to Configuring CloudFront to Cache Objects Based on Cookies.

### Whitelist Cookies (Amazon EC2 and Other Custom Origins Only)

If you chose **Whitelist** in the **Forward Cookies** list, then in the **Whitelist Cookies** field, enter the names of cookies that you want CloudFront to forward to your origin server for this cache behavior. Enter each cookie name on a new line.

You can specify the following wildcards to specify cookie names:

- * matches 0 or more characters in the cookie name
- ? matches exactly one character in the cookie name

For example, suppose viewer requests for an object include a cookie named:

`userid_member-number`

where each of your users has a unique value for *member-number*. You want CloudFront to cache a separate version of the object for each member. You could accomplish this by forwarding all cookies to your origin, but viewer requests include some cookies that you don't want CloudFront to cache. Alternatively, you could specify the following value as a cookie name, which causes CloudFront to forward to the applicable origin all of the cookies that begin with `userid_`:

`userid_*`

For the current limit on the number of cookie names that you can whitelist for each cache behavior or to request a higher limit, see Limits on Whitelisted Cookies (Web Distributions Only).

### Query String Forwarding and Caching

CloudFront can cache different versions of your content based on the values of query string parameters. Choose the applicable option:

**None (Improves Caching)**
Choose this option if your origin returns the same version of an object regardless of the values of query string parameters. This increases the likelihood that CloudFront can serve a request from the cache, which improves performance and reduces the load on your origin.

**Forward all, cache based on whitelist**
Choose this option if your origin server returns different versions of your objects based on one or more query string parameters. Then specify the parameters that you want CloudFront to use as a basis for caching in the Query String Whitelist field.

**Forward all, cache based on all**
Choose this option if your origin server returns different versions of your objects for all query string parameters.

For more information about caching based on query string parameters, including how to improve performance, see Configuring CloudFront to Cache Based on Query String Parameters.

## Query String Whitelist

If you chose **Forward all, cache based on whitelist** for Query String Forwarding and Caching, specify the query string parameters that you want CloudFront to use as a basis for caching.

## Smooth Streaming

Choose **Yes** if you want to distribute media files in the Microsoft Smooth Streaming format and you do not have an IIS server.

Choose **No** if you have a Microsoft IIS server that you want to use as an origin to distribute media files in the Microsoft Smooth Streaming format, or if you are not distributing Smooth Streaming media files.

**Note**
If you specify **Yes**, you can still distribute other content using this cache behavior if that content matches the value of **Path Pattern**.

For more information, see Configuring On-Demand Microsoft Smooth Streaming.

## Restrict Viewer Access (Use Signed URLs)

If you want requests for objects that match the `PathPattern` for this cache behavior to use public URLs, choose **No**.

If you want requests for objects that match the `PathPattern` for this cache behavior to use signed URLs, choose **Yes**. Then specify the AWS accounts that you want to use to create signed URLs; these accounts are known as trusted signers.

For more information about trusted signers, see Specifying the AWS Accounts That Can Create Signed URLs and Signed Cookies (Trusted Signers).

## Trusted Signers

Choose which AWS accounts you want to use as trusted signers for this cache behavior:

- **Self:** Use the account with which you're currently signed into the AWS Management Console as a trusted signer. If you're currently signed in as an IAM user, the associated AWS account is added as a trusted signer.
- **Specify Accounts:** Enter account numbers for trusted signers in the **AWS Account Numbers** field.

To create signed URLs, an AWS account must have at least one active CloudFront key pair.

**Important**
If you're updating a distribution that you're already using to distribute content, add trusted signers only when you're ready to start generating signed URLs for your objects. After you add trusted signers to a distribution, users must use signed URLs to access the objects that match the `PathPattern` for this cache behavior.

## AWS Account Numbers

If you want to create signed URLs using AWS accounts in addition to or instead of the current account, enter one AWS account number per line in this field. Note the following:

- The accounts that you specify must have at least one active CloudFront key pair. For more information, see Creating CloudFront Key Pairs for Your Trusted Signers.
- You can't create CloudFront key pairs for IAM users, so you can't use IAM users as trusted signers.

- For information about how to get the AWS account number for an account, see How Do I Get Security Credentials? in the *Amazon Web Services General Reference.*
- If you enter the account number for the current account, CloudFront automatically checks the **Self** checkbox and removes the account number from the **AWS Account Numbers** list.

**Compress Objects Automatically**

If you want CloudFront to automatically compress files of certain types when viewer requests include `Accept-Encoding: gzip` in the request header, choose **Yes**. When CloudFront compresses your content, downloads are faster because the files are smaller, and your web pages render faster for your users. For more information, see Serving Compressed Files.

**Event Type**

You can choose to run a Lambda function when one or more of the following CloudFront events occur:

- When CloudFront receives a request from a viewer (viewer request)
- Before CloudFront forwards a request to the origin (origin request)
- When CloudFront receives a response from the origin (origin response)
- Before CloudFront returns the response to the viewer (viewer response)

For more information, see How to Decide Which CloudFront Event to Use to Trigger a Lambda Function.

**Lambda Function ARN**

Specify the Amazon Resource Name (ARN) of the Lambda function that you want to add a trigger for. To learn how to get the ARN for a function, see step 1 of the procedure Adding Triggers by Using the CloudFront Console.

## Distribution Details

The following values apply to the entire distribution.

**Price Class**

Choose the price class that corresponds with the maximum price that you want to pay for CloudFront service. By default, CloudFront serves your objects from edge locations in all CloudFront regions.

For more information about price classes and about how your choice of price class affects CloudFront performance for your distribution, see Choosing the Price Class for a CloudFront Distribution. For information about CloudFront pricing, including how price classes map to CloudFront regions, go to Amazon CloudFront Pricing.

**AWS WAF Web ACL**

If you want to use AWS WAF to allow or block requests based on criteria that you specify, choose the web ACL to associate with this distribution.

AWS WAF is a web application firewall that lets you monitor the HTTP and HTTPS requests that are forwarded to CloudFront, and lets you control access to your content. Based on conditions that you specify, such as the IP addresses that requests originate from or the values of query strings, CloudFront responds to requests either with the requested content or with an HTTP 403 status code (Forbidden). You can also configure CloudFront to return a custom error page when a request is blocked. For more information about AWS WAF, see the AWS WAF Developer Guide.

**Alternate Domain Names (CNAMEs)**

Optional. Specify one or more domain names that you want to use for URLs for your objects instead of the domain name that CloudFront assigns when you create your distribution. For example, if you want the URL for the object:

`/images/image.jpg`

to look like this:

`http://www.example.com/images/image.jpg`

instead of like this:

`http://d111111abcdef8.cloudfront.net/images/image.jpg`

add a CNAME for `www.example.com`.

**Important**
If you add a CNAME for `www.example.com` to your distribution, you also need to create (or update) a CNAME record with your DNS service to route queries for `www.example.com` to `d111111abcdef8.cloudfront.net`. You must have permission to create a CNAME record with the DNS service provider for the domain. Typically, this means that you own the domain, but you may also be developing an application for the domain owner.

For the current limit on the number of alternate domain names that you can add to a distribution or to request a higher limit, see General Limits on Web Distributions.

For more information about alternate domain names, see Adding and Moving Alternate Domain Names (CNAMEs). For more information about CloudFront URLs, see Format of URLs for Objects.

**SSL Certificate**

If you want viewers to use HTTPS to access your objects, choose the applicable setting. In addition, if you choose **Custom SSL Certificate**, choose the certificate that you want to use:

- **Default CloudFront Certificate (\*.cloudfront.net)** – If you want to use the CloudFront domain name in the URLs for your objects, such as `https://d111111abcdef8.cloudfront.net/image1.jpg`, choose this option. Also choose this option if you want viewers to use HTTP to access your objects.

- **Custom SSL Certificate** – If you want to use your own domain name in the URLs for your objects, such as `https://example.com/image1.jpg`, choose this option and then choose the applicable certificate. The list can include certificates provided by AWS Certificate Manager, and certificates that you purchased from a third-party certificate authority and uploaded to ACM or to the IAM certificate store. For more information, see Using Alternate Domain Names and HTTPS.

  If you choose this setting, we recommend that you use only an alternate domain name in your object URLs (https://example/.com/logo/.jpg/)/. If you use your CloudFront distribution domain name (https://d111111abcdef8/.cloudfront/.net/logo/.jpg/) and the viewer supports SNI, then CloudFront behaves normally. However, a viewer that does not support SNI exhibits one of the following behaviors, depending on the value of **Clients Supported**:

  - **All Clients**: If the viewer doesn't support SNI, it displays a warning because the CloudFront domain name doesn't match the domain name in your SSL certificate.
  - **Only Clients that Support Server Name Indication (SNI)**: CloudFront drops the connection with the viewer without returning the object.

## Clients Supported

If you specified one or more alternate domain names and you specified an SSL certificate in the IAM certificate store, choose how you want CloudFront to serve HTTPS requests, either a method that works for all clients or one that works for most clients:

- **All Clients:** Any client can access your content. However, you must request permission to use this feature, and you incur additional monthly charges.
- **Only Clients that Support Server Name Indication (SNI):** All modern browsers can access your content because they all support SNI. However, some browsers still in use don't support SNI. Users with these browsers must access your content using some other method, for example, by getting your objects directly from the origin.

For more information, see Using Alternate Domain Names and HTTPS.

## Security Policy

Specify the security policy that you want CloudFront to use for HTTPS connections. A security policy determines two settings:

- The minimum SSL/TLS protocol that CloudFront uses to communicate with viewers
- The cipher that CloudFront uses to encrypt the content that it returns to viewers

The security policies that are available depend on the values that you specify for **SSL Certificate** and **Custom SSL Client Support**:

- When **SSL Certificate** is **Default CloudFront Certificate (\*.cloudfront.net)**, CloudFront automatically sets the value of **Security Policy** to **TLSv1**.
- When **SSL Certificate** is **Custom SSL Certificate (example.com)** and **Custom SSL Client Support** is **Only Clients that Support Server Name Indication (SNI)**, you must use TLSv1 or later. We recommend that you choose **TLSv1.1__2016** unless your users are using browsers or devices that don't support TLSv1.1 or later.
- When **SSL Certificate** is **Custom SSL Certificate (example.com)** and **Custom SSL Client Support** is **All Clients**, we recommend that you choose **TLSv1**. In this configuration, the **TLSv1__2016**, **TLSv1.1__2016**, and **TLSv1.2__2018** security policies aren't available.

For information about the relationship between the security policy that you choose and the protocols and ciphers that CloudFront uses to communicate with viewers, see Supported SSL/TLS Protocols and Ciphers for Communication Between Viewers and CloudFront.

## Minimum SSL Protocol Version

See Security Policy.

## Supported HTTP Versions

Choose the HTTP versions that you want viewers to use to communicate with CloudFront. Viewers use the latest version that you configure CloudFront to use. Viewers that don't support HTTP/2 will automatically use an earlier version.

For viewers and CloudFront to use HTTP/2, viewers must support TLS 1.2 or later, and must support Server Name Identification (SNI).

In general, configuring CloudFront to communicate with viewers using HTTP/2 reduces latency. You can improve performance by optimizing for HTTP/2. For more information, do an internet search for "http/2 optimization."

## Default Root Object

Optional. The object that you want CloudFront to request from your origin (for example, `index.html`) when a viewer requests the root URL of your distribution (`http://www.example.com/`) instead of an object in your distribution (`http://www.example.com/product-description.html`). Specifying a default root object avoids exposing the contents of your distribution.

The maximum length of the name is 255 characters. The name can contain any of the following characters:

- A-Z, a-z
- 0-9
- _ - . * $ / ~ " '
- &, passed and returned as `&amp;`

When you specify the default root object, enter only the object name, for example, `index.html`. Do not add a / before the object name.

For more information, see Specifying a Default Root Object (Web Distributions Only).

## Logging

Whether you want CloudFront to log information about each request for an object and store the log files in an Amazon S3 bucket. You can enable or disable logging at any time. There is no extra charge if you enable logging, but you accrue the usual Amazon S3 charges for storing and accessing the files in an Amazon S3 bucket. You can delete the logs at any time. For more information about CloudFront access logs, see Access Logs.

## Bucket for Logs

If you chose **On** for **Logging**, the Amazon S3 bucket that you want CloudFront to store access logs in, for example, `myawslogbucket.s3.amazonaws.com`. If you enable logging, CloudFront records information about each end-user request for an object and stores the files in the specified Amazon S3 bucket. You can enable or disable logging at any time. For more information about CloudFront access logs, see Access Logs.

### Note
You must have the permissions required to get and update Amazon S3 bucket ACLs, and the S3 ACL for the bucket must grant you `FULL_CONTROL`. This allows CloudFront to give the awsdatafeeds account permission to save log files in the bucket. For more information, see Permissions Required to Configure Logging and to Access Your Log Files.

## Log Prefix

Optional. If you chose **On** for **Logging**, specify the string, if any, that you want CloudFront to prefix to the access log filenames for this distribution, for example, `exampleprefix/`. The trailing slash ( / ) is optional but recommended to simplify browsing your log files. For more information about CloudFront access logs, see Access Logs.

## Cookie Logging

If you want CloudFront to include cookies in access logs, choose **On**. If you choose to include cookies in logs, CloudFront logs all cookies regardless of how you configure the cache behaviors for this distribution: forward all cookies, forward no cookies, or forward a specified list of cookies to the origin.

Amazon S3 doesn't process cookies, so unless your distribution also includes an Amazon EC2 or other custom origin, we recommend that you choose **Off** for the value of **Cookie Logging**.

For more information about cookies, go to Configuring CloudFront to Cache Objects Based on Cookies.

**Enable IPv6**

IPv6 is a new version of the IP protocol. It's the eventual replacement for IPv4 and uses a larger address space. CloudFront always responds to IPv4 requests. If you want CloudFront to respond to requests from IPv4 IP addresses (such as 192.0.2.44) and requests from IPv6 addresses (such as 2001:0db8:85a3:0000:0000:8a2e:0370:7334), select **Enable IPv6**.

In general, you should enable IPv6 if you have users on IPv6 networks who want to access your content. However, if you're using signed URLs or signed cookies to restrict access to your content, and if you're using a custom policy that includes the `IpAddress` parameter to restrict the IP addresses that can access your content, do not enable IPv6. If you want to restrict access to some content by IP address and not restrict access to other content (or restrict access but not by IP address), you can create two distributions. For information about creating signed URLs by using a custom policy, see Creating a Signed URL Using a Custom Policy. For information about creating signed cookies by using a custom policy, see Setting Signed Cookies Using a Custom Policy.

If you're using an Route 53 alias resource record set to route traffic to your CloudFront distribution, you need to create a second alias resource record set when both of the following are true:

- You enable IPv6 for the distribution
- You're using alternate domain names in the URLs for your objects

For more information, see Routing Traffic to an Amazon CloudFront Web Distribution by Using Your Domain Name in the *Amazon Route 53 Developer Guide.*

If you created a CNAME resource record set, either with Route 53 or with another DNS service, you don't need to make any changes. A CNAME record will route traffic to your distribution regardless of the IP address format of the viewer request.

If you enable IPv6 and CloudFront access logs, the `c-ip` column will include values in IPv4 and IPv6 format. For more information, see Access Logs.

**Note**
To maintain high customer availability, CloudFront will respond to viewer requests by using IPv4 if our data suggests that IPv4 will provide a better user experience. To find out what percentage of requests CloudFront is serving over IPv6, enable CloudFront logging for your distribution and parse the `c-ip` column, which contains the IP address of the viewer that made the request. This percentage should grow over time, but it will remain a minority of traffic as IPv6 is not yet supported by all viewer networks globally. Some viewer networks have excellent IPv6 support, but others don't support IPv6 at all. (A viewer network is analogous to your home internet or wireless carrier.)
For more information about our support for IPv6, see the CloudFront FAQ. For information about enabling access logs, see the fields Logging, Bucket for Logs, and Log Prefix.

**Comment**

Optional. When you create a distribution, you can include a comment of up to 128 characters. You can update the comment at any time.

**Distribution State**

Indicates whether you want the distribution to be enabled or disabled once it's deployed:

- *Enabled* means that as soon as the distribution is fully deployed you can deploy links that use the distribution's domain name and users can retrieve content. Whenever a distribution is enabled, CloudFront accepts and handles any end-user requests for content that use the domain name associated with that distribution.

When you create, modify, or delete a CloudFront distribution, it takes time for your changes to propagate to the CloudFront database. An immediate request for information about a distribution might not show the change. Propagation usually completes within minutes, but a high system load or network partition might increase this time.

- *Disabled* means that even though the distribution might be deployed and ready to use, users can't use it. Whenever a distribution is disabled, CloudFront doesn't accept any end-user requests that use the domain name associated with that distribution. Until you switch the distribution from disabled to enabled (by updating the distribution's configuration), no one can use it.

You can toggle a distribution between disabled and enabled as often as you want. Follow the process for updating a distribution's configuration. For more information, see Viewing and Updating CloudFront Distributions.

## Custom Error Pages and Error Caching

You can have CloudFront return an object to the viewer (for example, an HTML file) when your Amazon S3 or custom origin returns an HTTP 4xx or 5xx status code to CloudFront. You can also specify how long an error response from your origin or a custom error page is cached in CloudFront edge caches. For more information, see Customizing Error Responses.

**Note**
The following values aren't included in the Create Distribution wizard, so you can configure custom error pages only when you update a distribution.

### Error Code

The HTTP status code for which you want CloudFront to return a custom error page. You can configure CloudFront to return custom error pages for none, some, or all of the HTTP status codes that CloudFront caches.

### Response Page Path

The path to the custom error page (for example, `/4xx-errors/403-forbidden.html`) that you want CloudFront to return to a viewer when your origin returns the HTTP status code that you specified for **Error Code** (for example, 403). If you want to store your objects and your custom error pages in different locations, your distribution must include a cache behavior for which the following is true:

- The value of **Path Pattern** matches the path to your custom error messages. For example, suppose you saved custom error pages for 4xx errors in an Amazon S3 bucket in a directory named **/4xx-errors**. Your distribution must include a cache behavior for which the path pattern routes requests for your custom error pages to that location, for example, **/4xx-errors/\***.
- The value of **Origin** specifies the value of **Origin ID** for the origin that contains your custom error pages.

### Response Code

The HTTP status code that you want CloudFront to return to the viewer along with the custom error page.

### Error Caching Minimum TTL

The minimum amount of time that you want CloudFront to cache error responses from your origin server.

# Restrictions

If you need to prevent users in selected countries from accessing your content, you can configure your CloudFront distribution either to allow users in a whitelist of specified countries to access your content or to not allow users in a blacklist of specified countries to access your content. For more information, see Restricting the Geographic Distribution of Your Content.

**Note**
The following values aren't included in the Create Distribution wizard, so you can configure geo restrictions only when you update a distribution.

### Enable Geo Restriction

Whether you want to prevent users in selected countries from accessing your content. There is no additional charge for configuring geo restriction.

### Restriction Type

How you want to specify the countries from which your users can access your content:

- **Whitelist:** The **Countries** list includes all of the countries from which you *do* want your users to access your content.
- **Blacklist:** The **Countries** list includes all of the countries from which you *do not* want your users to access your content.

### Countries

The countries that you want to add to your whitelist or blacklist. To add a country, select it in the list on the left and choose **Add**. Note the following:

- To add multiple consecutive countries, select the first country, press and hold the Shift key, select the last country, and choose **Add**.
- To add multiple non-consecutive countries, select the first country, press and hold the Ctrl key, select the remaining countries, and choose **Add**.
- To find a country in the left list, enter the first few characters of the country's full name.
- The two-letter code before the name of each country is the value that you enter if you want to create or update a distribution by using the CloudFront API. We use the International Organization for Standardization country codes. For an easy-to-use list, sortable by code and by country name, see the Wikipedia entry ISO 3166-1 alpha-2.

# Values that CloudFront Displays in the Console When You Create or Update a Web Distribution

When you create a new web distribution or update an existing distribution, CloudFront displays the following information in the CloudFront console.

**Note**
Active trusted signers, the AWS accounts that have an active CloudFront key pair and can be used to create valid signed URLs, are currently not visible in the CloudFront console.

## Distribution ID (General Tab)

When you perform an action on a distribution using the CloudFront API, you use the distribution ID to specify which distribution you want to perform the action on, for example, EDFDVBD6EXAMPLE. You can't change the distribution ID.

## Distribution Status (General Tab)

The possible status values for a distribution are listed in the following table.

| Value | Description |
|---|---|
| **InProgress** | The distribution is still being created or updated. |
| **Deployed** | The distribution has been created or updated and the changes have been fully propagated through the CloudFront system. |

**Note**
In addition to ensuring that the status for a distribution is **Deployed**, you must enable the distribution before users can use CloudFront to access your content. For more information, see Distribution State.

## Last Modified (General Tab)

The date and time that the distribution was last modified, using ISO 8601 format, for example, 2012-05-19T19:37:58Z. For more information, go to http://www.w3.org/TR/NOTE-datetime.

## Domain Name (General Tab)

You use the distribution's domain name in the links to your objects. For example, if your distribution's domain name is d111111abcdef8.cloudfront.net, the link to /images/image.jpg would be http://d111111abcdef8.cloudfront.net/images/image.jpg. You can't change the CloudFront domain name for your distribution. For more information about CloudFront URLs for links to your objects, see Format of URLs for Objects.

If you specified one or more alternate domain names (CNAMEs), you can use your own domain names for links to your objects instead of using the CloudFront domain name. For more information about CNAMEs, see Alternate Domain Names (CNAMEs).

**Note**

CloudFront domain names are unique. Your distribution's domain name was never used for a previous distribution and will never be reused for another distribution in the future.

# Using Field-Level Encryption to Help Protect Sensitive Data

You can already configure CloudFront to help enforce secure end-to-end connections to origin servers by using HTTPS. Field-level encryption adds an additional layer of security along with HTTPS that lets you protect specific data throughout system processing so that only certain applications can see it.

Field-level encryption allows you to securely upload user-submitted sensitive information to your web servers. The sensitive information provided by your clients is encrypted at the edge closer to the user and remains encrypted throughout your entire application stack, ensuring that only applications that need the data—and have the credentials to decrypt it—are able to do so.

To use field-level encryption, you configure your CloudFront distribution to specify the set of fields in POST requests that you want to be encrypted, and the public key to use to encrypt them. You can encrypt up to 10 data fields in a request. (You can't encrypt all of the data in a request with field-level encryption; you must specify individual fields to encrypt.)

When the HTTPS request with field-level encryption is forwarded to the origin, and the request is routed throughout your origin sub-system, the sensitive data is still encrypted, reducing the risk of a data breach or accidental data loss of the sensitive data. Components that need access to the sensitive data for business reasons, such as a payment processing system needing access to a credit number, can use the appropriate private key to decrypt and access the data.

Be aware that in order to use field-level encryption, your origin must support chunked encoding.

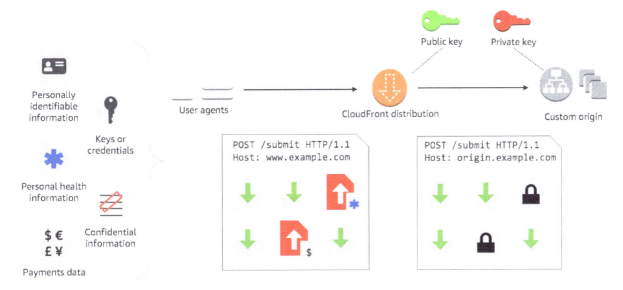

CloudFront field-level encryption uses asymmetric encryption, also known as public-key encryption. You provide a public key to CloudFront, and all sensitive data that you specify is encrypted automatically. The key you provide to CloudFront cannot be used to decrypt the encrypted values; only your private key can do that.

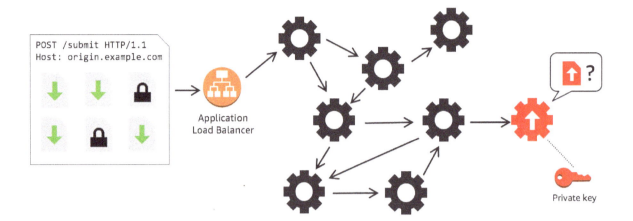

```
POST /submit HTTP/1.1
Host: origin.example.com
```

Application
Load Balancer

Private key

**Topics**

- Overview of Field-Level Encryption
- Setting Up Field-Level Encryption
- Decrypting Data Fields at Your Origin

## Overview of Field-Level Encryption

The following steps provide an overview of setting up field-level encryption. For specific steps, see Setting Up Field-Level Encryption.

---

1. **Get a public key-private key pair.** You must obtain and add the public key before you start setting up field-level encryption in CloudFront.

2. **Create a field-level encryption profile.** Field-level encryption profiles, which you create in CloudFront, define the fields that you want to be encrypted.

3. **Create a field-level encryption configuration.** A configuration specifies the profiles to use—based on the content type of the request or a query argument—for encrypting specific data fields. You can also choose the request-forwarding behavior options that you want for different scenarios; for example, when the profile name specified by the query argument in a request URL doesn't exist in CloudFront.

4. **Link to a cache behavior.** Link the configuration to a cache behavior for a distribution, to specify when CloudFront should encrypt data.

## Setting Up Field-Level Encryption

Follow these steps to get started using field-level encryption. To learn about limits in field-level encryption, see Limits.

- Step 1: Get an RSA Key Pair
- Step 2: Add Your Public Key to CloudFront
- Step 3: Create a Profile for Field-Level Encryption
- Step 4: Create a Configuration
- Step 5: Add a Configuration to a Cache Behavior

**Step 1: Get an RSA Key Pair**

To get started, you must obtain a RSA key pair that includes a public key, so CloudFront can encrypt data, and a private key, so components at your origin to decrypt the fields that have been encrypted. For example, you can use Open SSL or another tool to create a key pair. The key size must be 2048 bits. For more information, see To create an RSA key pair and upload the public key in the AWS Management Console.

**Step 2: Add Your Public Key to CloudFront**

After you get your RSA key pair, add your public key to CloudFront.

**To add your public key to CloudFront (console)**

1. Sign in to the AWS Management Console and open the CloudFront console at https://console.aws.amazon.com/cloudfront/.

2. In the navigation pane, choose **Public key**.

3. Choose **Add public key**.

4. For **Key name**, type a unique name for the key. The name can't have spaces and can include only alphanumeric characters, underscores (_), and hyphens (-). The maximum number of characters is 128.

5. For **Encoded key**, copy and paste the encoded key value for your public key, including the " -----BEGIN PUBLIC KEY-----" and "-----END PUBLIC KEY-----" lines.

6. For **Comment**, add an optional comment. For example, you could include the expiration date for the public key.

7. Choose **Add key**.

You can add more keys to use with CloudFront by repeating the steps in the procedure.

**Step 3: Create a Profile for Field-Level Encryption**

After you add at least one public key to CloudFront, create a profile that tells CloudFront which fields to encrypt.

**To create a profile for field-level encryption (console)**

1. In the navigation pane, choose **Field-level encryption**.

2. Choose **Create profile**.

3. Fill in the following fields:
   **Profile name**
   Type a unique name for the profile. The name can't have spaces and can include only alphanumeric characters, underscores (_), and hyphens (-). The maximum number of characters is 128.
   **Public key name**
   In the drop-down list, choose the name of a public key that you added to CloudFront in step 2. CloudFront uses the key to encrypt the fields that you specify in this profile.
   **Provider name**
   Type a phrase to help identify the key, such as the provider where you got the key pair. This information, along with the private key, will be needed when applications decrypt data fields. The provider name can't have spaces and can include only alphanumeric characters, colons (:), underscores (_), and hyphens (-). The maximum number of characters is 128.
   **Field name pattern to match**
   Type the names of the data fields, or patterns that identify data field names in the request, that you want CloudFront to encrypt. Choose the + option to add all the fields that you want to encrypt with this key. For the field name pattern, you can type the entire name of the data field, like DateOfBirth, or just the first part of the name with a wildcard character (*), like CreditCard*. The field name pattern must include

only alphanumeric characters, square brackets ([ and ]), periods (.), underscores (_), and hyphens (-), in addition to the optional wildcard character (*).

Make sure that you don't use overlapping characters for different field name patterns. For example, if you have a field name pattern of ABC*, you can't add another field name pattern that is AB*. In addition, note that field names are case sensitive and the maximum number of characters that you can use is 128.

**Comment**

(Optional) Type a comment about this profile. The maximum number of characters that you can use is 128.

4. After you fill in the fields, choose **Create profile**.

5. If you want to add more profiles, choose **Add profile**.

### Step 4: Create a Configuration

After you create one or more field-level encryption profiles, create a configuration that specifies the content type of the request that includes the data to be encrypted, the profile to use for encryption, and other options that specify how you want CloudFront to handle encryption.

For example, when CloudFront can't encrypt the data, you can specify whether CloudFront should block or forward a request to your origin in the following scenarios:

- **When a request's content type isn't in a configuration.** If you haven't added a content type to a configuration, you can specify whether CloudFront should forward the request with that content type to the origin without encrypting data fields, or block the request and return an error.

  Note: If you add a content type to a configuration but haven't specified a profile to use with that type, requests with that content type will always be forwarded to the origin.

- **When the profile name provided in a query argument is unknown.** When you specify the `fle -profile` query argument with a profile name that doesn't exist for your distribution, you can specify whether CloudFront should send the request to the origin without encrypting data fields, or block the request and return an error.

In a configuration, you can also specify whether providing a profile as a query argument in a URL overrides a profile that you've mapped to the content type for that query. By default, CloudFront uses the profile that you've mapped to a content type, if you specify one. This lets you have a profile that's used by default but decide for certain requests that you want to enforce a different profile.

So, for example, you might specify (in your configuration) SampleProfile as the query argument profile to use. Then you could use the URL `https://d1234.cloudfront.net?fle-profile=SampleProfile` instead of `https://d1234.cloudfront.net`, to have CloudFront use SampleProfile for this request, instead of the profile you'd set up for the content type of the request.

You can create up to 10 configurations for a single account, and then associate one of the configurations to the cache behavior of any distribution for the account.

**To create a configuration for field-level encryption (console)**

1. On the **Field-level encryption** page, choose **Create configuration**.

   Note: If you haven't created at least one profile, you won't see the option to create a configuration.

2. Fill in the following fields to specify the profile to use. (Some fields can't be changed.)
   **Content type (can't be changed)**
   The content type is set to `application/x-www-form-urlencoded` and can't be changed.
   **Default profile ID (optional)**
   In the drop-down list, choose the profile that you want to map to the content type in the **Content type** field.

**Content format (can't be changed)**
The content format is set to `URLencoded` and can't be changed.

3. If you want to change the CloudFront default behavior for the following options, select the appropriate check box.

   **Forward request to origin when request's content type is not configured**
   Select the check box if you want to allow the request to go to your origin *if you have not specified a profile to use for the content type of the request.*

   **Override the profile for a content type with a provided query argument**
   Select the check box if you want to allow a profile provided in a query argument to *override the profile that you've specified for a content type.*

4. If you select the check box to allow a query argument to override the default profile, you must complete the following additional fields for the configuration. You can create up to five of these query argument mappings to use with queries.

   **Query argument**
   Type the value that you want to include in URLs for the `fle-profile` query argument. This value tells CloudFront to use the profile ID (that you specify in the next field) associated with this query argument for field-level encryption for this query.

   The maximum number of characters that you can use is 128. The value can't include spaces, and must use only alphanumeric or the following characters: dash (-), period (.), underscore (_), asterisk (*), plus-sign (+), percent (%).

   **Profile ID**
   In the drop-down list, choose the profile that you want to associate with the value that you typed for **Query argument**.

   **Forward request to origin when the profile specified in a query argument does not exist**
   Select the check box if you want to allow the request to go to your origin *if the profile specified in a query argument isn't defined in CloudFront.*

**Step 5: Add a Configuration to a Cache Behavior**

To use field-level encryption, link a configuration to a cache behavior for a distribution by adding the configuration ID as a value for your distribution. Note that the Viewer Protocol Policy and Origin Protocol Policy must be HTTPS in order for you to link a configuration to a cache behavior.

For more information, see Values That You Specify When You Create or Update a Web Distribution.

# Decrypting Data Fields at Your Origin

CloudFront encrypts data fields by using the AWS Encryption SDK. The data remains encrypted throughout your application stack and can be accessed only by applications that have the credentials to decrypt it.

After encryption, the cipher text is base64 encoded. When your applications decrypt the text at the origin, they must first decode the cipher text, and then use the AWS Encryption SDK to decrypt the data.

The following code sample illustrates how applications can decrypt data at your origin. Note the following:

- To simplify the example, this sample loads public and private keys (in DER format) from files in the working directory. In practice, you would store the private key in a secure offline location, such as an offline hardware security module, and distribute the public key to your development team.
- CloudFront uses specific information while encrypting the data, and the same set of parameters should be used at the origin to decrypt it. Parameters CloudFront uses while initializing the MasterKey include the following:
  - PROVIDER_NAME: You specified this value when you created a field-level encryption profile. Use the same value here.

- KEY_NAME: You created a name for your public key when you uploaded it to CloudFront, and then specified the key name in the profile. Use the same value here.
  - ALGORITHM: CloudFront uses "RSA/ECB/OAEPWithSHA-256AndMGF1Padding" as the algorithm for encrypting, so you must use the same algorithm to decrypt the data.
- If you run the following sample program with cipher text as input, the decrypted data is output to your console. For more information, see the Java Example Code in the AWS Encryption SDK.

**Sample Code**

```
1  import java.nio.file.Files;
2  import java.nio.file.Paths;
3  import java.security.KeyFactory;
4  import java.security.PrivateKey;
5  import java.security.PublicKey;
6  import java.security.spec.PKCS8EncodedKeySpec;
7  import java.security.spec.X509EncodedKeySpec;
8
9  import org.apache.commons.codec.binary.Base64;
10
11 import com.amazonaws.encryptionsdk.AwsCrypto;
12 import com.amazonaws.encryptionsdk.CryptoResult;
13 import com.amazonaws.encryptionsdk.jce.JceMasterKey;
14
15 /**
16  * Sample example of decrypting data that has been encrypted by CloudFront Field-Level
         Encryption.
17  */
18 public class DecryptExample {
19
20     private static final String PRIVATE_KEY_FILENAME = "private_key.der";
21     private static final String PUBLIC_KEY_FILENAME = "public_key.der";
22     private static PublicKey publicKey;
23     private static PrivateKey privateKey;
24
25     // CloudFront uses the following values to encrypt data, and your origin must use same
            values to decrypt it.
26     // In your own code, for PROVIDER_NAME, use the provider name that you specified when you
            created your Field Level
27     // Encryption Profile. This sample uses 'DEMO' for the value.
28     private static final String PROVIDER_NAME = "DEMO";
29     // In your own code, use the Key name that you specified when you added your public key to
            CloudFront. This sample
30     // uses 'DEMOKEY' for the Key name.
31     private static final String KEY_NAME = "DEMOKEY";
32     // Cloudfront uses this algorithm when encrypting data.
33     private static final String ALGORITHM = "RSA/ECB/OAEPWithSHA-256AndMGF1Padding";
34
35     public static void main(final String[] args) throws Exception {
36
37         final String dataToDecrypt = args[0];
38
39         // This sample uses files to get public and private keys.
40         // In practice, you should distribute the public key and save the private key in secure
                storage.
```

```
41          populateKeyPair();
42
43          System.out.println(decrypt(debase64(dataToDecrypt)));
44      }
45
46      private static String decrypt(final byte[] bytesToDecrypt) throws Exception {
47          // You can decrypt the stream only by using the private key.
48
49          // 1. Instantiate the SDK
50          final AwsCrypto crypto = new AwsCrypto();
51
52          // 2. Instantiate a JCE master key
53          final JceMasterKey masterKey = JceMasterKey.getInstance(
54                  publicKey,
55                  privateKey,
56                  PROVIDER_NAME,
57                  KEY_NAME,
58                  ALGORITHM);
59
60          // 3. Decrypt the data
61          final CryptoResult <byte[], ? > result = crypto.decryptData(masterKey, bytesToDecrypt);
62          return new String(result.getResult());
63      }
64
65      // Function to decode base64 cipher text.
66      private static byte[] debase64(final String value) {
67          return Base64.decodeBase64(value.getBytes());
68      }
69
70      private static void populateKeyPair() throws Exception {
71          final byte[] PublicKeyBytes = Files.readAllBytes(Paths.get(PUBLIC_KEY_FILENAME));
72          final byte[] privateKeyBytes = Files.readAllBytes(Paths.get(PRIVATE_KEY_FILENAME));
73          publicKey = KeyFactory.getInstance("RSA").generatePublic(new X509EncodedKeySpec(
74              PublicKeyBytes));
            privateKey = KeyFactory.getInstance("RSA").generatePrivate(new PKCS8EncodedKeySpec(
                privateKeyBytes));
75      }
76 }
```

# Using AWS WAF to Control Access to Your Content

AWS WAF is a web application firewall that lets you monitor the HTTP and HTTPS requests that are forwarded to CloudFront, and lets you control access to your content. Based on conditions that you specify, such as the IP addresses that requests originate from or the values of query strings, CloudFront responds to requests either with the requested content or with an HTTP 403 status code (Forbidden). You can also configure CloudFront to return a custom error page when a request is blocked. For more information about AWS WAF, see the AWS WAF Developer Guide.

After you create an AWS WAF web access control list (web ACL), you create or update a web distribution and associate the distribution with a web ACL. You can associate as many CloudFront distributions as you want with the same web ACL or with different web ACLs. For information about creating a web distribution and associating it with a web ACL, see Creating a Web Distribution.

To associate or disassociate a web ACL and an existing distribution, or change the web ACL that is associated with a distribution, perform the following procedure.

**To associate or disassociate an AWS WAF web ACL and an existing CloudFront distribution by using the CloudFront console**

1. Sign in to the AWS Management Console and open the CloudFront console at https://console.aws.amazon.com/cloudfront/.

2. Choose the ID for the distribution that you want to update.

3. On the **General** tab, choose **Edit**.

4. On the **Distribution Settings** page, in the **AWS WAF Web ACL** list, choose the web ACL that you want to associate with this distribution.

   If you want to disassociate the distribution from all web ACLs, choose **None**. If you want to associate the distribution with a different web ACL, choose the new web ACL.

5. Choose **Yes, Edit**.

6. Repeat steps 2 through 5 for other distributions, if any, for which you want to add, delete, or change associations with AWS WAF web ACLs.

7. After you change settings, the value of the **Status** column for the distributions that you updated changes to **InProgress** while CloudFront propagates the changes to edge locations. When **Status** changes to **Deployed** for a distribution, the distribution is ready to use AWS WAF when it processes requests. (The value of the **State** column for the distribution must also be **Enabled**.) This should take less than 15 minutes after you save the last change to a distribution.

# Restricting the Geographic Distribution of Your Content

You can use *geo restriction*, also known as *geoblocking*, to prevent users in specific geographic locations from accessing content that you're distributing through a CloudFront web distribution. To use geo restriction, you have two options:

- Use the CloudFront geo restriction feature. Use this option to restrict access to all of the files that are associated with a distribution and to restrict access at the country level.
- Use a third-party geolocation service. Use this option to restrict access to a subset of the files that are associated with a distribution or to restrict access at a finer granularity than the country level.

**Topics**

- Using CloudFront Geo Restriction
- Using a Third-Party Geolocation Service

## Using CloudFront Geo Restriction

When a user requests your content, CloudFront typically serves the requested content regardless of where the user is located. If you need to prevent users in specific countries from accessing your content, you can use the CloudFront geo restriction feature to do one of the following:

- Allow your users to access your content only if they're in one of the countries on a whitelist of approved countries.
- Prevent your users from accessing your content if they're in one of the countries on a blacklist of banned countries.

For example, if a request comes from a country where, for copyright reasons, you are not authorized to distribute your content, you can use CloudFront geo restriction to block the request.

**Note**
CloudFront determines the location of your users by using a third-party GeoIP database. The accuracy of the mapping between IP addresses and countries varies by region. Based on recent tests, the overall accuracy is 99.8%. Be aware that if CloudFront can't determine a user's location, CloudFront will serve the content that the user has requested.

Here's how geo restriction works:

1. Suppose you have rights to distribute your content only in Liechtenstein. You update your CloudFront web distribution and add a whitelist that contains only Liechtenstein. (Alternatively, you could add a blacklist that contains every country except Liechtenstein.)

2. A user in Monaco requests your content, and DNS routes the request to the CloudFront edge location in Milan, Italy.

3. The edge location in Milan looks up your distribution and determines that the user in Monaco is not allowed to download your content.

4. CloudFront returns an HTTP status code of 403 (Forbidden) to the user.

You can optionally configure CloudFront to return a custom error message to the user, and you can specify how long you want CloudFront to cache the error response for the requested object; the default value is five minutes. For more information, see Customizing Error Responses.

Geo restriction applies to an entire web distribution. If you need to apply one restriction to part of your content and a different restriction (or no restriction) to another part of your content, you must either create separate CloudFront web distributions or use a third-party geolocation service.

If you enable CloudFront access logging, you can identify the requests that CloudFront rejected by searching for the log entries for which the value of `sc-status` (the HTTP status code) is 403. However, using only the access logs, you can't distinguish a request that CloudFront rejected based on the location of the user from a request that CloudFront rejected because the user didn't have permission to access the object for another reason. If you have a third-party geolocation service such as Digital Element or MaxMind, you can identify the location of requests based on the IP address in the `c-ip` (client IP) column in the access logs. For more information about CloudFront access logs, see Access Logs.

The following procedure explains how to use the CloudFront console to add geo restriction to an existing web distribution. For information about how to use the console to create a web distribution, see Working with Web Distributions.

**To use the CloudFront console to add geo restriction to your CloudFront web distribution**

1. Sign in to the AWS Management Console and open the CloudFront console at https://console.aws.amazon.com/cloudfront/.

2. Select the distribution that you want to update.

3. In the **Distribution Settings** pane, choose the **Restrictions** tab.

4. Choose **Edit**.

5. Enter the applicable values. For more information, see Restrictions.

6. Choose **Yes, Edit**.

## Using a Third-Party Geolocation Service

The CloudFront geo restriction feature lets you control distribution of your content at the country level for all files that you're distributing with a given web distribution. If you have geographic restrictions on where your content can be distributed and the restrictions don't follow country boundaries, or if you want to limit access to only some of the files that you're distributing through CloudFront, you can combine CloudFront with a third-party geolocation service. This can allow you to control access to your content based not only on country but also based on city, zip or postal code, or even latitude and longitude.

When you're using a third-party geolocation service, we recommend that you use CloudFront signed URLs, which let you specify an expiration date and time after which the URL is no longer valid. In addition, we recommend that you use an Amazon S3 bucket as your origin because you can then use a CloudFront origin access identity to prevent users from accessing your content directly from the origin. For more information about signed URLs and origin access identities, see Serving Private Content through CloudFront.

The following task list explains how to control access to your files by using a third-party geolocation service.

**Task list for restricting access to files in a CloudFront distribution based on geographic location**

1. Get an account with a geolocation service.

2. Upload your content to an Amazon Simple Storage Service (S3) bucket. For more information, see the Amazon S3 documentation.

3. Configure Amazon CloudFront and Amazon S3 to serve private content. For more information, see Serving Private Content through CloudFront.

4. Write your web application to do the following:

   1. Send the IP address for each user request to the geolocation service.

   2. Evaluate the return value from the geolocation service to determine whether the user is in a location to which you want CloudFront to distribute your content.

   3. Based on whether you want to distribute your content to the user's location, either generate a signed URL for your CloudFront content, or return HTTP status code 403 (Forbidden) to the user. Alternatively, you can configure CloudFront to return a custom error message. For more information, see Customizing Error Responses.

For more information, refer to the documentation for the geolocation service that you're using.

You can use a web server variable to get the IP addresses of the users who are visiting your website. Note the following caveats:

- If your web server is not connected to the internet through a load balancer, you can use a web server variable to get the remote IP address. However, this IP address isn't always the user's IP address—it can also be the IP address of a proxy server, depending on how the user is connected to the internet.
- If your web server is connected to the internet through a load balancer, a web server variable might contain the IP address of the load balancer, not the IP address of the user. In this configuration, we recommend that you use the last IP address in the `X-Forwarded-For` http header. This header typically contains more than one IP address, most of which are for proxies or load balancers. The last IP address in the list is the one most likely to be associated with the user's geographic location.

If your web server is not connected to a load balancer, we recommend that you use web server variables instead of the `X-Forwarded-For` header to avoid IP address spoofing.

# Configuring Video Streaming Web Distributions

You can use CloudFront to deliver on-demand video or live streaming video using any HTTP origin. One way you can set up video workflows in the cloud is by using CloudFront together with AWS Elemental Media Services.

**For on-demand video streaming**, your video content is stored on a server and viewers can watch it at any time. To make an asset that viewers can stream, use a transcoder, such as AWS Elemental MediaConvert, to convert your file into a streaming package. Common formats for packages are DASH, Apple HLS, and Microsoft (MS) Smooth.

These packages contain your audio, video, and captions content in small files called segments, each with a few seconds of content. They also contain manifest files, which players use to determine which segment to download and when to play it, in a specific order.

After your video is converted into the right formats, you can deliver it with CloudFront as viewers request it.

**For live video streaming**, you can either stream a live event or set up a 24x7 live channel delivery.

Examples of live events are live broadcasting and content aggregators streaming sports tournaments, awards ceremonies, and keynote addresses.

A 24x7 live channel might be set up for a studio, broadcaster, or paid TV service operator who wants to package and deliver a live linear channel over the internet, sending content directly to an audience without a third-party distribution platform.

There are also other companies that provide tools that you can use for delivering or viewing live video with CloudFront, such as Wowza and JW Player. For more information about using Wowza with CloudFront, see How to bring your Wowza Streaming Engine license to CloudFront live HTTP streaming on the Wowza website. For a tutorial on using JW Player with CloudFront, see On-Demand Video Streaming Using CloudFront and JW Player.

**Topics**

- Delivering On-Demand Video with CloudFront and AWS Media Services
- Delivering Live Streaming Video with CloudFront and AWS Media Services
- Configuring On-Demand Microsoft Smooth Streaming

# Delivering On-Demand Video with CloudFront and AWS Media Services

To use AWS products to deliver on-demand video streaming, you can use Amazon S3 to store the content in its original format, AWS Elemental MediaConvert to transcode the video files into streaming formats, and CloudFront to deliver the video to viewers.

To create the solution, follow these steps:

- **Step 1:** Upload your content to an Amazon S3 bucket. To learn more about working with S3, see the Amazon Simple Storage Service Developer Guide.
- **Step 2:**Use AWS Elemental MediaConvert to convert your video into the formats required by the players your viewers will be using. You can also create assets of that vary in size and quality for adaptive bitrate streaming, which adjusts the viewing quality depending on the viewer's available bandwidth. AWS Elemental MediaConvert takes content that you upload to an S3 bucket, transcodes it, and stores the result in another S3 bucket.
- **Step 3:** Deliver the converted content by using a CloudFront distribution, so viewers can watch it on any device, whenever they like. First, you put all segments and manifest files together in a single directory. Then you set up a CloudFront distribution to serve the content (see Configuring On-Demand Video with AWS Elemental MediaStore).

## Tip
To learn more about best practices when you implement a video on-demand workflow with AWS Cloud services, see Video on Demand on AWS.

You can also explore how to use an AWS CloudFormation template to deploy a video-on-demand AWS solution together with all the associated components. To see the steps for using the template, see Video on Demand Automated Deployment.

## Configuring On-Demand Video with AWS Elemental MediaStore

If you store on-demand videos in AWS Elemental MediaStore, you can create a CloudFront distribution to serve the content.

To get started, you grant CloudFront access to your AWS Elemental MediaStore container. Then you create a CloudFront distribution and configure it to work with AWS Elemental MediaStore.

1. Follow the procedure at Allowing Amazon CloudFront to Access Your AWS Elemental MediaStore Container, and then return to these steps to create your distribution.

2. Create a distribution with the following settings:
   **Origin Domain Name**
   The data endpoint that is assigned to your AWS Elemental MediaStore container. From the dropdown list, choose the AWS Elemental MediaStore container for your live video. The format of an AWS Elemental MediaStore origin is Container-OriginEndpointURL. For example, mymediastore.data.mediastore.us-east-1.amazonaws.com. For more information, see Origin Domain Name.
   **Origin Path**
   The folder structure in the AWS Elemental MediaStore container where your objects are stored. For more information, see Origin Path.
   **Origin Custom Headers**
   Add header names and values if you want CloudFront to include custom headers when it forwards requests to your origin.
   **Object Caching**
   If the transcoder that you use can't set cache controls on all objects, choose **Customize**. If your transcoder can set cache controls on all objects, choose **Origin Cache Headers**.
   **Minimum TTL, Maximum TTL, and Default TTL**

Set as appropriate for your caching needs and segment durations.

**Error Caching Minimum TTL**

Set to 5 seconds or less, to help prevent serving stale content.

For the other settings, you can set specific values based on other technical requirements or the needs of your business. For a list of all the options for web distributions and information about setting them, see Values That You Specify When You Create or Update a Web Distribution.

3. After you create your distribution and it's been provisioned, edit the cache behavior to set up cross-origin resource sharing (CORS) for your origin:

   1. Select the distribution, and then choose **Distribution Settings**.

   2. Choose **Behaviors**, select your origin, and then choose **Edit**.

   3. Under **Cache Based on Selected Request Headers**, choose **Whitelist**, and then, under **Whitelist Headers**, select **Origin**.

   To learn more about CORS, see *Configuring CloudFront to Respect Cross-Origin Resource Sharing (CORS) Settings* in Configuring CloudFront to Cache Objects Based on Request Headers.

4. For links in your application (for example, a media player), specify the name of the media file in the same format that you use for other objects that you're distributing using CloudFront.

# Delivering Live Streaming Video with CloudFront and AWS Media Services

To use AWS Media Services with CloudFront to deliver or broadcast live content to a global audience, follow the guidance included in this section.

AWS Elemental MediaLive encodes live video streams in real time. If you have a larger-sized live video source—for example, video coming from a ground encoder like Elemental Live—you can compress it by using AWS Elemental MediaLive into smaller versions ("encodes") that are then distributed to your viewers.

There are two main options for preparing and serving live streaming content:

- **Convert your content into required formats, and then serve it:** You can use AWS Elemental MediaPackage to convert your video content from a single format to multiple formats, and then package the content for different device types. AWS Elemental MediaPackage lets you implement video features for viewers such as start-over, pause, rewind, and so on. AWS Elemental MediaPackage can also protect your content from unauthorized copying by adding Digital Rights Management (DRM). For step-by-step instructions for using AWS Elemental MediaPackage with CloudFront, see Serving Live Video Formatted with AWS Elemental MediaPackage in this topic.
- **Store and serve your content using scalable origin:** If your encoder already outputs content in the formats required by all of the devices that your viewers use, you can serve the content by using a highly-scalable origin like an AWS Elemental MediaStore container. AWS Elemental MediaStore delivers the content to CloudFront, which then routes it to the audience for the event.

After you've set up your origin by using one of these options, you can distribute live streaming video to viewers by using CloudFront.

### Tip
To learn more about best practices when you implement a live video streaming workflow with AWS Cloud services, see Live Streaming Video.
You can also learn about an AWS solution that automatically deploys services for building a highly-available real-time viewing experience. To see the steps to automatically deploy this solution, see Live Streaming Automated Deployment.

## Serving Live Video Formatted with AWS Elemental MediaPackage

If you've used AWS Elemental MediaPackage to format a live stream for viewing, you can create a CloudFront distribution and configure cache behaviors to serve the live stream. This topic assumes that you have already created a channel and added endpoints for your live video using AWS Elemental MediaPackage.

To stream the video with CloudFront, create a web distribution for the channel, and then add each AWS Elemental MediaPackage endpoint as an origin for the distribution. For each origin, you must configure cache behaviors to route the video content correctly.

Follow these steps:

### Topics

- Step 1: Create and Configure a CloudFront Distribution for Live Video
- Step 2: Add the Other Endpoints as Origins for the Distribution
- Step 3: Configure Cache Behaviors for all Endpoints
- Step 4: Use CloudFront to Serve the Live Stream Channel

**Step 1: Create and Configure a CloudFront Distribution for Live Video**

Complete the following procedure to set up a CloudFront distribution for the live video channel that you created with AWS Elemental MediaPackage

**To create a web distribution for your live video channel**

1. Sign in to the AWS Management Console and open the CloudFront console at https://console.aws.amazon. com/cloudfront/.

2. Choose **Create Distribution**.

3. On the **Select a delivery method** page, in the **Web** section, choose **Get Started**.

4. Choose the settings for the distribution, including the following:
   **Origin Domain Name**
   The origin where your AWS Elemental MediaPackage live video channel and endpoints are. From the dropdown list, choose the AWS Elemental MediaPackage channel for your live video. The format of an AWS Elemental MediaPackage origin is ChannelID-OriginEndpointID-OriginEndpointURL. You can map one channel to several origin endpoints.
   If you created your channel using another AWS account, type the origin URL value into the field. The origin must be an HTTPS URL.
   For more information, see Origin Domain Name in the Values That You Specify When You Create or Update a Web Distribution topic.
   **Origin Path**
   The folder structure in the AWS Elemental MediaPackage where your objects are stored. When you choose a channel from the dropdown list, the path is filled in for you.
   Note that if you chose to use a channel from another AWS account for **Origin Domain Name**, the **Origin Path** field is not filled in for you. You must sign in to the other account and get the correct origin path so you that can enter it manually.
   For more information about how an origin path works, see Origin Path in the Values That You Specify When You Create or Update a Web Distribution topic.
   For the other distribution settings, set specific values based on other technical requirements or the needs of your business. For a list of all the options for web distributions and information about setting them, see Values That You Specify When You Create or Update a Web Distribution topic.

5. Specify the correct cache behavior settings for the channel that you chose for the origin. You'll add one or more additional origins later and edit cache behavior settings for them.

6. Wait until the value of the Status column for your distribution has changed from **In Progress** to **Deployed**, indicating that CloudFront has created your distribution.


**Step 2: Add the Other Endpoints as Origins for the Distribution**

Repeat the steps here to add each endpoint.

**To add other endpoints as origins**

1. On the CloudFront console, choose the distribution that you created for your channel, and then choose **Distribution Settings**.

2. On the **Origins** tab, choose **Create Origin**.

3. For **Origin Domain Name**, in the dropdown list, choose an AWS Elemental MediaPackage endpoint for your channel. The **Origin Path** field will be automatically filled in for you.

4. For the other settings, set the values based on other technical requirements or the needs of your business. For more information, see Origin Settings in the Values That You Specify When You Create or Update a Web Distribution topic.

5. Choose **Create**.

## Step 3: Configure Cache Behaviors for all Endpoints

For each endpoint, you must configure cache behaviors to add path patterns that route requests correctly. The path patterns that you specify depend on the video format that you're serving. The procedure in this topic includes the path pattern information to use for HLS, CMAF, DASH, and Microsoft Smooth formats.

You typically set up two cache behaviors for each endpoint:

- The parent manifest, which is the index to your files
- The child manifest, which is the video content itself

**To create a cache behavior for an endpoint**

1. On the CloudFront console, choose the distribution that you created for your channel, and then choose **Distribution Settings**.

2. On the **Behaviors** tab, choose **Create Behavior**.

3. In the **Cache Behavior Settings** section, for **Path Pattern**, type the first path pattern for the endpoint type for this origin, using the following path pattern guidance. For example, if it's a DASH endpoint, type *.mpd for **Path Pattern**.
   **Path Patterns**
   For an HLS or CMAF endpoint, create the following two cache behaviors:

   - A cache behavior with a path pattern of *.m3u8 (for the parent manifest)
   - A cache behavior with a path pattern of *.ts (for the child manifest) For a DASH endpoint, create the following two cache behaviors:
   - A cache behavior with a path pattern of *.mpd (for the parent manifest)
   - A cache behavior with a path pattern of *.mp4 (for the child manifest) For a Microsoft Smooth endpoint, only one manifest is served, so you create only one cache behavior:
   - A cache behavior with a path pattern of index.ism/* For all endpoint formats except for a Microsoft Smooth endpoint, you must repeat the steps, to add two cache behaviors.

4. Specify values for the following settings, for each cache behavior:
   **Viewer Protocol Policy**
   Choose **Redirect HTTP to HTTPS**.
   **Cache Based on Selected Request Headers**
   Choose **None (improves caching)**.
   For more information about improving caching, see Increasing the Proportion of Requests that Are Served from CloudFront Edge Caches.
   **Query String Forwarding and Caching**
   Choose **Forward all, cache based on whitelist**.
   **Query String Whitelist**
   Specify the letter m as the query string parameter that you want CloudFront to use as the basis for caching. The AWS Elemental MediaPackage response always includes the tag ?m=### to capture the modified time of the endpoint. If content is already cached with a different value for this tag, CloudFront requests a new manifest instead of serving the cached version.
   **Object Caching**
   AWS Elemental MediaPackage sets default Cache-Control headers that ensure correct playback behavior. If you want to use those values, choose Use Origin Cache Headers. However, you can cache headers for longer segments. For more information about customizing the time that objects stay in the CloudFront cache, see Object Caching in the Values That You Specify When You Create or Update a Web Distribution topic.

5. Choose **Create**.

6. If your endpoint is not a Microsoft Smooth endpoint, choose **Create Behavior**, and then repeat these steps to create a second cache behavior.

**Step 4: Use CloudFront to Serve the Live Stream Channel**

After you create the distribution, add the origins, and create the cache behaviors, you can serve the live stream channel using CloudFront. Content requests from viewers are routed to the correct AWS Elemental MediaPackage endpoints based on the settings that you configured for the cache behaviors.

For links in your application (for example, a media player), specify the URL for the media file in the standard format for CloudFront URLs. For more information, see Format of URLs for Objects.

# Configuring On-Demand Microsoft Smooth Streaming

You can use CloudFront for providing on-demand video by using files that you've transcoded into the Microsoft Smooth Streaming format. To distribute Smooth Streaming content on demand, you have two options:

- As the origin for your distribution, specify a web server running Microsoft IIS that can stream files that have been transcoded into Microsoft Smooth Streaming format.
- Enable Smooth Streaming in a CloudFront distribution. Smooth Streaming is a property of cache behaviors, which means that you can use one distribution to distribute Smooth Streaming media files as well as other content.

**Important**

If your origin is a web server running Microsoft IIS, do not enable Smooth Streaming when you create your CloudFront distribution. CloudFront can't use a Microsoft IIS server as an origin if you enable Smooth Streaming.

If you enable Smooth Streaming for an origin server (that is, you do not have a server that is running Microsoft IIS), note the following:

- You can still distribute other content using the same cache behavior if the content matches the value of **Path Pattern** for that cache behavior.
- CloudFront can use either an Amazon S3 bucket or a custom origin for Smooth Streaming media files. However, CloudFront cannot use a Microsoft IIS Server as an origin if the server is configured for Smooth Streaming.
- You cannot invalidate media files in the Smooth Streaming format. If you want to update files before they expire, you must rename them. For more information, see Adding, Removing, or Replacing Objects in a Distribution.

For information about Smooth Streaming clients, see Smooth Streaming Primer on the Microsoft website.

To use CloudFront to stream media files that have been encoded in the Microsoft Smooth Streaming format without using a Microsoft IIS web server that can stream files in Smooth Streaming format, do the following:

1. Transcode your media files into Smooth Streaming fragmented-MP4 format. For a list of applications that can transcode into Smooth Streaming format, see Smooth Streaming Primer on the Microsoft website.

2. Do one of the following:

    - **If you're using the CloudFront console:** When you create a web distribution, enable Smooth Streaming in the default cache behavior. Alternatively, you can enable Smooth Streaming in the default cache behavior and/or one or more custom cache behaviors in an existing CloudFront web distribution.
    - **If you're using the CloudFront API:** Add the `SmoothStreaming` element to the `DistributionConfig` complex type for the default cache behavior and/or one or more custom cache behaviors.

3. Upload the files in your Smooth Streaming presentations to the applicable origin.

4. Create either a `clientaccesspolicy.xml` or a `crossdomainpolicy.xml` file, and add it to a location that is accessible at the root of your distribution, for example, http://d111111abcdef8.cloudfront.net/ clientaccesspolicy.xml. The following is an example policy:

```
1 <?xml version="1.0" encoding="utf-8"?>
2 <access-policy>
3 <cross-domain-access>
4 <policy>
5 <allow-from http-request-headers="*">
6 <domain uri="*"/>
7 </allow-from>
8 <grant-to>
9 <resource path="/" include-subpaths="true"/>
```

```
10 </grant-to>
11 </policy>
12 </cross-domain-access>
13 </access-policy>
```

For more information, see Making a Service Available Across Domain Boundaries on the Microsoft Developer Network website.

5. For links in your application, specify the client manifest in the following format:

```
http://d111111abcdef8.cloudfront.net/video/presentation.ism/Manifest
```

# Using CloudFront with Lambda@Edge

Lambda@Edge is an extension of AWS Lambda, a compute service that lets you execute functions that customize the content that CloudFront delivers. You can author functions in one region and execute them in AWS locations globally that are closer to the viewer, without provisioning or managing servers. Lambda@Edge scales automatically, from a few requests per day to thousands per second. Processing requests at AWS locations closer to the viewer instead of on origin servers significantly reduces latency and improves the user experience.

When you associate a CloudFront distribution with a Lambda@Edge function, CloudFront intercepts requests and responses at CloudFront edge locations. You can execute Lambda functions when the following CloudFront events occur:

- When CloudFront receives a request from a viewer (viewer request)
- Before CloudFront forwards a request to the origin (origin request)
- When CloudFront receives a response from the origin (origin response)
- Before CloudFront returns the response to the viewer (viewer response)

There are many uses for Lambda@Edge processing. For example:

- A Lambda function can inspect cookies and rewrite URLs so that users see different versions of a site for A/B testing.
- CloudFront can return different objects to viewers based on the device they're using by checking the `User-Agent` header, which includes information about the devices. For example, CloudFront can return different images based on the screen size of their device. Similarly, the function could consider the value of the `Referer` header and cause CloudFront to return the images to bots that have the lowest available resolution.
- Or you could check cookies for other criteria. For example, on a retail website that sells clothing, if you use cookies to indicate which color a user chose for a jacket, a Lambda function can change the request so that CloudFront returns the image of a jacket in the selected color.
- A Lambda function can generate HTTP responses when CloudFront viewer request or origin request events occur.
- A function can inspect headers or authorization tokens, and insert a header to control access to your content before CloudFront forwards the request to your origin.
- A Lambda function can also make network calls to external resources to confirm user credentials, or fetch additional content to customize a response.

For sample code and additional examples, see Lambda@Edge Example Functions.

**Topics**

- Get Started Creating and Using Lambda@Edge Functions
- Setting IAM Permissions and Roles for Lambda@Edge
- Writing and Creating a Lambda@Edge Function
- Adding Triggers for a Lambda@Edge Function
- Testing and Debugging Lambda@Edge Functions
- CloudWatch Metrics and CloudWatch Logs for Lambda Functions
- Deleting Lambda@Edge Functions and Replicas
- Lambda@Edge Event Structure
- Generating HTTP Responses in Request Triggers
- Updating HTTP Responses in Origin-Response Triggers
- Lambda@Edge Example Functions
- Requirements and Restrictions on Lambda Functions

# Get Started Creating and Using Lambda@Edge Functions

You can use Lambda@Edge functions to do lots of useful things, but it can seem a little complicated when you're getting started. This section explains, at a high level, how Lambda@Edge works with CloudFront and provides a tutorial that steps through a simple example.

**Tip**

After you're familiar with how Lambda@Edge works and you've created a Lambda@Edge function, learn more about how you can use Lambda@Edge for your own custom solutions. Learn more about  creating and updating functions,  the event structure, and  adding CloudFront triggers. You can also find more ideas and get code samples in Lambda@Edge Example Functions.

Here's an overview of how to create and use Lambda functions with CloudFront:

1. In the AWS Lambda console, you create a Lambda function in the US East (N. Virginia) Region. (Or you can create the function programmatically, for example, by using one of the AWS SDKs.)

2. You save and publish a numbered version of the function.

   If you want to make changes to the function, you must edit the $LATEST version of the function in the US East (N. Virginia) Region. Then, before you set it up to work with CloudFront, you publish a new numbered version.

3. You choose the CloudFront distribution and cache behavior that the function applies to, and then specify one or more CloudFront events, known as *triggers*, that cause the function to execute. For example, you can create a trigger for the function to execute when CloudFront receives a request from a viewer.

4. When you create a trigger, Lambda replicates the function to AWS locations around the world.

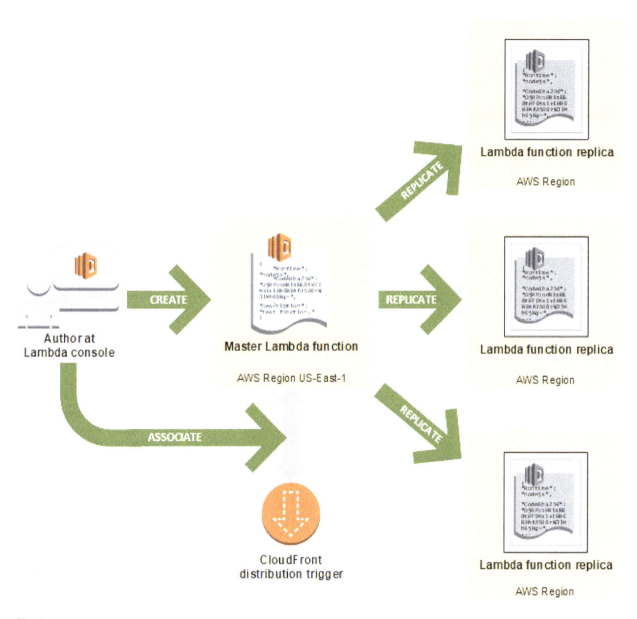

**Topics**

- Tutorial: Creating a Simple Lambda@Edge Function

# Tutorial: Creating a Simple Lambda@Edge Function

This tutorial shows you how to get started with Lambda@Edge by helping you create and add a sample Node.js function that runs in CloudFront. The example that we walk through adds HTTP security headers to a response, which can improve security and privacy for a website. (That said, you don't need a website for this walkthrough; we simply add security headers to a response when CloudFront retrieves a file.)

This example illustrates, step by step, how you create and configure a Lambda@Edge function. You will follow similar steps and choose from the same options for your own Lambda@Edge solution.

**Topics**

- Step 1: Sign Up for an AWS Account
- Step 2: Create a CloudFront Distribution
- Step 3: Create and Publish Your Function
- Step 4: Add a CloudFront Trigger that Runs the Function
- Step 5: Verify that the Function Runs
- Step 6: Troubleshoot Issues
- Step 7: Clean Up Your Example Resources
- Resources for Learning More

## Step 1: Sign Up for an AWS Account

If you haven't already done so, sign up for Amazon Web Services at https://aws/.amazon/.com//. Choose **Sign Up Now** and enter the required information.

## Step 2: Create a CloudFront Distribution

Before you create the example Lambda@Edge function, you must have a CloudFront environment to work with that includes an origin to serve content from.

**Are you new to CloudFront?** CloudFront delivers content through a worldwide network of edge locations. When you set up a Lambda function with CloudFront, the function can customize content closer to viewers, improving performance. If you're not familiar with CloudFront, take a few minutes before you complete the tutorial to read a short overview and learn a bit about how CloudFront caches and serves content.

For this example, you create a CloudFront distribution that is set up with an Amazon S3 bucket, the origin for your CloudFront distribution. If you already have an environment to use, you can skip this step.

**To create a CloudFront distribution with an Amazon S3 origin**

1. Create an Amazon S3 bucket with a file or two, such as image files, for sample content. You can follow the steps in Upload your content to Amazon S3. Make sure that you set permissions to grant public read access to the objects in your bucket.

2. Create a CloudFront distribution and add your S3 bucket as an origin, by following the steps in Create a CloudFront web distribution. If you already have a distribution, you can add the bucket as an origin for that distribution instead. **Tip**
   Make a note of your distribution ID. Later in this tutorial when you add a CloudFront trigger for your function, you must choose the ID for your distribution in a drop-down list—for example, E653W22221KDDL.

## Step 3: Create and Publish Your Function

In this step, you create a Lambda function, starting with a blueprint template that's provided in the Lambda Console. The function adds code to update security headers in your CloudFront distribution.

**Are you new to Lambda or Lambda@Edge?** Lambda@Edge lets you use CloudFront triggers to invoke a Lambda function. When you associate a CloudFront distribution with a Lambda function, CloudFront intercepts requests and responses at CloudFront edge locations and runs the function. Lambda functions can improve security or customize information close to your viewers, to improve performance. In this tutorial, the function we create updates the security headers in a CloudFront response.

There are several steps to take when you create a Lambda function. In this tutorial, you use a blueprint template as the basis for your function, and then update the function with code that sets the security headers. Finally, you save a new version of the function, which is a required step before you can add a CloudFront trigger to the function.

**To create a Lambda function**

1. Sign in to the AWS Management Console and open the AWS Lambda console at https://console.aws.amazon.com/lambda/. **Important**
   Make sure that you're in the US-East-1 (N. Virginia) Region. You must be in this region to create Lambda@Edge functions.

2. Choose **Create function**.

3. On the **Create function** page, choose **Blueprints**, and then filter for the CloudFront blueprints. Type `cloudfront` in the search field, and the press **Return**. The keyword `cloudfront` is shown, and all the blueprints that are tagged for CloudFront are listed.

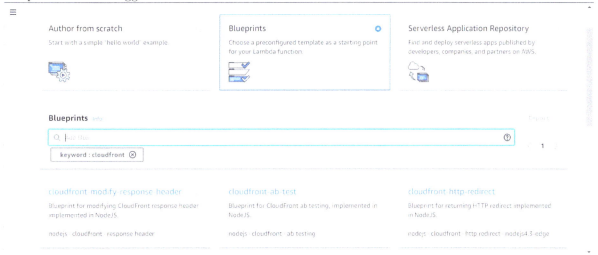

4. Choose the **cloudfront-modify-response-header** blueprint to use as the template for your function.

5. Enter the information about your function:
   **Name**
   Type a name for your function.
   **Role**
   Choose how to set the permissions for your function. It's easiest to get started by using the basic Lambda@Edge permissions policy template, so for this option, choose **Create new role from template(s)**.
   **Role name**
   Type a name for the role that will be created from the policy template, which you choose next, under **Policy templates**.
   **Policy templates**
   In the drop-down list, choose **Basic Edge Lambda permissions**. This template adds execution role permissions that allow CloudFront to run your Lambda function for you in CloudFront locations around the world. For more information, see Setting IAM Permissions and Roles for Lambda@Edge.

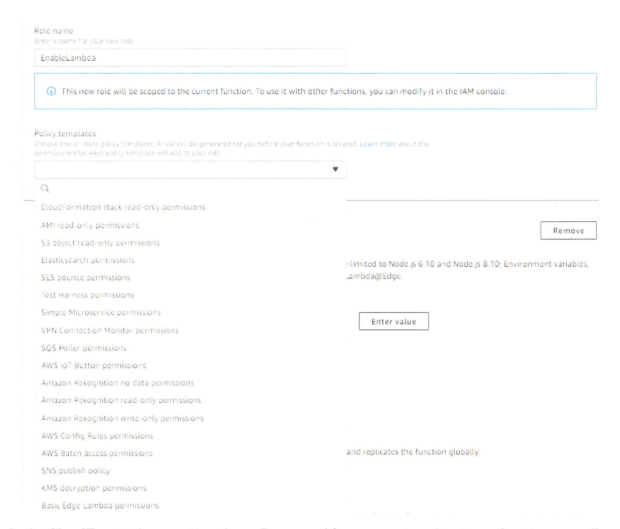

Role name
Enter a name for your new role

EnableLambda

ⓘ This new role will be scoped to the current function. To use it with other functions, you can modify it in the IAM console.

Policy templates
Choose one or more policy templates. A role will be generated for you before your function is created. Learn more about the permissions that each policy template will add to your role.

▼

🔍

CloudFormation stack read-only permissions

AMI read-only permissions

S3 object read-only permissions

Elasticsearch permissions

SES bounce permissions

Test Harness permissions

Simple Microservice permissions

VPN Connection Monitor permissions

SQS Poller permissions

AWS IoT Button permissions

Amazon Rekognition no data permissions

Amazon Rekognition read-only permissions

Amazon Rekognition write-only permissions

AWS Config Rules permissions

AWS Batch access permissions

SNS publish policy

KMS decryption permissions

Basic Edge Lambda permissions

Remove

: limited to Node.js 6.10 and Node.js 8.10; Environment variables,
.ambda@Edge.

Enter value

and replicates the function globally.

6. In the **CloudFront trigger** section, choose **Remove**. After you create and test your function, you will associate the function with your distribution and add a trigger so that the function will run.

For example, to add security headers, we will set the function to run when there's a CloudFront origin response. For more information about triggers, see CloudFront Events That Can Trigger a Lambda Function.

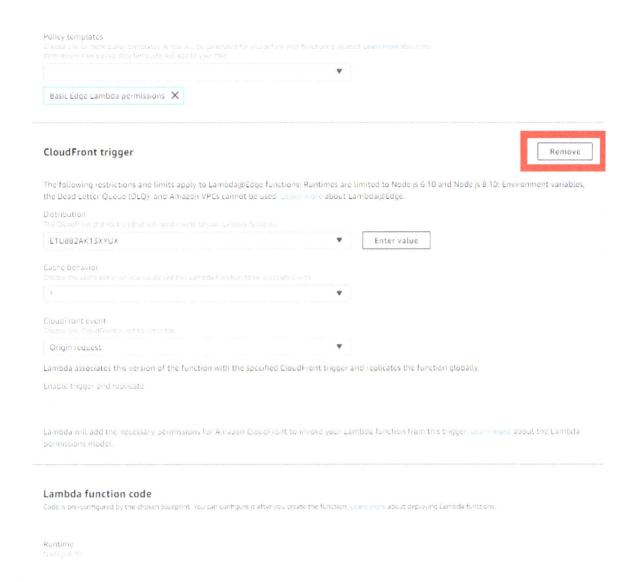

7. Choose **Create function**. Lambda creates the function, and on the next page, you see a Congratulations! success message box. In the next step, you'll update the function code, and then add a CloudFront trigger.

On the **Configuration** tab, there are three main areas: A diagram showing your function by name (for example, in our example, UpdateSecurityHeaders), any triggers you've added (there are none at this point), and logging information. There's also a list of trigger types you can choose from, and, at the bottom, the **Function code** section for adding or updating code.

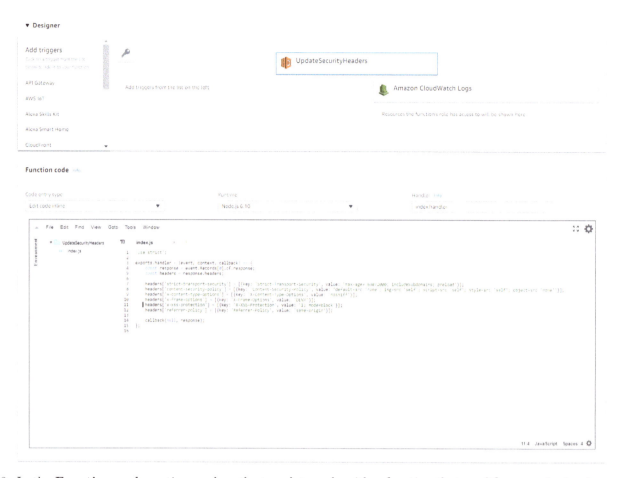

8. In the **Function code** section, replace the template code with a function that modifies security headers that are returned from your origin. For example, you could use code similar to the following:

```
1  'use strict';
2  exports.handler = (event, context, callback) => {
3
4      //Get contents of response
5      const response = event.Records[0].cf.response;
6      const headers = response.headers;
7
8  //Set new headers
9   headers['strict-transport-security'] = [{key: 'Strict-Transport-Security', value: 'max-age
        = 63072000
10  ; includeSubdomains; preload'}];
11  headers['content-security-policy'] = [{key: 'Content-Security-Policy', value: "default-src
        'none'; img-src 'self'; script-src 'self'; style-src 'self'; object-src 'none'"}];
12  headers['x-content-type-options'] = [{key: 'X-Content-Type-Options', value: 'nosniff'}];
13  headers['x-frame-options'] = [{key: 'X-Frame-Options', value: 'DENY'}];
14  headers['x-xss-protection'] = [{key: 'X-XSS-Protection', value: '1; mode=block'}];
15  headers['referrer-policy'] = [{key: 'Referrer-Policy', value: 'same-origin'}];
16
17      //Return modified response
18      callback(null, response);
19  };
```

9. Choose **Save** to save your updated code.

10. In the **Actions** drop-down list, choose **Publish new version**.

When you edit a Lambda function, you work with the $LATEST version. But you can't add a CloudFront trigger for the $LATEST version, so you must publish a new numbered version of the function, and then add the trigger.

## Step 4: Add a CloudFront Trigger that Runs the Function

Now that you have a Lambda function to update security headers, you create a CloudFront trigger that runs your function to add the headers in any response that CloudFront receives from the origin for your distribution.

**Tip**
Make sure that you're working in a numbered version for your function. If you left the console and then came back and opened your function again, your version will be $LATEST—even if you previously published a new version. To open a version that you can add a trigger to, do the following:
Choose **Qualifiers**. Choose the **Versions** tab, and then choose a version that isn't $LATEST, such as **1**.

## To create a CloudFront trigger for your function

1. Under **Add triggers**, choose **CloudFront**.

2. Under **Configure triggers**, enter the following information:
   **Distribution**
   The CloudFront distribution ID to associate with your function. In the drop-down list, choose the distribution ID.
   **Cache behavior**
   The cache behavior to use with the trigger. For this example, leave the value set to *, which applies your distribution's default cache behavior to all requests. For more information, see Cache Behavior Settings in the Values That You Specify When You Create or Update a Web Distribution topic.
   **CloudFront event**
   The trigger that specifies when your function will run. We want the security headers function to run whenever CloudFront returns a response from the origin. So in the drop-down list, choose **Origin response**. For more information, see Adding Triggers for a Lambda@Edge Function.
   **Enable trigger and replicate**
   Select this check box to add the trigger and replicate the function to AWS locations worldwide.

3. Choose **Add**, and then choose **Save**.

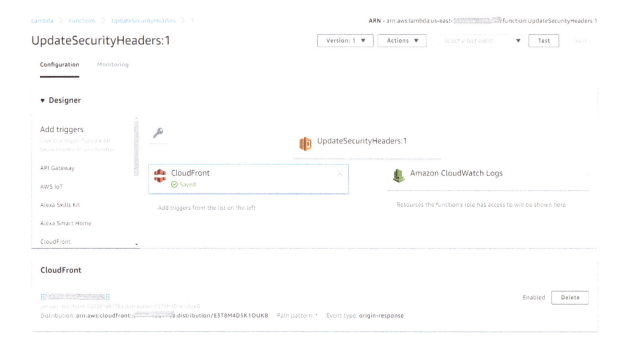

4. Wait for the function to replicate. This typically takes a few minutes but can take up to 15 minutes.

You can check to see if replication is finished by going to the CloudFront console and viewing your distribution:

- Go to the CloudFront console at https://console/.aws/.amazon/.com/cloudfront//.

Check for the distribution status to change from **In Progress** back to **Deployed**, which means that your function has been replicated. Then follow the steps in the next section to verify that the function works.

## Step 5: Verify that the Function Runs

Now that you've created your Lambda function and added a trigger to run it for a CloudFront distribution, check to make sure that the function is accomplishing what you expect it to. In this example, we check the HTTP headers that are returned from the origin, to make sure that the security headers are added.

**To verify that your Lambda@Edge function adds security headers**

1. In a browser, type the URL for a file in your S3 bucket. For example, you might use a URL similar to `http://d111111abcdef8.cloudfront.net/image.jpg`.

   For more information about the CloudFront domain name to use in the file URL, see Format of URLs for Objects.

2. Open your browser's Web Developer toolbar. For example, in your browser window in Chrome, open the context (right-click) menu, and then choose **Inspect**.

3. Choose the **Network** tab.

4. Reload the page to view your image, and then choose an HTTP request on the left pane. You will see the HTTP headers displayed in a separate pane.

5. Look through the list of HTTP headers to verify that the expected security headers are included in the list. For example, you might see headers similar to those shown in the following screenshot:

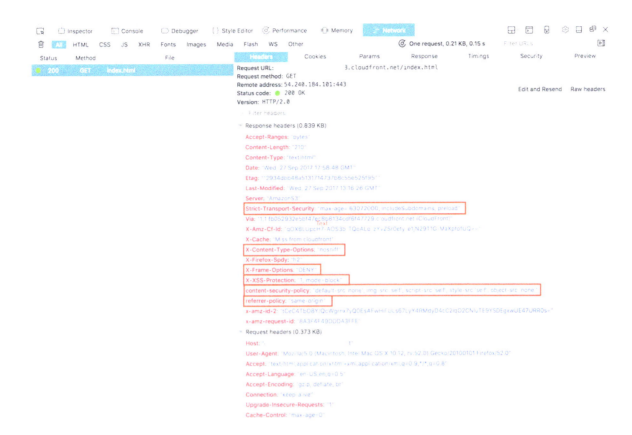

If the security headers are included in your headers list, great! You've successfully created your first Lambda@Edge function. If, on the other hand, CloudFront returns errors or there are other issues, continue to the next step to troubleshoot the issues.

## Step 6: Troubleshoot Issues

If CloudFront returns errors or doesn't add the security headers as expected, you can investigate your function's execution by looking at CloudWatch Logs. Be sure to use the logs stored in the AWS location that is closest to the location where the function is executed.

For example, if you view the file from London, try changing the Region in the CloudWatch console to EU (London).

### To examine CloudWatch logs for your Lambda@Edge function

1. Sign in to the AWS Management Console and open the CloudWatch console at https://console.aws.amazon.com/cloudwatch/.

2. Change **Region** to the region where the function is executing; that is, the location that is shown when you view the file in your browser.

3. In the left pane, choose **Logs** to view the logs for your distribution.

For more information, see Monitoring CloudFront Activity Using CloudWatch.

## Step 7: Clean Up Your Example Resources

If you created an S3 bucket and CloudFront distribution just for this tutorial, as a learning exercise, make sure to delete the AWS resources that you allocated so that you no longer accrue charges. After you delete your AWS resources, any content that you added is no longer available.

Tasks

- Delete the S3 Bucket
- Delete the CloudFront Distribution

**Delete the S3 Bucket**

Before you delete your S3 bucket, make sure that logging is disabled for the bucket. Otherwise, AWS continues to write logs to your bucket as you delete it.

**To disable logging for a bucket**

1. Open the Amazon S3 console at https://console.aws.amazon.com/s3/.

2. Select your bucket, and then choose **Properties**.

3. From **Properties**, choose **Logging**.

4. Clear the **Enabled** check box.

5. Choose **Save**.

Now, you can delete your bucket. For more information, see How Do I Delete an S3 Bucket? in the *Amazon Simple Storage Service Console User Guide.*

**Delete the CloudFront Distribution**

Before you delete a CloudFront distribution, you must disable it. A disabled distribution is no longer functional and does not accrue charges. You can enable a disabled distribution at any time. After you delete a disabled distribution, it's no longer available.

**To disable and delete a CloudFront distribution**

1. Open the CloudFront console at  https://console.aws.amazon.com/cloudfront/.

2. Select the distribution that you want to disable, and then choose **Disable**.

3. When prompted for confirmation, choose **Yes, Disable**.

4. Select the disabled distribution, and then choose **Delete**.

5. When prompted for confirmation, choose **Yes, Delete**.

## Resources for Learning More

Now that you have a basic idea of how Lambda@Edge functions work, learn more by reading the following:

- Lambda@Edge Example Functions
- Lambda@Edge Design Best Practices
- Reducing Latency and Shifting Compute to the Edge with Lambda@Edge

# Setting IAM Permissions and Roles for Lambda@Edge

Specific IAM permissions and an IAM execution role are required so that you can configure Lambda@Edge. Lambda@Edge also creates a service-linked role to replicate Lambda functions to CloudFront Regions.

**Topics**

- IAM Permissions Required to Associate Lambda Functions with CloudFront Distributions
- Function Execution Role for Service Principals
- Service-Linked Role for Lambda@Edge

## IAM Permissions Required to Associate Lambda Functions with CloudFront Distributions

In addition to the IAM permissions that you need to use AWS Lambda, the IAM user needs the following IAM permissions to associate Lambda functions with CloudFront distributions:

- `lambda:GetFunction`

  For the resource, specify the ARN of the function version that you want to execute when a CloudFront event occurs, as shown in the following example:

  `arn:aws:lambda:us-east-1:123456789012:function:TestFunction:2`

- `lambda:EnableReplication*`

  For the resource, specify the ARN of the function version that you want to execute when a CloudFront event occurs, as shown in the following example:

  `arn:aws:lambda:us-east-1:123456789012:function:TestFunction:2`

- `iam:CreateServiceLinkedRole`

  Used to create a service linked role used by Lambda@Edge to replicate Lambda functions in CloudFront. After this role has been created by the first distribution you use with Lambda@Edge, you do not need to add permission to other distributions you use with Lambda@Edge.

- `cloudfront:UpdateDistribution` or `cloudfront:CreateDistribution`

  Choose `cloudfront:UpdateDistribution` to update a distribution or `cloudfront:CreateDistribution` to create a distribution.

For more information, see the following documentation:

- Authentication and Access Control for CloudFront in this guide.
- Authentication and Access Control for AWS Lambda in the *AWS Lambda Developer Guide*

## Function Execution Role for Service Principals

You must create an IAM role that can be assumed by the service principals `lambda.amazonaws.com` and `edgelambda.amazonaws.com`. This role is assumed by the service principals when they execute your function. For more information, see Creating the Roles and Attaching the Policies (Console) in the topic "AWS Managed Policies for Job Functions" in the *IAM User Guide*.

You add this role under the **Trust Relationship** tab in IAM (do not add it under the **Permissions** tab).

Here's an example role trust policy:

```
1   {
2       "Version": "2012-10-17",
3       "Statement": [
4           {
5               "Effect": "Allow",
6               "Principal": {
7                   "Service": [
8                       "lambda.amazonaws.com",
9                       "edgelambda.amazonaws.com"
10                  ]
11              },
12              "Action": "sts:AssumeRole"
13          }
14      ]
15  }
```

For information about the permissions that you need to grant to the execution role, see Manage Permissions: Using an IAM Role (Execution Role) in the *AWS Lambda Developer Guide*. Note the following:

- By default, whenever a CloudFront event triggers a Lambda function, data is written to CloudWatch Logs. If you want to use these logs, the execution role needs permission to write data to CloudWatch Logs. You can use the predefined AWSLambdaBasicExecutionRole to grant permission to the execution role.

  For more information about CloudWatch Logs, see CloudWatch Metrics and CloudWatch Logs for Lambda Functions.

- If your Lambda function code accesses other AWS resources, such as reading an object from an S3 bucket, the execution role needs permission to perform that operation.

## Service-Linked Role for Lambda@Edge

Lambda@Edge uses an AWS Identity and Access Management (IAM) service-linked role. A service-linked role is a unique type of IAM role that is linked directly to Lambda@Edge. The service-linked role is predefined by Lambda@Edge and includes all of the permissions that the service requires so it can call other AWS services on your behalf.

When you first add a Lambda@Edge trigger in CloudFront, a role named AWSServiceRoleForLambdaReplicator is automatically created to allow Lambda@Edge to replicate functions to AWS Regions. This role is required for using Lambda@Edge functions. The ARN for the AWSServiceRoleForLambdaReplicator role looks like this:

`arn:aws:iam::123456789012:role/aws-service-role/replicator.lambda.amazonaws.com/`
`AWSServiceRoleForLambdaReplicator`

A service-linked role makes setting up Lambda@Edge easier because you don't have to manually add the necessary permissions. Lambda@Edge defines the permissions of its service-linked role, and only Lambda@Edge can assume the role. The defined permissions include the trust policy and the permissions policy. The permissions policy cannot be attached to any other IAM entity.

You must remove any associated CloudFront or Lambda@Edge resources before you can delete the service-linked role. This protects your Lambda@Edge resources because you can't inadvertently remove permission to access the resources.

For information about other services that support service-linked roles, see AWS Services That Work with IAM and look for the services that have **Yes **in the **Service-Linked Role** column.

## Service-Linked Role Permissions for Lambda@Edge

Lambda@Edge uses the service-linked role named **AWSServiceRoleForLambdaReplicator**. This service-linked role allows Lambda to replicate Lambda@Edge functions to AWS Regions.

The AWSServiceRoleForLambdaReplicator service-linked role trusts the following service to assume the role:

- `replicator.lambda.amazonaws.com`

The role permissions policy allows Lambda@Edge to complete the following actions on the specified resources:

- Action: `lambda:CreateFunction` on `arn:aws:lambda:*:*:function:*`
- Action: `lambda:DeleteFunction` on `arn:aws:lambda:*:*:function:*`
- Action: `lambda:DisableReplication` on `arn:aws:lambda:*:*:function:*`
- Action: `iam:PassRole` on all AWS resources
- Action: `cloudfront:ListDistributionsByLambdaFunction` on all AWS resources

You must configure permissions to allow an IAM entity (such as a user, group, or role) to create or delete a service-linked role. For more information, see Service-Linked Role Permissions in the *IAM User Guide*.

## Creating the Service-Linked Role for Lambda@Edge

You don't need to manually create the service-linked role for Lambda@Edge. When you first create a trigger, the service creates a role that allows Lambda to replicate Lambda@Edge functions to AWS Regions.

If you delete the service-linked role, the role will be created again when you add a new trigger for Lambda@Edge in a distribution.

## Editing the Service-Linked Role for Lambda@Edge

Lambda@Edge does not allow you to edit the AWSServiceRoleForLambdaReplicator service-linked role. After you create a service-linked role, you cannot change the name of the role because various entities might reference the role. However, you can edit the description of the role using IAM. For more information, see Editing a Service-Linked Role in the *IAM User Guide*.

## Deleting the Service-Linked Role for Lambda@Edge

If you no longer need to use Lambda@Edge, we recommend that you delete the service-linked role. That way you don't have an unused entity that is not actively monitored or maintained. However, you must clean up the Lambda@Edge resources in your account before you can manually delete the role.

### To delete Lambda@Edge resources used by the AWSServiceRoleForLambdaReplicator

To remove the service-linked role, you must remove all Lambda@Edge associations from your distributions. To do this, update your distributions to remove all Lambda@Edge function triggers, or remove the distributions that use Lambda@Edge functions. For more information, see Deleting Lambda@Edge Functions and Replicas.

After you have removed all Lambda@Edge function associations from your distributions and CloudFront has removed the function replicas from AWS locations, then you can use the CloudFront console to delete the AWSServiceRoleForLambdaReplicator service-linked role.

**Note**
If CloudFront hasn't finished updating, the service-linked role deletion might fail. If that happens, wait for a few minutes, and then try the steps again.

### To manually delete the Lambda@Edge service-linked role (CloudFront console)

1. Sign in to the AWS Management Console and open the CloudFront console at https://console.aws.amazon.com/cloudfront/.

2. On the **CloudFront Distributions** page, click the avatar in the upper right.

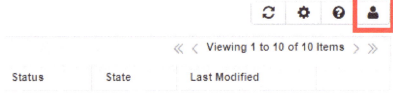

3. Choose **Delete**.

Role Management                                              ✕

CloudFront uses permissions defined in service-linked roles to manage AWS resources on your behalf. To delete these roles, you must first delete any resources that reference them.

- AWSServiceRoleForLambdaReplicator

Cancel    **Delete**

# Writing and Creating a Lambda@Edge Function

To use Lambda@Edge, you write the code for your Lambda function, then set up AWS Lambda to run the function based on specific CloudFront events (triggers). To set up Lambda to run your function, you use the create function option in Lambda.

You can use the AWS console to work with Lambda functions and CloudFront triggers, or you can work with Lambda@Edge programmatically by using APIs.

- If you use the AWS console, be aware that you can use only the AWS Lambda console to create Lambda functions. You can't use the CloudFront console to create a function.
- If you want to work with Lambda@Edge programmatically, there are several resources to help you. For more information, see Creating Lambda Functions and CloudFront Triggers Programmatically.

**Note**
You can use either the AWS Lambda console or CloudFront console to add triggers for Lambda@Edge functions.

**Topics**

- Writing Functions for Lambda@Edge
- Creating a Lambda@Edge Function in the Lambda Console
- Editing a Lambda Function for Lambda@Edge
- Creating Lambda Functions and CloudFront Triggers Programmatically

# Writing Functions for Lambda@Edge

There are several resources to help you with writing Lambda@Edge functions:

- For more information about writing Lambda functions that you can use with Lambda@Edge, see Requirements and Restrictions on Lambda Functions.
- To learn about the event structure to use with Lambda@Edge functions, see Lambda@Edge Event Structure.
- To see examples of Lambda@Edge functions, such as functions for A/B testing and generating an HTTP redirect, see Lambda@Edge Example Functions.

The programming model for using Node.js with Lambda@Edge is the same as using Lambda in an AWS Region. For more information, see Programming Model(Node.js).

In your Lambda@Edge code, include the `callback` parameter and return the applicable object for request or response events:

- **Request events** – Include the `cf.request` object in the response.

  If you're generating a response, include the `cf.response` object in the response. For more information, see Generating HTTP Responses in Request Triggers.

- **Response events** – Include the `cf.response` object in the response.

# Creating a Lambda@Edge Function in the Lambda Console

To set up AWS Lambda to run Lambda functions that are based on CloudFront events, follow this procedure.

**To create a Lambda@Edge function**

1. Sign in to the AWS Management Console and open the AWS Lambda console at https://console.aws.amazon.com/lambda/.

2. If you already have one or more Lambda functions, choose **Create function**.

   If you've don't have any functions, choose **Get Started Now**.

3. In the region list at the top of the page, choose **US East (N. Virginia)**.

4. Create a function using your own code or create a function starting with a CloudFront blueprint.

   - To create a function using your own code, choose **Author from scratch**.

   - To display a list of blueprints for CloudFront, type **cloudfront** in the filter field, and then press **Enter**.

     If you find a blueprint that you want to use, choose the name of the blueprint.

5. In the **Basic information** section, specify the following values:
   **Name**
   Type a name for your function.
   **Role**
   Choose **Create new role from template(s)**.
   Choosing this value will get your started quickly. Or you can choose **Choose an existing role** or **Create a custom role**. If you choose one of these, follow the prompts to complete the information for this section.
   **Role name**
   Type a name for the role.
   **Policy templates**
   Choose **Basic Edge Lambda permissions**.

6. If you chose **Author from scratch** in step 4, skip to step 7.

   If you chose a blueprint in step 4, the **cloudfront** section lets you create one trigger, which associates this function with a cache in a CloudFront distribution and a CloudFront event. We recommend that you choose **Remove** at this point, so there isn't a trigger for the function when it's created. Then you can add triggers later. **Important**
   Why add triggers later? Generally it's best to test and debug the function before you add triggers. If you choose instead to add a trigger now, the function will start to run as soon as you create the function and it finishes replicating to AWS locations around the world, and the corresponding distribution is deployed.

7. Choose **Create function**.

   Lambda creates two versions of your function: $LATEST and Version 1. You can edit only the $LATEST version, but the console initially displays Version 1.

8. To edit the function, choose **Version 1** near the top of the page, under the ARN for the function. Then, on the **Versions** tab, choose **$LATEST**. (If you left the function and then returned to it, the button label is **Qualifiers**.)

9. On the **Configuration** tab, choose the applicable **Code entry type**. Then follow the prompts to edit or upload your code.

10. For **Runtime**, choose the value based on your function's code.

11. In the **Tags** section, add any applicable tags.

12. Choose **Actions**, and then choose **Publish new version**.

13. Type a description for the new version of the function.

14. Choose **Publish**.

15. Test and debug the function. For more information, see the following in the *AWS Lambda Developer Guide*:
    - Using Amazon CloudWatch
    - Using AWS X-Ray
    - Test Your Serverless Applications Locally Using SAM Local (Public Beta)

16. When you're ready to have the function execute for CloudFront events, publish another version and edit the function to add triggers. For more information, see Adding Triggers for a Lambda@Edge Function.

# Editing a Lambda Function for Lambda@Edge

When you want to edit a Lambda function, note the following:

- The original version is labeled $LATEST.
- You can edit only the $LATEST version.
- Each time you edit the $LATEST version, you must publish a new numbered version.
- You can't create triggers for $LATEST.
- When you publish a new version of a function, Lambda doesn't automatically copy triggers from the previous version to the new version. You must reproduce the triggers for the new version.
- When you add a trigger for a CloudFront event to a function, if there's already a trigger for the same distribution, cache behavior, and event for an earlier version of the same function, Lambda deletes the trigger from the earlier version.
- After you make updates to a CloudFront distribution, like adding triggers, you must wait for the changes to propagate to edge locations before the functions you've specified in the triggers will work.

**To edit a Lambda function (AWS Lambda console)**

1. Sign in to the AWS Management Console and open the AWS Lambda console at https://console.aws. amazon.com/lambda/.

2. In the region list at the top of the page, choose **US East (N. Virginia)**.

3. In the list of functions, choose the name of the function that you want to edit.

   By default, the console displays the $LATEST version. You can view earlier versions (choose **Qualifiers**), but you can only edit $LATEST.

4. On the **Code** tab, for **Code entry type**, choose to edit the code in the browser, upload a .zip file, or upload a file from Amazon S3.

5. Choose either **Save** or **Save and test**.

6. Choose **Actions**, and choose **Publish new version**.

7. In the **Publish new version from $LATEST** dialog box, enter a description of the new version. This description appears in the list of versions, along with an automatically generated version number.

8. Choose **Publish**.

   The new version automatically becomes the latest version. The version number appears on the **Version** button in the upper-left corner of the page.

9. Choose the **Triggers** tab.

10. Choose **Add trigger**.

11. In the **Add trigger** dialog box, choose the dotted box, and then choose **CloudFront**. **Note** If you've already created one or more triggers for a function, CloudFront is the default service.

12. Specify the following values to indicate when you want the Lambda function to execute.
    **Distribution ID**
    Choose the ID of the distribution that you want to add the trigger to.
    **Cache behavior**
    Choose the cache behavior that specifies the objects that you want to execute the function on.
    **CloudFront event**
    Choose the CloudFront event that causes the function to execute.
    **Enable trigger and replicate**
    Select this check box so Lambda replicates the function to regions globally.

13. Choose **Submit**.

14. To add more triggers for this function, repeat steps 10 through 13.

# Creating Lambda Functions and CloudFront Triggers Programmatically

You can set up Lambda@Edge functions and CloudFront triggers programmatically instead of by using the AWS console. For more information, see the following:

- API Reference in the *AWS Lambda Developer Guide*
- Amazon CloudFront API Reference
- **AWS CLI**
  - Lambda create-function command
  - CloudFront create-distribution command
  - CloudFront create-distribution-with-tags command
  - CloudFront update-distribution command
- AWS SDKs (See the **SDKs & Toolkits** section.)
- AWS Tools for PowerShell Cmdlet Reference

# Adding Triggers for a Lambda@Edge Function

A Lambda@Edge trigger is one combination of CloudFront distribution, cache behavior, and event that causes a function to execute. You can specify one or more CloudFront triggers that cause the function to run. For example, you can create a trigger that causes the function to execute when CloudFront receives a request from a viewer for a specific cache behavior you set up for your distribution.

**Tip**
If you're not familiar with CloudFront cache behaviors, here's a brief overview. When you create a CloudFront distribution, you specify settings that tell CloudFront how to respond when it receives different requests. The default settings are called the default cache behavior for the distribution. You can set up additional cache behaviors that define how CloudFront responds under specific circumstances, for example, when it receives a request for a specific file type. For more information, see Cache Behavior Settings.

At the time that you create a Lambda function, you can specify only one trigger. But you can add more triggers to the same function later in one of two ways: by using the Lambda console or by editing the distribution in the CloudFront console.

- Using the Lambda console works well if you want to add more triggers to a function for the same CloudFront distribution.
- Using the CloudFront console can be better if you want to add triggers for multiple distributions because it's easier to find the distribution that you want to update. You can also update other CloudFront settings at the same time.

**Note**
If you want to work with Lambda@Edge programmatically, there are several resources to help you. For more information, see Creating Lambda Functions and CloudFront Triggers Programmatically.

**Topics**
- CloudFront Events That Can Trigger a Lambda Function
- How to Decide Which CloudFront Event to Use to Trigger a Lambda Function
- Adding Triggers by Using the Lambda Console
- Adding Triggers by Using the CloudFront Console

# CloudFront Events That Can Trigger a Lambda Function

For each cache behavior in a CloudFront distribution, you can add up to four triggers (associations) that cause a Lambda function to execute when specific CloudFront events occur. CloudFront triggers can be based on one of four CloudFront events, as shown in the following diagram.

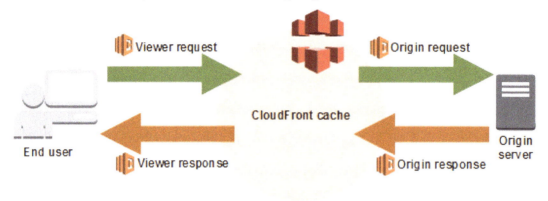

The CloudFront events that can be used to trigger Lambda@Edge functions are the following:

**Viewer Request**
The function executes when CloudFront receives a request from a viewer, before it checks to see whether the requested object is in the edge cache.

**Origin Request**
The function executes *only* when CloudFront forwards a request to your origin. When the requested object is in the edge cache, the function doesn't execute.

**Origin Response**
The function executes after CloudFront receives a response from the origin and before it caches the object in the response. Note that the function executes even if an error is returned from the origin.
The function doesn't execute in the following cases:

- When the requested file is in the edge cache
- When the response is generated from a function that was triggered by an origin request event

**Viewer Response**
The function executes before returning the requested file to the viewer. Note that the function executes regardless of whether the file is already in the edge cache.
The function doesn't execute in the following cases:

- When the origin returns an HTTP status code of 400 or higher
- When a custom error page is returned
- When the response is generated from a function that was triggered by a viewer request event
- When CloudFront automatically redirects an HTTP request to HTTPS (when the value of Viewer Protocol Policy is **Redirect HTTP to HTTPS**)

When you add multiple triggers to the same cache behavior, you can use them to run the same function or run different functions for each trigger. You can also associate the same function with more than one distribution.

**Note**
When a CloudFront event triggers the execution of a Lambda function, the function must finish before CloudFront can continue. For example, if when a Lambda function is triggered by a CloudFront viewer request event, CloudFront won't return a response to the viewer or forward the request to the origin until the Lambda function finishes running. This means that each request that triggers a Lambda function increases latency for the request, so you'll want the function to execute as fast as possible.

# How to Decide Which CloudFront Event to Use to Trigger a Lambda Function

When you're deciding which CloudFront event you want to use to trigger a Lambda function, consider the following:

**Do you want CloudFront to cache objects that are changed by a Lambda function?**
If you want CloudFront to cache an object that was modified by a Lambda function so that CloudFront can serve the object from the edge location the next time it's requested, use the origin request or origin response event. This reduces the load on the origin, reduces latency for subsequent requests, and reduces the cost of invoking Lambda@Edge on subsequent requests.
For example, if you want to add, remove, or change headers for objects that are returned by the origin and you want CloudFront to cache the result, use the origin response event.

**Do you want the function to execute for every request?**
If you want the function to execute for every request that CloudFront receives for the distribution, use the viewer request or viewer response events. Origin request and origin response events occur only when a requested object isn't cached in an edge location and CloudFront forwards a request to the origin.

**Does the function change the cache key?**
If you want the function to change a value that you're using as a basis for caching, use the viewer request event. For example, if a function changes the URL to include a language abbreviation in the path (for example, because the user chose their language from a dropdown list), use the viewer request event:

- **URL in the viewer request** – http://example/.com/en/index/.html
- **URL when the request comes from an IP address in Germany** – http://example/.com/de/index/ .html You also use the viewer request event if you're caching based on cookies or request headers.
  If the function changes cookies or headers, configure CloudFront to forward the applicable part of the request to the origin. For more information, see the following topics:
- Configuring CloudFront to Cache Objects Based on Cookies
- Configuring CloudFront to Cache Objects Based on Request Headers

**Does the function affect the response from the origin?**
If you want the function to change the request in a way that affects the response from the origin, use the origin request event. Typically, most viewer request events aren't forwarded to the origin; CloudFront responds to a request with an object that's already in the edge cache. If the function changes the request based on an origin request event, CloudFront caches the response to the changed origin request.

# Adding Triggers by Using the Lambda Console

**To add triggers to a Lambda@Edge function (AWS Lambda console)**

1. Sign in to the AWS Management Console and open the AWS Lambda console at https://console.aws. amazon.com/lambda/.

2. In the region list at the top of the page, choose **US East (N. Virginia)**.

3. On the **Functions** page, choose the name of the function that you want to add triggers for.

4. Choose **Qualifiers**, and then choose the **Versions** tab.

5. Choose the version that you want to add triggers to. **Important**
You can't create triggers for the $LATEST version, you must create them for a numbered version.

   After you choose a version, the name of the button changes to **Version: $LATEST** or **Version:** *version number.*

6. Choose the **Triggers** tab.

7. Choose **Add triggers**.

8. In the **Add trigger** dialog box, choose the dotted box, and then choose **CloudFront**. **Note**
If you've already created one or more triggers, CloudFront is the default service.

9. Specify the following values to indicate when you want the Lambda function to execute.
**Distribution ID**
Choose the ID of the distribution that you want to add the trigger to.
**Cache behavior**
Choose the cache behavior that specifies the objects that you want to execute the function on.
**CloudFront event**
Choose the CloudFront event that causes the function to execute.
**Enable trigger and replicate**
Select this check box so that AWS Lambda replicates the function to regions globally.

10. Choose **Submit**.

    The function starts to process requests for the specified CloudFront events when the updated CloudFront distribution is deployed. To determine whether a distribution is deployed, choose **Distributions** in the navigation pane. When a distribution is deployed, the value of the **Status** column for the distribution changes from **In Progress** to **Deployed**.

# Adding Triggers by Using the CloudFront Console

**To add triggers for CloudFront events to a Lambda function (CloudFront console)**

1. Get the ARN of the Lambda function that you want to add triggers for:

   1. Sign in to the AWS Management Console and open the AWS Lambda console at https://console.aws. amazon.com/lambda/.

   2. In the list of regions at the top of the page, choose **US East (N. Virginia)**.

   3. In the list of functions, choose name of the function that you want to add triggers to.

   4. Choose **Qualifiers**, choose the **Versions** tab, and choose the numbered version that you want to add triggers to. **Important**
   You can add triggers only to a numbered version, not to **$LATEST**.

   5. Copy the ARN that appears at the top of the page, for example:

      ```
      arn:aws:lambda:us-east-1:123456789012:function:TestFunction:2
      ```

      The number at the end (**2** in this example) is the version number of the function.

2. Open the CloudFront console at  https://console.aws.amazon.com/cloudfront/.

3. In the list of distributions, choose the ID of the distribution that you want to add triggers to.

4. Choose the **Behaviors** tab.

5. Select the check box for the cache behavior that you want to add triggers to, and then choose **Edit**.

6. At **Lambda Function Associations**, in the **Event Type** list, choose when you want the function to execute: for viewer requests, viewer responses, origin requests, or origin responses.

   For more information, see How to Decide Which CloudFront Event to Use to Trigger a Lambda Function.

7. Paste the ARN of the Lambda function that you want to execute when the chosen event occurs. This is the value that you copied in step 1.

8. To execute the same function for more event types, choose + and repeat steps 6 and 7.

9. Choose **Yes, Edit**.

10. To add triggers to more cache behaviors for this distribution, repeat steps 5 through 9.

    The function starts to process requests for the specified CloudFront events when the updated CloudFront distribution is deployed. To determine whether a distribution is deployed, choose **Distributions** in the navigation pane. When a distribution is deployed, the value of the **Status** column for the distribution changes from **In Progress** to **Deployed**.

# Testing and Debugging Lambda@Edge Functions

You can test Lambda@Edge functions on the Lambda console by using test events modeled on the CloudFront events. However, testing in the console only validates logic, and does not apply service limits that are specific to Lambda@Edge.

To monitor the execution of your function in CloudFront and help determine if it's working as expected, you can create logging statements for Lambda functions running on Lambda@Edge that will write to CloudWatch Logs.

When you check for the log files, be aware that log files are stored in the Region closest to the location where the function is executed. So if you visit a website from, for example, London, you must change the Region to view the CloudWatch Logs for the London Region.

For more information, see CloudWatch Metrics and CloudWatch Logs for Lambda Functions.

For more information, see the following topics:

- Lambda@Edge Event Structure
- Requirements and Restrictions on Lambda Functions

# CloudWatch Metrics and CloudWatch Logs for Lambda Functions

You can use CloudWatch metrics to monitor, in real time, the CloudFront requests that trigger Lambda functions. You can also use CloudWatch Logs to get aggregate data. There's no additional charge for metrics or logs.

**Topics**

- CloudWatch Metrics
- CloudWatch Logs

## CloudWatch Metrics

When you create a trigger for a CloudFront event, Lambda automatically begins to send metrics to CloudWatch. Metrics are available for all Lambda regions. The name of each metric is `/aws/lambda/us-east-1`.*function-name* where *function-name* is the name that you gave to the function when you created it. CloudWatch sends metrics to the region that's closest to the location where the function is executed.

For more information about CloudWatch metrics, see the Amazon CloudWatch User Guide.

## CloudWatch Logs

When you create a trigger, Lambda automatically starts to send data to CloudWatch Logs about the CloudFront requests that trigger Lambda functions. You use CloudWatch Logs tools to access the logs.

Lambda creates CloudWatch Logs log streams in the CloudWatch Logs regions closest to the locations where the function is executed. The format of the name for each log stream is `/aws/lambda/us-east-1`.*function-name* where *function-name* is the name that you gave to the function when you created it.

For information about the permissions required to send data to CloudWatch Logs, see Setting IAM Permissions and Roles for Lambda@Edge in the *IAM User Guide*.

For information about adding logging to a Lambda function, see Logging (Node.js) in the *AWS Lambda Developer Guide*.

For information about CloudWatch Logs limits, see Limits in the *Amazon CloudWatch Logs User Guide*.

Lambda@Edge throttles logs based on the request volume and the size of logs.

# Deleting Lambda@Edge Functions and Replicas

You can delete a Lambda@Edge function only when the replicas of the function have been deleted by CloudFront. Replicas of a Lambda function are automatically deleted in the following situations:

- After you have removed the last association for the function from all of your CloudFront distributions. If more than one distribution uses a function, the replicas are removed only after the function is disassociated from the last one.
- After you delete the last distribution that a function was associated with.

Replicas are typically deleted within a few hours.

You can also delete a specific version of a function if the version doesn't have any CloudFront distributions associated with it. If you remove the association for a function version, you can typically delete the function a few hours later.

Replicas cannot be manually deleted at this time. This helps prevent a situation where a replica is removed that you're still using, which would result in an error.

Note that it's important not to build applications that use function replicas outside of CloudFront because the replicas will be deleted whenever their associations with distributions are removed, or when distributions themselves are deleted. So the replica that an outside application depends on could be removed without warning, causing it to fail.

# Lambda@Edge Event Structure

The examples in this section show request and response events that CloudFront passes to or returns from a Lambda@Edge function when it's triggered.

**Topics**

- Content-Based Dynamic Origin Selection
- Request Event
- Response Event

## Content-Based Dynamic Origin Selection

You can use the path pattern in a cache behavior to route requests to an origin, based on the path and name of the requested object, such as images/*.jpg. Using Lambda@Edge, you can also route requests to an origin based on other characteristics, such as the values in request headers.

There are a number of ways this content-based dynamic origin selection can be useful. For example, you can distribute requests across origins in different geographic areas to help with global load balancing. Or you can selectively route requests to different origins that each serve a particular function: bot handling, SEO optimization, authentication, and so on. For code samples that demonstrate how to use this feature, see Example Functions for Content-Based Dynamic Origin Selection.

In the CloudFront origin request event, the origin element in the event structure contains information about the Amazon S3 or custom origin that the request would be routed to, based on the path pattern. You can update the values in the origin object to route a request to a different origin. The origin doesn't need to be defined in the distribution, and you can replace an Amazon S3 origin object with a custom origin object and vice versa.

You can specify either a custom origin or an Amazon S3 origin in a single request, but not both.

## Request Event

Here's the format of the event object that CloudFront passes to a Lambda function when the function is triggered by a CloudFront viewer request event or an origin request event:

```
1  {
2    "Records": [
3      {
4        "cf": {
5          "config": {
6            "distributionDomainName": "d123.cloudfront.net",
7            "distributionId": "EDFDVBD6EXAMPLE",
8            "eventType": "viewer-request",
9            "requestId": "MRVMF7KydIvxMWfJIglgwHQwZsbG2IhRJ07sn9AkKUFSHS9EXAMPLE=="
10         },
11         "request": {
12           "clientIp": "2001:0db8:85a3:0:0:8a2e:0370:7334",
13           "querystring": "size=large",
14           "uri": "/picture.jpg",
15           "method": "GET",
16           "headers": {
17             "host": [
18               {
19                 "key": "Host",
20                 "value": "d111111abcdef8.cloudfront.net"
```

```
21              }
22            ],
23            "user-agent": [
24              {
25                "key": "User-Agent",
26                "value": "curl/7.51.0"
27              }
28            ]
29          },
30          "origin": {
31            "custom": {
32              "customHeaders": {
33                "my-origin-custom-header": [
34                  {
35                    "key": "My-Origin-Custom-Header",
36                    "value": "Test"
37                  }
38                ]
39              },
40              "domainName": "example.com",
41              "keepaliveTimeout": 5,
42              "path": "/custom_path",
43              "port": 443,
44              "protocol": "https",
45              "readTimeout": 5,
46              "sslProtocols": [
47                "TLSv1",
48                "TLSv1.1"
49              ]
50            },
51            "s3": {
52              "authMethod": "origin-access-identity",
53              "customHeaders": {
54                "my-origin-custom-header": [
55                  {
56                    "key": "My-Origin-Custom-Header",
57                    "value": "Test"
58                  }
59                ]
60              },
61              "domainName": "my-bucket.s3.amazonaws.com",
62              "path": "/s3_path",
63              "region": "us-east-1"
64            }
65          }
66        }
67      }
68    }
69  ]
70 }
```

Request events include the following values:

**Config Values**

**distributionDomainName (read-only)**

The domain name of the distribution that's associated with the request.

**distributionID (read-only)**
The ID of the distribution that's associated with the request.

**eventType (read-only)**
The type of trigger that's associated with the request.

**requestId (read-only, viewer request events only)**
An encrypted string that uniquely identifies a request. The `requestId` value also appears in CloudFront access logs as `x-edge-request-id`. For more information, see Access Logs and Web Distribution Log File Format.

*Request Values - General*

**clientIp (read-only)**
The IP address of the viewer that made the request. If the viewer used an HTTP proxy or a load balancer to send the request, the value is the IP address of the proxy or load balancer.

**headers (read/write)**
The headers in the request. The keys in the `headers` object are lowercase versions of the header names in the HTTP request. These lowercase keys give you case-insensitive access to the header values. Each header (for example, `headers["accept"]` or `headers["host"]`) is an array of key-value pairs, where `key` is the case-sensitive name of the header as it appears in an HTTP request and `value` is a header value. The number of elements in the array is the number of times that a header is repeated in an HTTP request.
For information about restrictions on header usage, see Headers.

**method (read-only)**
The HTTP method of the viewer request.

**querystring**
The query string, if any, that CloudFront received in the viewer request. If the viewer request doesn't include a query string, the event structure still includes `querystring` with an empty value. For more information about query strings, see Configuring CloudFront to Cache Based on Query String Parameters.

**uri (read/write)**
The relative path of the requested object. Note the following:

- The new relative path must begin with a slash (like this: /).
- If a function changes the URI for a request, that changes the object that the viewer is requesting.
- If a function changes the URI for a request, that doesn't change the cache behavior for the request or the origin that the request is forwarded to.

*Request Values - Custom Origin*

You can specify either a custom origin or an Amazon S3 origin in a single request; not both.

**customHeaders**
You can include custom headers with the request by specifying a header name and value pair for each custom header. You can't add headers that are blacklisted for origin custom headers or hooks, and a header with the same name can't be present in request.headers or in request.origin.custom.customHeaders. The restrictions for request.headers also apply to custom headers. For more information, see Custom Headers that CloudFront Can't Forward to Your Origin and Blacklisted Headers.

**domainName**
The domain name of the origin server, like www.example.com. The domain name can't be empty, can't include a colon (:), and can't use the IPV4 address format. The domain name can be up to 253 characters.

**keepaliveTimeout**
How long, in seconds, that CloudFront should try to maintain the connection to your origin after receiving the last packet of a response. The value must be a number in the range of 1 to 60 seconds.

**path**

The directory path at the server where the request should locate content. The path should start with a slash (/) but should have no trailing / (like path/). The path should be URL encoded, with a maximum length of 255 characters.

**port**

The port at your custom origin. The port must be 80 or 443, or a number in the range of 1024 to 65535.

**protocol**

The origin protocol policy that CloudFront should use when fetching objects from your origin. The value can be `http` or `https`.

**readTimeout**

How long, in seconds, CloudFront should wait for a response after forwarding a request to the origin, and how long CloudFront should wait after receiving a packet of a response before receiving the next packet. The value must be a number in the range of 4 to 60 seconds.

**sslProtocols**

The SSL protocols that CloudFront can use when establishing an HTTPS connection with your origin. Values can be the following: `TLSv1.2`, `TLSv1.1`, `TLSv1`, `SSLv3`.

*Request Values - Amazon S3 Origin*

You can specify either a custom origin or an Amazon S3 origin in a single request, but not both.

**authMethod**

Set to `origin-access-identity` if your Amazon S3 bucket has an origin access identity (OAI) set up, or `none` if you aren't using OAI. If you set authMethod to `origin-access-identity`, there are several requirements:

- You must specify a region in your header.
- You must use the same OAI when you switch from one Amazon S3 origin to another.
- You can't use an OAI when you switch from a custom origin to an Amazon S3 origin. For more information about using an OAI, see Using an Origin Access Identity to Restrict Access to Your Amazon S3 Content.

**customHeaders**

You can include custom headers with the request by specifying a header name and value pair for each custom header. You can't add headers that are blacklisted for origin custom headers or hooks, and a header with the same name can't be present in request.headers or in request.origin.custom.customHeaders. The restrictions for request.headers also apply to custom headers. For more information, see Custom Headers that CloudFront Can't Forward to Your Origin and Blacklisted Headers.

**domainName**

The domain name of the Amazon S3 origin server, like `my-bucket.s3.amazonaws.com`. The domain name can't be empty, and must be an allowed bucket name (as defined by Amazon S3). Do not use a region-specific endpoint, like `my-bucket.s3-eu-west-1.amazonaws.com`. The name can be up to 128 characters, and must be all lowercase.

**path**

The directory path at the server where the request should locate content. The path should start with a slash (/) but should have no trailing / (like path/).

**region**

The region for your Amazon S3 bucket. This is required only if you use OAI.

# Response Event

Here's the format of the event object that CloudFront passes to a Lambda function when the function is triggered by a CloudFront viewer response event or an origin response event:

```
1  {
2      "Records": [
3          {
4              "cf": {
5                  "config": {
6                      "distributionDomainName": "d123.cloudfront.net",
7                      "distributionId": "EDFDVBD6EXAMPLE",
8                      "eventType": "viewer-response",
9                      "requestId": "xGN7KWpVEmB9Dp7ctcVFQC4E-nrcOcEKS3QyAez--06dV7TEXAMPLE=="
10                 },
11                 "request": {
12                     "clientIp": "2001:0db8:85a3:0:0:8a2e:0370:7334",
13                     "method": "GET",
14                     "uri": "/picture.jpg",
15                     "querystring": "size=large",
16                     "headers": {
17                         "host": [
18                             {
19                                 "key": "Host",
20                                 "value": "d111111abcdef8.cloudfront.net"
21                             }
22                         ],
23                         "user-agent": [
24                             {
25                                 "key": "User-Agent",
26                                 "value": "curl/7.18.1"
27                             }
28                         ]
29                     }
30                 },
31                 "response": {
32                     "status": "200",
33                     "statusDescription": "OK",
34                     "headers": {
35                         "server": [
36                             {
37                                 "key": "Server",
38                                 "value": "MyCustomOrigin"
39                             }
40                         ],
41                         "set-cookie": [
42                             {
43                                 "key": "Set-Cookie",
44                                 "value": "theme=light"
45                             },
46                             {
47                                 "key": "Set-Cookie",
48                                 "value": "sessionToken=abc123; Expires=Wed, 09 Jun 2021 10:18:14
                                      GMT"
49                             }
50                         ]
51                     }
52                 }
53             }
```

```
54        }
55     ]
56 }
```

Response events include the values that appear in the corresponding request event, and in addition, the following values. If your Lambda@Edge function generates an HTTP response, see Generating HTTP Responses in Request Triggers.

### distributionID (read-only)
The ID of the distribution that's associated with the request.

### eventType (read-only)
The type of trigger that's associated with the response.

### headers
Headers that you want CloudFront to return in the generated response. Note the following:

- The keys in the `headers` object are lowercase versions of standard HTTP header names. Using lowercase keys gives you case-insensitive access to the header values.
- Each header (for example, `headers["accept"]` or `headers["host"]`) is an array of key-value pairs. For a given header, the array contains one key-value pair for each value in the generated response.
- Specify `key` as the case-sensitive name of the header as it appears in an HTTP request; for example, `accept` or `host`.
- Specify `value` as a header value. For information about restrictions on header usage, see Headers.

### requestId (read-only, viewer response events only)
An encrypted string that uniquely identifies a request. The `requestId` value also appears in CloudFront access logs as the `x-edge-request-id`. For more information, see Access Logs and Web Distribution Log File Format.

### request – One of the following:

- Viewer response – The request that CloudFront received from the viewer and that might have been modified by the Lambda function that was triggered by a viewer request event
- Origin response – The request that CloudFront forwarded to the origin and that might have been modified by the Lambda function that was triggered by an origin request event If the Lambda function modifies the request object, the changes are ignored.

### response – One of the following:

- Viewer response – The response that CloudFront will return to the viewer for viewer response events.
- Origin response – The response that CloudFront received from the origin for origin response events.

### status
The HTTP status code that CloudFront returns to the viewer.

### statusDescription
The HTTP status description that CloudFront returns to the viewer.

# Generating HTTP Responses in Request Triggers

When CloudFront receives a request, you can use a Lambda function to generate an HTTP response that CloudFront returns directly to the viewer without forwarding the response to the origin. Generating HTTP responses reduces the load on the origin, and typically also reduces latency for the viewer.

Some common scenarios for generating HTTP responses include the following:

- Returning a small web page to the viewer
- Returning an HTTP 301 or 302 status code to redirect the user to another web page
- Returning an HTTP 401 status code to the viewer when the user hasn't authenticated

A Lambda@Edge function can generate an HTTP response when the following CloudFront events occur:

**Viewer request events**
When a function is triggered by a viewer request event, CloudFront returns the response to the viewer and doesn't cache it.

**Origin request events**
When a function is triggered by an origin request event, CloudFront checks the edge cache for a response that was previously generated by the function.

- If the response is in the cache, the function isn't executed and CloudFront returns the cached response to the viewer.
- If the response isn't in the cache, the function is executed, CloudFront returns the response to the viewer, and also caches it.

To see some sample code for generating HTTP responses, see field-level encryption. You can also replace the HTTP responses in response triggers. For more information, see Updating HTTP Responses in Origin-Response Triggers.

## Programming Model

This section describes the programming model for using Lambda@Edge to generate HTTP responses.

**Topics**

- Response Object
- Errors
- Required Fields

### Response Object

The response you return as the **result** parameter of the **callback** method should have the following structure (note that only the **status** field is required).

```
1  const response = {
2      body: 'content',
3      bodyEncoding: 'text' | 'base64',
4      headers: {
5          'header name in lowercase': [{
6              key: 'header name in standard case',
7              value: 'header value'
8          }],
9          ...
10     },
11     status: 'HTTP status code',
```

169

```
12    statusDescription: 'status description'
13 };
```

The response object can include the following values:

**body**

The body, if any, that you want CloudFront to return in the generated response.

**bodyEncoding**

The encoding for the value that you specified in the `body`. The only valid encodings are `text` and `base64`. If you include `body` in the `response` object but omit `bodyEncoding`, CloudFront treats the body as text. If you specify `bodyEncoding` as `base64` but the body is not valid base64, CloudFront returns an error.

**headers**

Headers that you want CloudFront to return in the generated response. Note the following:

- The keys in the `headers` object are lowercase versions of standard HTTP header names. Using lowercase keys gives you case-insensitive access to the header values.
- Each header (for example, `headers["accept"]` or `headers["host"]`) is an array of key-value pairs. For a given header, the array contains one key-value pair for each value in the generated response. For example, if you want to include 3 values in the host header, the `headers["host"]` array will contain 3 key-value pairs.
- `key` is the case-sensitive name of the header as it appears in an HTTP request; for example, `accept` or `host`.
- `value` is a header value. For information about restrictions on header usage, see Headers.

**status**

The HTTP status code that you want CloudFront to use for the following:

- Return in the response
- Cache in the CloudFront edge cache, when the response was generated by a function that was triggered by an origin request event
- Log in CloudFront Access Logs If the `status` value isn't between 200 and 599, CloudFront returns an error to the viewer.

**statusDescription**

The description that you want CloudFront to return in the response, to accompany the HTTP status code. You don't need to use standard descriptions, such as `OK` for an HTTP status code of 200.

**Errors**

The following are possible errors for generated HTTP responses.

**Response Contains a Body and Specifies 204 (No Content) for Status**

When a function is triggered by a viewer request, CloudFront returns an HTTP 502 status code (Bad Gateway) to the viewer when both of the following are true:

- The value of `status` is 204 (No Content)
- The response includes a value for `body` This is because Lambda@Edge imposes the optional restriction found in RFC 2616, which states that an `HTTP 204` response does not need to contain a message body.

**Limits on the Size of the Generated Response**

The maximum size of a response that is generated by a Lambda function (including the headers and body) depends on the event that triggered the function:

- **Viewer request events** – 40 KB
- **Origin request events** – 1 MB If the response is larger than the allowed size, CloudFront returns an HTTP 502 status code (Bad Gateway) to the viewer.

170

## Required Fields

The `status` field is required.

All other fields are optional.

# Updating HTTP Responses in Origin-Response Triggers

When CloudFront receives an HTTP response from the origin server, if there is an origin-response trigger associated with the cache behavior, you can modify the HTTP response to override what was returned from the origin.

Some common scenarios for updating HTTP responses include the following:

- Changing the status to set an HTTP 200 status code and creating static body content to return to the viewer when an origin returns an error status code (4xx or 5xx). For sample code, see Example: Using an Origin-Response Trigger to Update the Error Status Code to 200-OK.
- Changing the status to set an HTTP 301 or HTTP 302 status code, to redirect the user to another web site when an origin returns an error status code (4xx or 5xx). For sample code, see Example: Using an Origin-Response Trigger to Update the Error Status Code to 302-Found.

You can also replace the HTTP responses in viewer and origin request events. For more information, see Generating HTTP Responses in Request Triggers.

When you're working with the HTTP response, note that Lambda@Edge does not expose the HTML body that is returned by the origin server to the origin-response trigger. You can generate a static content body by setting it to the desired value, or remove the body inside the function by setting the value to be empty. If you don't update the body field in your function, the original body returned by the origin server is returned back to viewer.

# Lambda@Edge Example Functions

See the following sections for examples of using Lambda functions with CloudFront.

Note that each Lambda@Edge function must contain the `callback` parameter to successfully process a request or return a response. For more information, see Writing and Creating a Lambda@Edge Function.

**Topics**

- General Examples
- Generating Responses - Examples
- Working with Query Strings - Examples
- Personalize Content by Country or Device Type Headers - Examples
- Content-Based Dynamic Origin Selection - Examples
- Updating Error Statuses - Examples

## General Examples

### Example: A/B Testing

You can use the following example if you want to test two different versions of your home page, but you don't want to create redirects or change the URL. This example sets cookies when CloudFront receives a request, randomly assigns the user to version A or B, and then returns the corresponding version to the viewer.

```
1  'use strict';
2
3  exports.handler = (event, context, callback) => {
4      const request = event.Records[0].cf.request;
5      const headers = request.headers;
6
7      if (request.uri !== '/experiment-pixel.jpg') {
8          // do not process if this is not an A-B test request
9          callback(null, request);
10         return;
11     }
12
13     const cookieExperimentA = 'X-Experiment-Name=A';
14     const cookieExperimentB = 'X-Experiment-Name=B';
15     const pathExperimentA = '/experiment-group/control-pixel.jpg';
16     const pathExperimentB = '/experiment-group/treatment-pixel.jpg';
17
18     /*
19      * Lambda at the Edge headers are array objects.
20      *
21      * Client may send multiple Cookie headers, i.e.:
22      * > GET /viewerRes/test HTTP/1.1
23      * > User-Agent: curl/7.18.1 (x86_64-unknown-linux-gnu) libcurl/7.18.1 OpenSSL/1.0.1u zlib
              /1.2.3
24      * > Cookie: First=1; Second=2
25      * > Cookie: ClientCode=abc
26      * > Host: example.com
27      *
28      * You can access the first Cookie header at headers["cookie"][0].value
29      * and the second at headers["cookie"][1].value.
30      *
```

```
31       * Header values are not parsed. In the example above,
32       * headers["cookie"][0].value is equal to "First=1; Second=2"
33       */
34      let experimentUri;
35      if (headers.cookie) {
36          for (let i = 0; i < headers.cookie.length; i++) {
37              if (headers.cookie[i].value.indexOf(cookieExperimentA) >= 0) {
38                  console.log('Experiment A cookie found');
39                  experimentUri = pathExperimentA;
40                  break;
41              } else if (headers.cookie[i].value.indexOf(cookieExperimentB) >= 0) {
42                  console.log('Experiment B cookie found');
43                  experimentUri = pathExperimentB;
44                  break;
45              }
46          }
47      }
48
49      if (!experimentUri) {
50          console.log('Experiment cookie has not been found. Throwing dice...');
51          if (Math.random() < 0.75) {
52              experimentUri = pathExperimentA;
53          } else {
54              experimentUri = pathExperimentB;
55          }
56      }
57
58      request.uri = experimentUri;
59      console.log(`Request uri set to "${request.uri}"`);
60      callback(null, request);
61  };
```

### Example: Overriding a Response Header

The following example shows how to change the value of a response header based on the value of another header:

```
1  'use strict';
2
3  exports.handler = (event, context, callback) => {
4      const response = event.Records[0].cf.response;
5      const headers = response.headers;
6
7      const headerNameSrc = 'X-Amz-Meta-Last-Modified';
8      const headerNameDst = 'Last-Modified';
9
10     if (headers[headerNameSrc.toLowerCase()]) {
11         headers[headerNameDst.toLowerCase()] = [
12             headers[headerNameSrc.toLowerCase()][0],
13         ];
14         console.log(`Response header "${headerNameDst}" was set to ` +
15                 `"${headers[headerNameDst.toLowerCase()][0].value}"`);
16     }
17
18     callback(null, response);
```

```
19 };
```

## Generating Responses - Examples

### Example: Serving Static Content (Generated Response)

The following example shows how to use a Lambda function to serve static website content, which reduces the load on the origin server and reduces overall latency.

**Note**
You can generate HTTP responses for viewer request and origin request events. For more information, see Generating HTTP Responses in Request Triggers. You can also replace the HTTP response in origin and viewer response events. For more information, see Updating HTTP Responses in Origin-Response Triggers.

```
1  'use strict';
2
3  let content = `
4  <\!DOCTYPE html>
5  <html lang="en">
6    <head>
7      <meta charset="utf-8">
8      <title>Simple Lambda@Edge Static Content Response</title>
9    </head>
10   <body>
11     <p>Hello from Lambda@Edge!</p>
12   </body>
13 </html>
14 `;
15
16 exports.handler = (event, context, callback) => {
17     /*
18      * Generate HTTP OK response using 200 status code with HTML body.
19      */
20     const response = {
21         status: '200',
22         statusDescription: 'OK',
23         headers: {
24             'cache-control': [{
25                 key: 'Cache-Control',
26                 value: 'max-age=100'
27             }],
28             'content-type': [{
29                 key: 'Content-Type',
30                 value: 'text/html'
31             }],
32             'content-encoding': [{
33                 key: 'Content-Encoding',
34                 value: 'UTF-8'
35             }],
36         },
37         body: content,
38     };
39     callback(null, response);
40 };
```

**Example: Serving Static Website Content as Gzip Compressed Content (Generated Response)**

This function demonstrates how to use a Lambda function to serve static website content as gzip compressed content, which reduces the load on the origin server and reduces overall latency.

You can generate HTTP responses for viewer request and origin request events. For more information, see Generating HTTP Responses in Request Triggers.

```
1  'use strict';
2
3  const zlib = require('zlib');
4
5  let content = `
6  <\!DOCTYPE html>
7  <html lang="en">
8    <head>
9      <meta charset="utf-8">
10     <title>Simple Lambda@Edge Static Content Response</title>
11   </head>
12   <body>
13     <p>Hello from Lambda@Edge!</p>
14   </body>
15 </html>
16 `;
17
18 exports.handler = (event, context, callback) => {
19
20     /*
21      * Generate HTTP OK response using 200 status code with a gzip compressed content HTML body.
22      */
23
24     const buffer = zlib.gzipSync(content);
25     const base64EncodedBody = buffer.toString('base64');
26
27     var response = {
28         headers: {
29             'content-type': [{key:'Content-Type', value: 'text/html; charset=utf-8'}],
30             'content-encoding' : [{key:'Content-Encoding', value: 'gzip'}]
31         },
32         body: base64EncodedBody,
33         bodyEncoding: 'base64',
34         status: '200',
35         statusDescription: "OK"
36     }
37
38     callback(null, response);
39 };
```

**Example: Generating an HTTP Redirect (Generated Response)**

The following example shows how to generate an HTTP redirect.

**Note**
You can generate HTTP responses for viewer request and origin request events. For more information, see Generating HTTP Responses in Request Triggers.

```
1  'use strict';
2
3  exports.handler = (event, context, callback) => {
4      /*
5       * Generate HTTP redirect response with 302 status code and Location header.
6       */
7      const response = {
8          status: '302',
9          statusDescription: 'Found',
10         headers: {
11             location: [{
12                 key: 'Location',
13                 value: 'http://docs.aws.amazon.com/lambda/latest/dg/lambda-edge.html',
14             }],
15         },
16     };
17     callback(null, response);
18 };
```

## Working with Query Strings - Examples

### Example: Adding a Header Based on a Query String Parameter

The following example shows how to get the key-value pair of a query string parameter, and then add a header based on those values.

```
1  'use strict';
2
3  const querystring = require('querystring');
4  exports.handler = (event, context, callback) => {
5      const request = event.Records[0].cf.request;
6
7      /* When a request contains a query string key-value pair but the origin server
8       * expects the value in a header, you can use this Lambda function to
9       * convert the key-value pair to a header. Here's what the function does:
10      * 1. Parses the query string and gets the key-value pair.
11      * 2. Adds a header to the request using the key-value pair that the function got in step 1.
12      */
13
14     /* Parse request querystring to get javascript object */
15     const params = querystring.parse(request.querystring);
16
17     /* Move auth param from querystring to headers */
18     const headerName = 'Auth-Header';
19     request.headers[headerName.toLowerCase()] = [{ key: headerName, value: params.auth }];
20     delete params.auth;
21
22     /* Update request querystring */
23     request.querystring = querystring.stringify(params);
24
25     callback(null, request);
26 }
27
28
```

```
29 ;
```

## Example: Normalizing Query String Parameters to Improve the Cache Hit Ratio

The following example shows how to improve your cache hit ratio by making the following changes to query strings before CloudFront forwards requests to your origin:

- Alphabetize key-value pairs by the name of the parameter
- Change the case of key-value pairs to lowercase

For more information, see Configuring CloudFront to Cache Based on Query String Parameters.

```javascript
1  'use strict';
2
3  const querystring = require('querystring');
4
5  exports.handler = (event, context, callback) => {
6      const request = event.Records[0].cf.request;
7      /* When you configure a distribution to forward query strings to the origin and
8       * to cache based on a whitelist of query string parameters, we recommend
9       * the following to improve the cache-hit ratio:
10      * - Always list parameters in the same order.
11      * - Use the same case for parameter names and values.
12      *
13      * This function normalizes query strings so that parameter names and values
14      * are lowercase and parameter names are in alphabetical order.
15      *
16      * For more information, see:
17      * http://docs.aws.amazon.com/AmazonCloudFront/latest/DeveloperGuide/QueryStringParameters.
18         html
19      */
20
21      console.log('Query String: ', request.querystring);
22
23      /* Parse request query string to get javascript object */
24      const params = querystring.parse(request.querystring.toLowerCase());
25      const sortedParams = {};
26
27      /* Sort param keys */
28      Object.keys(params).sort().forEach(key => {
29          sortedParams[key] = params[key];
30      });
31
32      /* Update request querystring with normalized  */
33      request.querystring = querystring.stringify(sortedParams);
34
35      callback(null, request);
36  };
```

## Example: Redirecting Unauthenticated Users to a Sign-In Page

The following example shows how to redirect users to a sign-in page if they haven't entered their credentials.

```javascript
1  'use strict';
```

```
 2
 3  function parseCookies(headers) {
 4      const parsedCookie = {};
 5      if (headers.cookie) {
 6          headers.cookie[0].value.split(';').forEach((cookie) => {
 7              if (cookie) {
 8                  const parts = cookie.split('=');
 9                  parsedCookie[parts[0].trim()] = parts[1].trim();
10              }
11          });
12      }
13      return parsedCookie;
14  }
15
16  exports.handler = (event, context, callback) => {
17      const request = event.Records[0].cf.request;
18      const headers = request.headers;
19
20      /* Check for session-id in request cookie in viewer-request event,
21       * if session-id is absent, redirect the user to sign in page with original
22       * request sent as redirect_url in query params.
23       */
24
25      /* Check for session-id in cookie, if present then proceed with request */
26      const parsedCookies = parseCookies(headers);
27      if (parsedCookies && parsedCookies['session-id']) {
28          callback(null, request);
29      }
30
31      /* URI encode the original request to be sent as redirect_url in query params */
32      const encodedRedirectUrl = encodeURIComponent(`https://${headers.host[0].value}${request.uri
          }?${request.querystring}`);
33      const response = {
34          status: '302',
35          statusDescription: 'Found',
36          headers: {
37              location: [{
38                  key: 'Location',
39                  value: `http://www.example.com/signin?redirect_url=${encodedRedirectUrl}`,
40              }],
41          },
42      };
43      callback(null, response);
44  };
```

## Personalize Content by Country or Device Type Headers - Examples

### Example: Redirecting Viewer Requests to a Country-Specific URL

The following example shows how to generate an HTTP redirect response with a country-specific URL and return the response to the viewer. This is useful when you want to provide country-specific responses. For example:

- If you have country-specific subdomains, such as us.example.com and tw.example.com, you can generate a redirect response when a viewer requests example.com.

- If you're streaming video but you don't have rights to stream the content in a specific country, you can redirect users in that country to a page that explains why they can't view the video.

Note the following:

- You must configure your distribution to cache based on the `CloudFront-Viewer-Country` header. For more information, see Cache Based on Selected Request Headers.
- CloudFront adds the `CloudFront-Viewer-Country` header after the viewer request event. To use this example, you must create a trigger for the origin request event.

```
1  'use strict';
2
3  /* This is an origin request function */
4  exports.handler = (event, context, callback) => {
5      const request = event.Records[0].cf.request;
6      const headers = request.headers;
7
8      /*
9       * Based on the value of the CloudFront-Viewer-Country header, generate an
10      * HTTP status code 302 (Redirect) response, and return a country-specific
11      * URL in the Location header.
12      * NOTE: 1. You must configure your distribution to cache based on the
13      *          CloudFront-Viewer-Country header. For more information, see
14      *          http://docs.aws.amazon.com/console/cloudfront/cache-on-selected-headers
15      *       2. CloudFront adds the CloudFront-Viewer-Country header after the viewer
16      *          request event. To use this example, you must create a trigger for the
17      *          origin request event.
18      */
19
20      let url = 'https://example.com/';
21      if (headers['cloudfront-viewer-country']) {
22          const countryCode = headers['cloudfront-viewer-country'][0].value;
23          if (countryCode === 'TW') {
24              url = 'https://tw.example.com/';
25          } else if (countryCode === 'US') {
26              url = 'https://us.example.com/';
27          }
28      }
29
30      const response = {
31          status: '302',
32          statusDescription: 'Found',
33          headers: {
34              location: [{
35                  key: 'Location',
36                  value: url,
37              }],
38          },
39      };
40      callback(null, response);
41  };
```

## Example: Serving Different Versions of an Object Based on the Device

The following example shows how to serve different versions of an object based on the type of device that the user is using, for example, a mobile device or a tablet. Note the following:

- You must configure your distribution to cache based on the `CloudFront-Is-*-Viewer` headers. For more information, see Cache Based on Selected Request Headers.
- CloudFront adds the `CloudFront-Is-*-Viewer` headers after the viewer request event. To use this example, you must create a trigger for the origin request event.

```
1  'use strict';
2
3  /* This is an origin request function */
4  exports.handler = (event, context, callback) => {
5      const request = event.Records[0].cf.request;
6      const headers = request.headers;
7
8      /*
9       * Serve different versions of an object based on the device type.
10      * NOTE: 1. You must configure your distribution to cache based on the
11      *          CloudFront-Is-*-Viewer headers. For more information, see
12      *          the following documentation:
13      *          http://docs.aws.amazon.com/console/cloudfront/cache-on-selected-headers
14      *          http://docs.aws.amazon.com/console/cloudfront/cache-on-device-type
15      *       2. CloudFront adds the CloudFront-Is-*-Viewer headers after the viewer
16      *          request event. To use this example, you must create a trigger for the
17      *          origin request event.
18      */
19
20      const desktopPath = '/desktop';
21      const mobilePath = '/mobile';
22      const tabletPath = '/tablet';
23      const smarttvPath = '/smarttv';
24
25      if (headers['cloudfront-is-desktop-viewer']
26          && headers['cloudfront-is-desktop-viewer'][0].value === 'true') {
27          request.uri = desktopPath + request.uri;
28      } else if (headers['cloudfront-is-mobile-viewer']
29              && headers['cloudfront-is-mobile-viewer'][0].value === 'true') {
30          request.uri = mobilePath + request.uri;
31      } else if (headers['cloudfront-is-tablet-viewer']
32              && headers['cloudfront-is-tablet-viewer'][0].value === 'true') {
33          request.uri = tabletPath + request.uri;
34      } else if (headers['cloudfront-is-smarttv-viewer']
35              && headers['cloudfront-is-smarttv-viewer'][0].value === 'true') {
36          request.uri = smarttvPath + request.uri;
37      }
38      console.log(`Request uri set to "${request.uri}"`);
39
40      callback(null, request);
41  };
```

# Content-Based Dynamic Origin Selection - Examples

### Example: Using an Origin-Request Trigger to Change From a Custom Origin to an Amazon S3 Origin

This function demonstrates how an origin-request trigger can be used to change from a custom origin to an Amazon S3 origin from which the content is fetched, based on request properties.

```
1  'use strict';
2
3  const querystring = require('querystring');
4
5  exports.handler = (event, context, callback) => {
6      const request = event.Records[0].cf.request;
7
8      /**
9       * Reads query string to check if S3 origin should be used, and
10      * if true, sets S3 origin properties.
11      */
12
13      const params = querystring.parse(request.querystring);
14
15      if (params['useS3Origin']) {
16          if (params['useS3Origin'] === 'true') {
17              const s3DomainName = 'my-bucket.s3.amazonaws.com';
18
19              /* Set S3 origin fields */
20              request.origin = {
21                  s3: {
22                      domainName: s3DomainName,
23                      region: '',
24                      authMethod: 'none',
25                      path: '',
26                      customHeaders: {}
27                  }
28              };
29              request.headers['host'] = [{ key: 'host', value: s3DomainName}];
30          }
31      }
32
33      callback(null, request);
34  };
```

### Example: Using an Origin-Request Trigger to Change the Amazon S3 Origin Region

This function demonstrates how an origin-request trigger can be used to change the Amazon S3 origin from which the content is fetched, based on request properties.

In this example, we use the value of the CloudFront-Viewer-Country header to update the S3 bucket domain name to a bucket in a region that is closer to the viewer. This can be useful in several ways:

- It reduces latencies when the region specified is nearer to the viewer's country.
- It provides data sovereignty by making sure that data is served from an origin that's in the same country that the request came from.

To use this example, you must do the following:

- Configure your distribution to cache based on the CloudFront-Viewer-Country header. For more information, see Cache Based on Selected Request Headers.
- Create a trigger for this function in the origin request event. CloudFront adds the CloudFront-Viewer-Country header after the viewer request event, so to use this example, you must make sure the function executes for an origin request.

```
1   'use strict';
2
3   exports.handler = (event, context, callback) => {
4       const request = event.Records[0].cf.request;
5
6       /**
7        * This blueprint demonstrates how an origin-request trigger can be used to
8        * change the origin from which the content is fetched, based on request properties.
9        * In this example, we use the value of the CloudFront-Viewer-Country header
10       * to update the S3 bucket domain name to a bucket in a region that is closer to
11       * the viewer.
12       *
13       * This can be useful in several ways:
14       *      1) Reduces latencies when the region specified is nearer to the 'viewers
15       *         country.
16       *      2) Provides data sovereignty by making sure that data is served from an
17       *         origin 'thats in the same country that the request came from.
18       *
19       * NOTE: 1. You must configure your distribution to cache based on the
20       *          CloudFront-Viewer-Country header. For more information, see
21       *          http://docs.aws.amazon.com/console/cloudfront/cache-on-selected-headers
22       *       2. CloudFront adds the CloudFront-Viewer-Country header after the viewer
23       *          request event. To use this example, you must create a trigger for the
24       *          origin request event.
25       */
26
27       const countryToRegion = {
28           'DE': 'eu-central-1',
29           'IE': 'eu-west-1',
30           'GB': 'eu-west-2',
31           'FR': 'eu-west-3',
32           'JP': 'ap-northeast-1',
33           'IN': 'ap-south-1',
34           'CN': 'cn-north-1'
35       };
36
37       if (request.headers['cloudfront-viewer-country']) {
38           const countryCode = request.headers['cloudfront-viewer-country'][0].value;
39           const region = countryToRegion[countryCode];
40
41           /**
42            * If the viewer's country is not in the list you specify, the request
43            * goes to the default S3 bucket you've configured.
44            */
45           if (region) {
46               /**
47                * If 'youve set up OAI, the bucket policy in the destination bucket
48                * should allow the OAI GetObject operation, as configured by default
```

183

```
49          * for an S3 origin with OAI. Another requirement with OAI is to provide
50          * the region so it can be used for the SIGV4 signature. Otherwise, the
51          * region is not required.
52          */
53         request.origin.s3.region = region;
54         const domainName = `my-bucket-in-${region}.s3.amazonaws.com`;
55         request.origin.s3.domainName = domainName;
56         request.headers['host'] = [{ key: 'host', value: domainName }];
57     }
58   }
59
60   callback(null, request);
61 };
```

### Example: Using an Origin-Request Trigger to Change From an Amazon S3 Origin to a Custom Origin

This function demonstrates how an origin-request trigger can be used to change the custom origin from which the content is fetched, based on request properties.

```
1  'use strict';
2
3  const querystring = require('querystring');
4
5   exports.handler = (event, context, callback) => {
6       const request = event.Records[0].cf.request;
7
8       /**
9        * Reads query string to check if custom origin should be used, and
10       * if true, sets custom origin properties.
11       */
12
13      const params = querystring.parse(request.querystring);
14
15      if (params['useCustomOrigin']) {
16          if (params['useCustomOrigin'] === 'true') {
17
18              /* Set custom origin fields*/
19              request.origin = {
20                  custom: {
21                      domainName: 'www.example.com',
22                      port: 443,
23                      protocol: 'https',
24                      path: '',
25                      sslProtocols: ['TLSv1', 'TLSv1.1'],
26                      readTimeout: 5,
27                      keepaliveTimeout: 5,
28                      customHeaders: {}
29                  }
30              };
31              request.headers['host'] = [{ key: 'host', value: 'www.example.com'}];
32          }
33      }
34      callback(null, request);
```

```
35  };
```

## Example: Using an Origin-Request Trigger to Gradually Transfer Traffic From One Amazon S3 Bucket to Another

This function demonstrates how you can gradually transfer traffic from one Amazon S3 bucket to another, in a controlled way.

```
1  'use strict';
2
3      function getRandomInt(min, max) {
4          /* Random number is inclusive of min and max*/
5          return Math.floor(Math.random() * (max - min + 1)) + min;
6  }
7
8  exports.handler = (event, context, callback) => {
9      const request = event.Records[0].cf.request;
10     const BLUE_TRAFFIC_PERCENTAGE = 80;
11
12     /**
13      * This Lambda function demonstrates how to gradually transfer traffic from
14      * one S3 bucket to another in a controlled way.
15      * We define a variable BLUE_TRAFFIC_PERCENTAGE which can take values from
16      * 1 to 100. If the generated randomNumber less than or equal to BLUE_TRAFFIC_PERCENTAGE,
           traffic
17      * is re-directed to blue-bucket. If not, the default bucket that we've configured
18      * is used.
19      */
20
21     const randomNumber = getRandomInt(1, 100);
22
23  if (randomNumber <= BLUE_TRAFFIC_PERCENTAGE) {
24          const domainName = 'blue-bucket.s3.amazonaws.com';
25          request.origin.s3.domainName = domainName;
26          request.headers['host'] = [{ key: 'host', value: domainName}];
27      }
28      callback(null, request);
29  };
```

## Example: Using an Origin-Request Trigger to Change the Origin Domain Name Based on the Country Header

This function demonstrates how you can change the origin domain name based on the CloudFront-Viewer-Country header, so content is served from an origin closer to the viewer's country.

Implementing this functionality for your distribution can have advantages such as the following:

- Reducing latencies when the region specified is nearer to the viewer's country.
- Providing data sovereignty by making sure that data is served from an origin that's in the same country that the request came from.

Note that to enable this functionality you must configure your distribution to cache based on the CloudFront-Viewer-Country header. For more information, see Cache Based on Selected Request Headers.

```
1  'use strict';
2
3  exports.handler = (event, context, callback) => {
4      const request = event.Records[0].cf.request;
5
6    if (request.headers['cloudfront-viewer-country']) {
7          const countryCode = request.headers['cloudfront-viewer-country'][0].value;
8          if (countryCode === 'UK' || countryCode === 'DE' || countryCode === 'IE' ) {
9              const domainName = 'eu.example.com';
10             request.origin.custom.domainName = domainName;
11             request.headers['host'] = [{key: 'host', value: domainName}];
12         }
13     }
14
15     callback(null, request);
16 };
```

## Updating Error Statuses - Examples

### Example: Using an Origin-Response Trigger to Update the Error Status Code to 200-OK

This function demonstrates how you can update the response status to 200 and generate static body content to return to the viewer in the following scenario:

- The function is triggered in an origin response
- The response status from the origin server is an error status code (4xx or 5xx)

```
1  'use strict';
2
3  exports.handler = (event, context, callback) => {
4      const response = event.Records[0].cf.response;
5
6      /**
7       * This function updates the response status to 200 and generates static
8       * body content to return to the viewer in the following scenario:
9       * 1. The function is triggered in an origin response
10      * 2. The response status from the origin server is an error status code (4xx or 5xx)
11      */
12
13     if (response.status >= 400 && response.status <= 599) {
14         response.status = 200;
15         response.statusDescription = 'OK';
16         response.body = 'Body generation example';
17     }
18
19     callback(null, response);
20 };
```

### Example: Using an Origin-Response Trigger to Update the Error Status Code to 302-Found

This function demonstrates how you can update the HTTP status code to 302 to redirect to another path (cache behavior) that has a different origin configured. Note the following:

- The function is triggered in an origin response

- The response status from the origin server is an error status code (4xx or 5xx)

```
1  'use strict';
2
3  exports.handler = (event, context, callback) => {
4      const response = event.Records[0].cf.response;
5      const request = event.Records[0].cf.request;
6
7      /**
8       * This function updates the HTTP status code in the response to 302, to redirect to another
9       * path (cache behavior) that has a different origin configured. Note the following:
10      * 1. The function is triggered in an origin response
11      * 2. The response status from the origin server is an error status code (4xx or 5xx)
12      */
13
14      if (response.status >= 400 && response.status <= 599) {
15          const redirect_path = `/plan-b/path?${request.querystring}`;
16
17          response.status = 302;
18          response.statusDescription = 'Found';
19
20          /* Drop the body, as it is not required for redirects */
21          response.body = '';
22          response.headers['location'] = [{ key: 'Location', value: redirect_path }];
23      }
24
25      callback(null, response);
26  };
```

# Requirements and Restrictions on Lambda Functions

See the following sections for requirements and restrictions on using Lambda functions with CloudFront.

**Topics**

- CloudFront Distributions and Associations
- CloudFront Triggers for Lambda Functions
- CloudWatch Logs
- Headers
- HTTP Status Codes
- Lambda Function Configuration and Execution Environment
- Limits
- Microsoft Smooth Streaming
- Network Access
- Query String Parameters
- Tagging
- URI
- URI and Query String Encoding

## CloudFront Distributions and Associations

- You can create triggers (associations) for Lambda functions for a maximum of 25 distributions per AWS account.
- You can create a maximum of 100 triggers (associations) for a distribution.
- You cannot associate a Lambda function with a CloudFront distribution owned by another AWS account.

## CloudFront Triggers for Lambda Functions

- You can add triggers only for a numbered version, not for `$LATEST` or for aliases.
- You can add triggers only for functions in the US East (N. Virginia) Region.
- To add triggers, the IAM execution role associated with your Lambda function must be assumable by the service principals `lambda.amazonaws.com` and `edgelambda.amazonaws.com`. For more information, see Setting IAM Permissions and Roles for Lambda@Edge in the *IAM User Guide*.

## CloudWatch Logs

For information about Amazon CloudWatch Logs limits, see CloudWatch Logs Limits in the *Amazon CloudWatch User Guide*.

## Headers

Note the following requirements and restrictions on using headers with Lambda@Edge.

**Topics**

- Blacklisted Headers
- Read-only Headers
- CloudFront-* Headers

## Blacklisted Headers

Blacklisted headers aren't exposed and can't be added by Lambda@Edge functions. If your Lambda function adds a blacklisted header, the request fails CloudFront validation. CloudFront returns HTTP status code 502 (Bad Gateway) to the viewer.

- Connection
- Expect
- Keep-alive
- Proxy-Authenticate
- Proxy-Authorization
- Proxy-Connection
- Trailer
- Upgrade
- X-Accel-Buffering
- X-Accel-Charset
- X-Accel-Limit-Rate
- X-Accel-Redirect
- X-Amz-Cf-*
- X-Amzn-*
- X-Cache
- X-Edge-*
- X-Forwarded-Proto
- X-Real-IP

## Read-only Headers

Read-only headers can be read but not edited. You can use them as input to CloudFront caching logic, and your Lambda function can read the header values, but it can't change the values. If your Lambda function adds or edits a read-only header, the request fails CloudFront validation. CloudFront returns HTTP status code 502 (Bad Gateway) to the viewer.

### Read-only Headers for CloudFront Viewer Request Events

- Content-Length
- Host
- Transfer-Encoding
- Via

### Read-only Headers for CloudFront Origin Request Events

- Accept-Encoding
- Content-Length
- If-Modified-Since
- If-None-Match
- If-Range
- If-Unmodified-Since
- Range
- Transfer-Encoding
- Via

### Read-only Headers for CloudFront Origin Response Events

- Transfer-Encoding

- Via

**Read-only Headers for CloudFront Viewer Response Events**

- Content-Encoding
- Content-Length
- Transfer-Encoding
- Warning
- Via

**CloudFront-\* Headers**

A Lambda function can read, edit, remove, or add any of the following headers.

- CloudFront-Forwarded-Proto
- CloudFront-Is-Desktop-Viewer
- CloudFront-Is-Mobile-Viewer
- CloudFront-Is-SmartTV-Viewer
- CloudFront-Is-Tablet-Viewer
- CloudFront-Viewer-Country

Note the following:

- If you want CloudFront to add these headers, you must configure CloudFront to cache based on these headers. For information about configuring CloudFront to cache based on specified headers, see Cache Based on Selected Request Headers in the topic Values That You Specify When You Create or Update a Web Distribution.
- CloudFront adds the headers after the viewer request event.
- If the viewer adds headers that have these names, CloudFront overwrites the header values.
- For viewer events, CloudFront-Viewer-Country is blacklisted. Blacklisted headers aren't exposed and can't be added by Lambda@Edge functions. If your Lambda function adds a blacklisted header, the request fails CloudFront validation, and CloudFront returns HTTP status code 502 (Bad Gateway) to the viewer.

For more information, see the following examples:

- Example: Redirecting Viewer Requests to a Country-Specific URL
- Example: Serving Different Versions of an Object Based on the Device

## HTTP Status Codes

CloudFront doesn't execute Lambda functions for viewer response events if the origin returns HTTP status code 400 or higher.

## Lambda Function Configuration and Execution Environment

- You must create functions with the `nodejs6.10` or `nodejs8.10` runtime property.
- You can't configure your Lambda function to access resources inside your VPC.
- You can't associate your Lambda function to a CloudFront distribution owned by another AWS account.
- The Dead Letter Queue (DLQ) isn't supported.
- Environment variables aren't supported.

## Limits

For information about limits, see the following documentation:

- Limits on Lambda@Edge in this guide
- AWS Lambda Limits in the *AWS Lambda Developer Guide*

## Microsoft Smooth Streaming

You can't create triggers for a CloudFront distribution that you're using for on-demand streaming of media files that you've transcoded into the Microsoft Smooth Streaming format.

## Network Access

Functions triggered by origin request and response events as well as functions triggered by viewer request and response events can make network calls to resources on the internet, and to services in AWS regions such as Amazon S3 buckets, DynamoDB tables, or Amazon EC2 instances.

## Query String Parameters

- To access a query string in a Lambda function, use `event.Records[0].cf.request.querystring`.
- A function can update a query string for viewer and origin request events. The updated query string can't include spaces, control characters, or the fragment identifier (#).
- A function can read a query string only for origin and viewer response events.
- Configuring CloudFront to cache based on query string parameters affects whether a function can access the query string:
  - **Viewer request and response events** – A function can access a query string regardless of the setting for Query String Forwarding and Caching.
  - **Origin request and response events** – A function can access a query string only if Query String Forwarding and Caching is set either to **Forward All, Cache Based on Whitelist** or to **Forward All, Cache Based on All**.
- We recommend that you use percent encoding for the URI and query string. For more information, see URI and Query String Encoding.
- The total size of the URI (`event.Records[0].cf.request.uri`) and the query string (`event.Records[0].cf.request.querystring`) must be less than 8,192 characters.

For more information, see Configuring CloudFront to Cache Based on Query String Parameters.

## Tagging

Some AWS services, including Amazon CloudFront and AWS Lambda, support adding tags to resources within the service. However, at this time, you cannot apply tags to Lambda@Edge resources. To learn more about tagging in CloudFront, see Tagging Amazon CloudFront Distributions.

## URI

If a function changes the URI for a request, that doesn't change the cache behavior for the request or the origin that the request is forwarded to.

# URI and Query String Encoding

Lambda functions require the URI and query string to be UTF-8 encoded. (Percent encoding is compatible with UTF-8 encoding.) The behavior of CloudFront and Lambda depends on the following:

- The encoding of the URI and query string that CloudFront received in the request from the viewer
- Whether the URI or query string is changed by a function that is triggered by a viewer request or origin request event

### Values Are UTF-8 Encoded
CloudFront forwards the values to your Lambda function without changing them.

### Values Are ISO 8859-1 Encoded
CloudFront converts ISO 8859-1 character encoding to UTF-8 encoding before forwarding the values to your Lambda function.

### Values Are Encoded Using Some Other Character Encoding
If the values are encoded using any other character encoding, CloudFront assumes that they're ISO 8859-1 encoded and tries to convert from ISO 8859-1 encoding to UTF-8 encoding.

The converted version might be an inaccurate interpretation of the values in the original request. This can cause a Lambda function or your origin to produce an unintended result.

The value that CloudFront forwards to your origin server depends on whether functions that are triggered by viewer request or origin request events change the URI or query string:

- **If the functions don't change the URI or query string** – CloudFront forwards the values that CloudFront received in the request from the viewer to your origin server.
- **If the functions do change the URI or query string** – CloudFront forwards the UTF-8 encoded value.

In both cases, the behavior is unaffected by the character encoding of the request from the viewer.

# Working with RTMP Distributions

**Topics**

- How RTMP Distributions Work
- Task List for Streaming Media Files Using RTMP
- Creating an RTMP Distribution Using the CloudFront Console
- Values that You Specify When You Create or Update an RTMP Distribution
- Values that CloudFront Displays in the Console When You Create or Update an RTMP Distribution
- Configuring the Media Player
- Using an Amazon S3 Bucket as the Origin for an RTMP Distribution
- Creating Multiple RTMP Distributions for an Origin Server
- Restricting Access Using Crossdomain.xml
- Error Codes for RTMP Distributions
- Troubleshooting RTMP Distributions

This section describes how you configure and manage RTMP distributions. For information about how to create an RTMP distribution, see Task List for Streaming Media Files Using RTMP.

# How RTMP Distributions Work

To stream media files using CloudFront, you provide two types of files to your end users:

- Your media files
- A media player, for example, JW Player, Flowplayer, or Adobe Flash

End users view your media files using the media player that you provide for them; they do not use the media player (if any) that is already installed on their computer or other device.

When an end user streams your media file, the media player begins to play the content of the file while the file is still being downloaded from CloudFront. The media file is not stored locally on the end user's system.

To use CloudFront to serve both the media player and the media files, you need two types of distributions: a web distribution for the media player, and an RTMP distribution for the media files. Web distributions serve files over HTTP, while RTMP distributions stream media files over RTMP (or a variant of RTMP).

The following example assumes that your media files and your media player are stored in different buckets in Amazon S3, but that isn't required—you can store media files and your media player in the same Amazon S3 bucket. You can also make the media player available to end users in other ways, for example, using CloudFront and a custom origin. However, the media files must use an Amazon S3 bucket as the origin.

In the following diagram, your site serves a cached copy of the media player to each end user through the `d1234.cloudfront.net` domain. The media player then accesses cached copies of your media files through the `s5678.cloudfront.net` domain.

1. Your media player bucket holds the media player and is the origin server for a regular HTTP distribution. In this example, the domain name for the distribution is `d1234.cloudfront.net`. (The d in `d1234.cloudfront.net` indicates that this is a web distribution.)

2. Your streaming media bucket holds your media files and is the origin server for an RTMP distribution. In this example, the domain name for the distribution is `s5678.cloudfront.net`. (The s in `s5678.cloudfront.net` indicates that this is an RTMP distribution.)

When you configure CloudFront to distribute media files, CloudFront uses Adobe Flash Media Server as the streaming server and streams your media files using Adobe's Real-Time Messaging Protocol (RTMP). CloudFront accepts RTMP requests over port 1935 and port 80.

CloudFront supports the following variants of the RTMP protocol:

- **RTMP** – Adobe's Real-Time Message Protocol
- **RTMPT** – Adobe streaming tunneled over HTTP
- **RTMPE** – Adobe encrypted
- **RTMPTE** – Adobe encrypted tunneled over HTTP

# Task List for Streaming Media Files Using RTMP

This section summarizes the general process for configuring on-demand streaming using the Adobe RTMP protocol for any media player. If you're using JW Player for your media player, see On-Demand Video Streaming Using CloudFront and JW Player.

The following task list summarizes the process for creating a web distribution.

**To Create an RTMP Distribution**

1. Create an Amazon S3 bucket for your media files. If you are using a different Amazon S3 bucket for your media player, create an Amazon S3 bucket for the media player files, too.

   The names of your buckets must be all lowercase and cannot contain spaces.

2. Choose and configure a media player to play your media files. For more information, refer to the documentation for the media player.

3. Upload the files for your media player to the origin from which you want CloudFront to get the files. If you are using an Amazon S3 bucket as the origin for the media player, make the files (not the bucket) publicly readable.

4. Create a web distribution for your media player. (You can also use an existing distribution.) For more information, see Task List for Creating a Web Distribution.

5. Upload your media files to the Amazon S3 bucket that you created for the media files, and make the content (not the bucket) publicly readable. **Important**
   Media files in a Flash Video container must include the .flv filename extension, or the media will not stream.

   You can put media player files and media files in the same bucket.

6. Create an RTMP distribution for your media files:

   - For more information about creating a web distribution using the CloudFront console, see Creating an RTMP Distribution Using the CloudFront Console.
   - For information about creating a web distribution using the CloudFront API, go to CreateStreamingDistribution in the *Amazon CloudFront API Reference*.

7. Configure your media player. For more information, see Configuring the Media Player.

If you have trouble getting your content to play, see Troubleshooting RTMP Distributions.

195

# Creating an RTMP Distribution Using the CloudFront Console

The following procedure explains how to create an RTMP distribution using the CloudFront console. If you want to create an RTMP distribution using the CloudFront API, go to CreateStreamingDistribution in the *Amazon CloudFront API Reference*.

For the current limit on the number of RTMP distributions that you can create for each AWS account, see Amazon CloudFront Limits in the *Amazon Web Services General Reference*. To request a higher limit, go to https://console.aws.amazon.com/support/home#/case/create?issueType=service-limit-increase&limitType=service-code-cloudfront-distributions.

**To create an RTMP distribution using the CloudFront console**

1. Sign in to the AWS Management Console and open the CloudFront console at https://console.aws.amazon.com/cloudfront/.

2. Click **Create Distribution**.

3. On the first page of the **Create Distribution Wizard**, in the **RTMP** section, choose **Get Started**.

4. Specify settings for the distribution. For more information, see Values that You Specify When You Create or Update an RTMP Distribution.

5. Click **Create Distribution**.

6. After CloudFront creates your distribution, the value of the **Status** column for your distribution will change from **InProgress** to **Deployed**. If you chose to enable the distribution, it will then be ready to process requests. This should take less than 15 minutes.

   The domain name that CloudFront assigns to your distribution appears in the list of distributions. The domain name also appears on the **General** tab for a selected distribution.

# Values that You Specify When You Create or Update an RTMP Distribution

To stream media files using CloudFront, you create an RTMP distribution and specify the following values.

**Topics**

- Origin Domain Name (Amazon S3 Bucket)
- Restrict Bucket Access (Amazon S3 Only)
- Origin Access Identity (Amazon S3 Only)
- Comment for New Identity(Amazon S3 Only)
- Your Identities (Amazon S3 Only)
- Grant Read Permissions on Bucket (Amazon S3 Only)
- Price Class
- Alternate Domain Names (CNAMEs)
- Logging
- Bucket for Logs
- Log Prefix
- Comment
- Distribution State
- Restrict Viewer Access (Use Signed URLs)
- Trusted Signers
- AWS Account Numbers

## Origin Domain Name (Amazon S3 Bucket)

The DNS domain name of the Amazon S3 bucket from which you want CloudFront to get objects for this origin, for example, `myawsbucket.s3.amazonaws.com`. In the CloudFront console, click in the **Origin Domain Name** field, and a list enumerates the Amazon S3 buckets that are associated with the current AWS account. To use a bucket from a different AWS account, type the domain name of the bucket in the following format:

```
bucket-name.s3.amazonaws.com
```

If your bucket is in the US Standard region and you want Amazon S3 to route requests to a facility in Northern Virginia, use the following format:

```
bucket-name.s3-external-1.amazonaws.com
```

If you configured Amazon S3 Transfer Acceleration for your bucket, do not specify the `s3-accelerate` endpoint for **Origin Domain Name**.

The files must be publicly readable unless you secure your content in Amazon S3 by using a CloudFront origin access identity. For more information, see Using an Origin Access Identity to Restrict Access to Your Amazon S3 Content.

**Important**
The bucket name must conform to DNS naming requirements. For more information, go to Bucket Restrictions and Limitations in the *Amazon Simple Storage Service Developer Guide.*

When you change the bucket from which CloudFront gets objects for the current origin, CloudFront immediately begins replicating the change to CloudFront edge locations. Until the distribution configuration is updated in a given edge location, CloudFront will continue to forward requests to the previous Amazon S3 bucket. As soon as the distribution configuration is updated in that edge location, CloudFront begins to forward requests to the new Amazon S3 bucket.

Changing the bucket does not require CloudFront to repopulate edge caches with objects from the new origin. As long as the viewer requests in your application have not changed, CloudFront will continue to serve objects that are already in an edge cache until the TTL on each object expires or until seldom-requested objects are evicted.

For more information, see Using an Amazon S3 Bucket as the Origin for an RTMP Distribution.

## Restrict Bucket Access (Amazon S3 Only)

Click **Yes** if you want to require end users to access objects in an Amazon S3 bucket by using only CloudFront URLs, not by using Amazon S3 URLs. Then specify the applicable values.

Click **No** if you want end users to be able to access objects using either CloudFront URLs or Amazon S3 URLs.

For more information, see Using an Origin Access Identity to Restrict Access to Your Amazon S3 Content.

## Origin Access Identity (Amazon S3 Only)

If you chose **Yes** for **Restrict Bucket Access**, choose whether to create a new origin access identity or use an existing one that is associated with your AWS account. If you already have an origin access identity, we recommend that you reuse it to simplify maintenance. For more information about origin access identities, see Using an Origin Access Identity to Restrict Access to Your Amazon S3 Content.

## Comment for New Identity(Amazon S3 Only)

If you chose **Create a New Identity** for **Origin Access Identity**, enter a comment that identifies the new origin access identity. CloudFront will create the origin access identity when you create this distribution.

## Your Identities (Amazon S3 Only)

If you chose **Use an Existing Identity** for **Origin Access Identity**, choose the origin access identity that you want to use. You cannot use an origin access identity that is associated with another AWS account.

## Grant Read Permissions on Bucket (Amazon S3 Only)

If you want CloudFront to automatically grant the origin access identity the permission to read objects in your Amazon S3 bucket, click **Yes, Update Bucket Policy**.

**Important**
If you click **Yes, Update Bucket Policy**, CloudFront updates the bucket policy to grant the specified origin access identity the permission to read objects in your bucket. However, CloudFront does not remove existing permissions in the bucket policy or permissions on individual objects. If users currently have permission to access the objects in your bucket using Amazon S3 URLs, they will still have that permission after CloudFront updates your bucket policy. To view or change the existing bucket policy and the existing permissions on the objects in your bucket, use a method provided by Amazon S3. For more information, see Granting the Origin Access Identity Permission to Read Objects in Your Amazon S3 Bucket.

If you want to update permissions manually, for example, if you want to update ACLs on your objects instead of updating bucket permissions, click **No, I will Update Permissions**.

## Price Class

The price class that corresponds with the maximum price that you want to pay for CloudFront service. By default, CloudFront serves your objects from edge locations in all CloudFront regions.

For more information about price classes and about how your choice of price class affects CloudFront performance for your distribution, see Choosing the Price Class for a CloudFront Distribution. For information about CloudFront pricing, including how price classes map to CloudFront regions, go to Amazon CloudFront Pricing.

## Alternate Domain Names (CNAMEs)

Optional. You can associate one or more CNAME aliases with a distribution so that you can use your domain name (for example, example.com) in the URLs for your objects instead of using the domain name that CloudFront assigned when you created your distribution. For more information, see Adding and Moving Alternate Domain Names (CNAMEs).

## Logging

Whether you want CloudFront to log information about each request for an object and store the log files in an Amazon S3 bucket. You can enable or disable logging at any time. There is no extra charge if you enable logging, but you accrue the usual Amazon S3 charges for storing and accessing the files in an Amazon S3 bucket. You can delete the logs at any time. For more information about CloudFront access logs, see Access Logs.

## Bucket for Logs

If you chose **On** for **Logging**, the Amazon S3 bucket that you want CloudFront to store access logs in, for example, `myawslogbucket.s3.amazonaws.com`. If you enable logging, CloudFront records information about each end-user request for an object and stores the files in the specified Amazon S3 bucket. You can enable or disable logging at any time. For more information about CloudFront access logs, see Access Logs.

**Note**
You must have the permissions required to get and update Amazon S3 bucket ACLs, and the S3 ACL for the bucket must grant you `FULL_CONTROL`. This allows CloudFront to give the awsdatafeeds account permission to save log files in the bucket. For more information, see Permissions Required to Configure Logging and to Access Your Log Files.

## Log Prefix

Optional. If you chose **On** for **Logging**, specify the string, if any, that you want CloudFront to prefix to the access log filenames for this distribution, for example, `exampleprefix/`. The trailing slash ( / ) is optional but recommended to simplify browsing your log files. For more information about CloudFront access logs, see Access Logs.

## Comment

Optional. When you create a distribution, you can include a comment of up to 128 characters. You can update the comment at any time.

## Distribution State

When you create a distribution, you must specify whether you want the distribution to be enabled or disabled after it's created:

- *Enabled* means that as soon as the distribution is fully deployed you can deploy links that use the distribution's domain name and end users can retrieve content. Whenever a distribution is enabled, CloudFront accepts and processes any end-user requests for content that use the domain name associated with that distribution.

  When you create, modify, or delete a CloudFront distribution, it takes time for your changes to propagate to the CloudFront database. An immediate request for information about a distribution might not show the change. Propagation usually completes within minutes, but a high system load or network partition might increase this time.

- *Disabled* means that even though the distribution might be deployed and ready to use, end users can't use it. When a distribution is disabled, CloudFront doesn't accept any end-user requests that use the domain name associated with that distribution. Until you switch the distribution from disabled to enabled (by updating the distribution's configuration), no one can use it.

You can toggle a distribution between disabled and enabled as often as you want. For information about updating a distribution's configuration, see Viewing and Updating CloudFront Distributions.

## Restrict Viewer Access (Use Signed URLs)

If you want requests for objects served by this distribution to use public URLs, click **No**. If you want requests to use signed URLs, click **Yes**. Then specify the AWS accounts that you want to use to create signed URLs; these accounts are known as trusted signers.

For more information about trusted signers, see Specifying the AWS Accounts That Can Create Signed URLs and Signed Cookies (Trusted Signers).

## Trusted Signers

Choose which AWS accounts you want to use as trusted signers for this distribution:

- **Self:** Use the account with which you're currently signed into the AWS Management Console as a trusted signer. If you're currently signed in as an IAM user, the associated AWS account is added as a trusted signer.
- **Specify Accounts:** Enter account numbers for trusted signers in the **AWS Account Numbers** field.

To create signed URLs, an AWS account must have at least one active CloudFront key pair.

**Important**
If you're updating a distribution that you're already using to distribute content, add trusted signers only when you're ready to start generating signed URLs for your objects. After you add trusted signers to a distribution, users must use signed URLs to access the objects served by this distribution.

## AWS Account Numbers

If you want to create signed URLs using AWS accounts in addition to or instead of the current account, enter one AWS account number per line in this field. Note the following:

- The accounts that you specify must have at least one active CloudFront key pair. For more information, see Creating CloudFront Key Pairs for Your Trusted Signers.
- You can't create CloudFront key pairs for IAM users, so you can't use IAM users as trusted signers.
- For information about how to get the AWS account number for an account, see How Do I Get Security Credentials? in the *Amazon Web Services General Reference*.
- If you enter the account number for the current account, CloudFront automatically checks the **Self** checkbox and removes the account number from the **AWS Account Numbers** list.

# Values that CloudFront Displays in the Console When You Create or Update an RTMP Distribution

When you create a new RTMP distribution or update an existing distribution, CloudFront displays the following information in the CloudFront console.

**Note**
Active trusted signers, the AWS accounts that have an active CloudFront key pair and can be used to create valid signed URLs, are currently not visible in the CloudFront console.

## Distribution ID

When you perform an action on a distribution using the CloudFront API, you use the distribution ID to specify which distribution you want to perform the action on, for example, `EDFDVBD6EXAMPLE`. You can't change the distribution ID.

## Status

The possible status values for a distribution are listed in the following table.

| Value | Description |
|---|---|
| **InProgress** | The distribution is still being created or updated. |
| **Deployed** | The distribution has been created or updated and the changes have been fully propagated through the CloudFront system. |

In addition to ensuring that the status for a distribution is **Deployed**, you must enable the distribution before end users can use CloudFront to access your content. For more information, see Distribution State.

## Last Modified

The date and time that the distribution was last modified, using ISO 8601 format, for example, 2012-05-19T19:37:58Z. For more information, go to http://www.w3.org/TR/NOTE-datetime.

## Domain Name

You use the distribution's domain name in the links to your objects, unless you're using alternate domain names (CNAMEs). For example, if your distribution's domain name is `d111111abcdef8.cloudfront.net`, the link to the example `/images/image.jpg` file would be `http://d111111abcdef8.cloudfront.net/images/image.jpg`. You can't change the CloudFront domain name for your distribution. For more information about CloudFront URLs for links to your objects, see Format of URLs for Objects.

If you specified one or more alternate domain names (CNAMEs), you can use your own domain names for links to your objects instead of using the CloudFront domain name. For more information about CNAMEs, see Alternate Domain Names (CNAMEs).

**Note**

CloudFront domain names are unique. Your distribution's domain name was never used for a previous distribution and will never be reused for another distribution in the future.

# Configuring the Media Player

To play a media file, you must configure the media player with the correct path to the file. How you configure the media depends on which media player you're using and how you're using it.

When you configure the media player, the path you specify to the media file must contain the characters `cfx/st` immediately after the domain name, for example:

`rtmp://s5c39gqb8ow64r.cloudfront.net/cfx/st/mediafile.flv`.

**Note**
CloudFront follows Adobe's FMS naming requirements. Different players have their own rules about how to specify streams. The example above is for JW Player. Check your player's documentation. For example, Adobe's Flash Media Server does not allow the `.flv` extension to be present on the play path. Many players remove the `.flv` extension for you.

Your media player might ask for the path separate from the file name. For example, with the JW Player wizard, you specify a `streamer` and `file` variable:

- **streamer** – `rtmp://s5c39gqb8ow64r.cloudfront.net/cfx/st` (with no trailing slash)
- **file** – `mediafile.flv`

If you've stored the media files in a directory in your bucket (for example, `videos/mediafile.flv`), then the variables for JW Player would be:

- **streamer** – `rtmp://s5c39gqb8ow64r.cloudfront.net/cfx/st` (with no trailing slash)
- **file** – `videos/mediafile.flv`

To use the JW Player wizard, go to the Setup Wizard page on the JW Player website.

## MPEG Files

To serve MP3 audio files or H.264/MPEG-4 video files, you might need to prefix the file name with `mp3:` or `mp4:`. Some media players can be configured to add the prefix automatically. The media player might also require you to specify the file name without the file extension (for example, `magicvideo` instead of `magicvideo.mp4`).

# Using an Amazon S3 Bucket as the Origin for an RTMP Distribution

When you create a distribution, you specify where CloudFront gets the files that it distributes to edge locations. For an RTMP distribution, you must use an Amazon S3 bucket; custom origins are not supported. To get your objects into your bucket, you can use any method supported by Amazon S3, for example, the Amazon S3 API or a third-party tool. You can create a hierarchy in your bucket just as you would with any other Amazon S3 bucket. You incur regular Amazon S3 charges for storing the objects in the bucket. For more information about the charges to use CloudFront, see CloudFront Reports.

Using an existing Amazon S3 bucket as your CloudFront origin server doesn't change the bucket in any way; you can still use it as you normally would to store and access Amazon S3 objects (at the normal Amazon S3 prices).

You can use the same Amazon S3 bucket for both RTMP and web distributions.

**Note**
After you create an RTMP distribution, you can't change its origin server. If you need to change the Amazon S3 bucket for an RTMP distribution, you must create a new distribution that uses the new bucket and update either your links or your DNS records to use the domain name for the new distribution. You can then delete the original distribution. For more information, see Deleting a Distribution.

When you specify the name of the Amazon S3 bucket that you want CloudFront to get objects from, you generally use the following format:

`bucket-name.s3.amazonaws.com`

If your bucket is in the US Standard region and you want Amazon S3 to route requests to a facility in Northern Virginia, use the following format:

`bucket-name.s3-external-1.amazonaws.com`

Do not specify the name of the bucket using the following values:

- The Amazon S3 path style, `s3.amazonaws.com/bucket-name`
- The Amazon S3 CNAME, if any

**Important**
For your bucket to work with CloudFront, the name must conform to DNS naming requirements. For more information, go to Bucket Restrictions and Limitations in the *Amazon Simple Storage Service Developer Guide*.

# Creating Multiple RTMP Distributions for an Origin Server

You typically create one RTMP distribution per Amazon S3 bucket, but you can choose to create multiple RTMP distributions for the same bucket. For example, if you had two distributions for an Amazon S3 bucket, you could reference a single media file using either distribution. In this case, if you had a media file called `media.flv` in your origin server, CloudFront would work with each distribution as though it referenced an individual `media.flv` object: one `media.flv` accessible through one distribution, and another `media.flv` accessible through the other distribution.

# Restricting Access Using Crossdomain.xml

The Adobe Flash Media Server `crossdomain.xml` file specifies which domains can access media files in a particular domain. CloudFront supplies a default file that allows all domains to access the media files in your RTMP distribution, and you cannot change this behavior. If you include a more restrictive `crossdomain.xml` file in your Amazon S3 bucket, CloudFront ignores it.

# Error Codes for RTMP Distributions

The following table lists the error codes that CloudFront can send to your media player. The errors are part of the string returned with `Event.info.application.message` or `Event.info.description`.

| Error | Description |
| --- | --- |
| `DistributionNotFound` | The distribution was not found. |
| `DistributionTypeMismatch` | The distribution is not an RTMP distribution. |
| `InvalidInstance` | The instance is invalid. |
| `InvalidURI` | The URI is invalid. |

# Troubleshooting RTMP Distributions

If you're having trouble getting your media files to play, check the following items.

| Item to Check | Description |
| --- | --- |
| Separate distributions for the media player files and media files | The media player must be served by a regular HTTP distribution (for example, domain name d111111abcdef8.cloudfront.net), and media files must be served by an RTMP distribution (for example, domain name s5c39gqb8ow64r.cloudfront.net). Make sure you're not using the same distribution for both. |
| /cfx/st in the file path | Confirm that the path for the file includes /cfx/st. You don't need to include /cfx/st in the path to the object in the Amazon S3 bucket. For more information, see Configuring the Media Player. |
| File names in the file path | Some media players require that you include the file name extension (for example, mp4:) before the file name in the file path. Some media players also require that you exclude the file name extension (for example, .mp4) from the file path. For more information, see MPEG Files. The names of the media files in your Amazon S3 bucket must always include the applicable file name extension. |
| Port 1935 on your firewall | Adobe Flash Media Server uses port 1935 for RTMP. Make sure your firewall has this port open. If it doesn't, the typical message returned is "Unable to play video." You can also switch to RTMPT to tunnel over HTTP using port 80. |
| Adobe Flash Player messaging | By default, the Adobe Flash Player won't display a message if the video file it's trying to play is missing. Instead, it waits for the file to show up. You might want to change this behavior to give your end users a better experience. To instead have the player send a message if the video is missing, use play("vid",0,-1) instead of play("vid"). |

# Working with Objects

**Topics**

- Format of URLs for Objects
- How CloudFront Processes HTTP and HTTPS Requests
- Increasing the Proportion of Requests that Are Served from CloudFront Edge Caches
- Configuring CloudFront to Cache Based on Query String Parameters
- Configuring CloudFront to Cache Objects Based on Cookies
- Configuring CloudFront to Cache Objects Based on Request Headers
- Forwarding Custom Headers to Your Origin (Web Distributions Only)
- Adding, Removing, or Replacing Objects in a Distribution
- Customizing Error Responses
- How CloudFront Processes Partial Requests for an Object (Range GETs)
- Specifying a Default Root Object (Web Distributions Only)
- Serving Compressed Files

This section describes how you work with objects in CloudFront.

# Format of URLs for Objects

The domain name that you use in the URLs for objects on your web pages or in your web application can be either of the following:

- The domain name, such as `d111111abcdef8.cloudfront.net`, that CloudFront automatically assigns when you create a distribution
- Your own domain name, such as `example.com`

For example, you might use one of the following URLs to return the file `image.jpg`:

`http://d111111abcdef8.cloudfront.net/images/image.jpg`

`http://example.com/images/image.jpg`

You use the same URL format whether you store the content in Amazon S3 buckets or at a custom origin, like one of your own web servers.

**Note**
The URL format depends in part on the value that you specify for **Origin Path** in your distribution. This value gives CloudFront a top directory path for your objects. For more information about setting the origin path when you create a web distribution, see Origin Path.

For more information about URL formats, see the following sections.

**Topics**

- Using Your Own Domain Name (Example.com)
- Using a Trailing Slash (/) in URLs
- Creating URLs for Streaming
- Creating Signed URLs for Restricted Content

## Using Your Own Domain Name (Example.com)

Instead of using the default domain name that CloudFront assigns for you when you create a distribution, you can add an alternate domain name that's easier to work with, like `example.com`. By setting up your own domain name with CloudFront, you can use a URL like this for objects in your distribution:

`http://example.com/images/image.jpg`

If you plan to use HTTPS between viewers and CloudFront, see Using Alternate Domain Names and HTTPS.

## Using a Trailing Slash (/) in URLs

When you specify URLs for directories in your CloudFront distribution, choose either to always use a trailing slash or to never use a trailing slash. For example, choose only one of the following formats for all of your URLs:

`http://d111111abcdef8.cloudfront.net/images/`

`http://d111111abcdef8.cloudfront.net/images`

**Why does it matter?**

Both formats work to link to CloudFront objects, but being consistent can help prevent issues when you want to invalidate a directory later. CloudFront stores URLs exactly as they are defined, including trailing slashes. So if your format is inconsistent, you'll need to invalidate directory URLs with and without the slash, to ensure that CloudFront removes the directory.

It's inconvenient to have to invalidate both URL formats, and it can lead to additional costs. That's because if you must double up invalidations to cover both types of URLs, you might reach the limit for free invalidations for the month. And if that happens, you'll have to pay for all the invalidations, even if only one format for each directory URL exists in CloudFront.

## Creating URLs for Streaming

If your CloudFront distribution serves streaming content, you must include additional characters in the URLs for your objects. For more information, see Configuring the Media Player.

## Creating Signed URLs for Restricted Content

If you have content that you want to restrict access to, you can create signed URLs. For example, if you want to distribute your content only to users who have authenticated, you can create URLs that are valid only for a specified time period or that are available only from a specified IP address. For more information, see Serving Private Content through CloudFront.

# How CloudFront Processes HTTP and HTTPS Requests

For Amazon S3 origins, CloudFront accepts requests in both HTTP and HTTPS protocols for objects in a CloudFront distribution by default. CloudFront then forwards the requests to your Amazon S3 bucket using the same protocol in which the requests were made.

For custom origins, when you create your distribution, you can specify how CloudFront accesses your origin: HTTP only, or matching the protocol that is used by the viewer. For more information about how CloudFront handles HTTP and HTTPS requests for custom origins, see Protocols.

For information about how to restrict your web distribution so that end users can only access objects using HTTPS, see Using HTTPS with CloudFront. (This option doesn't apply to RTMP distributions, which use the RTMP protocol.)

**Note**
The charge for HTTPS requests is higher than the charge for HTTP requests. For more information about billing rates, go to the CloudFront pricing plan.

# Increasing the Proportion of Requests that Are Served from Cloud-Front Edge Caches

One of the purposes of using CloudFront is to reduce the number of requests that your origin server responds to. This reduces the load on your origin server and also reduces latency because more objects are served from CloudFront edge locations, which are closer to your users. The more requests that CloudFront is able to serve from edge caches as a proportion of all requests (the greater the cache hit ratio), the fewer requests that CloudFront needs to forward to your origin to get the latest version or a unique version of an object.

You can view the percentage of viewer requests that are hits, misses, and errors in the CloudFront console. For more information, see CloudFront Cache Statistics Reports in the *Amazon CloudFront Developer Guide.*

The following sections explain how to improve your cache hit ratio.

**Topics**

- Specifying How Long CloudFront Caches Your Objects
- Caching Based on Query String Parameters
- Caching Based on Cookie Values
- Caching Based on Request Headers
- Serving Media Content by Using HTTP

## Specifying How Long CloudFront Caches Your Objects

To increase your cache hit ratio, you can configure your origin to add a `Cache-Control max-age` directive to your objects, and specify the longest practical value for `max-age`. The shorter the cache duration, the more frequently CloudFront forwards another request to your origin to determine whether the object has changed and, if so, to get the latest version. For more information, see Specifying How Long Objects Stay in a CloudFront Edge Cache (Expiration).

## Caching Based on Query String Parameters

If you configure CloudFront to cache based on query string parameters, you can improve caching if you do the following:

- Configure CloudFront to forward only the query string parameters for which your origin will return unique objects.
- Use the same case (uppercase or lowercase) for all instances of the same parameter. For example, if one request contains `parameter1=A` and another contains `parameter1=a`, CloudFront forwards separate requests to your origin when a request contains `parameter1=A` and when a request contains `parameter1=a`. CloudFront then separately caches the corresponding objects returned by your origin separately even if the objects are identical. If you use just `A` or `a`, CloudFront forwards fewer requests to your origin.
- List parameters in the same order. As with differences in case, if one request for an object contains the query string `parameter1=a&parameter2=b` and another request for the same object contains `parameter2=b&parameter1=a`, CloudFront forwards both requests to your origin and separately caches the corresponding objects even if they're identical. If you always use the same order for parameters, CloudFront forwards fewer requests to your origin.

For more information, see Configuring CloudFront to Cache Based on Query String Parameters. If you want to review the query strings that CloudFront forwards to your origin, enable CloudFront access logs and see the values in the `cs-uri-query` column of your log files. For more information, see Access Logs.

## Caching Based on Cookie Values

If you configure CloudFront to cache based on cookie values, you can improve caching if you do the following:

- Configure CloudFront to forward only specified cookies instead of forwarding all cookies. For the cookies that you configure CloudFront to forward to your origin, CloudFront forwards every combination of cookie name and value, and separately caches the objects that your origin returns, even if they're all identical.

  For example, suppose that viewers include two cookies in every request, that each cookie has three possible values, and that all combinations of cookie values are possible. CloudFront forwards up to six different requests to your origin for each object. If your origin returns different versions of an object based on only one of the cookies, then CloudFront is forwarding more requests to your origin than necessary and is needlessly caching multiple identical versions of the object.

- Create separate cache behaviors for static and dynamic content, and configure CloudFront to forward cookies to your origin only for dynamic content.

  For example, suppose you have just one cache behavior for your distribution and that you're using the distribution both for dynamic content, such as .js files, and for .css files that rarely change. CloudFront caches separate versions of your .css files based on cookie values, so each CloudFront edge location forwards a request to your origin for every new cookie value or combination of cookie values.

  If you create a cache behavior for which the path pattern is *.css and for which CloudFront doesn't cache based on cookie values, then CloudFront forwards requests for .css files to your origin only for the first request that an edge location receives for a given .css file and for the first request after a .css file expires.

- If possible, create separate cache behaviors for dynamic content for which cookie values are unique for each user (such as a user ID) and dynamic content that varies based on a smaller number of unique values.

For more information, see Configuring CloudFront to Cache Objects Based on Cookies. If you want to review the cookies that CloudFront forwards to your origin, enable CloudFront access logs and see the values in the `cs(Cookie)` column of your log files. For more information, see Access Logs.

## Caching Based on Request Headers

If you configure CloudFront to cache based on request headers, you can improve caching if you do the following:

- Configure CloudFront to forward and cache based only specified headers instead of forwarding and caching based on all headers. For the headers that you specify, CloudFront forwards every combination of header name and value and separately caches the objects that your origin returns even if they're all identical.
  **Note**
  CloudFront always forwards to your origin the headers specified in the following topics:
  How CloudFront Processes and Forwards Requests to Your Amazon S3 Origin Server > HTTP Request Headers That CloudFront Removes or Updates How CloudFront Processes and Forwards Requests to Your Custom Origin Server > HTTP Request Headers and CloudFront Behavior (Custom and S3 Origins)

  When you configure CloudFront to cache based on request headers, you don't change the headers that CloudFront forwards, only whether CloudFront caches objects based on the header values.

- Try to avoid caching based on request headers that have large numbers of unique values.

  For example, if you want to serve different sizes of an image based on the user's device, then don't configure CloudFront to cache based on the `User-Agent` header, which has an enormous number of possible values. Instead, configure CloudFront to cache based on the CloudFront device-type headers `CloudFront-Is-Desktop-Viewer`, `CloudFront-Is-Mobile-Viewer`, `CloudFront-Is-SmartTV-Viewer`, and `CloudFront-Is-Tablet-Viewer`. In addition, if you're returning the same version of the image for tablets and desktops, then forward only the `CloudFront-Is-Tablet-Viewer` header, not the `CloudFront-Is-Desktop-Viewer` header.

For more information, see Configuring CloudFront to Cache Objects Based on Request Headers.

214

## Serving Media Content by Using HTTP

When you use HTTP to serve media content, we recommend that you use an HTTP-based dynamic streaming protocol such as Apple HTTP Dynamic Streaming (Apple HDS), Apple HTTP Live Streaming (Apple HLS), Microsoft Smooth Streaming, or MPEG-DASH. For dynamic-streaming protocols, a video is divided into a lot of small segments that are typically just a few seconds long each. If your users commonly stop watching before the end of a video (for example, because they close their viewer during the credits), CloudFront has still cached all of the small segments up to that point in the video. If you're using a protocol for which a video is served in a single, large file and a user stops watching before the end, CloudFront might not cache the entire video, and it might need to request the video from your origin again the next time that CloudFront receives a request for it.

# Configuring CloudFront to Cache Based on Query String Parameters

Some web applications use query strings to send information to the origin. A query string is the part of a web request that appears after a ? character; the string can contain one or more parameters separated by & characters. In the following example, the query string includes two parameters, *color=red* and *size=large*:

`http://d111111abcdef8.cloudfront.net/images/image.jpg?color=red&size=large`

For web distributions, you can choose whether you want CloudFront to forward query strings to your origin and, if so, whether to cache your content based on all parameters or on selected parameters.

Suppose your website is available in five languages. The directory structure and file names for all five versions of the website are identical. As a user views your website, requests that are forwarded to CloudFront include a language query string parameter based on the language that the user chose. You can configure CloudFront to forward query strings to the origin and to cache based on the language parameter. If you configure your web server to return the version of a given page that corresponds with the selected language, CloudFront will cache each language version separately, based on the value of the language query string parameter.

In this example, if the main page for your website is main.html, the following five requests will cause CloudFront to cache main.html five times, once for each value of the language query string parameter:

- `http://d111111abcdef8.cloudfront.net/main.html?language=de`
- `http://d111111abcdef8.cloudfront.net/main.html?language=en`
- `http://d111111abcdef8.cloudfront.net/main.html?language=es`
- `http://d111111abcdef8.cloudfront.net/main.html?language=fr`
- `http://d111111abcdef8.cloudfront.net/main.html?language=jp`

Note the following:

- For RTMP distributions, you cannot configure CloudFront to forward query string parameters to your origin. Before CloudFront forwards a request to the origin server, it removes any query string parameters.
- Some HTTP servers don't process query string parameters and, therefore, don't return different versions of an object based on parameter values. For these origins, if you configure CloudFront to forward query string parameters to the origin, CloudFront will still cache based on the parameter values even though the origin returns identical versions of the object to CloudFront for every parameter value.
- You must use the & character as the delimiter between query string parameters. If you use a different delimiter, caching depends on which parameters you want CloudFront to use as a basis for caching and the order in which they appear in the query string. The following examples show what happens if you configure CloudFront to cache based only on the `color` parameter:
    - In the following request, CloudFront caches your content based on the value of the `color` parameter, but CloudFront interprets the value as *red;size=large*:
    `http://d111111abcdef8.cloudfront.net/images/image.jpg?color=red;size=large`
    - In the following request, CloudFront caches your content but doesn't base caching on the query string parameters. This is because you configured CloudFront to cache based on the `color` parameter, but CloudFront interprets the following string as containing only a `size` parameter that has a value of *large;color=red*:
    `http://d111111abcdef8.cloudfront.net/images/image.jpg?size=large;color=red`

You can configure CloudFront do to one of the following:

- Don't forward query strings to the origin at all. If you don't forward query strings, CloudFront doesn't cache based on query string parameters.
- Forward query strings to the origin, and cache based on all parameters in the query string.
- Forward query strings to the origin, and cache based on specified parameters in the query string.

For more information, see Optimizing Caching.

**Topics**

- Console and API Settings for Query String Forwarding and Caching

- Optimizing Caching
- Query String Parameters and CloudFront Access Logs

## Console and API Settings for Query String Forwarding and Caching

To configure query string forwarding and caching in the CloudFront console, see the following settings in Values That You Specify When You Create or Update a Web Distribution:

- Query String Forwarding and Caching
- Query String Whitelist

To configure query string forwarding and caching with the CloudFront API, see the following settings in DistributionConfig Complex Type and in DistributionConfigWithTags Complex Type in the *Amazon CloudFront API Reference*:

- `QueryString`
- `QueryStringCacheKeys`

## Optimizing Caching

When you configure CloudFront to cache based on query string parameters, here's how you can reduce the number of requests that CloudFront forwards to your origin, which reduces the load on your origin server and also reduces latency because more objects are served from CloudFront edge locations.

**Cache Based Only on Parameters for Which Your Origin Returns Different Versions of an Object**
For each query string parameter that your web application forwards to CloudFront, CloudFront forwards requests to your origin for every parameter value and caches a separate version of the object for every parameter value. This is true even if your origin always returns the same object regardless of the parameter value. For multiple parameters, the number of requests and the number of objects multiply: if requests for an object include two parameters that each have three different values, CloudFront will cache six versions of that object, assuming you follow the other recommendations in this section.
We recommend that you configure CloudFront to cache based only on the query string parameters for which your origin returns different versions, and that you carefully consider the merits of caching based on each parameter. For example, suppose you have a retail website. You have pictures of a jacket in six different colors, and the jacket comes in ten different sizes. The pictures that you have of the jacket show the different colors but not the different sizes. To optimize caching, you should configure CloudFront to cache based only on the color parameter, not on the size parameter. This increases the likelihood that CloudFront can serve a request from the cache, which improves performance and reduces the load on your origin.

**Always List Parameters in the Same Order**
The order of parameters matters in query strings. In the following example, the query strings are identical except that the parameters are in a different order. This will cause CloudFront to forward two separate requests for image.jpg to your origin and to cache two separate versions of the object:

- `http://d111111abcdef8.cloudfront.net/images/image.jpg?color=red&size=large`
- `http://d111111abcdef8.cloudfront.net/images/image.jpg?size=large&color=red` We recommend that you always list parameter names in the same order, such as alphabetical order.

**Always Use the Same Case for Parameter Names and Values**
CloudFront considers the case of parameter names and values when caching based on query string parameters. In the following example, the query strings are identical except for the case of parameter names and values. This will cause CloudFront to forward four separate requests for image.jpg to your origin and to cache four separate versions of the object:

- `http://d111111abcdef8.cloudfront.net/images/image.jpg?color=red`
- `http://d111111abcdef8.cloudfront.net/images/image.jpg?color=Red`
- `http://d111111abcdef8.cloudfront.net/images/image.jpg?Color=red`

- `http://d111111abcdef8.cloudfront.net/images/image.jpg?Color=Red` We recommend that you use case consistently for parameter names and values, such as all lowercase.

**Don't Use Parameter Names that Conflict with Signed URLs**

If you're using signed URLs to restrict access to your content (if you added trusted signers to your distribution), CloudFront removes the following query string parameters before forwarding the rest of the URL to your origin:

- `Expires`
- `Key-Pair-Id`
- `Policy`
- `Signature` If you're using signed URLs and you want to configure CloudFront to forward query strings to your origin, your own query string parameters cannot be named `Expires`, `Key-Pair-Id`, `Policy`, or `Signature`.

## Query String Parameters and CloudFront Access Logs

For web and RTMP distributions, if you enable logging, CloudFront logs the full URL, including query string parameters. For web distributions, this is true regardless of whether you have configured CloudFront to forward query strings to the origin. For more information about CloudFront logging, see Access Logs.

# Configuring CloudFront to Cache Objects Based on Cookies

For web distributions, you can choose whether you want CloudFront to forward cookies to your origin and to cache separate versions of your objects based on cookie values in viewer requests.

For Real Time Messaging Protocol (RTMP) distributions, you cannot configure CloudFront to process cookies. When CloudFront requests an object from the origin server, it removes any cookies before forwarding the request to your origin. If your origin returns any cookies along with the object, CloudFront removes them before returning the object to the viewer. For RTMP distributions, CloudFront does not cache cookies in edge caches.

**Important**
Amazon S3 and some HTTP servers do not process cookies. Do not configure CloudFront cache behaviors to forward cookies to an origin that doesn't process cookies, or you'll adversely affect cacheability and, therefore, performance. For more information about cache behaviors, see Cache Behavior Settings.

For HTTP and HTTPS web distributions, you can choose whether you want CloudFront to forward cookies to your origin. For RTMP distributions, you cannot configure CloudFront to process cookies.

For web distributions, CloudFront by default doesn't consider cookies when caching your objects in edge locations. If your origin returns two objects and they differ only by the values in the `Set-Cookie` header, CloudFront caches only one version of the object.

You can configure CloudFront to forward to your origin some or all of the cookies in viewer requests. CloudFront uses the cookies in viewer requests to uniquely identify an object in the cache. For example, suppose that requests for `locations.html` contain a `country` cookie that has a value of either `uk` or `fr`. When you configure CloudFront to cache your objects based on the value of the `country` cookie, CloudFront forwards requests for `locations.html` to the origin and includes the `country` cookie and cookie values. Your origin returns `locations.html`, and CloudFront caches the object once for requests in which the value of the `country` cookie is `uk` and once for requests in which the value is `fr`.

**Note**
If you configure CloudFront to forward cookies to your origin, CloudFront caches based on cookie values. This is true even if your origin ignores the cookie values in the request and, in the previous example, always returns the same version of `locations.html` to CloudFront. As a result, CloudFront forwards more requests to your origin server for the same object, which slows performance and increases the load on your origin server. If your origin server does not vary its response based on the value of a given cookie, we recommend that you do not configure CloudFront to forward that cookie to your origin.

You can configure each cache behavior in a web distribution to do one of the following:

- **Forward all cookies to your origin – ** CloudFront forwards viewer requests to your origin, including all cookies. When your origin returns a response, CloudFront caches the response, and the cookies and cookie values in the viewer request. (If your origin returns cookies that were not in the viewer request, CloudFront does not cache them.) CloudFront returns to the viewer the requested object and all cookies and cookie values, including cookies that were not in the viewer request.

- **Forward a whitelist of cookies that you specify – ** CloudFront removes any cookies that aren't on the whitelist before forwarding requests to your origin. CloudFront caches the response from your origin as well as the specified cookies and their values. (If your origin returns both whitelisted cookies and cookies that aren't on your whitelist, CloudFront caches only the whitelisted cookies.) CloudFront also returns to the viewer the object, including the specified cookies and cookie values. If the response from the origin includes cookies that aren't on the whitelist, CloudFront returns those cookies to the viewer, too.

    For information about specifying wildcards in cookie names, see Whitelist Cookies (Amazon EC2 and Other Custom Origins Only).

    For the current limit on the number of cookie names that you can whitelist for each cache behavior, see Amazon CloudFront Limits in the *Amazon Web Services General Reference*. To request a higher limit, go to https://console.aws.amazon.com/support/home#/case/create?issueType=service-limit-increase&limitType=service-code-cloudfront-distributions.

- **Don't forward cookies to your origin – **CloudFront doesn't cache your objects based on cookie values. In addition, CloudFront removes the `Cookie` header from requests that it forwards to your origin and removes the `Set-Cookie` header from responses that it returns to your viewers.

Note the following about specifying the cookies that you want to forward:

**Access Logs**

If you configure CloudFront to log requests and to log cookies, CloudFront logs all cookies and all cookie attributes, even if you configure CloudFront not to forward cookies to your origin or if you configure CloudFront to forward only a specified list of cookies. For more information about CloudFront logging, see Access Logs.

**Case Sensitivity**

Cookie names and values are both case sensitive. For example, if two cookies for the same object are identical except for case, CloudFront will cache the object twice.

**CloudFront Sorts Cookies**

CloudFront sorts the cookies in natural order by cookie name before forwarding the request to your origin.

**If-Modified-Since and If-None-Match**

`If-Modified-Since` and `If-None-Match` conditional requests are not supported.

**Suspending Caching Based on Cookies**

If you want CloudFront to temporarily stop caching cookies and cookie attributes, configure your origin server to add the following header in responses to CloudFront:
`no-cache="Set-Cookie"`

**Total Length of Cookie Names**

The total number of bytes in all of the cookie names that you configure CloudFront to forward to your origin can't exceed:
`512 (the number of cookies that you're forwarding)`
For example, if you configure CloudFront to forward 10 cookies to your origin, the combined length of the names of the 10 cookies can't exceed 502 bytes (512 – 10). If you configure CloudFront to forward all cookies to your origin, the length of cookie names doesn't matter.

For information about using the CloudFront console to update a distribution so CloudFront forwards cookies to the origin, see Viewing and Updating CloudFront Distributions. For information about using the CloudFront API to update a distribution, see UpdateDistribution in the *Amazon CloudFront API Reference*.

# Configuring CloudFront to Cache Objects Based on Request Headers

For web distributions, CloudFront lets you choose whether you want CloudFront to forward headers to your origin and to cache separate versions of a specified object based on the header values in viewer requests. This allows you to serve different versions of your content based on the device the user is using, the location of the viewer, the language the viewer is using, and a variety of other criteria. For RTMP distributions, you cannot configure CloudFront to cache based on header values.

**Topics**

- Headers and Web Distributions
- Headers and RTMP Distributions

## Headers and Web Distributions

By default, CloudFront doesn't consider headers when caching your objects in edge locations. If your origin returns two objects and they differ only by the values in the request headers, CloudFront caches only one version of the object.

You can configure CloudFront to forward headers to the origin, which causes CloudFront to cache multiple versions of an object based on the values in one or more request headers. To configure CloudFront to cache objects based on the values of specific headers, you specify cache behavior settings for your distribution. For more information, see Cache Based on Selected Request Headers.

For example, suppose viewer requests for `logo.jpg` contain a custom `Product` header that has a value of either `Acme` or `Apex`. When you configure CloudFront to cache your objects based on the value of the `Product` header, CloudFront forwards requests for `logo.jpg` to the origin and includes the `Product` header and header values. CloudFront caches `logo.jpg` once for requests in which the value of the `Product` header is `Acme` and once for requests in which the value is `Apex`.

You can configure each cache behavior in a web distribution to do one of the following:

- Forward all headers to your origin **Important**
  If you configure CloudFront to forward all headers to your origin, CloudFront doesn't cache the objects associated with this cache behavior. Instead, it sends every request to the origin.
- Forward a whitelist of headers that you specify. CloudFront caches your objects based on the values in all of the specified headers. CloudFront also forwards the headers that it forwards by default, but it caches your objects based only on the headers that you specify.
- Forward only the default headers. In this configuration, CloudFront doesn't cache your objects based on the values in the request headers.

For the current limit on the number of headers that you can whitelist for each cache behavior, see Amazon CloudFront Limits in the *Amazon Web Services General Reference*. To request a higher limit, go to https://console.aws.amazon.com/support/home#/case/create?issueType=service-limit-increase&limitType=service-code-cloudfront-distributions.

For information about using the CloudFront console to update a distribution so CloudFront forwards headers to the origin, see Viewing and Updating CloudFront Distributions. For information about using the CloudFront API to update an existing web distribution, see UpdateDistribution in the *Amazon CloudFront API Reference*.

**Topics**

- Selecting the Headers on Which You Want CloudFront to Base Caching
- Configuring CloudFront to Respect Cross-Origin Resource Sharing (CORS) Settings
- Configuring CloudFront to Cache Objects Based on the Device Type
- Configuring CloudFront to Cache Objects Based on the Language of the Viewer
- Configuring CloudFront to Cache Objects Based on the Location of the Viewer
- Configuring CloudFront to Cache Objects Based on the Protocol of the Request

- How Caching Based on Headers Affects Performance
- How the Case of Headers and Header Values Affects Caching
- Headers that CloudFront Returns to the Viewer

**Selecting the Headers on Which You Want CloudFront to Base Caching**

The headers that you can forward to the origin and that CloudFront bases caching on depend on whether your origin is an Amazon S3 bucket or a custom origin.

- **Amazon S3 – **You can configure CloudFront to forward and to cache your objects based on a number of specific headers (see a list of exceptions below). However, we recommend that you avoid whitelisting headers with an Amazon S3 origin unless you need to implement cross-origin resource sharing (CORS) or you want to personalize content by using Lambda@Edge in origin-facing events.

  - To configure CORS, you must forward headers that allow CloudFront to distribute content for websites that are enabled for cross-origin resource sharing (CORS). For more information, see Configuring CloudFront to Respect Cross-Origin Resource Sharing (CORS) Settings.

  - To personalize content by using headers that you forward to your Amazon S3 origin, you write and add Lambda@Edge functions and associate them with your CloudFront distribution to be triggered by an origin-facing event. For more information about working with headers to personalize content, see Personalize Content by Country or Device Type Headers - Examples.

    We recommend that you avoid whitelisting headers that you aren't using to personalize content because forwarding extra headers can reduce your cache hit ratio. That is, CloudFront won't be able to serve as many requests from edge caches, as a proportion of all requests.

- **Custom origin ** – You can configure CloudFront to cache based on the value of any request header except the following:

  - `Accept-Encoding`
  - `Connection`
  - `Cookie` – If you want to forward and cache based on cookies, you use a separate setting in your distribution. For more information, see Configuring CloudFront to Cache Objects Based on Cookies.
  - `Host (for Amazon S3 origins)`
  - `Proxy-Authorization`
  - `TE`
  - `Upgrade`

  You can configure CloudFront to cache objects based on values in the `Date` and `User-Agent` headers, but we don't recommend it. These headers have a lot of possible values, and caching based on their values would cause CloudFront to forward significantly more requests to your origin.

For a full list of HTTP request headers and how CloudFront processes them, see HTTP Request Headers and CloudFront Behavior (Custom and S3 Origins).

**Configuring CloudFront to Respect Cross-Origin Resource Sharing (CORS) Settings**

If you have enabled cross-origin resource sharing (CORS) on an Amazon S3 bucket or a custom origin, you must choose specific headers to forward, to respect the CORS settings. The headers that you must forward differ depending on the origin (Amazon S3 or custom) and whether you want to cache `OPTIONS` responses.

**Amazon S3**

- If you want `OPTIONS` responses to be cached, do the following:
  - Choose the options for default cache behavior settings that enable caching for `OPTIONS` responses.
  - Configure CloudFront to forward the following headers: `Origin`, `Access-Control-Request-Headers`, and `Access-Control-Request-Method`.

- If you don't want `OPTIONS` responses to be cached, configure CloudFront to forward the `Origin` header, together with any other headers required by your origin.

**Custom origins** – Forward the `Origin` header along with any other headers required by your origin.

For more information about CORS and Amazon S3, see Enabling Cross-Origin Resource Sharing in the *Amazon Simple Storage Service Developer Guide.*

## Configuring CloudFront to Cache Objects Based on the Device Type

If you want CloudFront to cache different versions of your objects based on the device a user is using to view your content, configure CloudFront to forward the applicable headers to your custom origin:

- `CloudFront-Is-Desktop-Viewer`
- `CloudFront-Is-Mobile-Viewer`
- `CloudFront-Is-SmartTV-Viewer`
- `CloudFront-Is-Tablet-Viewer`

Based on the value of the `User-Agent` header, CloudFront sets the value of these headers to `true` or `false` before forwarding the request to your origin. If a device falls into more than one category, more than one value might be `true`. For example, for some tablet devices, CloudFront might set both `CloudFront-Is-Mobile-Viewer` and `CloudFront-Is-Tablet-Viewer` to `true`.

## Configuring CloudFront to Cache Objects Based on the Language of the Viewer

If you want CloudFront to cache different versions of your objects based on the language specified in the request, program your application to include the language in the `Accept-Language` header, and configure CloudFront to forward the `Accept-Language` header to your origin.

## Configuring CloudFront to Cache Objects Based on the Location of the Viewer

If you want CloudFront to cache different versions of your objects based on the country that the request came from, configure CloudFront to forward the `CloudFront-Viewer-Country` header to your origin. CloudFront automatically converts the IP address that the request came from into a two-letter country code. For an easy-to-use list of country codes, sortable by code and by country name, see the Wikipedia entry ISO 3166-1 alpha-2.

## Configuring CloudFront to Cache Objects Based on the Protocol of the Request

If you want CloudFront to cache different versions of your objects based on the protocol of the request, HTTP or HTTPS, configure CloudFront to forward the `CloudFront-Forwarded-Proto` header to your origin.

## How Caching Based on Headers Affects Performance

When you configure CloudFront to cache based on one or more headers and the headers have more than one possible value, CloudFront forwards more requests to your origin server for the same object. This slows performance and increases the load on your origin server. If your origin server returns the same object regardless of the value of a given header, we recommend that you don't configure CloudFront to cache based on that header.

If you configure CloudFront to forward more than one header, the order of the headers in viewer requests doesn't affect caching as long as the values are the same. For example, if one request contains the headers A:1,B:2 and another request contains B:2,A:1, CloudFront caches just one copy of the object.

### How the Case of Headers and Header Values Affects Caching

When CloudFront caches based on header values, it doesn't consider the case of the header name, but it does consider the case of the header value:

- If viewer requests include both `Product:Acme` and `product:Acme`, CloudFront caches an object only once. The only difference between them is the case of the header name, which doesn't affect caching.
- If viewer requests include both `Product:Acme` and `Product:acme`, CloudFront caches an object twice, because the value is `Acme` in some requests and `acme` in others.

### Headers that CloudFront Returns to the Viewer

Configuring CloudFront to forward and cache headers does not affect which headers CloudFront returns to the viewer. CloudFront returns all of the headers that it gets from the origin with a few exceptions. For more information, see the applicable topic:

- **Amazon S3 origins – ** See HTTP Response Headers That CloudFront Removes or Updates.
- **Custom origins – ** See HTTP Response Headers that CloudFront Removes or Updates.

## Headers and RTMP Distributions

For RTMP distributions, you cannot configure CloudFront to cache your content based on the headers in viewer requests.

# Forwarding Custom Headers to Your Origin (Web Distributions Only)

You can configure CloudFront to include custom headers whenever it forwards a request to your origin. You can specify the names and values of custom headers for each origin, both for custom origins and for Amazon S3 buckets. Custom headers have a variety of uses, such as the following:

- You can identify the requests that are forwarded to your custom origin by CloudFront. This is useful if you want to know whether users are bypassing CloudFront or if you're using more than one CDN and you want information about which requests are coming from each CDN. (If you're using an Amazon S3 origin and you enable Amazon S3 server access logging, the logs don't include header information.)
- If you've configured more than one CloudFront distribution to use the same origin, you can specify different custom headers for the origins in each distribution and use the logs for your web server to distinguish between the requests that CloudFront forwards for each distribution.
- If some of your users use viewers that don't support cross-origin resource sharing (CORS), you can configure CloudFront to forward the `Origin` header to your origin. That will cause your origin to return the `Access-Control-Allow-Origin` header for every request.
- You can use custom headers together and, optionally, signed URLs or signed cookies, to control access to content on a custom origin. If you configure your custom origin to respond to requests only if they include a custom header, you can prevent users from bypassing CloudFront and submitting requests directly to your origin.

**Topics**

- Configuring CloudFront to Forward Custom Headers to Your Origin
- Custom Headers that CloudFront Can't Forward to Your Origin
- Using Custom Headers for Cross-Origin Resource Sharing (CORS)
- Using Custom Headers to Restrict Access to Your Content on a Custom Origin

## Configuring CloudFront to Forward Custom Headers to Your Origin

To configure a web distribution to forward custom headers to your origin, you update the configuration of the applicable origins by using one of the following methods:

**CloudFront console**
When you create or update a distribution, specify header names and values in the **Origin Custom Headers** settings. For more information, see Creating a Web Distribution.

**CloudFront API**
For each origin that you want to forward custom headers to, add header names and values to the `CustomHeaders` section of the `DistributionConfig` complex type. For more information, see CreateDistribution (to create a new distribution) or UpdateDistribution (to update an existing distribution).

If the header names and values that you specify are not already present in the viewer request, CloudFront adds them. If a header is present, CloudFront overwrites the header value before forwarding the request to the origin.

For the current limits related to forwarding custom headers to the origin, see Limits.

## Custom Headers that CloudFront Can't Forward to Your Origin

You can't configure CloudFront to forward the following custom headers to your origin.

| | |
|---|---|
| Accept-Encoding | Proxy-Authenticate |
| Cache-Control | Proxy-Authorization |

| | |
|---|---|
| Connection | Proxy-Connection |
| Content-Length | Range |
| Cookie | Request-Range |
| Host | TE |
| If-Match | Trailer |
| If-Modified-Since | Transfer-Encoding |
| If-None-Match | Upgrade |
| If-Range | Via |
| If-Unmodified-Since | Headers that begin with X-Amz-* |
| Max-Forwards | Headers that begin with X-Edge-* |
| Pragma | X-Real-Ip |

## Using Custom Headers for Cross-Origin Resource Sharing (CORS)

You can configure CloudFront to always forward the applicable headers to your origin to accommodate viewers that don't automatically include those headers in requests. You also need to configure CloudFront to respect CORS settings. For more information, see Configuring CloudFront to Respect Cross-Origin Resource Sharing (CORS) Settings.

## Using Custom Headers to Restrict Access to Your Content on a Custom Origin

If you're using a custom origin, you can use custom headers to prevent users from bypassing CloudFront and requesting content directly from your origin. You can also optionally restrict access to your content by requiring that your users access your objects by using either signed URLs or signed cookies. For more information about private content, see Serving Private Content through CloudFront.

To require that users access your content through CloudFront, change the following settings in your CloudFront distributions:

**Origin Custom Headers**
Configure CloudFront to forward custom headers to your origin. See Configuring CloudFront to Forward Custom Headers to Your Origin.

**Viewer Protocol Policy**
Configure your distribution to require viewers to use HTTPS to access CloudFront. See Viewer Protocol Policy.

**Origin Protocol Policy**
Configure your distribution to require CloudFront to use the same protocol as viewers to forward requests to the origin. See Origin Protocol Policy (Amazon EC2, Elastic Load Balancing, and Other Custom Origins Only).

The combination of **Viewer Protocol Policy** and **Origin Protocol Policy** ensure that your custom headers are encrypted between the viewer and your origin. However, we recommend that you periodically perform the following tasks to rotate the custom headers that CloudFront forwards to your origin:

1. Update your CloudFront distribution to begin forwarding a new header to your custom origin.

2. Update your application to accept the new header as confirmation that the request is coming from CloudFront.

3. When viewer requests no longer include the header that you're replacing, update your application to no longer accept the old header as confirmation that the request is coming from CloudFront.

# Adding, Removing, or Replacing Objects in a Distribution

For information about adding objects to a distribution, see Adding Objects that You Want CloudFront to Distribute.

When you replace objects in your distribution, we recommend that you use versioned object names. For more information, see Updating Existing Objects Using Versioned Object Names. You can also replace objects with objects that have the same name. See Updating Existing Objects Using the Same Object Names. Regardless of how you choose to replace objects in your distribution, we recommend that you specify when objects should be removed from the CloudFront cache. For more information, see Specifying How Long Objects Stay in a CloudFront Edge Cache (Expiration).

If you need to quickly remove objects from a distribution, you can invalidate them. For more information, see Invalidating Objects (Web Distributions Only).

# Adding Objects that You Want CloudFront to Distribute

When you want CloudFront to start distributing additional objects, you add the objects to one of the origins that you specified for the distribution, and you expose a CloudFront link to the objects. A CloudFront edge location doesn't fetch the new objects from an origin until the edge location receives viewer requests for the objects. For more information, see How CloudFront Delivers Content.

When you add an object that you want CloudFront to distribute, ensure that you add it to one of the Amazon S3 buckets specified in your distribution or, for a custom origin, to a directory in the specified domain. In addition, confirm that the path pattern in the applicable cache behavior sends requests to the correct origin. For example, suppose the path pattern for a cache behavior is `*.html`. If no other cache behaviors are configured to forward requests to that origin, CloudFront will never distribute .jpg files that you upload to the origin.

CloudFront servers don't determine the MIME type for the objects they serve. When you upload an object to your origin, you should set the `Content-Type` header field for the object.

# Updating Existing Objects Using Versioned Object Names

When you update existing objects in a CloudFront distribution, we recommend that you include some sort of version identifier either in your object names or in your directory names to give yourself better control over your content. This identifier might be a date-time stamp, a sequential number, or some other method of distinguishing two versions of the same object.

For example, instead of naming a graphic file image.jpg, you might call it image_1.jpg. When you want to start serving a new version of the file, you'd name the new file image_2.jpg, and you'd update the links in your web application or website to point to image_2.jpg. Alternatively, you might put all graphics in an images_v1 directory and, when you want to start serving new versions of one or more graphics, you'd create a new images_v2 directory, and you'd update your links to point to that directory. With versioning, you don't have to wait for an object to expire before CloudFront begins to serve a new version of it, and you don't have to pay for object invalidation.

Even if you version your objects, we still recommend that you set an expiration date. For more information, see Specifying How Long Objects Stay in a CloudFront Edge Cache (Expiration).

**Note**
Specifying versioned object names or directory names is not related to Amazon S3 object versioning.

# Updating Existing Objects Using the Same Object Names

Although you can update existing objects in a CloudFront distribution and use the same object names, we don't recommend it. CloudFront distributes objects to edge locations only when the objects are requested, not when you put new or updated objects in your origin. If you update an existing object in your origin with a newer version that has the same name, an edge location won't get that new version from your origin until both of the following occur:

- The old version of the object in the cache expires. For more information, see Specifying How Long Objects Stay in a CloudFront Edge Cache (Expiration).
- There's an end user request for the object at that edge location.

If you use the same names when you replace objects, you can't control when CloudFront starts to serve the new files. By default, CloudFront caches objects in edge locations for 24 hours. (For more information, see Specifying How Long Objects Stay in a CloudFront Edge Cache (Expiration).) For example, if you're replacing all of the objects on an entire website:

- Objects for the less popular pages may not be in any edge locations. The new versions of these objects will start being served on the next request.
- Objects for some pages may be in some edge locations and not in others, so your end users will see different versions depending on which edge location they're served from.
- New versions of the objects for the most popular pages might not be served for up to 24 hours because CloudFront might have retrieved the objects for those pages just before you replaced the objects with new versions.

# Specifying How Long Objects Stay in a CloudFront Edge Cache (Expiration)

You can control how long your objects stay in a CloudFront cache before CloudFront forwards another request to your origin. Reducing the duration allows you to serve dynamic content. Increasing the duration means your users get better performance because your objects are more likely to be served directly from the edge cache. A longer duration also reduces the load on your origin.

Typically, CloudFront serves an object from an edge location until the cache duration that you specified passes—that is, until the object expires. After it expires, the next time the edge location gets a user request for the object, CloudFront forwards the request to the origin server to verify that the cache contains the latest version of the object. The response from the origin depends on whether the object has changed:

- If the CloudFront cache already has the latest version, the origin returns a 304 status code (Not Modified).
- If the CloudFront cache does not have the latest version, the origin returns a 200 status code (OK) and the latest version of the object.

If an object in an edge location isn't frequently requested, CloudFront might evict the object—remove the object before its expiration date—to make room for objects that have been requested more recently.

By default, each object automatically expires after 24 hours. For web distributions, you can change the default behavior in two ways:

- To change the cache duration for all objects that match the same path pattern, you can change the CloudFront settings for **Minimum TTL**, **Maximum TTL**, and **Default TTL** for a cache behavior. For information about the individual settings, see Minimum TTL, Maximum TTL, and Default TTL. To use these settings, you must choose the **Customize** option for the Object Caching setting.
- To change the cache duration for an individual object, you can configure your origin to add a `Cache-Control max-age` or `Cache-Control s-maxage` directive, or an `Expires` header field to the object. For more information, see Using Headers to Control Cache Duration for Individual Objects.

For more information about how **Minimum TTL**, **Default TTL**, and **Maximum TTL** interact with `Cache -Control max-age` and `Cache-Control s-maxage` directives and the `Expires` header field, see Specifying the Amount of Time that CloudFront Caches Objects for Web Distributions.

You can also control how long errors (for example, 404, Not Found) stay in a CloudFront cache before CloudFront tries again to get the requested object by forwarding another request to your origin. For more information, see How CloudFront Processes and Caches HTTP 4xx and 5xx Status Codes from Your Origin.

### Topics

- Using Headers to Control Cache Duration for Individual Objects
- Specifying the Amount of Time that CloudFront Caches Objects for Web Distributions
- Specifying the Minimum Time that CloudFront Caches Objects for RTMP Distributions
- Adding Headers to Your Objects Using the Amazon S3 Console

## Using Headers to Control Cache Duration for Individual Objects

You can use the `Cache-Control` and `Expires` headers to control how long objects stay in the cache. Settings for **Minimum TTL**, **Default TTL**, and \*\*Maximum TTL \*\* also affect cache duration, but here's an overview of how headers can affect cache duration:

- The `Cache-Control max-age` directive lets you specify how long (in seconds) that you want an object to remain in the cache before CloudFront gets the object again from the origin server. The minimum expiration time CloudFront supports is 0 seconds for web distributions and 3600 seconds for RTMP distributions. The maximum value is 100 years. Specify the value in the following format:

`Cache-Control: max-age=`*seconds*

For example, the following directive tells CloudFront to keep the associated object in the cache for 3600 seconds (one hour):

```
Cache-Control: max-age=3600
```

If you want objects to stay in CloudFront edge caches for a different duration than they stay in browser caches, you can use the `Cache-Control max-age` and `Cache-Control s-maxage` directives together. For more information, see Specifying the Amount of Time that CloudFront Caches Objects for Web Distributions.

- The `Expires` header field lets you specify an expiration date and time using the format specified in RFC 2616, Hypertext Transfer Protocol -- HTTP/1.1 Section 3.3.1, Full Date, for example:

```
Sat, 27 Jun 2015 23:59:59 GMT
```

We recommend that you use the `Cache-Control max-age` directive instead of the `Expires` header field to control object caching. If you specify values both for `Cache-Control max-age` and for `Expires`, CloudFront uses only the value of `Cache-Control max-age`.

For more information, see Specifying the Amount of Time that CloudFront Caches Objects for Web Distributions.

You cannot use the HTTP `Cache-Control` or `Pragma` header fields in a `GET` request from a viewer to force CloudFront to go back to the origin server for the object. CloudFront ignores those header fields in viewer requests.

For more information about the `Cache-Control` and `Expires` header fields, see the following sections in *RFC 2616, Hypertext Transfer Protocol -- HTTP/1.1*:

- Section 14.9 Cache Control
- Section 14.21 Expires

For an example of how to add `Cache-Control` and `Expires` header fields using the AWS SDK for PHP, see Upload an Object Using the AWS SDK for PHP in the *Amazon Simple Storage Service Developer Guide*. Some third-party tools are also able to add these fields.

## Specifying the Amount of Time that CloudFront Caches Objects for Web Distributions

For web distributions, you can use `Cache-Control` or `Expires` headers, and CloudFront minimum, maximum, and default TTL values to control the amount of time in seconds that CloudFront keeps an object in the cache before forwarding another request to the origin. Headers values also determine how long a browser keeps an object in the cache before forwarding another request to CloudFront.

**Important**
If you configure CloudFront to forward all headers to your origin for a cache behavior, CloudFront never caches the associated objects. Instead, CloudFront forwards all requests for those objects to the origin. In that configuration, the value of minimum TTL must be 0. For more information, see Configuring CloudFront to Cache Objects Based on Request Headers.

To specify values for Minimum TTL, Maximum TTL, and Default TTL, you must choose the **Customize** option for the Object Caching setting.

| Origin Configuration | Minimum TTL = 0 Seconds | Minimum TTL > 0 Seconds |
| --- | --- | --- |
| **The origin adds a Cache-Control max-age directive to objects** | **CloudFront caching** CloudFront caches objects for the lesser of the value of the `Cache-Control max-age` directive or the value of the CloudFront maximum TTL. **Browser caching** Browsers cache objects for the value of the `Cache-Control max-age` directive. | **CloudFront caching** CloudFront caching depends on the values of the CloudFront minimum TTL and maximum TTL and the `Cache-Control max-age` directive: [See the AWS documentation website for more details] **Browser caching** Browsers cache objects for the value of the `Cache-Control max-age` directive. |
| **The origin does not add a Cache-Control max-age directive to objects** | **CloudFront caching** CloudFront caches objects for the value of the CloudFront default TTL. **Browser caching** Depends on the browser. | **CloudFront caching** CloudFront caches objects for the greater of the value of the CloudFront minimum TTL or default TTL. **Browser caching** Depends on the browser. |
| **The origin adds Cache-Control max-age and Cache-Control s-maxage directives to objects** | **CloudFront caching** CloudFront caches objects for the lesser of the value of the `Cache-Control s-maxage` directive or the value of the CloudFront maximum TTL. **Browser caching** Browsers cache objects for the value of the `Cache-Control max-age` directive. | **CloudFront caching** CloudFront caching depends on the values of the CloudFront minimum TTL and maximum TTL and the `Cache-Control s-maxage` directive: [See the AWS documentation website for more details] **Browser caching** Browsers cache objects for the value of the `Cache-Control max-age` directive. |
| **The origin adds an Expires header to objects** | **CloudFront caching** CloudFront caches objects until the date in the `Expires` header or for the value of the CloudFront maximum TTL, whichever is sooner. **Browser caching** Browsers cache objects until the date in the `Expires` header. | **CloudFront caching** CloudFront caching depends on the values of the CloudFront minimum TTL and maximum TTL and the `Expires` header: [See the AWS documentation website for more details] **Browser caching** Browsers cache objects until the date and time in the `Expires` header. |
| **Origin adds Cache-Control: no-cache, no-store, and/or private directives to objects** | CloudFront and browsers respect the headers. For an exception to how CloudFront handles the `Cache-Control: no-cache` header, see Simultaneous Requests for the Same Object (Traffic Spikes). | **CloudFront caching** CloudFront caches objects for the value of the CloudFront minimum TTL. **Browser caching** Browsers respect the headers. |

For information about how to change settings for web distributions using the CloudFront console, see Viewing and Updating CloudFront Distributions. For information about how to change settings for web distributions using the CloudFront API, see UpdateDistribution.

## Specifying the Minimum Time that CloudFront Caches Objects for RTMP Distributions

For RTMP distributions, CloudFront keeps objects in edge caches for 24 hours by default. You can add `Cache-Control` or `Expires` headers to your objects to change the amount of time that CloudFront keeps objects in edge caches before it forwards another request to the origin. The minimum duration is 3600 seconds (one hour). If you specify a lower value, CloudFront uses 3600 seconds.

## Adding Headers to Your Objects Using the Amazon S3 Console

**Note**
Using the Amazon S3 console, you can only add headers to one object at a time, but with some third-party tools, you can add headers to multiple Amazon S3 objects at a time. For more information about third-party tools that support Amazon S3, perform a web search on **AWS S3 third party tools**.

**To add a `Cache-Control` or `Expires` header field to Amazon S3 objects using the Amazon S3 console**

1. Sign in to the AWS Management Console and open the Amazon S3 console at https://console.aws.amazon.com/s3.

2. In the Amazon S3 console, in the buckets list, choose the name of the bucket that contains the files.

3. In the list of objects, select the check box for one or more objects that you want to add a header to.

4. Choose **More** and choose **Change metadata**.

5. In the **Key** list, choose **Cache-Control** or **Expires**, as applicable.

6. In the **Value** field, type the applicable value:

    - For a `Cache-Control` field, type:

      `max-age=number of seconds that you want objects to stay in a CloudFront edge cache`

    - For an **Expires** field, type a date and time in HTML format.

7. Choose **Save**.

# Invalidating Objects (Web Distributions Only)

If you need to remove an object from CloudFront edge caches before it expires, you can do one of the following:

- Invalidate the object from edge caches. The next time a viewer requests the object, CloudFront returns to the origin to fetch the latest version of the object.
- Use object versioning to serve a different version of the object that has a different name. For more information, see Updating Existing Objects Using Versioned Object Names.

**Important**
You can invalidate most types of objects that are served by a web distribution, but you cannot invalidate media files in the Microsoft Smooth Streaming format when you have enabled Smooth Streaming for the corresponding cache behavior. In addition, you cannot invalidate objects that are served by an RTMP distribution.

To invalidate objects, you can specify either the path for individual objects or a path that ends with the * wildcard, which might apply to one object or to many, as shown in the following examples:

- `/images/image1.jpg`
- `/images/image*`
- `/images/*`

**Note**
If you use the AWS command line interface (CLI) for invalidating objects and you specify a path that includes the * wildcard, you must use quotes (") around the path.
For example: `aws cloudfront create-invalidation --distribution-id $CDN_DISTRIBUTION_ID --paths "/*"`

You can submit a specified number of invalidation paths each month for free. If you submit more than the allotted number of invalidation paths in a month, you pay a fee for each invalidation path that you submit. For more information about the charges for invalidation, see Paying for Object Invalidation.

**Topics**

- Choosing Between Invalidating Objects and Using Versioned Object Names
- Determining Which Objects to Invalidate
- Specifying the Objects to Invalidate
- Invalidating Objects and Displaying Information about Invalidations
- Third-Party Tools for Invalidating Objects
- Invalidation Limits
- Paying for Object Invalidation

## Choosing Between Invalidating Objects and Using Versioned Object Names

To control the versions of objects that are served from your distribution, you can either invalidate objects or give them versioned file names. If you'll want to update your objects frequently, we recommend that you primarily use object versioning for the following reasons:

- Versioning enables you to control which object a request returns even when the user has a version cached either locally or behind a corporate caching proxy. If you invalidate the object, the user might continue to see the old version until it expires from those caches.
- CloudFront access logs include the names of your objects, so versioning makes it easier to analyze the results of object changes.
- Versioning provides a way to serve different versions of objects to different users.
- Versioning simplifies rolling forward and back between object revisions.
- Versioning is less expensive. You still have to pay for CloudFront to transfer new versions of your objects to edge locations, but you don't have to pay for invalidating objects.

For more information about object versioning, see Updating Existing Objects Using Versioned Object Names.

## Determining Which Objects to Invalidate

If you want to invalidate multiple objects such as all of the objects in a directory or all of the objects whose names begin with the same characters, you can include the * wildcard at the end of the invalidation path. For more information about using the * wildcard, see Invalidation paths.

If you want to invalidate selected objects but your users don't necessarily access every object on your origin, you can determine which objects viewers have requested from CloudFront and invalidate only those objects. To determine which objects viewers have requested, enable CloudFront access logging. For more information about access logs, see Access Logs.

## Specifying the Objects to Invalidate

Whether you invalidate objects by using the CloudFront console or the CloudFront API, the requirements and limitations for specifying objects are the same. Note the following about specifying the objects that you want to invalidate.

**Case sensitivity**
Invalidation paths are case sensitive, so /images/image.jpg and /images/Image.jpg specify two different objects.

**Changing the URI Using a Lambda Function**
If your CloudFront distribution triggers a Lambda function on viewer request events, and if the function changes the URI of the requested object, you must invalidate both URIs to remove the object from CloudFront edge caches:

- The URI in the viewer request
- The URI after the function changed it For example, suppose your Lambda function changes the URI for an object from this:
  http://d111111abcdef8.cloudfront.net/index.html
  to a URI that includes a language directory:
  http://d111111abcdef8.cloudfront.net/en/index.html
  To invalidate the object, you must specify the following paths:
- index.html
- en/index.html For more information, see Invalidation paths.

**Default root object**
To invalidate the default root object, specify the path the same way that you specify the path for any other object.

**Distribution types**
You can invalidate only objects that are associated with a web distribution.

**Forwarding cookies**
If you configured CloudFront to forward cookies to your origin, CloudFront edge caches might contain several versions of the object. When you invalidate an object, CloudFront invalidates every cached version of the object regardless of its associated cookies. You can't selectively invalidate some versions and not others based on the associated cookies. For more information, see Configuring CloudFront to Cache Objects Based on Cookies.

**Forwarding headers**
If you configured CloudFront to forward a whitelist of headers to your origin and to cache based on the values of the headers, CloudFront edge caches might contain several versions of the object. When you invalidate an object, CloudFront invalidates every cached version of the object regardless of the header values. You can't selectively invalidate some versions and not others based on header values. (If you configure CloudFront to forward all headers to your origin, CloudFront doesn't cache your objects.) For more information, see Configuring CloudFront to Cache Objects Based on Request Headers.

## Forwarding query strings

If you configured CloudFront to forward query strings to your origin, you must include the query strings when invalidating objects, as shown in the following examples:

- `images/image.jpg?parameter1=a`
- `images/image.jpg?parameter1=b` If client requests include five different query strings for the same object, you can either invalidate the object five times, once for each query string, or you can use the * wildcard in the invalidation path, as shown in the following example:

  `/images/image.jpg*`

  For more information about using wildcards in the invalidation path, see Invalidation paths. For more information about query strings, see Configuring CloudFront to Cache Based on Query String Parameters. To determine which query strings are in use, you can enable CloudFront logging. For more information, see Access Logs.

## Limits

For information about limits on invalidations, see Invalidation Limits.

## Microsoft Smooth Streaming files

You cannot invalidate media files in the Microsoft Smooth Streaming format when you have enabled Smooth Streaming for the corresponding cache behavior.

## Non-ASCII or unsafe characters in the path

If the path includes non-ASCII characters or unsafe characters as defined in RFC 1783 (http://www.ietf.org/rfc/rfc1738.txt), URL-encode those characters. Do not URL-encode any other characters in the path, or CloudFront will not invalidate the old version of the updated object.

## Invalidation paths

The path is relative to the distribution. A leading / is optional. For example, to invalidate the object at `http://d111111abcdef8.cloudfront.net/images/image2.jpg`, you would specify the following:

`/images/image2.jpg`

or

`images/image2.jpg`

You can also invalidate multiple objects simultaneously by using the * wildcard. The *, which replaces 0 or more characters, must be the last character in the invalidation path. Also, if you use the AWS command line interface (CLI) for invalidating objects and you specify a path that includes the * wildcard, you must use quotes (") around the path (like "/*").

The following are some examples:

- To invalidate all of the objects in a directory:

  */directory-path/**

- To invalidate a directory, all of its subdirectories, and all of the objects in the directory and subdirectories:

  */directory-path**

- To invalidate all files that have the same name but different file name extensions, such as logo.jpg, logo.png, and logo.gif:

  */directory-path/file-name.**

- To invalidate all of the files in a directory for which the file name starts with the same characters (such as all of the files for a video in HLS format), regardless of the file name extension:

  */directory-path/initial-characters-in-file-name**

- When you configure CloudFront to cache based on query string parameters and you want to invalidate every version of an object:

  */directory-path/file-name.file-name-extension**

- To invalidate all of the objects in a distribution:

/\* The maximum length of a path is 4,000 characters. You can't use a wildcard within the path; only at the end of the path.

For information about invalidating objects if you use a Lambda function to change the URI, see Changing the URI Using a Lambda Function.

The charge to submit an invalidation path is the same regardless of the number of objects you're invalidating: a single object (/images/logo.jpg) or all of the objects that are associated with a distribution (/\*). For more information, see Amazon CloudFront Pricing.

If the invalidation path is a directory and if you have not standardized on a method for specifying directories—with or without a trailing slash (/)—we recommend that you invalidate the directory both with and without a trailing slash, for example, /images and /images/.

**Signed URLs**

If you are using signed URLs, invalidate an object by including only the portion of the URL before the question mark (?).

## Invalidating Objects and Displaying Information about Invalidations

You can use the CloudFront console or CloudFront API actions to create and run an invalidation, display a list of the invalidations that you submitted previously, and display detailed information about an individual invalidation. You can also copy an existing invalidation, edit the list of object paths, and run the edited invalidation.

See the applicable topic:

- Invalidating Objects Using the CloudFront Console
- Copying, Editing, and Rerunning an Existing Invalidation Using the CloudFront Console
- Canceling Invalidations
- Listing Invalidations (Console)
- Displaying Information about an Invalidation Using the CloudFront Console
- Invalidating Objects and Displaying Information about Invalidations Using the CloudFront API

### Invalidating Objects Using the CloudFront Console

To invalidate objects using the CloudFront console, do the following procedure.

**To invalidate objects using the CloudFront console**

1. Sign in to the AWS Management Console and open the CloudFront console at https://console.aws.amazon.com/cloudfront/.

2. Choose the distribution for which you want to invalidate objects.

3. Choose **Distribution Settings**.

4. Choose the **Invalidations** tab.

5. Choose **Create Invalidation**.

6. For the objects that you want to invalidate, enter one invalidation path per line. For information about specifying invalidation paths, see Specifying the Objects to Invalidate. **Important**
   Specify object paths carefully. You can't cancel an invalidation request after you start it.

7. Choose **Invalidate**.

### Copying, Editing, and Rerunning an Existing Invalidation Using the CloudFront Console

You can copy an invalidation that you created previously, update the list of invalidation paths, and run the updated invalidation. You cannot copy an existing invalidation, update the invalidation paths, and save the updated invalidation without running it.

**Important**

If you copy an invalidation that is still in progress, update the list of invalidation paths, and run the updated invalidation, CloudFront will not stop or delete the invalidation that you copied. If any invalidation paths appear in the original and in the copy, CloudFront will try to invalidate the objects twice, and both invalidations will count against your maximum number of free invalidations for the month. If you've already reached the maximum number of free invalidations, you'll be charged for both invalidations of each object. For more information, see Invalidation Limits.

**To copy, edit, and rerun an existing invalidation using the CloudFront console**

1. Sign in to the AWS Management Console and open the CloudFront console at https://console.aws.amazon.com/cloudfront/.

2. Choose the distribution that contains the invalidation that you want to copy.

3. Choose **Distribution Settings**.

4. Choose the **Invalidations** tab.

5. Choose the invalidation that you want to copy.

   If you aren't sure which invalidation you want to copy, you can choose an invalidation and choose **Details** to display detailed information about that invalidation.

6. Choose **Copy**.

7. Update the list of invalidation paths if applicable.

8. Choose **Invalidate**.

## Canceling Invalidations

When you submit an invalidation request to CloudFront, CloudFront forwards the request to all edge locations within a few seconds, and each edge location starts processing the invalidation immediately. As a result, you can't cancel an invalidation after you submit it.

## Listing Invalidations (Console)

Using the console, you can display a list of the last 100 invalidations that you've created and run for a distribution. If you want to get a list of more than 100 invalidations, use the ListInvalidations API action. For more information, see ListInvalidations in the *Amazon CloudFront API Reference*.

**To list invalidations using the CloudFront console**

1. Sign in to the AWS Management Console and open the CloudFront console at https://console.aws.amazon.com/cloudfront/.

2. Choose the distribution for which you want to display a list of invalidations.

3. Choose **Distribution Settings**.

4. Choose the **Invalidations** tab.

## Displaying Information about an Invalidation Using the CloudFront Console

You can display detailed information about an invalidation, including distribution ID, invalidation ID, the status of the invalidation, the date and time that the invalidation was created, and a complete list of the invalidation paths.

**To display information about an invalidation using the CloudFront console**

1. Sign in to the AWS Management Console and open the CloudFront console at https://console.aws.amazon.com/cloudfront/.

2. Choose the distribution that contains the invalidation that you want to display detailed information for.

3. Choose **Distribution Settings**.

4. Choose the **Invalidations** tab.

5. Choose the applicable invalidation.

6. Choose **Details**.

**Invalidating Objects and Displaying Information about Invalidations Using the CloudFront API**

For information about invalidating objects and about displaying information about invalidations using the CloudFront API, see the applicable topic in the *Amazon CloudFront API Reference*:

- Invalidating objects: CreateInvalidation
- Getting a list of your invalidations: ListInvalidations
- Getting information about a specific invalidation: GetInvalidation

## Third-Party Tools for Invalidating Objects

In addition to the invalidation methods provided by CloudFront, several third-party tools provide ways to invalidate objects. For a list of tools, see Invalidating Objects.

## Invalidation Limits

If you're invalidating objects individually, you can have invalidation requests for up to 3,000 objects per distribution in progress at one time. This can be one invalidation request for up to 3,000 objects, up to 3,000 requests for one object each, or any other combination that doesn't exceed 3,000 objects. For example, you can submit 30 invalidation requests that invalidate 100 objects each. As long as all 30 invalidation requests are still in progress, you can't submit any more invalidation requests. If you exceed the limit, CloudFront returns an error message.

If you're using the * wildcard, you can have requests for up to 15 invalidation paths in progress at one time. You can also have invalidation requests for up to 3,000 individual objects per distribution in progress at the same time; the limit on wildcard invalidation requests is independent of the limit on invalidating objects individually.

## Paying for Object Invalidation

The first 1,000 invalidation paths that you submit per month are free; you pay for each invalidation path over 1,000 in a month. An invalidation path can be for a single object (such as /images/logo.jpg) or for multiple objects (such as /images/*). A path that includes the * wildcard counts as one path even if it causes CloudFront to invalidate thousands of objects.

This limit of 1000 invalidation paths per month applies to the total number of invalidation paths across all of the distributions that you create with one AWS account. For example, if you use the AWS account john@example.com to create three distributions, and you submit 600 invalidation paths for each distribution in a given month (for a total of 1,800 invalidation paths), AWS will charge you for 800 invalidation paths in that month. For specific information about invalidation pricing, see Amazon CloudFront Pricing. For more information about invalidation paths, see Invalidation paths.

# Customizing Error Responses

**Topics**

- Creating or Updating a Cache Behavior for Custom Error Pages
- Changing Response Codes
- Controlling How Long CloudFront Caches Errors
- How CloudFront Responds When a Custom Error Page Is Unavailable
- Pricing for Custom Error Pages
- Configuring Error Response Behavior

If the objects that you're serving through CloudFront are unavailable for some reason, your web server typically returns an HTTP status code to CloudFront. For example, if a viewer specifies an invalid URL, your web server returns a 404 status code to CloudFront, and CloudFront returns that status code to the viewer. The viewer displays a brief and sparsely formatted default message similar to this:

```
Not Found: The requested URL /myfilename.html was not found on this server.
```

If you'd rather display a custom error message, possibly using the same formatting as the rest of your website, you can have CloudFront return to the viewer an object (for example, an HTML file) that contains your custom error message.

You can specify a different object for each supported HTTP status code, or you can use the same object for all of the supported status codes. You can also choose to specify objects for some status codes and not for others.

The objects that you're serving through CloudFront can be unavailable for a variety of reasons. These fall into two broad categories:

- **Client errors** indicate a problem with the request. For example, an object with the specified name isn't available, or the user doesn't have the permissions required to get an object in your Amazon S3 bucket. When a client error occurs, the origin returns an HTTP status code in the 400 range to CloudFront.
- **Server errors** indicate a problem with the origin server. For example, the HTTP server is busy or unavailable. When a server error occurs, either your origin server returns an HTTP status code in the 500 range to CloudFront, or CloudFront doesn't get a response from your origin server for a certain period of time and assumes a 504 status code (gateway timeout).

The HTTP status codes for which CloudFront can return a custom error page include the following:

- 400, 403, 404, 405, 414, 416
- 500, 501, 502, 503, 504

**Note**
You can create a custom error page for HTTP status code 416 (Requested Range Not Satisfiable), and you can change the HTTP status code that CloudFront returns to viewers when your origin returns a status code 416 to CloudFront. (For more information, see Changing Response Codes.) However, CloudFront doesn't cache status code 416 responses, so you can specify a value for **Error Caching Minimum TTL** for status code 416, but CloudFront doesn't use it.

For a detailed explanation of how CloudFront handles error responses from your origin, see How CloudFront Processes and Caches HTTP 4xx and 5xx Status Codes from Your Origin.

## Creating or Updating a Cache Behavior for Custom Error Pages

If you want to store your objects and your custom error pages in different locations, your distribution must include a cache behavior for which the following is true:

- The value of **Path Pattern** matches the path to your custom error messages. For example, suppose you saved custom error pages for 4xx errors in an Amazon S3 bucket in a directory named `/4xx-errors`. Your distribution must include a cache behavior for which the path pattern routes requests for your custom error pages to that location, for example, `/4xx-errors/*`.
- The value of **Origin** specifies the value of **Origin ID** for the origin that contains your custom error pages.

For more information, see Cache Behavior Settings in the topic Values That You Specify When You Create or Update a Web Distribution.

## Changing Response Codes

You can choose the HTTP status code CloudFront returns along with a custom error page for a given HTTP status code. For example, if your origin returns a 500 status code to CloudFront, you might want CloudFront to return a custom error page and a 200 status code (OK) to the viewer. There are a variety of reasons that you might want CloudFront to return a status code to the viewer that is different from the one that your origin returned to CloudFront:

- Some internet devices (some firewalls and corporate proxies, for example) intercept HTTP 4xx and 5xx and prevent the response from being returned to the viewer. If you substitute 200, the response typically won't be intercepted.
- If you don't care about distinguishing among different client errors or server errors, you can specify **400** or **500** as the value that CloudFront returns for all 4xx or 5xx status codes.
- You might want to return a 200 status code (OK) and static website so your customers don't know that your website is down.

If you enable CloudFront access logs and you configure CloudFront to change the HTTP status code in the response, the value of the `sc-status` column in access logs will contain the status code that you specify. However, the value of the `x-edge-result-type` column will not be affected; it will still contain the result type of the response from the origin. For example, suppose you configure CloudFront to return a status code of 200 to the viewer when the origin returns 404 (Not Found) to CloudFront. When the origin responds to a request with a 404 status code, the value in the `sc-status` column in the access log will be 200, but the value in the `x-edge-result-type` column will be `Error`.

You can configure CloudFront to return any of the following HTTP status codes along with a custom error page:

- 200
- 400, 403, 404, 405, 414, 416
- 500, 501, 502, 503, 504

## Controlling How Long CloudFront Caches Errors

By default, when your origin returns an HTTP 4xx or 5xx status code, CloudFront caches these error responses for five minutes and then submits the next request for the object to your origin to see whether the problem that caused the error has been resolved and the requested object is now available.

**Note**
You can create a custom error page for HTTP status code 416 (Requested Range Not Satisfiable), and you can change the HTTP status code that CloudFront returns to viewers when your origin returns a status code 416 to CloudFront. (For more information, see Changing Response Codes.) However, CloudFront doesn't cache status code 416 responses, so you can specify a value for **Error Caching Minimum TTL** for status code 416, but CloudFront doesn't use it.

You can specify the error-caching duration—the **Error Caching Minimum TTL**—for each 4xx and 5xx status code that CloudFront caches. For a procedure, see Configuring Error Response Behavior. When you specify a duration, note the following:

- If you specify a short error-caching duration, CloudFront forwards more requests to your origin than if you specify a longer duration. For 5xx errors, this may aggravate the problem that originally caused your origin to return an error.
- When your origin returns an error for an object, CloudFront responds to requests for the object either with the error response or with your custom error page until the error-caching duration elapses. If you specify a long error-caching duration, CloudFront might continue to respond to requests with an error response or your custom error page for a long time after the object becomes available again.

If you want to control how long CloudFront caches errors for individual objects, you can configure your origin server to add the applicable header to the error response for that object:

- **If the origin adds a `Cache-Control max-age` or `Cache-Control s-maxage` directive, or an `Expires` header:** CloudFront caches error responses for the greater of the value in the header or the value of **Error Caching Minimum TTL**.

  Be aware that `Cache-Control max-age` and `Cache-Control s-maxage` values cannot be greater than the **Maximum TTL** value set for the cache behavior for which the error page is being fetched.

- **If the origin adds other `Cache-Control` directives or adds no headers:** CloudFront caches error responses for the value of **Error Caching Minimum TTL**.

If the expiration time for a 4xx or 5xx status code for an object is longer than you want to wait, you can invalidate the status code by using the URL of the requested object. If your origin is returning an error response for multiple objects, you need to invalidate each object separately. For more information about invalidating objects, see Invalidating Objects (Web Distributions Only).

## How CloudFront Responds When a Custom Error Page Is Unavailable

If you configure CloudFront to return a custom error page for an HTTP status code but the custom error page isn't available, CloudFront returns to the viewer the status code that CloudFront received from the origin that contains the custom error pages. For example, suppose your custom origin returns a 500 status code and you have configured CloudFront to get a custom error page for a 500 status code from an Amazon S3 bucket. However, someone accidentally deleted the custom error page from your bucket. CloudFront will return an HTTP 404 status code (not found) to the viewer that requested the object.

## Pricing for Custom Error Pages

When CloudFront returns a custom error page to a viewer, you pay the standard CloudFront charges for the custom error page, not the charges for the requested object. For more information about CloudFront charges, see Amazon CloudFront Pricing.

## Configuring Error Response Behavior

You can use either the CloudFront API or console to configure CloudFront error responses. For information about using the CloudFront API to configure error responses, go to UpdateDistribution in the *Amazon CloudFront API Reference*, and see the `CustomErrorResponses` element.

**To configure CloudFront error responses using the console**

1. Create the custom error pages that you want CloudFront to return to viewers when your origin returns HTTP 4xx or 5xx errors. Save the pages in a location that is accessible to CloudFront.

   We recommend that you store custom error pages in an Amazon S3 bucket even if you're using a custom origin. If you store custom error pages on an HTTP server and the server starts to return 5xx errors, CloudFront can't get the files that you want to return to viewers because the origin server is unavailable.

2. Confirm that you have granted CloudFront at least **read** permission to your custom error page objects.

   For more information about Amazon S3 permissions, see Access Control in the *Amazon Simple Storage Service Developer Guide*. For information on using the Amazon S3 console to update permissions, go to the http://docs.aws.amazon.com/AmazonS3/latest/UG/Welcome.html.

3. (Optional) Configure your origin server to add **Cache-Control** directives or an **Expires** header along with the error response for specific objects, if applicable. For more information, see Controlling How Long CloudFront Caches Errors.

4. Sign in to the AWS Management Console and open the CloudFront console at https://console.aws.amazon.com/cloudfront/.

5. In the list of distributions, select the distribution to update and choose **Distribution Settings**.

6. Choose the **Error Pages** tab. Then either choose **Create Custom Error Response**, or choose an existing error code and choose **Edit**.

7. Enter the applicable values. For more information, see Custom Error Pages and Error Caching.

8. If you configured CloudFront to return custom error pages, add or update the applicable cache behaviors. For more information, see Creating or Updating a Cache Behavior for Custom Error Pages.

9. To save your changes, choose **Yes, Edit**.

# How CloudFront Processes Partial Requests for an Object (Range GETs)

For a large object, an end user's browser or client might make multiple `GET` requests and use the `Range` request header to download the object in smaller units. These requests for ranges of bytes, sometimes known as `Range GET` requests, improve the efficiency of partial downloads and the recovery from partially failed transfers.

When CloudFront receives a `Range GET` request, it checks the cache in the edge location that received the request. If the cache in that edge location already contains the entire object or the requested portion of the object, CloudFront immediately serves the requested range from the cache.

If the cache doesn't contain the requested range, CloudFront forwards the request to the origin. (To optimize performance, CloudFront may request a larger range than the client requested in the `Range GET`.) What happens next depends on whether the origin supports `Range GET` requests:

- **If the origin supports `Range GET` requests:** It returns the requested range. CloudFront serves the requested range and also caches it for future requests. (Amazon S3 supports `Range GET` requests, as do some HTTP servers, for example, Apache and IIS. For information about whether your HTTP server does, see the documentation for your HTTP server.)
- **If the origin doesn't support `Range GET` requests:** It returns the entire object. CloudFront serves the entire object and also caches the entire object for future requests. After CloudFront caches the entire object in an edge cache, it responds to `Range GET` requests by serving the requested range.

In either case, CloudFront begins to serve the requested range or object to the end user as soon as the first byte arrives from the origin.

**Note**
If the viewer makes a `Range GET` request and the origin returns `Transfer-Encoding: chunked`, CloudFront returns the entire object to the viewer instead of the requested range.

CloudFront generally follows the RFC specification for the `Range` header. However, if your `Range` headers don't adhere to the following requirements, CloudFront will return HTTP status code 200 with the full object instead of status code 206 with the specified ranges:

- The ranges must be listed in ascending order. For example, `100-200,300-400` is valid, `300-400,100-200` is not valid.
- The ranges must not overlap. For example, `100-200,150-250` is not valid.
- All of the ranges specifications must be valid. For example, you can't specify a negative value as part of a range.

For more information about the `Range` request header, see "Section 14.35 Range" in *Hypertext Transfer Protocol -- HTTP/1.1* at http://www.w3.org/Protocols/rfc2616/rfc2616-sec14.html#sec14.35.

# Specifying a Default Root Object (Web Distributions Only)

You can configure CloudFront to return a specific object (the default root object) when an end user requests the root URL for your distribution instead of an object in your distribution. Specifying a default root object avoids exposing the contents of your distribution.

For example, the following request points to the object `image.jpg`:

`http://d111111abcdef8.cloudfront.net/image.jpg`

The following request points to the root URL of the same distribution instead of to a specific object:

`http://d111111abcdef8.cloudfront.net/`

When you define a default root object, an end-user request that calls the root of your distribution returns the default root object. For example, if you designate the file `index.html` as your default root object, a request for:

`http://d111111abcdef8.cloudfront.net/`

returns:

`http://d111111abcdef8.cloudfront.net/index.html`

However, if you define a default root object, an end-user request for a subdirectory of your distribution does not return the default root object. For example, suppose `index.html` is your default root object and that CloudFront receives an end-user request for the `install` directory under your CloudFront distribution:

`http://d111111abcdef8.cloudfront.net/install/`

CloudFront will not return the default root object even if a copy of `index.html` appears in the `install` directory.

If you configure your distribution to allow all of the HTTP methods that CloudFront supports, the default root object applies to all methods. For example, if your default root object is index.php and you write your application to submit a `POST` request to the root of your domain (http://example/.com/), CloudFront will send the request to http://example/.com/index/.php/.

The behavior of CloudFront default root objects is different from the behavior of Amazon S3 index documents. When you configure an Amazon S3 bucket as a website and specify the index document, Amazon S3 returns the index document even if a user requests a subdirectory in the bucket. (A copy of the index document must appear in every subdirectory.) For more information about configuring Amazon S3 buckets as websites and about index documents, see the Hosting Websites on Amazon S3 chapter in the *Amazon Simple Storage Service Developer Guide*.

**Important**
Remember that a default root object applies only to your CloudFront distribution. You still need to manage security for your origin. For example, if you are using an Amazon S3 origin, you still need to set your Amazon S3 bucket ACLs appropriately to ensure the level of access you want on your bucket.

If you don't define a default root object, requests for the root of your distribution pass to your origin server. If you are using an Amazon S3 origin, any of the following might be returned:

- **A list of the contents of your Amazon S3 bucket**—Under any of the following conditions, the contents of your origin are visible to anyone who uses CloudFront to access your distribution:
  - Your bucket is not properly configured.
  - The Amazon S3 permissions on the bucket associated with your distribution and on the objects in the bucket grant access to *everyone*.
  - An end user accesses your origin using your origin root URL.
- **A list of the private contents of your origin**—If you configure your origin as a private distribution (only you and CloudFront have access), the contents of the Amazon S3 bucket associated with your distribution are visible to anyone who has the credentials to access your distribution through CloudFront. In this case, users are not able to access your content through your origin root URL. For more information about distributing private content, see Serving Private Content through CloudFront.

- **Error 403 Forbidden**—CloudFront returns this error if the permissions on the Amazon S3 bucket associated with your distribution or the permissions on the objects in that bucket deny access to CloudFront and to everyone.

To avoid exposing the contents of your web distribution or returning an error, perform the following procedure to specify a default root object for your distribution.

**To specify a default root object for your distribution**

1. Upload the default root object to the origin that your distribution points to.

   The file can be any type supported by CloudFront. For a list of constraints on the file name, see the description of the `DefaultRootObject` element in DistributionConfig. **Note**
   If the file name of the default root object is too long or contains an invalid character, CloudFront returns the error `HTTP 400 Bad Request - InvalidDefaultRootObject`. In addition, CloudFront caches the code for five minutes and writes the results to the access logs.

2. Confirm that the permissions for the object grant CloudFront at least `read` access.

   For more information about Amazon S3 permissions, see Access Control in the *Amazon Simple Storage Service Developer Guide*. For information on using the Amazon S3 console to update permissions, go to the http://docs.aws.amazon.com/AmazonS3/latest/UG/Welcome.html.

3. Update your distribution to refer to the default root object using the CloudFront console or the CloudFront API.

   To specify a default root object using the CloudFront console:

   1. Sign in to the AWS Management Console and open the CloudFront console at https://console.aws.amazon.com/cloudfront/.

   2. In the list of distributions in the top pane, select the distribution to update.

   3. In the **Distribution Details** pane, on the **General** tab, choose **Edit**.

   4. In the **Edit Distribution** dialog box, in the **Default Root Object** field, enter the file name of the default root object.

      Enter only the object name, for example, `index.html`. Do not add a / before the object name.

   5. To save your changes, choose **Yes, Edit**.

   To update your configuration using the CloudFront API, you specify a value for the `DefaultRootObject` element in your distribution. For information about using the CloudFront API to specify a default root object, see UpdateDistribution in the *Amazon CloudFront API Reference*.

4. Confirm that you have enabled the default root object by requesting your root URL. If your browser doesn't display the default root object, perform the following steps:

   1. Confirm that your distribution is fully deployed by viewing the status of your distribution in the CloudFront console.

   2. Repeat Steps 2 and 3 to verify that you granted the correct permissions and that you correctly updated the configuration of your distribution to specify the default root object.

# Serving Compressed Files

You can configure CloudFront to automatically compress files of certain types and serve the compressed files when viewer requests include `Accept-Encoding: gzip` in the request header. When content is compressed, downloads are faster because the files are smaller—in some cases, less than a quarter the size of the original. Especially for JavaScript and CSS files, faster downloads translates into faster rendering of web pages for your users. In addition, because the cost of CloudFront data transfer is based on the total amount of data served, serving compressed files is less expensive than serving uncompressed files.

**Important**
A viewer request must include `Accept-Encoding: gzip` in the request header, or CloudFront won't compress the requested file.

If you're using a custom origin, you can configure your origin to compress files with or without CloudFront compression. Your origin can compress file types that CloudFront doesn't compress. (See File Types that CloudFront Compresses.) If your origin returns a compressed file to CloudFront, CloudFront detects that the file is compressed based on the value of the `Content-Encoding` header and doesn't compress the file again.

**Topics**

- Using CloudFront to Compress Your Content
- Using a Custom Origin to Compress Your Content

## Using CloudFront to Compress Your Content

CloudFront can compress files both for Amazon S3 origins and for custom origins. When you configure CloudFront to compress your content, you specify the setting in your cache behaviors.

When you configure CloudFront to compress your content, here's how CloudFront serves your content:

1. You create or update a CloudFront distribution and configure CloudFront to compress content.

2. A viewer requests a file. The viewer adds the `Accept-Encoding: gzip` header to the request. This indicates that the viewer supports compressed content.

3. At the edge location, CloudFront checks the cache for a compressed version of the file that is referenced in the request.

4. If the compressed file is already in the cache, CloudFront returns the file to the viewer and skips the remaining steps.

5. If the compressed file is not in the cache, CloudFront forwards the request to the origin server, which can be either an Amazon S3 bucket or a custom origin. **Note**
If CloudFront has an uncompressed version of the file in the cache, it still forwards a request to the origin.

6. The origin server returns an uncompressed version of the requested file to CloudFront.

7. CloudFront determines whether the file is compressible:

   - The file must be of a type that CloudFront compresses.
   - The file size must be between 1,000 and 10,000,000 bytes.
   - The response must include a `Content-Length` header so CloudFront can determine whether the size of the file is in the range that CloudFront compresses. If the `Content-Length` header is missing, CloudFront won't compress the file.
   - The response must not include a `Content-Encoding` header.

8. If the file is compressible, CloudFront compresses it, returns the compressed file to the viewer, and adds it to the cache.

9. The viewer uncompresses the file.

Note the following:

**File types that CloudFront compresses**
CloudFront compresses files in a large number of file types. For a complete list, see File Types that CloudFront Compresses.

**Size of files that CloudFront compresses**
CloudFront compresses files that are between 1,000 bytes and 10,000,000 bytes in size.

**Content-Length header**
The origin must include a `Content-Length` header in the response so CloudFront can determine whether the size of the file is in the range that CloudFront compresses. If the `Content-Length` header is missing, CloudFront won't compress the file.

**Etag header**
If you configure CloudFront to compress content, CloudFront removes the `ETag` response header from the files that it compresses. When the `ETag` header is present, CloudFront and your origin can use it to determine whether the version of a file in a CloudFront edge cache is identical to the version on the origin server. However, after compression the two versions are no longer identical. As a result, when a compressed file expires and CloudFront forwards another request to your origin, your origin always returns the file to CloudFront instead of an HTTP status code 304 (Not Modified).

**Content already in edge locations when you configure CloudFront to compress files**
CloudFront compresses files in each edge location when it gets the files from your origin. When you configure CloudFront to compress your content, it doesn't compress files that are already in edge locations. In addition, when a file expires in an edge location and CloudFront forwards another request for the file to your origin, CloudFront doesn't compress the file if your origin returns an HTTP status code 304, which means that the edge location already has the latest version of the file. If you want CloudFront to compress the files that are already in edge locations, you'll need to invalidate those files. For more information, see Invalidating Objects (Web Distributions Only).

**Custom origin is already configured to compress files**
If you configure CloudFront to compress files and CloudFront is forwarding requests to a custom origin that is also configured to compress files, the custom origin will include a `Content-Encoding: gzip` header, which indicates that the file that the origin returned to CloudFront has already been compressed. CloudFront returns the cached file to the viewer and caches it in the edge location.
CloudFront does not compress a file if the response includes a `Content-Encoding` header, regardless of the value.

**Request doesn't include Accept-Encoding: gzip**
If the `Accept-Encoding` header is missing from the request, CloudFront serves uncompressed content. If the `Accept-Encoding` header includes additional values such as `deflate` or `sdch`, CloudFront removes them before forwarding the request to the origin server.

**CloudFront is busy**
In rare cases, when a CloudFront edge location is unusually busy, some files might not be compressed.

### Configuring a CloudFront Distribution to Compress Content

To configure a web distribution to compress your content, you update the applicable cache behaviors by using one of the following methods:

- **CloudFront console** – Update the **Compress objects automatically** setting. For more information, see Creating a Web Distribution.
- **CloudFront API** – Change the value of the `Compress` element to `true`. For more information, see CreateDistribution (to create a new distribution) or UpdateDistribution (to update an existing distribution).
- **One of the AWS SDKs** – See the applicable SDK documentation on the AWS Documentation page.
- **The AWS CLI** – For more information, see create-distribution or update-distribution in the *AWS CLI Command Reference.*

### File Types that CloudFront Compresses

If you configure CloudFront to compress your content, CloudFront compresses files that have the following values in the `Content-Type` header:

| | |
|---|---|
| application/eot | application/x-otf |
| application/font | application/x-perl |
| application/font-sfnt | application/x-ttf |
| application/javascript | font/eot |
| application/json | font/ttf |
| application/opentype | font/otf |
| application/otf | font/opentype |
| application/pkcs7-mime | image/svg+xml |
| application/truetype | text/css |
| application/ttf | text/csv |
| application/vnd.ms-fontobject | text/html |
| application/xhtml+xml | text/javascript |
| application/xml | text/js |
| application/xml+rss | text/plain |
| application/x-font-opentype | text/richtext |
| application/x-font-truetype | text/tab-separated-values |
| application/x-font-ttf | text/xml |
| application/x-httpd-cgi | text/x-script |
| application/x-javascript | text/x-component |
| application/x-mpegurl | text/x-java-source |
| application/x-opentype | |

## Using a Custom Origin to Compress Your Content

If you want to compress file types that CloudFront doesn't compress, you can configure your custom origin to compress files of those types using gzip. CloudFront doesn't support other compression algorithms. When your origin returns the compressed file to CloudFront, it will include a `Content-Encoding: gzip` header, which indicates to CloudFront that the file is already compressed.

**Note**
CloudFront does not compress a file if the response includes a `Content-Encoding` header, regardless of the value.

### Serving Compressed Files When Your Origin Server Is Running IIS

By default, IIS does not serve compressed content for requests that come through proxy servers such as CloudFront. If you're using IIS and if you configured IIS to compress content by using the `httpCompression` element, change the value of the `noCompressionForProxies` attribute to `false` so IIS will return compressed content to CloudFront.

In addition, if you have compressed objects that are requested less frequently than every few seconds, you might have to change the values of `frequentHitThreshold` and `frequentHitTimePeriod`.

For more information, refer to the IIS documentation on the Microsoft website.

**Serving Compressed Files When Your Origin Server Is Running NGINX**

When CloudFront forwards a request to the origin server, it includes a `Via` header. This causes NGINX to interpret the request as proxied and, by default, NGINX disables compression for proxied requests. If your version of NGINX includes the `gzip_proxied` setting, change the value to `any` so that NGINX will return compressed content to CloudFront. For more information, see the NGINX documentation for the module `ngx_http_gzip_module`.

# Request and Response Behavior

The following sections explain how CloudFront processes viewer requests and forwards the requests to your Amazon S3 or custom origin, and how CloudFront processes responses from your origin, including how CloudFront processes and caches 4xx and 5xx HTTP status codes.

**Topics**

- Request and Response Behavior for Amazon S3 Origins
- Request and Response Behavior for Custom Origins
- How CloudFront Processes HTTP 3xx Status Codes from Your Origin
- How CloudFront Processes and Caches HTTP 4xx and 5xx Status Codes from Your Origin

# Request and Response Behavior for Amazon S3 Origins

**Topics**

- How CloudFront Processes and Forwards Requests to Your Amazon S3 Origin Server
- How CloudFront Processes Responses from Your Amazon S3 Origin Server

## How CloudFront Processes and Forwards Requests to Your Amazon S3 Origin Server

This topic contains information about how CloudFront processes viewer requests and forwards the requests to your Amazon S3 origin.

**Topics**

- Caching Duration and Minimum TTL
- Client IP Addresses
- Conditional GETs
- Cookies
- Cross-Origin Resource Sharing (CORS)
- GET Requests That Include a Body
- HTTP Methods
- HTTP Request Headers That CloudFront Removes or Updates
- Maximum Length of a Request and Maximum Length of a URL
- OCSP Stapling
- Protocols
- Query Strings
- Origin Response Timeout
- Simultaneous Requests for the Same Object (Traffic Spikes)

### Caching Duration and Minimum TTL

For web distributions, to control how long your objects stay in a CloudFront cache before CloudFront forwards another request to your origin, you can:

- Configure your origin to add a `Cache-Control` or an `Expires` header field to each object.
- Specify a value for Minimum TTL in CloudFront cache behaviors.
- Use the default value of 24 hours.

For more information, see Specifying How Long Objects Stay in a CloudFront Edge Cache (Expiration).

### Client IP Addresses

If a viewer sends a request to CloudFront and does not include an `X-Forwarded-For` request header, CloudFront gets the IP address of the viewer from the TCP connection, adds an `X-Forwarded-For` header that includes the IP address, and forwards the request to the origin. For example, if CloudFront gets the IP address `192.0.2.2` from the TCP connection, it forwards the following header to the origin:

`X-Forwarded-For: 192.0.2.2`

If a viewer sends a request to CloudFront and includes an `X-Forwarded-For` request header, CloudFront gets the IP address of the viewer from the TCP connection, appends it to the end of the `X-Forwarded-For` header, and forwards the request to the origin. For example, if the viewer request includes `X-Forwarded-For: 192.0.2.4,192.0.2.3` and CloudFront gets the IP address `192.0.2.2` from the TCP connection, it forwards the following header to the origin:

```
X-Forwarded-For: 192.0.2.4,192.0.2.3,192.0.2.2
```
**Note**

The `X-Forwarded-For` header contains IPv4 addresses (such as 192.0.2.44) and IPv6 addresses (such as 2001:0db8:85a3:0000:0000:8a2e:0370:7334), as applicable.

### Conditional GETs

When CloudFront receives a request for an object that has expired from an edge cache, it forwards the request to the Amazon S3 origin either to get the latest version of the object or to get confirmation from Amazon S3 that the CloudFront edge cache already has the latest version. When Amazon S3 originally sent the object to CloudFront, it included an `ETag` value and a `LastModified` value in the response. In the new request that CloudFront forwards to Amazon S3, CloudFront adds one or both of the following:

- An `If-Match` or `If-None-Match` header that contains the `ETag` value for the expired version of the object.
- An `If-Modified-Since` header that contains the `LastModified` value for the expired version of the object.

Amazon S3 uses this information to determine whether the object has been updated and, therefore, whether to return the entire object to CloudFront or to return only an HTTP 304 status code (not modified).

### Cookies

Amazon S3 doesn't process cookies. If you configure a cache behavior to forward cookies to an Amazon S3 origin, CloudFront forwards the cookies, but Amazon S3 ignores them. All future requests for the same object, regardless if you vary the cookie, are served from the existing object in the cache.

### Cross-Origin Resource Sharing (CORS)

If you want CloudFront to respect Amazon S3 cross-origin resource sharing settings, configure CloudFront to forward selected headers to Amazon S3. For more information, see Configuring CloudFront to Cache Objects Based on Request Headers.

### GET Requests That Include a Body

If a viewer `GET` request includes a body, CloudFront returns an HTTP status code 403 (Forbidden) to the viewer.

### HTTP Methods

If you configure CloudFront to process all of the HTTP methods that it supports, CloudFront accepts the following requests from viewers and forwards them to your Amazon S3 origin:

- DELETE
- GET
- HEAD
- OPTIONS
- PATCH
- POST
- PUT

CloudFront always caches responses to `GET` and `HEAD` requests. You can also configure CloudFront to cache responses to `OPTIONS` requests. CloudFront does not cache responses to requests that use the other methods.

If you use an Amazon S3 bucket as the origin for your distribution and if you use CloudFront origin access identities, `POST` requests aren't supported in some Amazon S3 regions and `PUT` requests in those regions require an additional header. For more information, see Using an Origin Access Identity in Amazon S3 Regions that Support Only Signature Version 4 Authentication.

If you want to use multi-part uploads to add objects to an Amazon S3 bucket, you must add a CloudFront origin access identity to your distribution and grant the origin access identity the applicable permissions. For more information, see Using an Origin Access Identity to Restrict Access to Your Amazon S3 Content.

**Important**
If you configure CloudFront to accept and forward to Amazon S3 all of the HTTP methods that CloudFront supports, you must create a CloudFront origin access identity to restrict access to your Amazon S3 content and grant the origin access identity the applicable permissions. For example, if you configure CloudFront to accept and forward these methods because you want to use PUT, you must configure Amazon S3 bucket policies or ACLs to handle DELETE requests appropriately so viewers can't delete resources that you don't want them to. For more information, see Using an Origin Access Identity to Restrict Access to Your Amazon S3 Content.

For information about the operations supported by Amazon S3, see the Amazon S3 documentation.

## HTTP Request Headers That CloudFront Removes or Updates

CloudFront removes or updates some headers before forwarding requests to your Amazon S3 origin. For most headers this behavior is the same as for custom origins. For a full list of HTTP request headers and how CloudFront processes them, see HTTP Request Headers and CloudFront Behavior (Custom and S3 Origins).

## Maximum Length of a Request and Maximum Length of a URL

The maximum length of a request, including the path, the query string (if any), and headers, is 20,480 bytes.

CloudFront constructs a URL from the request. The maximum length of this URL is 8192 bytes.

If a request or a URL exceeds these limits, CloudFront returns HTTP status code 413, Request Header Fields Too Large, to the viewer, and then terminates the TCP connection to the viewer.

## OCSP Stapling

When a viewer submits an HTTPS request for an object, either CloudFront or the viewer must confirm with the certificate authority (CA) that the SSL certificate for the domain has not been revoked. OCSP stapling speeds up certificate validation by allowing CloudFront to validate the certificate and to cache the response from the CA, so the client doesn't need to validate the certificate directly with the CA.

The performance improvement of OCSP stapling is more pronounced when CloudFront receives a lot of HTTPS requests for objects in the same domain. Each server in a CloudFront edge location must submit a separate validation request. When CloudFront receives a lot of HTTPS requests for the same domain, every server in the edge location soon has a response from the CA that it can "staple" to a packet in the SSL handshake; when the viewer is satisfied that the certificate is valid, CloudFront can serve the requested object. If your distribution doesn't get much traffic in a CloudFront edge location, new requests are more likely to be directed to a server that hasn't validated the certificate with the CA yet. In that case, the viewer separately performs the validation step and the CloudFront server serves the object. That CloudFront server also submits a validation request to the CA, so the next time it receives a request that includes the same domain name, it has a validation response from the CA.

## Protocols

CloudFront forwards HTTP or HTTPS requests to the origin server based on the protocol of the viewer request, either HTTP or HTTPS.

**Important**

If your Amazon S3 bucket is configured as a website endpoint, you cannot configure CloudFront to use HTTPS to communicate with your origin because Amazon S3 doesn't support HTTPS connections in that configuration.

### Query Strings

For web distributions, you can configure whether CloudFront forwards query string parameters to your Amazon S3 origin. For RTMP distributions, CloudFront does not forward query string parameters. For more information, see Configuring CloudFront to Cache Based on Query String Parameters.

### Origin Response Timeout

The origin response timeout, also known as the origin read timeout or origin request timeout, applies to both of the following values:

- The amount of time, in seconds, that CloudFront waits for a response after forwarding a request to Amazon S3
- The amount of time, in seconds, that CloudFront waits after receiving a packet of a response from S3 and before receiving the next packet

CloudFront behavior depends on the HTTP method:

- `GET` and `HEAD` requests – If Amazon S3 doesn't respond within 30 seconds or stops responding for 30 seconds, CloudFront drops the connection and makes two additional attempts to contact the origin. If the origin doesn't reply during the third attempt, CloudFront doesn't try again until it receives another request for content on the same CloudFront origin.
- `DELETE`, `OPTIONS`, `PATCH`, `PUT`, and `POST` requests – If Amazon S3 doesn't respond within 30 seconds, CloudFront drops the connection and doesn't try again to contact the origin. The client can resubmit the request if necessary.

For all requests, CloudFront attempts to establish a connection with S3. If the connection fails within 10 seconds, CloudFront drops the connection and makes two additional attempts to contact S3. If the origin doesn't reply during the third attempt, CloudFront doesn't try again until it receives another request for content on the same origin.

The response timeout for S3 can't be changed.

### Simultaneous Requests for the Same Object (Traffic Spikes)

When a CloudFront edge location receives a request for an object and either the object isn't currently in the cache or the object has expired, CloudFront immediately sends the request to your Amazon S3 origin. If there's a traffic spike—if additional requests for the same object arrive at the edge location before Amazon S3 responds to the first request—CloudFront pauses briefly before forwarding additional requests for the object to your origin. Typically, the response to the first request will arrive at the CloudFront edge location before the response to subsequent requests. This brief pause helps to reduce unnecessary load on Amazon S3. If additional requests are not identical because, for example, you configured CloudFront to cache based on request headers or query strings, CloudFront forwards all of the unique requests to your origin.

When the response from the origin includes a `Cache-Control: no-cache` header, CloudFront typically forwards the next request for the same object to the origin to determine whether the object has been updated. However, when there's a traffic spike and CloudFront pauses after forwarding the first request to your origin, multiple viewer requests might arrive before CloudFront receives a response from the origin. When CloudFront receives a response that contains a `Cache-Control: no-cache` header, it sends the object in the response to the viewer that made the original request and to all of the viewers that requested the object during the pause. After the response arrives from the origin, CloudFront forwards the next viewer request for the same object to the origin.

In CloudFront access logs, the first request is identified as a `Miss` in the `x-edge-result-type` column, and all subsequent requests that CloudFront received during the pause are identified as a `Hit`. For more information about access log file format, see Web Distribution Log File Format.

# How CloudFront Processes Responses from Your Amazon S3 Origin Server

This topic contains information about how CloudFront processes responses from your Amazon S3 origin.

**Topics**

- Canceled Requests
- HTTP Response Headers That CloudFront Removes or Updates
- Maximum File Size
- Redirects

### Canceled Requests

If an object is not in the edge cache, and if a viewer terminates a session (for example, closes a browser) after CloudFront gets the object from your origin but before it can deliver the requested object, CloudFront does not cache the object in the edge location.

### HTTP Response Headers That CloudFront Removes or Updates

CloudFront removes or updates the following header fields before forwarding the response from your Amazon S3 origin to the viewer:

- `Set-Cookie` – If you configure CloudFront to forward cookies, it will forward the `Set-Cookie` header field to clients. For more information, see Configuring CloudFront to Cache Objects Based on Cookies.

- `Trailer`

- `Transfer-Encoding` – If your Amazon S3 origin returns this header field, CloudFront sets the value to `chunked` before returning the response to the viewer.

- `Upgrade`

- `Via` – CloudFront sets the value to:

  `Via: 1.1`*alphanumeric-string*`.cloudfront.net (CloudFront)`

  before returning the response to the viewer. For example:

  `Via: 1.1 1026589cc7887e7a0dc7827b4example.cloudfront.net (CloudFront)`

### Maximum File Size

The maximum size of a response body that CloudFront will return to the viewer is 20 GB. This includes chunked transfer responses that don't specify the `Content-Length` header value.

### Redirects

You can configure an Amazon S3 bucket to redirect all requests to another host name; this can be another Amazon S3 bucket or an HTTP server. If you configure a bucket to redirect all requests and if the bucket is the origin for a CloudFront distribution, we recommend that you configure the bucket to redirect all requests to a CloudFront distribution using either the domain name for the distribution (for example, d111111abcdef8.cloudfront.net) or an alternate domain name (a CNAME) that is associated with a distribution (for example, example.com). Otherwise, viewer requests bypass CloudFront, and the objects are served directly from the new origin.

**Note**

If you redirect requests to an alternate domain name, you must also update the DNS service for your domain by adding a CNAME record. For more information, see Adding and Moving Alternate Domain Names (CNAMEs).

Here's what happens when you configure a bucket to redirect all requests:

1. A viewer (for example, a browser) requests an object from CloudFront.

2. CloudFront forwards the request to the Amazon S3 bucket that is the origin for your distribution.

3. Amazon S3 returns an HTTP status code 301 (Moved Permanently) as well as the new location.

4. CloudFront caches the redirect status code and the new location, and returns the values to the viewer. CloudFront does not follow the redirect to get the object from the new location.

5. The viewer sends another request for the object, but this time the viewer specifies the new location that it got from CloudFront:

   - If the Amazon S3 bucket is redirecting all requests to a CloudFront distribution, using either the domain name for the distribution or an alternate domain name, CloudFront requests the object from the Amazon S3 bucket or the HTTP server in the new location. When the new location returns the object, CloudFront returns it to the viewer and caches it in an edge location.
   - If the Amazon S3 bucket is redirecting requests to another location, the second request bypasses CloudFront. The Amazon S3 bucket or the HTTP server in the new location returns the object directly to the viewer, so the object is never cached in a CloudFront edge cache.

# Request and Response Behavior for Custom Origins

**Topics**

- How CloudFront Processes and Forwards Requests to Your Custom Origin Server
- How CloudFront Processes Responses from Your Custom Origin Server

## How CloudFront Processes and Forwards Requests to Your Custom Origin Server

This topic contains information about how CloudFront processes viewer requests and forwards the requests to your custom origin.

**Topics**

- Authentication
- Caching Duration and Minimum TTL
- Client IP Addresses
- Client-Side SSL Authentication
- Compression
- Conditional Requests
- Cookies
- Cross-Origin Resource Sharing (CORS)
- Encryption
- GET Requests That Include a Body
- HTTP Methods
- HTTP Request Headers and CloudFront Behavior (Custom and S3 Origins)
- HTTP Version
- Maximum Length of a Request and Maximum Length of a URL
- OCSP Stapling
- Persistent Connections
- Protocols
- Query Strings
- Origin Response Timeout
- Simultaneous Requests for the Same Object (Traffic Spikes)
- User-Agent Header

### Authentication

For `DELETE`, `GET`, `HEAD`, `PATCH`, `POST`, and `PUT` requests, if you configure CloudFront to forward the `Authorization` header to your origin, you can configure your origin server to request client authentication.

For `OPTIONS` requests, you can configure your origin server to request client authentication only if you use the following CloudFront settings:

- Configure CloudFront to forward the `Authorization` header to your origin
- Configure CloudFront to *not* cache the response to `OPTIONS` requests

You can configure CloudFront to forward requests to your origin using either HTTP or HTTPS; for more information, see Using HTTPS with CloudFront.

### Caching Duration and Minimum TTL

For web distributions, to control how long your objects stay in a CloudFront cache before CloudFront forwards another request to your origin, you can:

- Configure your origin to add a `Cache-Control` or an `Expires` header field to each object.
- Specify a value for Minimum TTL in CloudFront cache behaviors.
- Use the default value of 24 hours.

For more information, see Specifying How Long Objects Stay in a CloudFront Edge Cache (Expiration).

### Client IP Addresses

If a viewer sends a request to CloudFront and does not include an `X-Forwarded-For` request header, CloudFront gets the IP address of the viewer from the TCP connection, adds an `X-Forwarded-For` header that includes the IP address, and forwards the request to the origin. For example, if CloudFront gets the IP address `192.0.2.2` from the TCP connection, it forwards the following header to the origin:

`X-Forwarded-For: 192.0.2.2`

If a viewer sends a request to CloudFront and includes an `X-Forwarded-For` request header, CloudFront gets the IP address of the viewer from the TCP connection, appends it to the end of the `X-Forwarded-For` header, and forwards the request to the origin. For example, if the viewer request includes `X-Forwarded-For: 192.0.2.4,192.0.2.3` and CloudFront gets the IP address `192.0.2.2` from the TCP connection, it forwards the following header to the origin:

`X-Forwarded-For: 192.0.2.4,192.0.2.3,192.0.2.2`

Some applications, such as load balancers (including Elastic Load Balancing), web application firewalls, reverse proxies, intrusion prevention systems, and API Gateway, append the IP address of the CloudFront edge server that forwarded the request onto the end of the `X-Forwarded-For` header. For example, if CloudFront includes `X-Forwarded-For: 192.0.2.2` in a request that it forwards to ELB and if the IP address of the CloudFront edge server is 192.0.2.199, the request that your EC2 instance receives contains the following header:

`X-Forwarded-For: 192.0.2.2,192.0.2.199`

### Note
The `X-Forwarded-For` header contains IPv4 addresses (such as 192.0.2.44) and IPv6 addresses (such as 2001:0db8:85a3:0000:0000:8a2e:0370:7334), as applicable.

### Client-Side SSL Authentication

CloudFront does not support client authentication with client-side SSL certificates. If an origin requests a client-side certificate, CloudFront drops the request.

### Compression

CloudFront forwards requests that have the `Accept-Encoding` field values `"identity"` and `"gzip"`. For more information, see Serving Compressed Files.

### Conditional Requests

When CloudFront receives a request for an object that has expired from an edge cache, it forwards the request to the origin either to get the latest version of the object or to get confirmation from the origin that the CloudFront edge cache already has the latest version. Typically, when the origin last sent the object to CloudFront, it included an `ETag` value, a `LastModified` value, or both values in the response. In the new request that CloudFront forwards to the origin, CloudFront adds one or both of the following:

- An `If-Match` or `If-None-Match` header that contains the `ETag` value for the expired version of the object.
- An `If-Modified-Since` header that contains the `LastModified` value for the expired version of the object.

The origin uses this information to determine whether the object has been updated and, therefore, whether to return the entire object to CloudFront or to return only an HTTP 304 status code (not modified).

## Cookies

You can configure CloudFront to forward cookies to your origin. For more information, see Configuring CloudFront to Cache Objects Based on Cookies.

## Cross-Origin Resource Sharing (CORS)

If you want CloudFront to respect cross-origin resource sharing settings, configure CloudFront to forward the Origin header to your origin. For more information, see Configuring CloudFront to Cache Objects Based on Request Headers.

## Encryption

You can require viewers to use HTTPS to send requests to CloudFront and require CloudFront to forward requests to your custom origin by using the protocol that is used by the viewer. For more information, see the following distribution settings:

- Viewer Protocol Policy
- Origin Protocol Policy (Amazon EC2, Elastic Load Balancing, and Other Custom Origins Only)

CloudFront forwards HTTPS requests to the origin server using the SSLv3, TLSv1.0, TLSv1.1, and TLSv1.2 protocols. For custom origins, you can choose the SSL protocols that you want CloudFront to use when communicating with your origin:

- If you're using the CloudFront console, choose protocols by using the **Origin SSL Protocols** check boxes. For more information, see Creating a Web Distribution.
- If you're using the CloudFront API, specify protocols by using the OriginSslProtocols element. For more information, see  OriginSslProtocols and  DistributionConfig in the *Amazon CloudFront API Reference*.

If the origin is an Amazon S3 bucket, CloudFront always uses TLSv1.2.

### Important
Other versions of SSL and TLS are not supported.

For more information about using HTTPS with CloudFront, see Using HTTPS with CloudFront. For lists of the ciphers that CloudFront supports for HTTPS communication between viewers and CloudFront, and between CloudFront and your origin, see Supported SSL/TLS Protocols and Ciphers for Communication Between Viewers and CloudFront.

## GET Requests That Include a Body

If a viewer GET request includes a body, CloudFront returns an HTTP status code 403 (Forbidden) to the viewer.

## HTTP Methods

If you configure CloudFront to process all of the HTTP methods that it supports, CloudFront accepts the following requests from viewers and forwards them to your custom origin:

- DELETE
- GET
- HEAD
- OPTIONS

- `PATCH`
- `POST`
- `PUT`

CloudFront always caches responses to `GET` and `HEAD` requests. You can also configure CloudFront to cache responses to `OPTIONS` requests. CloudFront does not cache responses to requests that use the other methods.

For information about configuring whether your custom origin processes these methods, see the documentation for your origin.

**Important**

If you configure CloudFront to accept and forward to your origin all of the HTTP methods that CloudFront supports, configure your origin server to handle all methods. For example, if you configure CloudFront to accept and forward these methods because you want to use `POST`, you must configure your origin server to handle `DELETE` requests appropriately so viewers can't delete resources that you don't want them to. For more information, see the documentation for your HTTP server.

## HTTP Request Headers and CloudFront Behavior (Custom and S3 Origins)

The following table lists HTTP request headers that you can forward to both custom and Amazon S3 origins (with the exceptions that are noted). For each header, the table includes information about the following:

- CloudFront behavior if you don't configure CloudFront to forward the header to your origin, which causes CloudFront to cache your objects based on header values.

- Whether you can configure CloudFront to cache objects based on header values for that header.

  You can configure CloudFront to cache objects based on values in the `Date` and `User-Agent` headers, but we don't recommend it. These headers have a lot of possible values, and caching based on their values would cause CloudFront to forward significantly more requests to your origin.

For more information about caching based on header values, see Configuring CloudFront to Cache Objects Based on Request Headers.

| Header | Behavior If You Don't Configure CloudFront to Cache Based on Header Values | Caching Based on Header Values Is Supported |
|---|---|---|
| Other-defined headers | CloudFront forwards the headers to your origin. | Yes |
| `Accept` | CloudFront removes the header. | Yes |
| `Accept-Charset` | CloudFront removes the header. | Yes |
| `Accept-Encoding` | If the value contains `gzip`, CloudFront forwards `Accept -Encoding: gzip` to your origin. If the value does not contain `gzip`, CloudFront removes the `Accept-Encoding` header field before forwarding the request to your origin. | No |
| `Accept-Language` | CloudFront removes the header. | Yes |
| `Authorization` | [See the AWS documentation website for more details] | Yes |

262

| Header | Behavior If You Don't Configure CloudFront to Cache Based on Header Values | Caching Based on Header Values Is Supported |
| --- | --- | --- |
| Cache-Control | CloudFront forwards the header to your origin. | No |
| CloudFront-Forwarded-Proto | CloudFront does not add the header before forwarding the request to your origin. For more information, see Configuring CloudFront to Cache Objects Based on the Protocol of the Request. | Yes |
| CloudFront-Is-Desktop-Viewer | CloudFront does not add the header before forwarding the request to your origin. For more information, see Configuring CloudFront to Cache Objects Based on the Device Type. | Yes |
| CloudFront-Is-Mobile-Viewer | CloudFront does not add the header before forwarding the request to your origin. For more information, see Configuring CloudFront to Cache Objects Based on the Device Type. | Yes |
| CloudFront-Is-Tablet-Viewer | CloudFront does not add the header before forwarding the request to your origin. For more information, see Configuring CloudFront to Cache Objects Based on the Device Type. | Yes |
| CloudFront-Viewer-Country | CloudFront does not add the header before forwarding the request to your origin. | Yes |
| Connection | CloudFront replaces this header with **Connection: Keep-Alive** before forwarding the request to your origin. | No |
| Content-Length | CloudFront forwards the header to your origin. | No |
| Content-MD5 | CloudFront forwards the header to your origin. | Yes |
| Content-Type | CloudFront forwards the header to your origin. | Yes |

| Header | Behavior If You Don't Configure CloudFront to Cache Based on Header Values | Caching Based on Header Values Is Supported |
| --- | --- | --- |
| Cookie | If you configure CloudFront to forward cookies, it will forward the `Cookie` header field to your origin. If you don't, CloudFront removes the `Cookie` header field. For more information, see Configuring CloudFront to Cache Objects Based on Cookies. | No |
| Date | CloudFront forwards the header to your origin. | Yes, but not recommended |
| Expect | CloudFront removes the header. | Yes |
| From | CloudFront forwards the header to your origin. | Yes |
| Host | CloudFront sets the value to the domain name of the origin that is associated with the requested object. You can't cache based on the Host header for Amazon S3 origins. | Yes (custom) No (S3) |
| If-Match | CloudFront forwards the header to your origin. | Yes |
| If-Modified-Since | CloudFront forwards the header to your origin. | Yes |
| If-None-Match | CloudFront forwards the header to your origin. | Yes |
| If-Range | CloudFront forwards the header to your origin. | Yes |
| If-Unmodified-Since | CloudFront forwards the header to your origin. | Yes |
| Max-Forwards | CloudFront forwards the header to your origin. | No |
| Origin | CloudFront forwards the header to your origin. | Yes |
| Pragma | CloudFront forwards the header to your origin. | No |
| Proxy-Authenticate | CloudFront removes the header. | No |
| Proxy-Authorization | CloudFront removes the header. | No |
| Proxy-Connection | CloudFront removes the header. | No |
| Range | CloudFront forwards the header to your origin. For more information, see How CloudFront Processes Partial Requests for an Object (Range GETs). | Yes, by default |
| Referer | CloudFront removes the header. | Yes |

| Header | Behavior If You Don't Configure CloudFront to Cache Based on Header Values | Caching Based on Header Values Is Supported |
| --- | --- | --- |
| Request-Range | CloudFront forwards the header to your origin. | No |
| TE | CloudFront removes the header. | No |
| Trailer | CloudFront removes the header. | No |
| Transfer-Encoding | CloudFront forwards the header to your origin. | No |
| Upgrade | CloudFront removes the header. | No |
| User-Agent | CloudFront replaces the value of this header field with `Amazon CloudFront`. If you want CloudFront to cache your content based on the device the user is using, see Configuring CloudFront to Cache Objects Based on the Device Type. | Yes, but not recommended |
| Via | CloudFront forwards the header to your origin. | Yes |
| Warning | CloudFront forwards the header to your origin. | Yes |
| X-Amz-Cf-Id | CloudFront adds the header to the viewer request before forwarding the request to your origin. The header value contains an encrypted string that uniquely identifies the request. | No |
| X-Edge-* | CloudFront removes all X-Edge-* headers. | No |
| X-Forwarded-For | CloudFront forwards the header to your origin. For more information, see Client IP Addresses. | Yes |
| X-Forwarded-Proto | CloudFront removes the header. | Yes |
| X-Real-IP | CloudFront removes the header. | No |

**HTTP Version**

CloudFront forwards requests to your custom origin using HTTP/1.1.

**Maximum Length of a Request and Maximum Length of a URL**

The maximum length of a request, including the path, the query string (if any), and headers, is 20,480 bytes.

CloudFront constructs a URL from the request. The maximum length of this URL is 8192 bytes.

If a request or a URL exceeds these limits, CloudFront returns HTTP status code 413, Request Header Fields Too Large, to the viewer, and then terminates the TCP connection to the viewer.

## OCSP Stapling

When a viewer submits an HTTPS request for an object, either CloudFront or the viewer must confirm with the certificate authority (CA) that the SSL certificate for the domain has not been revoked. OCSP stapling speeds up certificate validation by allowing CloudFront to validate the certificate and to cache the response from the CA, so the client doesn't need to validate the certificate directly with the CA.

The performance improvement of OCSP stapling is more pronounced when CloudFront receives a lot of HTTPS requests for objects in the same domain. Each server in a CloudFront edge location must submit a separate validation request. When CloudFront receives a lot of HTTPS requests for the same domain, every server in the edge location soon has a response from the CA that it can "staple" to a packet in the SSL handshake; when the viewer is satisfied that the certificate is valid, CloudFront can serve the requested object. If your distribution doesn't get much traffic in a CloudFront edge location, new requests are more likely to be directed to a server that hasn't validated the certificate with the CA yet. In that case, the viewer separately performs the validation step and the CloudFront server serves the object. That CloudFront server also submits a validation request to the CA, so the next time it receives a request that includes the same domain name, it has a validation response from the CA.

## Persistent Connections

When CloudFront gets a response from your origin, it tries to maintain the connection for several seconds in case another request arrives during that period. Maintaining a persistent connection saves the time required to re-establish the TCP connection and perform another TLS handshake for subsequent requests.

For more information, including how to configure the duration of persistent connections, see Origin Keep-alive Timeout (Amazon EC2, Elastic Load Balancing, and Other Custom Origins Only) in the section Values That You Specify When You Create or Update a Web Distribution.

## Protocols

CloudFront forwards HTTP or HTTPS requests to the origin server based on the following:

- The protocol of the request that the viewer sends to CloudFront, either HTTP or HTTPS.
- The value of the **Origin Protocol Policy** field in the CloudFront console or, if you're using the CloudFront API, the OriginProtocolPolicy element in the DistributionConfig complex type. In the CloudFront console, the options are **HTTP Only**, **HTTPS Only**, and **Match Viewer**.

If you specify **HTTP Only** or **HTTPS Only**, CloudFront forwards requests to the origin server using the specified protocol, regardless of the protocol in the viewer request.

If you specify **Match Viewer**, CloudFront forwards requests to the origin server using the protocol in the viewer request. Note that CloudFront caches the object only once even if viewers make requests using both HTTP and HTTPS protocols.

**Important**
If CloudFront forwards a request to the origin using the HTTPS protocol, and if the origin server returns an invalid certificate or a self-signed certificate, CloudFront drops the TCP connection.

For information about how to update a distribution using the CloudFront console, see Viewing and Updating CloudFront Distributions. For information about how to update a distribution using the CloudFront API, go to UpdateDistribution in the *Amazon CloudFront API Reference*.

## Query Strings

You can configure whether CloudFront forwards query string parameters to your origin. For more information, see Configuring CloudFront to Cache Based on Query String Parameters.

## Origin Response Timeout

The origin response timeout, also known as the origin request timeout or origin read timeout, applies to both of the following values:

- The amount of time, in seconds, that CloudFront waits for a response after forwarding a request to a custom origin
- The amount of time, in seconds, that CloudFront waits after receiving a packet of a response from the origin and before receiving the next packet

For more information, including how to configure the origin response timeout, see Origin Response Timeout (Amazon EC2, Elastic Load Balancing, and Other Custom Origins Only) in the section Values That You Specify When You Create or Update a Web Distribution.

## Simultaneous Requests for the Same Object (Traffic Spikes)

When a CloudFront edge location receives a request for an object and either the object isn't currently in the cache or the object has expired, CloudFront immediately sends the request to your origin. If there's a traffic spike—if additional requests for the same object arrive at the edge location before your origin responds to the first request—CloudFront pauses briefly before forwarding additional requests for the object to your origin. Typically, the response to the first request will arrive at the CloudFront edge location before the response to subsequent requests. This brief pause helps to reduce unnecessary load on your origin server. If additional requests are not identical because, for example, you configured CloudFront to cache based on request headers or cookies, CloudFront forwards all of the unique requests to your origin.

## User-Agent Header

If you want CloudFront to cache different versions of your objects based on the device a user is using to view your content, we recommend that you configure CloudFront to forward the applicable headers to your custom origin:

- `CloudFront-Is-Desktop-Viewer`
- `CloudFront-Is-Mobile-Viewer`
- `CloudFront-Is-SmartTV-Viewer`
- `CloudFront-Is-Tablet-Viewer`

Based on the value of the `User-Agent` header, CloudFront sets the value of these headers to `true` or `false` before forwarding the request to your origin. If a device falls into more than one category, more than one value might be `true`. For example, for some tablet devices, CloudFront might set both `CloudFront-Is-Mobile-Viewer` and `CloudFront-Is-Tablet-Viewer` to `true`. For more information about configuring CloudFront to cache based on request headers, see Configuring CloudFront to Cache Objects Based on Request Headers.

You can configure CloudFront to cache objects based on values in the `User-Agent` header, but we don't recommend it. The `User-Agent` header has a lot of possible values, and caching based on those values would cause CloudFront to forward significantly more requests to your origin.

If you do not configure CloudFront to cache objects based on values in the `User-Agent` header, CloudFront CloudFront adds a `User-Agent` header with the following value before it forwards a request to your origin:

`User-Agent = Amazon CloudFront`

CloudFront adds this header regardless of whether the request from the viewer includes a `User-Agent` header. If the request from the viewer includes a `User-Agent` header, CloudFront removes it.

# How CloudFront Processes Responses from Your Custom Origin Server

This topic contains information about how CloudFront processes responses from your custom origin.

**Topics**

- 100-Continue Responses
- Caching
- Canceled Requests
- Content Negotiation
- Cookies
- Dropped TCP Connections
- HTTP Response Headers that CloudFront Removes or Updates
- Maximum File Size
- Origin Unavailable
- Redirects
- Transfer Encoding

## 100-Continue Responses

Your origin cannot send more than one 100-Continue response to CloudFront. After the first 100-Continue response, CloudFront expects an HTTP 200 OK response. If your origin sends another 100-Continue response after the first one, CloudFront will return an error.

## Caching

- Ensure that the origin server sets valid and accurate values for the `Date` and `Last-Modified` header fields.
- If requests from viewers include the `If-Match` or `If-None-Match` request header fields, set the `ETag` response header field. If you do not specify an `ETag` value, CloudFront ignores subsequent `If-Match` or `If-None-Match` headers.
- CloudFront normally respects a `Cache-Control: no-cache` header in the response from the origin. For an exception, see Simultaneous Requests for the Same Object (Traffic Spikes).

## Canceled Requests

If an object is not in the edge cache, and if a viewer terminates a session (for example, closes a browser) after CloudFront gets the object from your origin but before it can deliver the requested object, CloudFront does not cache the object in the edge location.

## Content Negotiation

If your origin returns `Vary:*` in the response, and if the value of **Minimum TTL** for the corresponding cache behavior is **0**, CloudFront caches the object but still forwards every subsequent request for the object to the origin to confirm that the cache contains the latest version of the object. CloudFront doesn't include any conditional headers, such as `If-None-Match` or `If-Modified-Since`. As a result, your origin returns the object to CloudFront in response to every request.

If your origin returns `Vary:*` in the response, and if the value of **Minimum TTL** for the corresponding cache behavior is any other value, CloudFront processes the `Vary` header as described in HTTP Response Headers that CloudFront Removes or Updates.

## Cookies

If you enable cookies for a cache behavior, and if the origin returns cookies with an object, CloudFront caches both the object and the cookies. Note that this reduces cacheability for an object. For more information, see Configuring CloudFront to Cache Objects Based on Cookies.

## Dropped TCP Connections

If the TCP connection between CloudFront and your origin drops while your origin is returning an object to CloudFront, CloudFront behavior depends on whether your origin included a `Content-Length` header in the response:

- **Content-Length header** – CloudFront returns the object to the viewer as it gets the object from your origin. However, if the value of the `Content-Length` header doesn't match the size of the object, CloudFront doesn't cache the object.
- **Transfer-Encoding: Chunked** – CloudFront returns the object to the viewer as it gets the object from your origin. However, if the chunked response is not complete, CloudFront does not cache the object.
- **No Content-Length header** – CloudFront returns the object to the viewer and caches it, but the object may not be complete. Without a `Content-Length` header, CloudFront cannot determine whether the TCP connection was dropped accidentally or on purpose.

We recommend that you configure your HTTP server to add a `Content-Length` header to prevent CloudFront from caching partial objects.

## HTTP Response Headers that CloudFront Removes or Updates

CloudFront removes or updates the following header fields before forwarding the response from your origin to the viewer:

- `Set-Cookie` – If you configure CloudFront to forward cookies, it will forward the `Set-Cookie` header field to clients. For more information, see Configuring CloudFront to Cache Objects Based on Cookies.

- `Trailer`

- `Transfer-Encoding` – If your origin returns this header field, CloudFront sets the value to `chunked` before returning the response to the viewer.

- `Upgrade`

- `Vary` – Note the following:

  - If you configure CloudFront to forward any of the device-specific headers to your origin (`CloudFront-Is-Desktop-Viewer`, `CloudFront-Is-Mobile-Viewer`, `CloudFront-Is-SmartTV-Viewer`, `CloudFront-Is-Tablet-Viewer`) and you configure your origin to return `Vary:User-Agent` to CloudFront, CloudFront returns `Vary:User-Agent` to the viewer. For more information, see Configuring CloudFront to Cache Objects Based on the Device Type.
  - If you configure your origin to include either `Accept-Encoding` or `Cookie` in the `Vary` header, CloudFront includes the values in the response to the viewer.
  - If you configure CloudFront to forward a whitelist of headers to your origin, and if you configure your origin to return the header names to CloudFront in the `Vary` header (for example, `Vary: Accept-Charset,Accept-Language`), CloudFront returns the `Vary` header with those value to the viewer.
  - For information about how CloudFront processes a value of * in the `Vary` header, see Content Negotiation.
  - If you configure your origin to include any other values in the `Vary` header, CloudFront removes the values before returning the response to the viewer.

- `Via` – Regardless of whether your origin returns this header field to CloudFront, CloudFront sets the value to:

  `Via: 1.1`*alphanumeric-string*`.cloudfront.net (CloudFront)`

  before returning the response to the viewer. For example:

  `Via: 1.1 1026589cc7887e7a0dc7827b4example.cloudfront.net (CloudFront)`

## Maximum File Size

The maximum size of a response body that CloudFront will return to the viewer is 20 GB. This includes chunked transfer responses that don't specify the `Content-Length` header value.

## Origin Unavailable

If your origin server is unavailable and CloudFront gets a request for an object that is in the edge cache but that has expired (for example, because the period of time specified in the `Cache-Control max-age` directive has passed), CloudFront either serves the expired version of the object or serves a custom error page. For more information, see How CloudFront Processes and Caches HTTP 4xx and 5xx Status Codes from Your Origin.

In some cases, an object that is seldom requested is evicted and is no longer available in the edge cache. CloudFront can't serve an object that has been evicted.

## Redirects

If you change the location of an object on the origin server, you can configure your web server to redirect requests to the new location. After you configure the redirect, the first time a viewer submits a request for the object, CloudFront Front sends the request to the origin, and the origin responds with a redirect (for example, `302 Moved Temporarily`). CloudFront caches the redirect and returns it to the viewer. CloudFront does not follow the redirect.

You can configure your web server to redirect requests to one of the following locations:

- The new URL of the object on the origin server. When the viewer follows the redirect to the new URL, the viewer bypasses CloudFront and goes straight to the origin. As a result, we recommend that you not redirect requests to the new URL of the object on the origin.
- The new CloudFront URL for the object. When the viewer submits the request that contains the new CloudFront URL, CloudFront gets the object from the new location on your origin, caches it at the edge location, and returns the object to the viewer. Subsequent requests for the object will be served by the edge location. This avoids the latency and load associated with viewers requesting the object from the origin. However, every new request for the object will incur charges for two requests to CloudFront.

## Transfer Encoding

CloudFront supports only the `chunked` value of the `Transfer-Encoding` header. If your origin returns `Transfer -Encoding: chunked`, CloudFront returns the object to the client as the object is received at the edge location, and caches the object in chunked format for subsequent requests.

If the viewer makes a `Range GET` request and the origin returns `Transfer-Encoding: chunked`, CloudFront returns the entire object to the viewer instead of the requested range.

We recommend that you use chunked encoding if the content length of your response cannot be predetermined. For more information, see Dropped TCP Connections.

# How CloudFront Processes HTTP 3xx Status Codes from Your Origin

When CloudFront requests an object from your Amazon S3 bucket or custom origin server, your origin sometimes returns an HTTP 3xx status code, which typically indicates either that the URL has changed (301, Moved Permanently, or 307, Temporary Redirect) or that the object hasn't changed since the last time CloudFront requested it (304, Not Modified). CloudFront caches 3xx responses for the duration specified by the settings in your CloudFront distribution and by the header fields that your origin returns along with an object. For more information, see Specifying How Long Objects Stay in a CloudFront Edge Cache (Expiration).

If your origin returns a 301 or 307 status code, CloudFront doesn't follow the redirect to the new location.

# How CloudFront Processes and Caches HTTP 4xx and 5xx Status Codes from Your Origin

**Topics**

- How CloudFront Processes Errors When You Have Configured Custom Error Pages
- How CloudFront Processes Errors When You Have Not Configured Custom Error Pages
- HTTP 4xx and 5xx Status Codes that CloudFront Caches

When CloudFront requests an object from your Amazon S3 bucket or custom origin server, your origin sometimes returns an HTTP 4xx or 5xx status code, which indicates an error has occurred. CloudFront behavior depends on:

- Whether you have configured custom error pages.
- Whether you have configured how long you want CloudFront to cache error responses from your origin (error caching minimum TTL).
- The status code.
- For 5xx status codes, whether the requested object is currently in the CloudFront edge cache.

CloudFront always caches responses to `GET` and `HEAD` requests. You can also configure CloudFront to cache responses to `OPTIONS` requests. CloudFront does not cache responses to requests that use the other methods.

For information about settings for custom error pages in the CloudFront console, see Custom Error Pages and Error Caching. For information about the error caching minimum TTL in the CloudFront console, see Error Caching Minimum TTL.

For a list of the HTTP status codes that CloudFront caches, see HTTP 4xx and 5xx Status Codes that CloudFront Caches.

If you have enabled logging, CloudFront writes the results to the logs regardless of the HTTP status code.

## How CloudFront Processes Errors When You Have Configured Custom Error Pages

If you have configured custom error pages, CloudFront behavior depends on whether the requested object is in the edge cache.

### The Requested Object Is Not in the Edge Cache

CloudFront continues to try to get the requested object from your origin when all of the following are true:

- A viewer requests an object
- The object isn't in the edge cache
- Your origin returns an HTTP 4xx or 5xx status code instead of returning a 304 status code (Not Modified) or an updated version of the object

CloudFront does the following:

1. In the CloudFront edge cache that received the viewer request, CloudFront checks your distribution configuration and gets the path of the custom error page that corresponds with the status code that your origin returned.

2. CloudFront finds the first cache behavior in your distribution that has a path pattern that matches the path of the custom error page.

3. The CloudFront edge location sends a request for the custom error page to the origin that is specified in the cache behavior.

4. The origin returns the custom error page to the edge location.

5. CloudFront returns the custom error page to the viewer that made the request, and also caches the custom error page for the amount of time specified by the error caching minimum TTL (five minutes by default).

6. After the error caching minimum TTL has elapsed, CloudFront tries again to get the requested object by forwarding another request to your origin. CloudFront continues to retry at intervals specified by the error caching minimum TTL.

### The Requested Object Is in the Edge Cache

CloudFront continues to serve the object that is currently in the edge cache when all of the following are true:

- A viewer requests an object
- The object is in the edge cache but it has expired
- Your origin returns an HTTP 5xx status code instead of returning a 304 status code (Not Modified) or an updated version of the object

CloudFront does the following:

1. If your origin returns a 5xx status code, CloudFront serves the object even though it has expired. For the duration of the error caching minimum TTL, CloudFront continues to respond to viewer requests by serving the object from the edge cache.

   If your origin returns a 4xx status code, CloudFront returns the status code, not the requested object, to the viewer.

2. After the error caching minimum TTL has elapsed, CloudFront tries again to get the requested object by forwarding another request to your origin. Note that if the object is not requested frequently, CloudFront might evict it from the edge cache while your origin server is still returning 5xx responses. For information about how long objects stay in CloudFront edge caches, see Specifying How Long Objects Stay in a CloudFront Edge Cache (Expiration).

## How CloudFront Processes Errors When You Have Not Configured Custom Error Pages

If you have not configured custom error pages, CloudFront behavior depends on whether the requested object is in the edge cache.

### The Requested Object Is Not in the Edge Cache

CloudFront continues to try to get the requested object from your origin when all of the following are true:

- A viewer requests an object
- The object isn't in the edge cache
- Your origin returns an HTTP 4xx or 5xx status code instead of returning a 304 status code (Not Modified) or an updated version of the object

CloudFront does the following:

1. CloudFront returns the 4xx or 5xx status code to the viewer.

2. CloudFront also caches the status code in the edge cache that received the request.

3. For the duration of the error caching minimum TTL (five minutes by default), CloudFront responds to subsequent viewer requests for the same object with the cached 4xx or 5xx status code.

4. After the error caching minimum TTL has elapsed, CloudFront tries again to get the requested object by forwarding another request to your origin.

**The Requested Object Is in the Edge Cache**

CloudFront continues to serve the object that is currently in the edge cache when all of the following are true:

- A viewer requests an object
- The object is in the edge cache but it has expired
- Your origin returns an HTTP 5xx status code instead of returning a 304 status code (Not Modified) or an updated version of the object

CloudFront does the following:

1. If your origin returns a 5xx error code, CloudFront serves the object even though it has expired. For the duration of the error caching minimum TTL (five minutes by default), CloudFront continues to respond to viewer requests by serving the object from the edge cache.

   If your origin returns a 4xx status code, CloudFront returns the status code, not the requested object, to the viewer.

2. After the error caching minimum TTL has elapsed, CloudFront tries again to get the requested object by forwarding another request to your origin. Note that if the object is not requested frequently, CloudFront might evict it from the edge cache while your origin server is still returning 5xx responses. For information about how long objects stay in CloudFront edge caches, see Specifying How Long Objects Stay in a CloudFront Edge Cache (Expiration).

## HTTP 4xx and 5xx Status Codes that CloudFront Caches

CloudFront caches the following HTTP 4xx and 5xx status codes returned by Amazon S3 or your custom origin server. If you have configured a custom error page for an HTTP status code, CloudFront caches the custom error page.

| | |
|---|---|
| 400 | Bad Request |
| 403 | Forbidden |
| 404 | Not Found |
| 405 | Method Not Allowed |
| 414 | Request-URI Too Large |
| 500 | Internal Server Error |
| 501 | Not Implemented |
| 502 | Bad Gateway |
| 503 | Service Unavailable |
| 504 | Gateway Time-out |

# Serving Private Content through CloudFront

Many companies that distribute content via the internet want to restrict access to documents, business data, media streams, or content that is intended for selected users, for example, users who have paid a fee. To securely serve this private content using CloudFront, you can do the following:

- Require that your users access your private content by using special CloudFront signed URLs or signed cookies.
- Require that your users access your Amazon S3 content using CloudFront URLs, not Amazon S3 URLs. Requiring CloudFront URLs isn't required, but we recommend it to prevent users from bypassing the restrictions that you specify in signed URLs or signed cookies.

### Topics

- Overview of Private Content
- Using an HTTP Server for Private Content
- Task List: Serving Private Content
- Using an Origin Access Identity to Restrict Access to Your Amazon S3 Content
- Specifying the AWS Accounts That Can Create Signed URLs and Signed Cookies (Trusted Signers)
- Choosing Between Signed URLs and Signed Cookies
- Using Signed URLs
- Using Signed Cookies
- Using a Linux Command and OpenSSL for Base64-Encoding and Encryption
- Code Examples for Creating a Signature for a Signed URL

## Overview of Private Content

You can control user access to your private content in two ways, as shown in the following illustration:

1. Restrict access to objects in CloudFront edge caches

2. Restrict access to objects in your Amazon S3 bucket

### Restricting Access to Objects in CloudFront Edge Caches

You can configure CloudFront to require that users access your objects using either **signed URLs** or **signed cookies**. You then develop your application either to create and distribute signed URLs to authenticated users or to send `Set-Cookie` headers that set signed cookies on the viewers for authenticated users. (To give a few users long-term access to a limited number of objects, you can also create signed URLs manually.)

When you create signed URLs or signed cookies to control access to your objects, you can specify the following restrictions:

- An ending date and time, after which the URL is no longer valid.
- (Optional) The date and time that the URL becomes valid.
- (Optional) The IP address or range of addresses of the computers that can be used to access your content.

One part of a signed URL or a signed cookie is hashed and signed using the private key from a public/private key pair. When someone uses a signed URL or signed cookie to access an object, CloudFront compares the signed and unsigned portions of the URL or cookie. If they don't match, CloudFront doesn't serve the object.

### Restricting Access to Objects in Amazon S3 Buckets

You can optionally secure the content in your Amazon S3 bucket so users can access it through CloudFront but cannot access it directly by using Amazon S3 URLs. This prevents anyone from bypassing CloudFront and using the Amazon S3 URL to get content that you want to restrict access to. This step isn't required to use signed URLs, but we recommend it.

To require that users access your content through CloudFront URLs, you perform the following tasks:

- Create a special CloudFront user called an **origin access identity**.
- Give the origin access identity permission to read the objects in your bucket.
- Remove permission for anyone else to use Amazon S3 URLs to read the objects.

## Using an HTTP Server for Private Content

You can use signed URLs or signed cookies for any CloudFront distribution, regardless of whether the origin is an Amazon S3 bucket or an HTTP server. However, for CloudFront to get your objects from an HTTP server, the objects must remain publicly accessible. When the objects are publicly accessible, anyone who has the URL for an object on your HTTP server can access the object without logging in or paying for your content. If you use signed URLs or signed cookies and your origin is an HTTP server, do not give the URLs for the objects on your HTTP server to your customers or to others outside your organization.

# Task List: Serving Private Content

To configure CloudFront to serve private content, perform the following tasks:

1. (Optional but recommended) Require your users to access your content only through CloudFront. The method that you use depends on whether you're using Amazon S3 or custom origins:

    - **Amazon S3** – See Using an Origin Access Identity to Restrict Access to Your Amazon S3 Content.
    - **Custom origin** – See Using Custom Headers to Restrict Access to Your Content on a Custom Origin.

2. Specify the AWS accounts that you want to use to create signed URLs or signed cookies. For more information, see Specifying the AWS Accounts That Can Create Signed URLs and Signed Cookies (Trusted Signers).

3. Write your application to respond to requests from authorized users either with signed URLs or with `Set-Cookie` headers that set signed cookies. Follow the steps in one of the following topics:

    - Using Signed URLs
    - Using Signed Cookies

    If you're not sure which method to use, see Choosing Between Signed URLs and Signed Cookies.

# Using an Origin Access Identity to Restrict Access to Your Amazon S3 Content

**Topics**

- Creating a CloudFront Origin Access Identity and Adding it to Your Distribution
- Granting the Origin Access Identity Permission to Read Objects in Your Amazon S3 Bucket
- Using an Origin Access Identity in Amazon S3 Regions that Support Only Signature Version 4 Authentication

Typically, if you're using an Amazon S3 bucket as the origin for a CloudFront distribution, you grant everyone permission to read the objects in your bucket. This allows anyone to access your objects either through CloudFront or using the Amazon S3 URL. CloudFront doesn't expose Amazon S3 URLs, but your users might have those URLs if your application serves any objects directly from Amazon S3 or if anyone gives out direct links to specific objects in Amazon S3.

**Note**

You can also restrict access to content on a custom origin by using custom headers. For more information, see Using Custom Headers to Restrict Access to Your Content on a Custom Origin.

If you want to use CloudFront signed URLs or signed cookies to provide access to objects in your Amazon S3 bucket, you probably also want to prevent users from accessing your Amazon S3 objects using Amazon S3 URLs. If users access your objects directly in Amazon S3, they bypass the controls provided by CloudFront signed URLs or signed cookies, for example, control over the date and time that a user can no longer access your content and control over which IP addresses can be used to access content. In addition, if users access objects both through CloudFront and directly by using Amazon S3 URLs, CloudFront access logs are less useful because they're incomplete.

**Note**

To create origin access identities, you must use the CloudFront console or CloudFront API version 2009-09-09 or later.

To ensure that your users access your objects using only CloudFront URLs, regardless of whether the URLs are signed, perform the following tasks:

1. Create an origin access identity, which is a special CloudFront user, and associate the origin access identity with your distribution. (For web distributions, you associate the origin access identity with origins, so you can secure all or just some of your Amazon S3 content.) You can also create an origin access identity and add it to your distribution when you create the distribution. For more information, see Creating a CloudFront Origin Access Identity and Adding it to Your Distribution.

2. Change the permissions either on your Amazon S3 bucket or on the objects in your bucket so only the origin access identity has read permission (or read and download permission). When your users access your Amazon S3 objects through CloudFront, the CloudFront origin access identity gets the objects on behalf of your users. If your users request objects directly by using Amazon S3 URLs, they're denied access. The origin access identity has permission to access objects in your Amazon S3 bucket, but users don't. For more information, see Granting the Origin Access Identity Permission to Read Objects in Your Amazon S3 Bucket.

For detailed information about setting up a private Amazon S3 bucket to use with CloudFront, see How to Set Up and Serve Private Content Using S3 and Amazon CloudFront.

## Creating a CloudFront Origin Access Identity and Adding it to Your Distribution

An AWS account can have up to 100 CloudFront origin access identities. However, you can add an origin access identity to as many distributions as you want, so one origin access identity is usually sufficient.

If you didn't create an origin access identity and add it to your distribution when you created the distribution, you can create and add one now using either the CloudFront console or the CloudFront API:

- **If you're using the CloudFront console** – You can create an origin access identity and add it to your distribution at the same time. For more information, see Creating an Origin Access Identity and Adding it to Your Distribution Using the CloudFront Console.
- **If you're using the CloudFront API** – You create an origin access identity and then you add it to your distribution. Perform the procedure in each of the following topics:
  - Creating an Origin Access Identity Using the CloudFront API
  - Adding an Origin Access Identity to Your Distribution Using the CloudFront API

### Creating an Origin Access Identity and Adding it to Your Distribution Using the CloudFront Console

If you didn't create an origin access identity when you created your distribution, perform the following procedure.

**To create a CloudFront origin access identity using the CloudFront console**

1. Sign in to the AWS Management Console and open the CloudFront console at https://console.aws.amazon.com/cloudfront/.

2. Click the ID of the distribution that you want to add an origin access identity to.

3. Change to edit mode:

   - **Web distributions** – Click the **Origins** tab, select the origin that you want to edit, and click **Edit**. You can only create an origin access identity for origins for which **Origin Type** is **S3 Origin**.
   - **RTMP distributions** – Click **Edit**.

4. For **Restrict Bucket Access**, click **Yes**.

5. If you already have an origin access identity that you want to use, click **Use an Existing Identity**. Then select the identity in the **Your Identities** list. **Note** If you already have an origin access identity, we recommend that you reuse it to simplify maintenance.

   If you want to create an identity, click **Create a New Identity**. Then enter a description for the identity in the **Comment** field.

6. If you want CloudFront to automatically give the origin access identity permission to read the objects in the Amazon S3 bucket specified in **Origin Domain Name**, click **Yes, Update Bucket Policy**. **Important** If you click **Yes, Update Bucket Policy**, CloudFront updates bucket permissions to grant the specified origin access identity the permission to read objects in your bucket. However, CloudFront does not remove existing permissions. If users currently have permission to access the objects in your bucket using Amazon S3 URLs, they will still have that permission after CloudFront updates your bucket permissions. To view or remove existing bucket permissions, use a method provided by Amazon S3. For more information, see Granting the Origin Access Identity Permission to Read Objects in Your Amazon S3 Bucket.

   If you want to manually update permissions on your Amazon S3 bucket, click **No, I Will Update Permissions**.

7. Click **Yes, Edit**.

8. If you're adding an origin access identity to a web distribution and you have more than one origin, repeat step 3 through step 7 as applicable.

### Creating an Origin Access Identity Using the CloudFront API

If you already have an origin access identity and you want to reuse it instead of creating another one, skip to Adding an Origin Access Identity to Your Distribution Using the CloudFront API.

To create a CloudFront origin access identity using the CloudFront API, use the `POST Origin Access Identity` API action. The response includes an `Id` and an `S3CanonicalUserId` for the new origin access identity. Make note of these values because you will use them later in the process:

- **Id element** – You use the value of the `Id` element to associate an origin access ID with your distribution.
- **S3CanonicalUserId element** – You use the value of the `S3CanonicalUserId` element when you give CloudFront access to your Amazon S3 bucket or objects.

For more information, see CreateCloudFrontOriginAccessIdentity in the *Amazon CloudFront API Reference*.

### Adding an Origin Access Identity to Your Distribution Using the CloudFront API

You can use the CloudFront API to add a CloudFront origin access identity to an existing distribution or to create a new distribution that includes an origin access identity. In either case, include an `OriginAccessIdentity` element. This element contains the value of the `Id` element that the `POST Origin Access Identity` API action returned when you created the origin access identity. For web distributions, add the `OriginAccessIdentity` element to one or more origins. For RTMP distributions, add the `OriginAccessIdentity` element to the distribution.

See the applicable topic in the *Amazon CloudFront API Reference*:
- **Create a new web distribution** – CreateDistribution
- **Update an existing web distribution** – UpdateDistribution
- **Create a new RTMP distribution** – CreateStreamingDistribution
- **Update an existing RTMP distribution** – UpdateStreamingDistribution

## Granting the Origin Access Identity Permission to Read Objects in Your Amazon S3 Bucket

When you create or update a distribution, you can add an origin access identity and automatically update the bucket policy to give the origin access identity permission to access your bucket. Alternatively, you can choose to manually change the bucket policy or change ACLs, which control permissions on individual objects in your bucket.

Whichever method you use, you should still review the bucket policy for your bucket and review the permissions on your objects to ensure that:
- CloudFront can access objects in the bucket on behalf of users who are requesting your objects through CloudFront.
- Users can't use Amazon S3 URLs to access your objects.

**Important**
If you configure CloudFront to accept and forward to Amazon S3 all of the HTTP methods that CloudFront supports, create a CloudFront origin access identity to restrict access to your Amazon S3 content, and grant the origin access identity the applicable permissions. For example, if you configure CloudFront to accept and forward these methods because you want to use the `PUT` method, you must configure Amazon S3 bucket policies or ACLs to handle `DELETE` requests appropriately so users can't delete resources that you don't want them to.

Note the following:
- You might find it easier to update Amazon S3 bucket policies than ACLs because you can add objects to the bucket without updating permissions. However, ACLs give you more fine-grained control because you're granting permissions on each object.
- By default, your Amazon S3 bucket and all of the objects in it are private—only the AWS account that created the bucket has permission to read or write the objects in it.
- If you're adding an origin access identity to an existing distribution, modify the bucket policy or any object ACLs as appropriate to ensure that the objects are not publicly available.
- Grant additional permissions to one or more secure administrator accounts so you can continue to update the contents of the Amazon S3 bucket.

**Important**

There might be a brief delay between when you save your changes to Amazon S3 permissions and when the changes take effect. Until the changes take effect, you can get permission-denied errors when you try to access objects in your bucket.

## Updating Amazon S3 Bucket Policies

You can update the Amazon S3 bucket policy using either the AWS Management Console or the Amazon S3 API:

- Grant the CloudFront origin access identity the applicable permissions on the bucket.

  To specify an origin access identity, use the value of **Amazon S3 Canonical User ID** on the **Origin Access Identity** page in the CloudFront console. If you're using the CloudFront API, use the value of the `S3CanonicalUserId` element that was returned when you created the origin access identity.

- Deny access to anyone that you don't want to have access using Amazon S3 URLs.

For more information, go to Using Bucket Policies and User Policies in the *Amazon Simple Storage Service Developer Guide*.

For an example, see "Granting Permission to an Amazon CloudFront Origin Identity" in the topic Bucket Policy Examples, also in the *Amazon Simple Storage Service Developer Guide*.

## Updating Amazon S3 ACLs

Using either the AWS Management Console or the Amazon S3 API, change the Amazon S3 ACL:

- Grant the CloudFront origin access identity the applicable permissions on each object that the CloudFront distribution serves.

  To specify an origin access identity, use the value of **Amazon S3 Canonical User ID** on the **Origin Access Identity** page in the CloudFront console. If you're using the CloudFront API, use the value of the `S3CanonicalUserId` element that was returned when you created the origin access identity.

- Deny access to anyone that you don't want to have access using Amazon S3 URLs.

If another AWS account uploads objects to your bucket, that account is the owner of those objects. Bucket policies only apply to objects that the bucket owner owns. This means that if another account uploads objects to your bucket, the bucket policy that you created for your OAI will not be evaluated for those objects.

For more information, see Managing Access with ACLs in the *Amazon Simple Storage Service Developer Guide*.

You can also change the ACLs programmatically by using one of the AWS SDKs. For an example, see the downloadable sample code in Create a URL Signature Using C# and the .NET Framework.

## Using an Origin Access Identity in Amazon S3 Regions that Support Only Signature Version 4 Authentication

Newer Amazon S3 regions require that you use signature version 4 for authenticated requests. (For the versions of signature supported in each Amazon S3 region, see Amazon Simple Storage Service (S3) in the topic Regions and Endpoints in the *Amazon Web Services General Reference*.) However, when you create an origin access identity and add it to a CloudFront distribution, CloudFront typically uses signature version 2 for authentication when it requests objects in your Amazon S3 bucket. If you're using an origin access identity and if your bucket is in one of the regions that requires signature version 4 for authentication, note the following:

- `DELETE`, `GET`, `HEAD`, `OPTIONS`, and `PATCH` requests are supported without qualifications.

- If you want to submit `PUT` requests to CloudFront to upload objects to your Amazon S3 bucket, you must add an `x-amz-content-sha256` header to the request, and the header value must contain a SHA256 hash of the body of the request. For more information, see the documentation about the `x-amz-content-sha256` header on the Common Request Headers page in the *Amazon Simple Storage Service API Reference*.
- `POST` requests are not supported.

# Specifying the AWS Accounts That Can Create Signed URLs and Signed Cookies (Trusted Signers)

**Topics**

- Creating CloudFront Key Pairs for Your Trusted Signers
- Reformatting the CloudFront Private Key (.NET and Java Only)
- Adding Trusted Signers to Your Distribution
- Verifying that Trusted Signers Are Active (Optional)
- Rotating CloudFront Key Pairs

To create signed URLs or signed cookies, you need at least one AWS account that has an active CloudFront key pair. This account is known as a trusted signer. The trusted signer has two purposes:

- As soon as you add the AWS account ID for your trusted signer to your distribution, CloudFront starts to require that users use signed URLs or signed cookies to access your objects.
- When you create signed URLs or signed cookies, you use the private key from the trusted signer's key pair to sign a portion of the URL or the cookie. When someone requests a restricted object, CloudFront compares the signed portion of the URL or cookie with the unsigned portion to verify that the URL or cookie hasn't been tampered with. CloudFront also verifies that the URL or cookie is valid, meaning, for example, that the expiration date and time hasn't passed.

When you specify trusted signers, you also indirectly specify the objects that require signed URLs or signed cookies:

- **Web distributions** – You add trusted signers to cache behaviors. If your distribution has only one cache behavior, users must use signed URLs or signed cookies to access any object associated with the distribution. If you create multiple cache behaviors and add trusted signers to some cache behaviors and not to others, you can require that users use signed URLs or signed cookies to access some objects and not others.
- **RTMP distributions (signed URLs only)** – You add trusted signers to a distribution. After you add trusted signers to an RTMP distribution, users must use signed URLs to access any object associated with the distribution.

**Note**
To specify trusted signers for a distribution, you must use the CloudFront console or CloudFront API version 2009-09-09 or later.

To specify the accounts that are allowed to create signed URLs or signed cookies and to add the accounts to your CloudFront distribution, perform the following tasks:

1. Decide which AWS accounts you want to use as trusted signers. Most CloudFront customers use the account that they used to create the distribution.

2. For each of the accounts that you selected in Step 1, create a CloudFront key pair. For more information, see Creating CloudFront Key Pairs for Your Trusted Signers.

3. If you're using .NET or Java to create signed URLs or signed cookies, reformat the CloudFront private key. For more information, see Reformatting the CloudFront Private Key (.NET and Java Only).

4. In the distribution for which you're creating signed URLs or signed cookies, specify the AWS account IDs of your trusted signers. For more information, see Adding Trusted Signers to Your Distribution.

5. (Optional) Verify that CloudFront recognizes that your trusted signers have active CloudFront key pairs. For more information, see Verifying that Trusted Signers Are Active (Optional).

## Creating CloudFront Key Pairs for Your Trusted Signers

Each of the AWS accounts that you use to create CloudFront signed URLs or signed cookies—your trusted signers—must have its own CloudFront key pair, and the key pair must be active. Note that you can't substitute an Amazon EC2 key pair for a CloudFront key pair. When you create a CloudFront signed URL or signed cookie, you include the key pair ID for the trusted signer's key pair in the URL. Amazon EC2 does not make key pair IDs available.

To help secure your applications, we recommend that you change CloudFront key pairs every 90 days or more often. For more information, see Rotating CloudFront Key Pairs.

You can create a key pair in the following ways:

- Create a key pair in the AWS Management Console and download the private key. See the procedure To create CloudFront key pairs in the AWS Management Console.
- Create an RSA key pair by using an application such as OpenSSL, and upload the public key to the AWS Management Console. See the procedure To create an RSA key pair and upload the public key in the AWS Management Console.

**To create CloudFront key pairs in the AWS Management Console**

1. Sign in to the AWS Management Console using the root credentials for an AWS account. **Important** IAM users can't create CloudFront key pairs. You must log in using root credentials to create key pairs.

2. On the *account-name* menu, click **Security Credentials**.

3. Expand **CloudFront Key Pairs**.

4. Confirm that you have no more than one active key pair. You can't create a key pair if you already have two active key pairs.

5. Click **Create New Key Pair**.

6. In the **Create Key Pair** dialog box, click **Download Private Key File**.

7. In the **Opening** dialog box, accept the default value of **Save File**, and click **OK** to download and save the private key for your CloudFront key pair. **Important** Save the private key for your CloudFront key pair in a secure location, and set permissions on the file so that only the desired administrator users can read it. If someone gets your private key, they can generate valid signed URLs and signed cookies and download your content. You cannot get the private key again, so if you lose or delete it, you must create a new CloudFront key pair.

8. Record the key pair ID for your key pair. (In the AWS Management Console, this is called the access key ID.) You'll use it when you create signed URLs or signed cookies.

**To create an RSA key pair and upload the public key in the AWS Management Console**

1. Use OpenSSL or another tool to create a key pair.

   For example, if you're using OpenSSL, you can use the following command to generate a key pair with a length of 4096 bits and save it in the file `private_key.pem`:

   ```
   $ openssl genrsa -out private_key.pem 4096
   ```

   The resulting file contains both the public and the private key. To extract the public key from that file, run the following command:

   ```
   $ openssl rsa -pubout -in private_key.pem -out public_key.pem
   ```

   The public key is the file that you upload later in this procedure

   Note the following requirements for the key:

   - The key pair must be an SSH-2 RSA key pair.
   - The key pair must be in base64 encoded PEM format.

- The supported key lengths are 1024, 2048, and 4096 bits.

2. Sign in to the AWS Management Console using the root credentials for an AWS account. **Important** IAM users can't create CloudFront key pairs. You must log in using root credentials to create key pairs.

3. On the *account-name* menu, click **Security Credentials**.

4. Expand **CloudFront Key Pairs**.

5. Confirm that you have no more than one active key pair. You can't upload your own key pair if you already have two active key pairs.

6. Click **Upload Your Own Key Pair**.

7. In the **Upload Your Own Key Pair** dialog box, click **Choose File** and choose the public key file that you created in step 1.

8. Click **Upload**.

   The **Upload Key Pair** dialog box clears, and the new key pair appears at the top of the list of CloudFront key pairs.

9. Record the key pair ID for your key pair. (In the AWS Management Console, this is called the access key ID.) You'll use it when you create signed URLs or signed cookies.

## Reformatting the CloudFront Private Key (.NET and Java Only)

If you're using .NET or Java to create signed URLs or signed cookies, you cannot use the private key from your key pair in the default .pem format to create the signature:

- **.NET framework** – Convert the private key to the XML format that the .NET framework uses. Several tools are available.

- **Java** – Convert the private key to DER format. To do this, you can use OpenSSL:

  ```
  $ openssl pkcs8 -topk8 -nocrypt -in origin.pem -inform PEM -out new.der -outform DER
  ```

  To ensure that the encoder works correctly, add the jar for the Bouncy Castle Java cryptography APIs to your project and then add the Bouncy Castle provider.

## Adding Trusted Signers to Your Distribution

Trusted signers are the AWS accounts that can create signed URLs and signed cookies for a distribution. By default, no account, not even the account that created the distribution, is allowed to create signed URLs or signed cookies. To specify the AWS accounts that you want to use as trusted signers, add the accounts to your distribution:

- **Web distributions** – Trusted signers are associated with cache behaviors. This allows you to require signed URLs or signed cookies for some objects and not for others in the same distribution. Trusted signers can only create signed URLs or cookies for objects that are associated with the corresponding cache behaviors. For example, if you have one trusted signer for one cache behavior and a different trusted signer for a different cache behavior, neither trusted signer can create signed URLs or cookies for objects that are associated with the other cache behavior.
- **RTMP distributions (signed URLs only)** – Trusted signers are associated with the distribution. After you add trusted signers to an RTMP distribution, users must use signed URLs or signed cookies to access any of the objects associated with the distribution.

**Important**
Define path patterns and their sequence carefully so you don't either give users unintended access to your content or prevent them from accessing content that you want to be available to everyone. For example, suppose a

request matches the path pattern for two cache behaviors. The first cache behavior does not require signed URLs or signed cookies and the second cache behavior does. Users will be able to access the objects without using signed URLs or signed cookies because CloudFront processes the cache behavior that is associated with the first match.

For more information about path patterns, see Path Pattern.

**Important**

If you're updating a distribution that you're already using to distribute content, add trusted signers only when you're ready to start generating signed URLs or signed cookies for your objects, or CloudFront will reject the requests:
**Web distributions** – After you add trusted signers to a cache behavior for a web distribution, users must use signed URLs or signed cookies to access the objects that are associated with the cache behavior. **RTMP distributions (signed URLs only)** – After you add trusted signers to an RTMP distribution, users must use signed URLs to access any of the objects associated with the distribution.

The maximum number of trusted signers depends on the type of distribution:

- **Web distributions** – A maximum of five for each cache behavior
- **RTMP distributions** – A maximum of five for the distribution

You can add trusted signers to your distribution using either the CloudFront console or the CloudFront API. See the applicable topic:

- Adding Trusted Signers to Your Distribution Using the CloudFront Console
- Adding Trusted Signers to Your Distribution Using the CloudFront API

**Adding Trusted Signers to Your Distribution Using the CloudFront Console**

**To add trusted signers to your distribution using the CloudFront console**

1. If you want to use only the AWS account that created the distribution as a trusted signer, skip to Step 2.

   If you want to use other AWS accounts, get the AWS account ID for each account:

   1. Sign in to the AWS Management Console at https://console.aws.amazon.com/console/home using an account that you want to use as a trusted signer.

   2. In the upper-right corner of the console, click the name associated with the account, and click **My Account**.

   3. Under **Account Settings**, make note of the account ID.

   4. Sign out of the AWS Management Console.

   5. Repeat steps a through d for the other accounts that you want to use as trusted signers.

2. Open the Amazon CloudFront console at https://console.aws.amazon.com/cloudfront/, and sign in using the account that you used to create the distribution that you want to add trusted signers to.

3. Click the distribution ID.

4. Change to edit mode:

   - **Web distributions** – Click the **Behaviors** tab, click the behavior that you want to edit, and click **Edit**.
   - **RTMP distributions** – Click **Edit**.

5. For **Restrict Viewer Access (Use Signed URLs or Signed Cookies)**, click **Yes**.

6. For **Trusted Signers**, check the applicable check boxes:

   - **Self** – Check this check box if you want to use the current account (the account that you used to create the distribution).

- **Specify Accounts** – Check this check box if you want to use other AWS accounts.

7. If you checked the **Specify Accounts** check box, enter AWS account IDs in the **AWS Account Number** field. These are the account IDs that you got in the first step of this procedure. Enter one account ID per line.

8. Click **Yes, Edit**.

9. If you're adding trusted signers to a web distribution and you have more than one cache behavior, repeat steps 4 through 8 as applicable.

### Adding Trusted Signers to Your Distribution Using the CloudFront API

You can use the CloudFront API to add the AWS account IDs for trusted signers to an existing distribution or to create a new distribution that includes trusted signers. In either case, specify the applicable values in the `TrustedSigners` element. For web distributions, add the `TrustedSigners` element to one or more cache behaviors. For RTMP distributions, add the `TrustedSigners` element to the distribution.

See the applicable topic in the *Amazon CloudFront API Reference*:

- **Create a new web distribution** – CreateDistribution
- **Update an existing web distribution** – UpdateDistribution
- **Create a new RTMP distribution** – CreateStreamingDistribution
- **Update an existing RTMP distribution** – UpdateStreamingDistribution

## Verifying that Trusted Signers Are Active (Optional)

After you add trusted signers to your distribution, you might want to verify that the signers are active. For a trusted signer to be active, the following must be true:

- The AWS account must have at least one active key pair. If you're rotating key pairs, the account will temporarily have two active key pairs, the old key pair and the new one.
- CloudFront must be aware of the active key pair. After you create a key pair, there can be a short period of time before CloudFront is aware that the key pair exists.

**Note**
To display a list of active trusted signers for a distribution, you currently must use the CloudFront API. A list of active trusted signers is not available in the CloudFront console.

### Verifying that Trusted Signers Are Active Using the CloudFront API

To determine which trusted signers have active key pairs (are active trusted signers), you get the distribution and review the values in the `ActiveTrustedSigners` element. This element lists the AWS account ID of each account that the distribution identifies as a trusted signer. If the trusted signer has one or more active CloudFront key pairs, the `ActiveTrustedSigners` element also lists the key pair IDs. For more information, see the applicable topic in the *Amazon CloudFront API Reference*:

- **Web distributions** – GetDistribution
- **RTMP distributions** – GetStreamingDistribution

## Rotating CloudFront Key Pairs

AWS recommends that you rotate (change) your active CloudFront key pairs every 90 days. To rotate CloudFront key pairs that you're using to create signed URLs or signed cookies without invalidating URLs or cookies that haven't expired yet, perform the following tasks:

1. Create a new key pair for each of the accounts that you're using to create signed URLs. For more information, see Creating CloudFront Key Pairs for Your Trusted Signers.

2. Verify that CloudFront is aware of the new key pairs. For more information, see Verifying that Trusted Signers Are Active (Optional).

3. Update your application to create signatures using the private keys from the new key pairs.

4. Confirm that URLs or cookies that you're signing using the new private keys are working.

5. Wait until the expiration date has passed in URLs or cookies that were signed using the old CloudFront key pairs.

6. Change the old CloudFront key pairs to **Inactive**:

   1. Sign in to the AWS Management Console using the root credentials for an AWS account for which you want to make key pairs inactive.

   2. On the *account-name* menu, click **Security Credentials**.

   3. Expand **CloudFront Key Pairs**.

   4. For the applicable key pairs, click **Make Inactive**.

   5. Repeat steps a through d for each of the AWS accounts for which you want to make key pairs inactive.

7. Reconfirm that URLs or cookies that you're signing using the new private keys are working.

8. Delete the old CloudFront key pairs:

   1. Go to the Your Security Credentials page.

   2. Expand **CloudFront Key Pairs**.

   3. For the applicable key pairs, click **Delete**.

9. Delete the old private keys from the location where you stored them.

# Choosing Between Signed URLs and Signed Cookies

CloudFront signed URLs and signed cookies provide the same basic functionality: they allow you to control who can access your content. If you want to serve private content through CloudFront and you're trying to decide whether to use signed URLs or signed cookies, consider the following.

Use signed URLs in the following cases:

- You want to use an RTMP distribution. Signed cookies aren't supported for RTMP distributions.
- You want to restrict access to individual files, for example, an installation download for your application.
- Your users are using a client (for example, a custom HTTP client) that doesn't support cookies.

Use signed cookies in the following cases:

- You want to provide access to multiple restricted files, for example, all of the files for a video in HLS format or all of the files in the subscribers' area of a website.
- You don't want to change your current URLs.

If you are not currently using signed URLs and if your URLs contain any of the following query string parameters, you cannot use either signed URLs or signed cookies:

- Expires
- Policy
- Signature
- Key-Pair-Id

CloudFront assumes that URLs that contain any of those query string parameters are signed URLs and therefore won't look at signed cookies.

## Using Both Signed URLs and Signed Cookies

If you use both signed URLs and signed cookies to control access to the same objects and a viewer uses a signed URL to request an object, CloudFront determines whether to return the object to the viewer based only on the signed URL.

# Using Signed URLs

**Topics**

- Choosing Between Canned and Custom Policies for Signed URLs
- How Signed URLs Work
- Choosing How Long Signed URLs Are Valid
- When Does CloudFront Check the Expiration Date and Time in a Signed URL?
- Sample Code and Third-Party Tools
- Creating a Signed URL Using a Canned Policy
- Creating a Signed URL Using a Custom Policy

A signed URL includes additional information, for example, an expiration date and time, that gives you more control over access to your content. This additional information appears in a policy statement, which is based on either a canned policy or a custom policy. The differences between canned and custom policies are explained in the next two sections.

**Note**
You can create some signed URLs using canned policies and create some signed URLs using custom policies for the same distribution.

## Choosing Between Canned and Custom Policies for Signed URLs

When you create a signed URL, you write a policy statement in JSON format that specifies the restrictions on the signed URL, for example, how long the URL is valid. You can use either a canned policy or a custom policy. Here's how canned and custom policies compare:

| Description | Canned Policy | Custom Policy |
| --- | --- | --- |
| You can reuse the policy statement for multiple objects. To reuse the policy statement, you must use wildcard characters in the `Resource` object. For more information, see Values that You Specify in the Policy Statement for a Signed URL That Uses a Custom Policy.) | No | Yes |
| You can specify the date and time that users can begin to access your content. | No | Yes (optional) |
| You can specify the date and time that users can no longer access your content. | Yes | Yes |
| You can specify the IP address or range of IP addresses of the users who can access your content. | No | Yes (optional) |
| The signed URL includes a base64-encoded version of the policy, which results in a longer URL. | No | Yes |

For information about creating signed URLs using a canned policy, see Creating a Signed URL Using a Canned Policy.

For information about creating signed URLs using a custom policy, see Creating a Signed URL Using a Custom Policy.

## How Signed URLs Work

Here's an overview of how you configure CloudFront and Amazon S3 for signed URLs and how CloudFront responds when a user uses a signed URL to request an object.

1. In your CloudFront distribution, specify one or more trusted signers, which are the AWS accounts that you want to have permission to create signed URLs.

   For more information, see Specifying the AWS Accounts That Can Create Signed URLs and Signed Cookies (Trusted Signers).

2. You develop your application to determine whether a user should have access to your content and to create signed URLs for the objects or parts of your application that you want to restrict access to. For more information, see the applicable topic:

   - Creating a Signed URL Using a Canned Policy
   - Creating a Signed URL Using a Custom Policy

3. A user requests an object for which you want to require signed URLs.

4. Your application verifies that the user is entitled to access the object: they've signed in, they've paid for access to the content, or they've met some other requirement for access.

5. Your application creates and returns a signed URL to the user.

6. The signed URL allows the user to download or stream the content.

   This step is automatic; the user usually doesn't have to do anything additional to access the content. For example, if a user is accessing your content in a web browser, your application returns the signed URL to the browser. The browser immediately uses the signed URL to access the object in the CloudFront edge cache without any intervention from the user.

7. CloudFront uses the public key to validate the signature and confirm that the URL hasn't been tampered with. If the signature is invalid, the request is rejected.

   If the signature is valid, CloudFront looks at the policy statement in the URL (or constructs one if you're using a canned policy) to confirm that the request is still valid. For example, if you specified a beginning and ending date and time for the URL, CloudFront confirms that the user is trying to access your content during the time period that you want to allow access.

   If the request meets the requirements in the policy statement, CloudFront performs the standard operations: determines whether the object is already in the edge cache, forwards the request to the origin if necessary, and returns the object to the user.

## Choosing How Long Signed URLs Are Valid

You can distribute private content using a signed URL that is valid for only a short time—possibly for as little as a few minutes. Signed URLs that are valid for such a short period are good for distributing content on-the-fly to a user for a limited purpose, such as distributing movie rentals or music downloads to customers on demand. If your signed URLs will be valid for just a short period, you'll probably want to generate them automatically using an application that you develop. When the user starts to download an object or starts to play a media file, CloudFront compares the expiration time in the URL with the current time to determine whether the URL is still valid.

You can also distribute private content using a signed URL that is valid for a longer time, possibly for years. Signed URLs that are valid for a longer period are useful for distributing private content to known users, such as distributing a business plan to investors or distributing training materials to employees. You can develop an application to generate these longer-term signed URLs for you, or you can use one of the third-party GUI tools listed in Tools and Code Examples for Configuring Private Content.

## When Does CloudFront Check the Expiration Date and Time in a Signed URL?

When CloudFront checks the expiration date and time in a signed URL to determine whether the URL is still valid depends on whether the URL is for a web distribution or an RTMP distribution:

- **Web distributions** – CloudFront checks the expiration date and time in a signed URL at the time of the HTTP request. If a client begins to download a large object immediately before the expiration time, the download should complete even if the expiration time passes during the download. If the TCP connection drops and the client tries to restart the download after the expiration time passes, the download will fail.

  If a client uses Range GETs to get an object in smaller pieces, any GET request that occurs after the expiration time passes will fail. For more information about Range GETs, see How CloudFront Processes Partial Requests for an Object (Range GETs).

- **RTMP distributions** – CloudFront checks the expiration time in a signed URL at the start of a play event. If a client starts to play a media file before the expiration time passes, CloudFront allows the entire media file to play. However, depending on the media player, pausing and restarting might trigger another play event. Skipping to another position in the media file will trigger another play event. If the subsequent play event occurs after the expiration time passes, CloudFront won't serve the media file.

## Sample Code and Third-Party Tools

For sample code that creates the hashed and signed part of signed URLs, see the following topics:

- Create a URL Signature Using Perl
- Create a URL Signature Using PHP
- Create a URL Signature Using C# and the .NET Framework
- Create a URL Signature Using Java

For information about third-party tools that support private content, including creating signed URLs, see Tools and Code Examples for Configuring Private Content.

# Creating a Signed URL Using a Canned Policy

To create a signed URL using a canned policy, perform the following procedure.

**To create a signed URL using a canned policy**

1. If you're using .NET or Java to create signed URLs, and if you haven't reformatted the private key for your key pair from the default .pem format to a format compatible with .NET or with Java, do so now. For more information, see Reformatting the CloudFront Private Key (.NET and Java Only).

2. Concatenate the following values in the specified order, and remove the whitespace (including tabs and newline characters) between the parts. You might have to include escape characters in the string in application code. All values have a type of String. Each part is keyed by number (  ) to the two examples that follow.

   **❶** *Base URL for the object*

   The base URL is the CloudFront URL that you would use to access the object if you were not using signed URLs, including your own query string parameters, if any. For more information about the format of URLs for web distributions, see Format of URLs for Objects.

   The following examples show values that you specify for web distributions.

   - The following CloudFront URL is for an object in a web distribution (using the CloudFront domain name). Note that `image.jpg` is in an `images` directory. The path to the object in the URL must match the path to the object on your HTTP server or in your Amazon S3 bucket.

     `http://d111111abcdef8.cloudfront.net/images/image.jpg`

   - The following CloudFront URL includes a query string:

     `http://d111111abcdef8.cloudfront.net/images/image.jpg?size=large`

   - The following CloudFront URLs are for objects in a web distribution. Both use an alternate domain name; the second one includes a query string:

     `http://www.example.com/images/image.jpg`

     `http://www.example.com/images/image.jpg?color=red`

   - The following CloudFront URL is for an objects in a web distribution that uses an alternate domain name and the HTTPS protocol:

     `https://www.example.com/images/image.jpg` For RTMP distributions, the following examples are for objects in two different video formats, MP4 and FLV:

   - **MP4** – `mp4:sydney-vacation.mp4`

   - **FLV** – `sydney-vacation`

   - **FLV** – `sydney-vacation.flv` For .flv files, whether you include the `.flv` filename extension depends on your player. To serve MP3 audio files or H.264/MPEG-4 video files, you might need to prefix the file name with `mp3:` or `mp4:`. Some media players can be configured to add the prefix automatically. The media player might also require you to specify the file name without the file extension (for example, sydney-vacation instead of sydney-vacation.mp4).

   **❷** `?`

   The `?` indicates that query string parameters follow the base URL. Include the `?` even if you don't have any query string parameters of your own.

   **❸** *Your query string parameters, if any*`&****`

   This value is optional. If you want to add your own query string parameters, for example:

   `color=red&size=medium`

   then add the parameters after the `?` (see **❷**) and before the `Expires` parameter. In certain rare circumstances, you might need to put your query string parameters after `Key-Pair-Id`.

Your parameters cannot be named `Expires`, `Signature`, or `Key-Pair-Id`. If you add your own parameters, append an **&** after each one, including the last one.

**④** `Expires=`*date and time in Unix time format (in seconds) and Coordinated Universal Time (UTC)*

The date and time that you want the URL to stop allowing access to the object.

Specify the expiration date and time in Unix time format (in seconds) and Coordinated Universal Time (UTC). For example, January 1, 2013 10:00 am UTC converts to 1357034400 in Unix time format. To use epoch time, use a 32-bit integer for a date which can be no later than 2147483647 (January 19th, 2038 at 03:14:07 UTC). For information about UTC, see *RFC 3339, Date and Time on the Internet: Timestamps*, http://tools.ietf.org/html/rfc3339.

**⑤** `&Signature=`*hashed and signed version of the policy statement*

A hashed, signed, and base64-encoded version of the JSON policy statement. For more information, see Creating a Signature for a Signed URL That Uses a Canned Policy.

**⑥** `&Key-Pair-Id=`*active CloudFront key pair Id for the key pair that you're using to generate the signature*

The ID for an active CloudFront key pair, for example, APKA9ONS7QCOWEXAMPLE. The CloudFront key pair ID tells CloudFront which public key to use to validate the signed URL. CloudFront compares the information in the signature with the information in the policy statement to verify that the URL has not been tampered with.

The key pair ID that you include in CloudFront signed URLs must be the ID of an active key pair for one of your trusted signers:

- **Web distributions** – The key pair must be associated with an AWS account that is one of the trusted signers for the applicable cache behavior.

- **RTMP distributions** – The key pair must be associated with an AWS account that is one of the trusted signers for the distribution. For more information, see Specifying the AWS Accounts That Can Create Signed URLs and Signed Cookies (Trusted Signers).

  If you make a key pair inactive while rotating CloudFront key pairs, and if you're generating signed URLs programmatically, you must update your application to use a new active key pair for one of your trusted signers. If you're generating signed URLs manually, you must create new signed URLs. For more information about rotating key pairs, see Rotating CloudFront Key Pairs.

Example signed URL for a web distribution:

```
**    ①    http://d111111abcdef8.cloudfront.net/image.jpg    ②    ?    ③    color=red&size=
medium&    ④    Expires=1357034400    ⑤    &Signature=nitfHRCrtziwO2HwPfWw~yYDhUF5EwRunQA
-j19DzZrvDh6hQ73lDx~-ar3UocvvRQVw6EkC~GdpGQyyOSKQim-TxAnW7d8F5Kkai9HVxOFIu-5
jcQbOUEmatEXAMPLE3ReXySpLSMj0yCd3ZAB4UcBCAqEijkytL6f3fVYNGQI6    ⑥    &Key-Pair-Id=
APKA9ONS7QCOWEXAMPLE **
```

Example signed URL for an RTMP distribution:

```
**    ①    videos/mediafile.flv    ②    ?    ③    color=red&size=medium&    ④
Expires=1357034400    ⑤    &Signature=nitfHRCrtziwO2HwPfWw~yYDhUF5EwRunQA-
j19DzZrvDh6hQ73lDx~-ar3UocvvRQVw6EkC~GdpGQyyOSKQim-TxAnW7d8F5Kkai9HVxOFIu-5
jcQbOUEmatEXAMPLE3ReXySpLSMj0yCd3ZAB4UcBCAqEijkytL6f3fVYNGQI6    ⑥    &Key-Pair-Id=
APKA9ONS7QCOWEXAMPLE **
```

## Creating a Signature for a Signed URL That Uses a Canned Policy

To create the signature for a signed URL that uses a canned policy, you perform the following procedures:

1. Create a policy statement. See Creating a Policy Statement for a Signed URL That Uses a Canned Policy.

2. Sign the policy statement to create a signature. See Creating a Signature for a Signed URL That Uses a Canned Policy.

## Creating a Policy Statement for a Signed URL That Uses a Canned Policy

When you create a signed URL using a canned policy, the `Signature` parameter is a hashed and signed version of a policy statement. For signed URLs that use a canned policy, you don't include the policy statement in the URL, as you do for signed URLs that use a custom policy. To create the policy statement, perform the following procedure.

### To create the policy statement for a signed URL that uses a canned policy

1. Construct the policy statement using the following JSON format and using UTF-8 character encoding. Include all punctuation and other literal values exactly as specified. For information about the `Resource` and `DateLessThan` parameters, see Values that You Specify in the Policy Statement for a Signed URL That Uses a Canned Policy.

```
1  {
2     "Statement":[
3        {
4           "Resource":"base URL or stream name",
5           "Condition":{
6              "DateLessThan":{
7                 "AWS:EpochTime":ending date and time in Unix time format and UTC
8              }
9           }
10       }
11    ]
12 }
```

2. Remove all whitespace (including tabs and newline characters) from the policy statement. You might have to include escape characters in the string in application code.

## Values that You Specify in the Policy Statement for a Signed URL That Uses a Canned Policy

When you create a policy statement for a canned policy, you specify the following values.

### Resource
The value that you specify depends on whether you're creating the signed URL for a web distribution or an RTMP distribution.
You can specify only one value for `Resource`.
### Web distributions
The base URL including your query strings, if any, but excluding the CloudFront `Expires`, `Signature`, and `Key-Pair-Id` parameters, for example:
`http://d111111abcdef8.cloudfront.net/images/horizon.jpg?size=large&license=yes`
Note the following:

- **Protocol** – The value must begin with `http://` or `https://`.
- **Query string parameters** – If you have no query string parameters, omit the question mark.
- **Alternate domain names** – If you specify an alternate domain name (CNAME) in the URL, you must specify the alternate domain name when referencing the object in your web page or application. Do not specify the Amazon S3 URL for the object.
  ### RTMP distributions
  Include only the stream name. For example, if the full URL for a streaming video is:
  `rtmp://s5c39gqb8ow64r.cloudfront.net/videos/cfx/st/mp3_name.mp3`
  then use the following value for `Resource`:

```
videos/mp3_name
```
Do not include a prefix such as `mp3:` or `mp4:`. Also, depending on the player you're using, you might have to omit the file extension from the value of `Resource`. For example, you might need to use `sydney-vacation` instead of `sydney-vacation.flv`.

### DateLessThan

The expiration date and time for the URL in Unix time format (in seconds) and Coordinated Universal Time (UTC). For example, January 1, 2013 10:00 am UTC converts to 1357034400 in Unix time format.

This value must match the value of the `Expires` query string parameter in the signed URL. Do not enclose the value in quotation marks.

For more information, see When Does CloudFront Check the Expiration Date and Time in a Signed URL?.

### Example Policy Statement for a Signed URL That Uses a Canned Policy

When you use the following example policy statement in a signed URL, a user can access the object `http://d111111abcdef8.cloudfront.net/horizon.jpg` until January 1, 2013 10:00 am UTC:

```
1  {
2      "Statement":[
3          {
4              "Resource":"http://d111111abcdef8.cloudfront.net/horizon.jpg?size=large&license=yes",
5              "Condition":{
6                  "DateLessThan":{
7                      "AWS:EpochTime":1357034400
8                  }
9              }
10         }
11     ]
12 }
```

### Creating a Signature for a Signed URL That Uses a Canned Policy

To create the value for the `Signature` parameter in a signed URL, you hash and sign the policy statement that you created in Creating a Policy Statement for a Signed URL That Uses a Canned Policy. There are two versions of this procedure. Perform the applicable procedure:

- Option 1: To create a signature for a web distribution or for an RTMP distribution (without Adobe Flash Player) by using a canned policy
- Option 2: To create a signature for an RTMP distribution by using a canned policy (Adobe Flash Player)

For additional information and examples of how to hash, sign, and encode the policy statement, see:

- Using a Linux Command and OpenSSL for Base64-Encoding and Encryption
- Code Examples for Creating a Signature for a Signed URL
- Tools and Code Examples for Configuring Private Content

#### Option 1: To create a signature for a web distribution or for an RTMP distribution (without Adobe Flash Player) by using a canned policy

1. Use the SHA-1 hash function and RSA to hash and sign the policy statement that you created in the procedure To create the policy statement for a signed URL that uses a canned policy. Use the version of the policy statement that no longer includes whitespace.

   For the private key that is required by the hash function, use the private key that is associated with the applicable active trusted signer. **Note**
   The method that you use to hash and sign the policy statement depends on your programming language and platform. For sample code, see Code Examples for Creating a Signature for a Signed URL.

2. Remove whitespace (including tabs and newline characters) from the hashed and signed string.

3. Base64-encode the string using MIME base64 encoding. For more information, see Section 6.8, Base64 Content-Transfer-Encoding in *RFC 2045, MIME (Multipurpose Internet Mail Extensions) Part One: Format of Internet Message Bodies.*

4. Replace characters that are invalid in a URL query string with characters that are valid. The following table lists invalid and valid characters.

---

[See the AWS documentation website for more details]

1. Append the resulting value to your signed URL after `&Signature=`, and return to To create a signed URL using a canned policy to finish concatenating the parts of your signed URL.

## Option 2: To create a signature for an RTMP distribution by using a canned policy (Adobe Flash Player)

1. Use the SHA-1 hash function and RSA to hash and sign the policy statement that you created in the To create the policy statement for a signed URL that uses a canned policy procedure. Use the version of the policy statement that no longer includes whitespace.

   For the private key that is required by the hash function, use the private key that is associated with the applicable active trusted signer. **Note**
   The method that you use to hash and sign the policy statement depends on your programming language and platform. For sample code, see Code Examples for Creating a Signature for a Signed URL.

2. Remove whitespace (including tabs and newline characters) from the hashed and signed string.

   Continue on to Step 3 if you're using Adobe Flash Player and the stream name is passed in from a web page.

   If you're using Adobe Flash Player and if the stream name is not passed in from a web page, skip the rest of this procedure. For example, if you wrote your own player that fetches stream names from within the Adobe Flash .swf file, skip the rest of this procedure.

3. Base64-encode the string using MIME base64 encoding. For more information, see Section 6.8, Base64 Content-Transfer-Encoding in *RFC 2045, MIME (Multipurpose Internet Mail Extensions) Part One: Format of Internet Message Bodies.*

4. Replace characters that are invalid in a URL query string with characters that are valid. The following table lists invalid and valid characters.

---

[See the AWS documentation website for more details]

1. Some versions of Adobe Flash Player require that you URL-encode the characters ?, =, and &. For information about whether your version of Adobe Flash Player requires this character substitution, refer to the Adobe website.

   If your version of Flash does not require URL-encoding those character, skip to Step 6.

   If your version of Flash requires URL-encoding those characters, replace them as indicated in the following table. (You already replaced = in the previous step.)

---

[See the AWS documentation website for more details]

1. Append the resulting value to your signed URL after `&Signature=`, and return to To create a signed URL using a canned policy to finish concatenating the parts of your signed URL.

# Creating a Signed URL Using a Custom Policy

**Topics**

- Creating a Policy Statement for a Signed URL That Uses a Custom Policy
- Example Policy Statements for a Signed URL That Uses a Custom Policy
- Creating a Signature for a Signed URL That Uses a Custom Policy

To create a signed URL using a custom policy, perform the following procedure.

**To create a signed URL using a custom policy**

1. If you're using .NET or Java to create signed URLs, and if you haven't reformatted the private key for your key pair from the default .pem format to a format compatible with .NET or with Java, do so now. For more information, see Reformatting the CloudFront Private Key (.NET and Java Only).

2. Concatenate the following values in the specified order, and remove the whitespace (including tabs and newline characters) between the parts. You might have to include escape characters in the string in application code. All values have a type of String. Each part is keyed by number () to the two examples that follow.

    *Base URL for the object*

   The base URL is the CloudFront URL that you would use to access the object if you were not using signed URLs, including your own query string parameters, if any. For more information about the format of URLs for web distributions, see Format of URLs for Objects.

   The following examples show values that you specify for web distributions.

   - The following CloudFront URL is for an object in a web distribution (using the CloudFront domain name). Note that `image.jpg` is in an `images` directory. The path to the object in the URL must match the path to the object on your HTTP server or in your Amazon S3 bucket.

     `http://d111111abcdef8.cloudfront.net/images/image.jpg`

   - The following CloudFront URL includes a query string:

     `http://d111111abcdef8.cloudfront.net/images/image.jpg?size=large`

   - The following CloudFront URLs are for objects in a web distribution. Both use an alternate domain name; the second one includes a query string:

     `http://www.example.com/images/image.jpg`

     `http://www.example.com/images/image.jpg?color=red`

   - The following CloudFront URL is for an objects in a web distribution that uses an alternate domain name and the HTTPS protocol:

     `https://www.example.com/images/image.jpg` For RTMP distributions, the following examples are for objects in two different video formats, MP4 and FLV:

   - **MP4** – `mp4:sydney-vacation.mp4`

   - **FLV** – `sydney-vacation`

   - **FLV** – `sydney-vacation.flv` For .flv files, whether you include the `.flv` filename extension depends on your player. To serve MP3 audio files or H.264/MPEG-4 video files, you might need to prefix the file name with **mp3:** or **mp4:**. Some media players can be configured to add the prefix automatically. The media player might also require you to specify the file name without the file extension (for example, sydney-vacation instead of sydney-vacation.mp4).

     **2** ?

     The **?** indicates that query string parameters follow the base URL. Include the **?** even if you don't have any query string parameters of your own.

298

**③** *Your query string parameters, if any* &****

This value is optional. If you want to add your own query string parameters, for example:

`color=red&size=medium`

then add them after the `?` (see **②**) and before the `Policy` parameter. In certain rare circumstances, you might need to put your query string parameters after `Key-Pair-Id`.

Your parameters cannot be named `Policy`, `Signature`, or `Key-Pair-Id`. If you add your own parameters, append an `&` after each one, including the last one.

**④** `Policy=`*base64 encoded version of policy statement*

Your policy statement in JSON format, with white space removed, then base64 encoded. For more information, see Creating a Policy Statement for a Signed URL That Uses a Custom Policy.

The policy statement controls the access that a signed URL grants to a user: the URL of the object (for web distributions) or the stream name (for RTMP distributions), an expiration date and time, an optional date and time that the URL becomes valid, and an optional IP address or range of IP addresses that are allowed to access the object.

**⑤** `&Signature=`*hashed and signed version of the policy statement*

A hashed, signed, and base64-encoded version of the JSON policy statement. For more information, see Creating a Signature for a Signed URL That Uses a Custom Policy.

**⑥** `&Key-Pair-Id=`*active CloudFront key pair Id for the key pair that you're using to sign the policy statement*

The ID for an active CloudFront key pair, for example, APKA9ONS7QCOWEXAMPLE. The CloudFront key pair ID tells CloudFront which public key to use to validate the signed URL. CloudFront compares the information in the signature with the information in the policy statement to verify that the URL has not been tampered with.

The key pair ID that you include in CloudFront signed URLs must be the ID of an active key pair for one of your trusted signers:

- **Web distributions** – The key pair must be associated with an AWS account that is one of the trusted signers for the applicable cache behavior.

- **RTMP distributions** – The key pair must be associated with an AWS account that is one of the trusted signers for the distribution. For more information, see Specifying the AWS Accounts That Can Create Signed URLs and Signed Cookies (Trusted Signers).

  If you make a key pair inactive while rotating CloudFront key pairs, and if you're generating signed URLs programmatically, you must update your application to use a new active key pair for one of your trusted signers. If you're generating signed URLs manually, you must create new signed URLs. For more information about rotating key pairs, see Rotating CloudFront Key Pairs.

Example signed URL for a web distribution:

`**` **①** `http://d111111abcdef8.cloudfront.net/image.jpg` **②** `?` **③** `color=red&size=`
`medium&` **④** `Policy=eyANCiAgICEXAMPLEW1lbnQiOiBbeyANCiAgICAgICJSZXNvdXJjZSI6ImhOdHA`
`6Ly9kemJlc3FtN3VuMW0wLmNsb3VkZnJvbnQubVOL2RlbW8ucGhwIiwgDQogICAgICAiQ`
`29uZGl0aW9uIjp7IA0KICAgICAgICAgIklwQWRkcmVzcyI6eyJBV1M6U291cmNlSXAiOiI`
`yMDcuMTcxLjE4MC4xMDEvMzIifSwNCiAgICAgICJEYXRlR3JlYXRlclRoYW4iOnsiQ`
`VdTOkVwb2NoVGltZSI6MTI5Njg2MDE3NnOsDQogICAgICAiRGF0ZUxlc3NUaGFuIjp 7`

`IkFXUzpFcG9jaFRpbWUiOjEyOTY4NjAyMjZ9DQogICAgICB9IA0KICAgIAGfV0gDQp9DQo` **⑤** `&Signature=`
`nitfHRCrtziwO2HwPfWw~yYDhUF5EwRunQA-j19DzZrvDh6hQ731Dx~ -ar3UocvvRQVw6EkC~GdpGQyyOSKQim-`

`TxAnW7d8F5Kkai9HVx0FIu-5jcQb0UEmat EXAMPLE3ReXySpLSMj0yCd3ZAB4UcBCAqEijkytL6f3fVYNGQI6` **⑥** `&`
`Key-Pair-Id=APKA9ONS7QCOWEXAMPLE**`

Example signed URL for an RTMP distribution:

`**` **①** `videos/mediafile.flv` **②** `?` **③** `color=red&size=medium&` **④** `Policy=eyANCiAgICEXAMPLEW1lbnQiOiBbeyAl`
`6Ly9kemJlc3FtN3VuMW0wLmNsb3VkZnJvbnQubVOL2RlbW8ucGhwIiwgDQogICAgICAiQ`
`29uZGl0aW9uIjp7IA0KICAgICAgICAgIklwQWRkcmVzcyI6eyJBV1M6U291cmNlSXAiOiI`

yMDcuMTcxLjE4MC4xMDEvMzIifSwNCiAgICAgICAgICJEYXRlR3JlYXRlclRoYW4iOnsiQ
VdTOkVwb2NoVGltZSI6MTI5Njg2MDE3Nn0sDQogICAgICAgICAiRGF0ZUxlc3NUaGFuIjp 7

IkFXUzpFcG9jaFRpbWUiOjEyOTY4NjAyMjZ9DQogICAgICB9IA0KICAgAgfVOgDQp9DQo⑤&Signature=
nitfHRCrtziwO2HwPfWw~yYDhUF5EwRunQA-j19DzZrvDh6hQ73lDx~ -ar3UocvvRQVw6EkC~GdpGQyyOSKQim-

TxAnW7d8F5Kkai9HVxOFIu-5jcQbOUEmat EXAMPLE3ReXySpLSMj0yCd3ZAB4UcBCAqEijkytL6f3fVYNGQI6⑥&
Key-Pair-Id=APKA9ONS7QCOWEXAMPLE**

## Creating a Policy Statement for a Signed URL That Uses a Custom Policy

To create a policy statement for a custom policy, perform the following procedure. For several example policy statements that control access to objects in a variety of ways, see Example Policy Statements for a Signed URL That Uses a Custom Policy.

**To create the policy statement for a signed URL that uses a custom policy**

1. Construct the policy statement using the following JSON format. For more information, see Values that You Specify in the Policy Statement for a Signed URL That Uses a Custom Policy.

```
1  {
2    "Statement": [
3      {
4        "Resource":"URL or stream name of the object",
5        "Condition":{
6          "DateLessThan":{"AWS:EpochTime":required ending date and time in Unix time
                format and UTC},
7          "DateGreaterThan":{"AWS:EpochTime":optional beginning date and time in Unix
                time format and UTC},
8          "IpAddress":{"AWS:SourceIp":"optional IP address"}
9        }
10     }
11   ]
12 }
```

Note the following:

- You can include only one statement.
- Use UTF-8 character encoding.
- Include all punctuation and parameter names exactly as specified. Abbreviations for parameter names are not accepted.
- The order of the parameters in the `Condition` section doesn't matter.
- For information about the values for `Resource`, `DateLessThan`, `DateGreaterThan`, and `IpAddress`, see Values that You Specify in the Policy Statement for a Signed URL That Uses a Custom Policy.

2. Remove all whitespace (including tabs and newline characters) from the policy statement. You might have to include escape characters in the string in application code.

3. Base64-encode the policy statement using MIME base64 encoding. For more information, see Section 6.8, Base64 Content-Transfer-Encoding in *RFC 2045, MIME (Multipurpose Internet Mail Extensions) Part One: Format of Internet Message Bodies*.

4. Replace characters that are invalid in a URL query string with characters that are valid. The following table lists invalid and valid characters.

---

[See the AWS documentation website for more details]

1. Append the resulting value to your signed URL after `Policy=`.

2. Create a signature for the signed URL by hashing, signing, and base64-encoding the policy statement. For more information, see Creating a Signature for a Signed URL That Uses a Custom Policy.

**Values that You Specify in the Policy Statement for a Signed URL That Uses a Custom Policy**

When you create a policy statement for a custom policy, you specify the following values.

**Resource**
The value that you specifies depends on whether you're creating signed URLs for web or RTMP distributions. You can specify only one value for `Resource`.

**Web distributions (optional but recommended)**
The base URL including your query strings, if any, but excluding the CloudFront `Policy`, `Signature`, and `Key-Pair-Id` parameters, for example:
`http://d111111abcdef8.cloudfront.net/images/horizon.jpg?size=large&license=yes`
If you omit the Resource parameter for a web distribution, users can access all of the objects associated with any distribution that is associated with the key pair that you use to create the signed URL. Note the following:

- **Protocol** – The value must begin with `http://`, `https://`, or `*`.

- **Query string parameters** – If you have no query string parameters, omit the question mark.

- **Wildcard characters** – You can use the wildcard character that matches zero or more characters (`*`) or the wild-card character that matches exactly one character (`?`) anywhere in the string. For example, the value:

    `http://d111111abcdef8.cloudfront.net/*game_download.zip*`

    would include (for example) the following objects:

    - `http://d111111abcdef8.cloudfront.net/game_download.zip`
    - `http://d111111abcdef8.cloudfront.net/example_game_download.zip?license=yes`
    - `http://d111111abcdef8.cloudfront.net/test_game_download.zip?license=temp`

- **Alternate domain names** – If you specify an alternate domain name (CNAME) in the URL, you must specify the alternate domain name when referencing the object in your web page or application. Do not specify the Amazon S3 URL for the object.

**RTMP distributions**
Include only the stream name. For example, if the full URL for a streaming video is:
`rtmp://s5c39gqb8ow64r.cloudfront.net/videos/cfx/st/mp3_name.mp3`
then use the following value for `Resource`:
`videos/mp3_name`
Do not include a prefix such as `mp3:` or `mp4:`. Also, depending on the player you're using, you might have to omit the file extension from the value of `Resource`. For example, you might need to use `sydney-vacation` instead of `sydney-vacation.flv`.

**DateLessThan**
The expiration date and time for the URL in Unix time format (in seconds) and Coordinated Universal Time (UTC). Do not enclose the value in quotation marks. For information about UTC, see *RFC 3339, Date and Time on the Internet: Timestamps*, http://tools.ietf.org/html/rfc3339.
For example, January 1, 2013 10:00 am UTC converts to 1357034400 in Unix time format.
This is the only required parameter in the `Condition` section. CloudFront requires this value to prevent users from having permanent access to your private content.
For more information, see When Does CloudFront Check the Expiration Date and Time in a Signed URL?

**DateGreaterThan (Optional)**
An optional start date and time for the URL in Unix time format (in seconds) and Coordinated Universal Time (UTC). Users are not allowed to access the object before the specified date and time. Do not enclose the value in quotation marks.

**IpAddress (Optional)**

The IP address of the client making the GET request. Note the following:

- To allow any IP address to access the object, omit the `IpAddress` parameter.

- You can specify either one IP address or one IP address range. For example, you can't set the policy to allow access if the client's IP address is in one of two separate ranges.

- To allow access from a single IP address, you specify:

  *"IPv4 IP address*/32"

- You must specify IP address ranges in standard IPv4 CIDR format (for example, `192.0.2.0/24`). For more information, see *RFC 4632, Classless Inter-domain Routing (CIDR): The Internet Address Assignment and Aggregation Plan*, http://tools.ietf.org/html/rfc4632. **Important** IP addresses in IPv6 format, such as 2001:0db8:85a3:0000:0000:8a2e:0370:7334, are not supported.

  If you're using a custom policy that includes `IpAddress`, do not enable IPv6 for the distribution. If you want to restrict access to some content by IP address and support IPv6 requests for other content, you can create two distributions. For more information, see Enable IPv6 in the topic Values That You Specify When You Create or Update a Web Distribution.

## Example Policy Statements for a Signed URL That Uses a Custom Policy

The following example policy statements show how to control access to a specific object, all of the objects in a directory, or all of the objects associated with a key pair ID. The examples also show how to control access from an individual IP address or a range of IP addresses, and how to prevent users from using the signed URL after a specified date and time.

If you copy and paste any of these examples, remove any whitespace (including tabs and newline characters), replace the applicable values with your own values, and include a newline character after the closing brace ( } ).

For more information, see Values that You Specify in the Policy Statement for a Signed URL That Uses a Custom Policy.

**Topics**

- Example Policy Statement: Accessing One Object from a Range of IP Addresses
- Example Policy Statement: Accessing All Objects in a Directory from a Range of IP Addresses
- Example Policy Statement: Accessing All Objects Associated with a Key Pair ID from One IP Address

**Example Policy Statement: Accessing One Object from a Range of IP Addresses**

The following example custom policy in a signed URL specifies that a user can access the object `http://d111111abcdef8.cloudfront.net/game_download.zip` from IP addresses in the range `192.0.2.0/24` until January 1, 2013 10:00 am UTC:

```
1  {
2      "Statement": [
3          {
4              "Resource":"http://d111111abcdef8.cloudfront.net/game_download.zip",
5              "Condition":{
6                  "IpAddress":{"AWS:SourceIp":"192.0.2.0/24"},
7                  "DateLessThan":{"AWS:EpochTime":1357034400}
8              }
9          }
10     ]
11 }
```

**Example Policy Statement: Accessing All Objects in a Directory from a Range of IP Addresses**

The following example custom policy allows you to create signed URLs for any object in the `training` directory, as indicated by the * wildcard character in the `Resource` parameter. Users can access the object from an IP address in the range 192.0.2.0/24 until January 1, 2013 10:00 am UTC:

```
1  {
2     "Statement": [
3        {
4           "Resource":"http://d111111abcdef8.cloudfront.net/training/*",
5           "Condition":{
6              "IpAddress":{"AWS:SourceIp":"192.0.2.0/24"},
7              "DateLessThan":{"AWS:EpochTime":1357034400}
8           }
9        }
10    ]
11 }
```

Each signed URL in which you use this policy includes a base URL that identifies a specific object, for example:

`http://d111111abcdef8.cloudfront.net/training/orientation.pdf`

**Example Policy Statement: Accessing All Objects Associated with a Key Pair ID from One IP Address**

The following sample custom policy allows you to create signed URLs for any object associated with any distribution, as indicated by the * wildcard character in the `Resource` parameter. The user must use the IP address 192.0.2.10/32. (The value 192.0.2.10/32 in CIDR notation refers to a single IP address, 192.0.2.10.) The objects are available only from January 1, 2013 10:00 am UTC until January 2, 2013 10:00 am UTC:

```
1  {
2     "Statement": [
3        {
4           "Resource":"http://*",
5           "Condition":{
6              "IpAddress":{"AWS:SourceIp":"192.0.2.10/32"},
7              "DateGreaterThan":{"AWS:EpochTime":1357034400},
8              "DateLessThan":{"AWS:EpochTime":1357120800}
9           }
10       }
11    ]
12 }
```

Each signed URL in which you use this policy includes a base URL that identifies a specific object in a specific CloudFront distribution, for example:

`http://d111111abcdef8.cloudfront.net/training/orientation.pdf`

The signed URL also includes a key pair ID, which must be associated with a trusted signer in the distribution (d111111abcdef8.cloudfront.net) that you specify in the base URL.

## Creating a Signature for a Signed URL That Uses a Custom Policy

The signature for a signed URL that uses a custom policy is a hashed, signed, and base64-encoded version of the policy statement. To create a signature for a custom policy, perform the applicable procedure. The version that you choose depends on your distribution type (web or RTMP) and, for RTMP distributions, the media player that you're using (Adobe Flash Player or another media player):

- Option 1: To create a signature for a web distribution or for an RTMP distribution (without Adobe Flash Player) by using a custom policy
- Option 2: To create a signature for an RTMP distribution by using a custom policy (Adobe Flash Player)

For additional information and examples of how to hash, sign, and encode the policy statement, see:

- Using a Linux Command and OpenSSL for Base64-Encoding and Encryption
- Code Examples for Creating a Signature for a Signed URL
- Tools and Code Examples for Configuring Private Content

## Option 1: To create a signature for a web distribution or for an RTMP distribution (without Adobe Flash Player) by using a custom policy

1. Use the SHA-1 hash function and RSA to hash and sign the JSON policy statement that you created in the procedure To create the policy statement for a signed URL that uses a custom policy. Use the version of the policy statement that no longer includes whitespace but that has not yet been base64-encoded.

   For the private key that is required by the hash function, use the private key that is associated with the applicable active trusted signer. **Note**
   The method that you use to hash and sign the policy statement depends on your programming language and platform. For sample code, see Code Examples for Creating a Signature for a Signed URL.

2. Remove whitespace (including tabs and newline characters) from the hashed and signed string.

3. Base64-encode the string using MIME base64 encoding. For more information, see Section 6.8, Base64 Content-Transfer-Encoding in *RFC 2045, MIME (Multipurpose Internet Mail Extensions) Part One: Format of Internet Message Bodies*.

4. Replace characters that are invalid in a URL query string with characters that are valid. The following table lists invalid and valid characters.

---

[See the AWS documentation website for more details]

1. Append the resulting value to your signed URL after `&Signature=`, and return to To create a signed URL using a custom policy to finish concatenating the parts of your signed URL.

## Option 2: To create a signature for an RTMP distribution by using a custom policy (Adobe Flash Player)

1. Use the SIIA-1 hash function and RSA to hash and sign the JSON policy statement that you created in the To create the policy statement for a signed URL that uses a custom policy procedure. Use the version of the policy statement that no longer includes whitespace but that has not yet been base64-encoded.

   For the private key that is required by the hash function, use the private key that is associated with the applicable active trusted signer. **Note**
   The method that you use to hash and sign the policy statement depends on your programming language and platform. For sample code, see Code Examples for Creating a Signature for a Signed URL.

2. Remove whitespace (including tabs and newline characters) from the hashed and signed string.

   Continue on to Step 3 if the stream name is passed in from a web page.

   If the stream name is not passed in from a web page, skip the rest of this procedure. For example, if you wrote your own player that fetches stream names from within the Adobe Flash .swf file, skip the rest of this procedure.

3. Base64-encode the string using MIME base64 encoding. For more information, see Section 6.8, Base64 Content-Transfer-Encoding in *RFC 2045, MIME (Multipurpose Internet Mail Extensions) Part One: Format of Internet Message Bodies*.

4. Replace characters that are invalid in a URL query string with characters that are valid. The following table lists invalid and valid characters.

---

[See the AWS documentation website for more details]

1. Some versions of Adobe Flash Player require that you URL-encode the characters ?, =, and &. For information about whether your version of Adobe Flash Player requires this character substitution, refer to the Adobe website.

   If your version of Adobe Flash Player does not require that you URL-encode the characters ?, =, and &, skip to Step 6.

   If your version of Adobe Flash Player requires URL-encoding those characters, replace them as indicated in the following table. (You already replaced = in the previous step.)

---

[See the AWS documentation website for more details]

1. Append the resulting value to your signed URL after `&Signature=`, and return to To create a signed URL using a custom policy to finish concatenating the parts of your signed URL.

# Using Signed Cookies

CloudFront signed cookies allow you to control who can access your content when you don't want to change your current URLs or when you want to provide access to multiple restricted files, for example, all of the files in the subscribers' area of a website. This topic explains the considerations when using signed cookies and describes how to set signed cookies using canned and custom policies.

**Topics**

- Choosing Between Canned and Custom Policies for Signed Cookies
- How Signed Cookies Work
- Preventing Misuse of Signed Cookies
- When Does CloudFront Check the Expiration Date and Time in a Signed Cookie?
- Sample Code and Third-Party Tools
- Setting Signed Cookies Using a Canned Policy
- Setting Signed Cookies Using a Custom Policy

## Choosing Between Canned and Custom Policies for Signed Cookies

When you create a signed cookie, you write a policy statement in JSON format that specifies the restrictions on the signed cookie, for example, how long the cookie is valid. You can use canned policies or custom policies. The following table compares canned and custom policies:

| Description | Canned Policy | Custom Policy |
| --- | --- | --- |
| You can reuse the policy statement for multiple objects. To reuse the policy statement, you must use wildcard characters in the `Resource` object. For more information, see Values That You Specify in the Policy Statement for a Custom Policy for Signed Cookies.) | No | Yes |
| You can specify the date and time that users can begin to access your content | No | Yes (optional) |
| You can specify the date and time that users can no longer access your content | Yes | Yes |
| You can specify the IP address or range of IP addresses of the users who can access your content | No | Yes (optional) |

For information about creating signed cookies using a canned policy, see Setting Signed Cookies Using a Canned Policy.

For information about creating signed cookies using a custom policy, see Setting Signed Cookies Using a Custom Policy.

# How Signed Cookies Work

Here's an overview of how you configure CloudFront for signed cookies and how CloudFront responds when a user submits a request that contains a signed cookie.

1. In your CloudFront distribution, you specify one or more trusted signers, which are the AWS accounts that you want to have permission to create signed URLs and signed cookies.

   For more information, see Specifying the AWS Accounts That Can Create Signed URLs and Signed Cookies (Trusted Signers).

2. You develop your application to determine whether a user should have access to your content and, if so, to send three `Set-Cookie` headers to the viewer. (Each `Set-Cookie` header can contain only one name-value pair, and a CloudFront signed cookie requires three name-value pairs.) You must send the `Set-Cookie` headers to the viewer before the viewer requests your private content. If you set a short expiration time on the cookie, you might also want to send three more `Set-Cookie` headers in response to subsequent requests, so that the user continues to have access.

   Typically, your CloudFront distribution will have at least two cache behaviors, one that doesn't require authentication and one that does. The error page for the secure portion of the site includes a redirector or a link to a login page.

   If you configure your distribution to cache objects based on cookies, CloudFront doesn't cache separate objects based on the attributes in signed cookies.

3. A user signs in to your website and either pays for content or meets some other requirement for access.

4. Your application returns the `Set-Cookie` headers in the response, and the viewer stores the name-value pairs.

5. The user requests an object.

   The user's browser or other viewer gets the name-value pairs from step 4 and adds them to the request in a `Cookie` header. This is the signed cookie.

6. CloudFront uses the public key to validate the signature in the signed cookie and to confirm that the cookie hasn't been tampered with. If the signature is invalid, the request is rejected.

   If the signature in the cookie is valid, CloudFront looks at the policy statement in the cookie (or constructs one if you're using a canned policy) to confirm that the request is still valid. For example, if you specified a beginning and ending date and time for the cookie, CloudFront confirms that the user is trying to access your content during the time period that you want to allow access.

   If the request meets the requirements in the policy statement, CloudFront serves your content as it does for content that isn't restricted: it determines whether the object is already in the edge cache, forwards the request to the origin if necessary, and returns the object to the user.

# Preventing Misuse of Signed Cookies

If you specify the `Domain` parameter in a `Set-Cookie` header, specify the most precise value possible to limit potential access by someone with the same root domain name. For example, apex.example.com is preferable to example.com, especially when you don't control example.com. This helps prevent someone from accessing your content from nadir.example.com.

To prevent this type of attack, do the following:

- Exclude the `Expires` and `Max-Age` cookie attributes, so that the `Set-Cookie` header creates a session cookie. Session cookies are automatically deleted when the user closes the browser, which reduces the possibility of someone getting unauthorized access to your content.
- Include the `Secure` attribute, so that the cookie is encrypted when a viewer includes it in a request.
- When possible, use a custom policy and include the IP address of the viewer.

- In the `CloudFront-Expires` attribute, specify the shortest reasonable expiration time based on how long you want users to have access to your content.

## When Does CloudFront Check the Expiration Date and Time in a Signed Cookie?

To determine whether a signed cookie is still valid, CloudFront checks the expiration date and time in the cookie at the time of the HTTP request. If a client begins to download a large object immediately before the expiration time, the download should complete even if the expiration time passes during the download. If the TCP connection drops and the client tries to restart the download after the expiration time passes, the download will fail.

If a client uses Range GETs to get an object in smaller pieces, any GET request that occurs after the expiration time passes will fail. For more information about Range GETs, see How CloudFront Processes Partial Requests for an Object (Range GETs).

## Sample Code and Third-Party Tools

The sample code for private content shows only how to create the signature for signed URLs. However, the process for creating a signature for a signed cookie is very similar, so much of the sample code is still relevant. For more information, see the following topics:

- Create a URL Signature Using Perl
- Create a URL Signature Using PHP
- Create a URL Signature Using C# and the .NET Framework
- Create a URL Signature Using Java

For information about third-party tools that support private content, including creating signed URLs, see Tools and Code Examples for Configuring Private Content.

# Setting Signed Cookies Using a Canned Policy

To set a signed cookie by using a canned policy, complete the following steps. To create the signature, see Creating a Signature for a Signed Cookie That Uses a Canned Policy.

**To set a signed cookie using a canned policy**

1. If you're using .NET or Java to create signed cookies, and if you haven't reformatted the private key for your key pair from the default .pem format to a format compatible with .NET or with Java, do so now. For more information, see Reformatting the CloudFront Private Key (.NET and Java Only).

2. Program your application to send three `Set-Cookie` headers to approved viewers. You need three `Set-Cookie` headers because each `Set-Cookie` header can contain only one name-value pair, and a CloudFront signed cookie requires three name-value pairs. The name-value pairs are: `CloudFront-Expires`, `CloudFront-Signature`, and `CloudFront-Key-Pair-Id`. The values must be present on the viewer before a user makes the first request for an object that you want to control access to. **Note**
In general, we recommend that you exclude `Expires` and `Max-Age` attributes. Excluding the attributes causes the browser to delete the cookie when the user closes the browser, which reduces the possibility of someone getting unauthorized access to your content. For more information, see Preventing Misuse of Signed Cookies.

   **The names of cookie attributes are case sensitive**.

   Line breaks are included only to make the attributes more readable.

```
1 Set-Cookie:
2 Domain=optional domain name;
3 Path=/optional directory path;
4 Secure;
5 HttpOnly;
6 CloudFront-Expires=date and time in Unix time format (in seconds) and Coordinated Universal
      Time (UTC)
7
8 Set-Cookie:
9 Domain=optional domain name;
10 Path=/optional directory path;
11 Secure;
12 HttpOnly;
13 CloudFront-Signature=hashed and signed version of the policy statement
14
15 Set-Cookie:
16 Domain=optional domain name;
17 Path=/optional directory path;
18 Secure;
19 HttpOnly;
20 CloudFront-Key-Pair-Id=active CloudFront key pair Id for the key pair that you are using to
      generate the signature
```

**(Optional) `Domain`**
The domain name for the requested object. If you don't specify a `Domain` attribute, the default value is the domain name in the URL, and it applies only to the specified domain name, not to subdomains. If you specify a `Domain` attribute, it also applies to subdomains. A leading dot in the domain name (for example, `Domain=.example.com`) is optional. In addition, if you specify a `Domain` attribute, the domain name in the URL and the value of the `Domain` attribute must match.
You can specify the domain name that CloudFront assigned to your distribution, for example, d111111abcdef8.cloudfront.net, but you can't specify *.cloudfront.net for the domain name.
If you want to use an alternate domain name such as example.com in URLs, you must add the alternate domain

name to your distribution regardless of whether you specify the `Domain` attribute. For more information, see Alternate Domain Names (CNAMEs) in the topic Values That You Specify When You Create or Update a Web Distribution.

**(Optional) `Path`**

The path for the requested object. If you don't specify a `Path` attribute, the default value is the path in the URL.

**`Secure`**

Requires that the viewer encrypt cookies before sending a request. We recommend that you send the `Set-Cookie` header over an HTTPS connection to ensure that the cookie attributes are protected from man-in-the-middle attacks.

**`HttpOnly`**

Requires that the viewer send the cookie only in HTTP or HTTPS requests.

**`CloudFront-Expires`**

Specify the expiration date and time in Unix time format (in seconds) and Coordinated Universal Time (UTC). For example, January 1, 2013 10:00 am UTC converts to 1357034400 in Unix time format. To use epoch time, use a 32-bit integer for a date which can be no later than 2147483647 (January 19th, 2038 at 03:14:07 UTC). For information about UTC, see *RFC 3339, Date and Time on the Internet: Timestamps*, http://tools.ietf.org/html/rfc3339.

**`CloudFront-Signature`**

A hashed, signed, and base64-encoded version of a JSON policy statement. For more information, see Creating a Signature for a Signed Cookie That Uses a Canned Policy.

**`CloudFront-Key-Pair-Id`**

The ID for an active CloudFront key pair, for example, APKA9ONS7QCOWEXAMPLE. The CloudFront key pair ID tells CloudFront which public key to use to validate the signed cookie. CloudFront compares the information in the signature with the information in the policy statement to verify that the URL has not been tampered with.

The key pair ID that you include in CloudFront signed cookies must be associated with an AWS account that is one of the trusted signers for the applicable cache behavior.

For more information, see Specifying the AWS Accounts That Can Create Signed URLs and Signed Cookies (Trusted Signers).

If you make a key pair inactive while rotating CloudFront key pairs, you must update your application to use a new active key pair for one of your trusted signers. For more information about rotating key pairs, see Rotating CloudFront Key Pairs.

The following example shows `Set-Cookie` headers for one signed cookie when you're using the domain name that is associated with your distribution in the URLs for your objects:

```
1 Set-Cookie: Domain=d111111abcdef8.cloudfront.net; Path=/images/*; Secure; HttpOnly; CloudFront-
      Expires=1426500000
2 Set-Cookie: Domain=d111111abcdef8.cloudfront.net; Path=/images/*; Secure; HttpOnly; CloudFront-
      Signature=yXrSIgyQoeE4FBI4eMKF6ho~CA8_
3 Set-Cookie: Domain=d111111abcdef8.cloudfront.net; Path=/images/*; Secure; HttpOnly; CloudFront-
      Key-Pair-Id=APKA9ONS7QCOWEXAMPLE
```

The following example shows `Set-Cookie` headers for one signed cookie when you're using the alternate domain name example.org in the URLs for your objects:

```
1 Set-Cookie: Domain=example.org; Path=/images/*; Secure; HttpOnly; CloudFront-Expires=1426500000
2 Set-Cookie: Domain=example.org; Path=/images/*; Secure; HttpOnly; CloudFront-Signature=
      yXrSIgyQoeE4FBI4eMKF6ho~CA8_
3 Set-Cookie: Domain=example.org; Path=/images/*; Secure; HttpOnly; CloudFront-Key-Pair-Id=
      APKA9ONS7QCOWEXAMPLE
```

If you want to use an alternate domain name such as example.com in URLs, you must add the alternate domain name to your distribution regardless of whether you specify the `Domain` attribute. For more information, see Alternate Domain Names (CNAMEs) in the topic Values That You Specify When You Create or Update a Web Distribution.

# Creating a Signature for a Signed Cookie That Uses a Canned Policy

To create the signature for a signed cookie that uses a canned policy, do the following:

1. Create a policy statement. See Creating a Policy Statement for a Signed Cookie That Uses a Canned Policy.

2. Sign the policy statement to create a signature. See Signing the Policy Statement to Create a Signature for a Signed Cookie That Uses a Canned Policy.

## Creating a Policy Statement for a Signed Cookie That Uses a Canned Policy

When you set a signed cookie that uses a canned policy, the `CloudFront-Signature` attribute is a hashed and signed version of a policy statement. For signed cookies that use a canned policy, you don't include the policy statement in the `Set-Cookie` header, as you do for signed cookies that use a custom policy. To create the policy statement, perform the following procedure.

**To create a policy statement for a signed cookie that uses a canned policy**

1. Construct the policy statement using the following JSON format and using UTF-8 character encoding. Include all punctuation and other literal values exactly as specified. For information about the `Resource` and `DateLessThan` parameters, see Values That You Specify in the Policy Statement for a Canned Policy for Signed Cookies.

```
1  {
2     "Statement":[
3        {
4           "Resource":"base URL or stream name",
5           "Condition":{
6              "DateLessThan":{
7                 "AWS:EpochTime":ending date and time in Unix time format and UTC
8              }
9           }
10       }
11    ]
12 }
```

2. Remove all whitespace (including tabs and newline characters) from the policy statement. You might have to include escape characters in the string in application code.

## Values That You Specify in the Policy Statement for a Canned Policy for Signed Cookies

When you create a policy statement for a canned policy, you specify the following values:

**Resource**
The base URL including your query strings, if any, for example:
`http://d111111abcdef8.cloudfront.net/images/horizon.jpg?size=large&license=yes`
You can specify only one value for `Resource`.
Note the following:

- **Protocol** – The value must begin with `http://` or `https://`.
- **Query string parameters** – If you have no query string parameters, omit the question mark.
- **Alternate domain names** – If you specify an alternate domain name (CNAME) in the URL, you must specify the alternate domain name when referencing the object in your web page or application. Do not specify the Amazon S3 URL for the object.

**DateLessThan**
The expiration date and time for the URL in Unix time format (in seconds) and Coordinated Universal Time

(UTC). Do not enclose the value in quotation marks.

For example, March 16, 2015 10:00 am UTC converts to 1426500000 in Unix time format.

This value must match the value of the `CloudFront-Expires` attribute in the `Set-Cookie` header. Do not enclose the value in quotation marks.

For more information, see When Does CloudFront Check the Expiration Date and Time in a Signed Cookie?.

## Example Policy Statement for a Canned Policy

When you use the following example policy statement in a signed cookie, a user can access the object `http://d111111abcdef8.cloudfront.net/horizon.jpg` until March 16, 2015 10:00 am UTC:

```
1  {
2     "Statement":[
3        {
4           "Resource":"http://d111111abcdef8.cloudfront.net/horizon.jpg?size=large&license=yes",
5           "Condition":{
6              "DateLessThan":{
7                 "AWS:EpochTime":1426500000
8              }
9           }
10       }
11    ]
12 }
```

## Signing the Policy Statement to Create a Signature for a Signed Cookie That Uses a Canned Policy

To create the value for the `CloudFront-Signature` attribute in a `Set-Cookie` header, you hash and sign the policy statement that you created in To create a policy statement for a signed cookie that uses a canned policy.

For additional information and examples of how to hash, sign, and encode the policy statement, see the following topics:

- Using a Linux Command and OpenSSL for Base64-Encoding and Encryption
- Code Examples for Creating a Signature for a Signed URL
- Tools and Code Examples for Configuring Private Content

### To create a signature for a signed cookie using a canned policy

1. Use the SHA-1 hash function and RSA to hash and sign the policy statement that you created in the procedure To create a policy statement for a signed cookie that uses a canned policy. Use the version of the policy statement that no longer includes whitespace.

   For the private key that is required by the hash function, use the private key that is associated with the applicable active trusted signer. **Note**
   The method that you use to hash and sign the policy statement depends on your programming language and platform. For sample code, see Code Examples for Creating a Signature for a Signed URL.

2. Remove whitespace (including tabs and newline characters) from the hashed and signed string.

3. Base64-encode the string using MIME base64 encoding. For more information, see Section 6.8, Base64 Content-Transfer-Encoding in *RFC 2045, MIME (Multipurpose Internet Mail Extensions) Part One: Format of Internet Message Bodies*.

4. Replace characters that are invalid in a URL query string with characters that are valid. The following table lists invalid and valid characters.

---

[See the AWS documentation website for more details]

1. Include the resulting value in the `Set-Cookie` header for the `CloudFront-Signature` name-value pair. Then return to To set a signed cookie using a canned policy add the `Set-Cookie` header for `CloudFront-Key-Pair-Id`.

# Setting Signed Cookies Using a Custom Policy

## Topics

- Creating a Policy Statement for a Signed Cookie That Uses a Custom Policy
- Example Policy Statements for a Signed Cookie That Uses a Custom Policy
- Creating a Signature for a Signed Cookie That Uses a Custom Policy

To set a signed cookie that uses a custom policy, perform the following procedure.

### To set a signed cookie using a custom policy

1. If you're using .NET or Java to create signed URLs, and if you haven't reformatted the private key for your key pair from the default .pem format to a format compatible with .NET or with Java, do so now. For more information, see Reformatting the CloudFront Private Key (.NET and Java Only).

2. Program your application to send three `Set-Cookie` headers to approved viewers. You need three `Set-Cookie` headers because each `Set-Cookie` header can contain only one name-value pair, and a CloudFront signed cookie requires three name-value pairs. The name-value pairs are: `CloudFront-Policy`, `CloudFront-Signature`, and `CloudFront-Key-Pair-Id`. The values must be present on the viewer before a user makes the first request for an object that you want to control access to. **Note**
In general, we recommend that you exclude `Expires` and `Max-Age` attributes. This causes the browser to delete the cookie when the user closes the browser, which reduces the possibility of someone getting unauthorized access to your content. For more information, see Preventing Misuse of Signed Cookies.

   **The names of cookie attributes are case sensitive**.

   Line breaks are included only to make the attributes more readable.

```
 1 Set-Cookie:
 2 Domain=optional domain name;
 3 Path=/optional directory path;
 4 Secure;
 5 HttpOnly;
 6 CloudFront-Policy=base64 encoded version of the policy statement
 7
 8 Set-Cookie:
 9 Domain=optional domain name;
10 Path=/optional directory path;
11 Secure;
12 HttpOnly;
13 CloudFront-Signature=hashed and signed version of the policy statement
14
15 Set-Cookie:
16 Domain=optional domain name;
17 Path=/optional directory path;
18 Secure;
19 HttpOnly;
20 CloudFront-Key-Pair-Id=active CloudFront key pair Id for the key pair that you are using to
          generate the signature
```

### (Optional) `Domain`

The domain name for the requested object. If you don't specify a `Domain` attribute, the default value is the domain name in the URL, and it applies only to the specified domain name, not to subdomains. If you specify a `Domain` attribute, it also applies to subdomains. A leading dot in the domain name (for example, `Domain=.example.com`) is optional. In addition, if you specify a `Domain` attribute, the domain name in the URL and the value of the `Domain` attribute must match.

You can specify the domain name that CloudFront assigned to your distribution, for example, d111111abcdef8.cloudfront.net, but you can't specify *.cloudfront.net for the domain name.

If you want to use an alternate domain name such as example.com in URLs, you must add the alternate domain name to your distribution regardless of whether you specify the `Domain` attribute. For more information, see Alternate Domain Names (CNAMEs) in the topic Values That You Specify When You Create or Update a Web Distribution.

**(Optional) `Path`**

The path for the requested object. If you don't specify a `Path` attribute, the default value is the path in the URL.

**`Secure`**

Requires that the viewer encrypt cookies before sending a request. We recommend that you send the `Set-Cookie` header over an HTTPS connection to ensure that the cookie attributes are protected from man-in-the-middle attacks.

**`HttpOnly`**

Requires that the viewer send the cookie only in HTTP or HTTPS requests.

**`CloudFront-Policy`**

Your policy statement in JSON format, with white space removed, then base64 encoded. For more information, see Creating a Signature for a Signed Cookie That Uses a Custom Policy.

The policy statement controls the access that a signed cookie grants to a user: the objects that the user can access, an expiration date and time, an optional date and time that the URL becomes valid, and an optional IP address or range of IP addresses that are allowed to access the object.

**`CloudFront-Signature`**

A hashed, signed, and base64-encoded version of the JSON policy statement. For more information, see Creating a Signature for a Signed Cookie That Uses a Custom Policy.

**`CloudFront-Key-Pair-Id`**

The ID for an active CloudFront key pair, for example, APKA9ONS7QCOWEXAMPLE. The CloudFront key pair ID tells CloudFront which public key to use to validate the signed cookie. CloudFront compares the information in the signature with the information in the policy statement to verify that the URL has not been tampered with.

The key pair ID that you include in CloudFront signed cookies must be associated with an AWS account that is one of the trusted signers for the applicable cache behavior.

For more information, see Specifying the AWS Accounts That Can Create Signed URLs and Signed Cookies (Trusted Signers).

If you make a key pair inactive while rotating CloudFront key pairs, you must update your application to use a new active key pair for one of your trusted signers. For more information about rotating key pairs, see Rotating CloudFront Key Pairs.

Example `Set-Cookie` headers for one signed cookie when you're using the domain name that is associated with your distribution in the URLs for your objects:

```
1 Set-Cookie: Domain=d111111abcdef8.cloudfront.net; Path=/; Secure; HttpOnly; CloudFront-Policy=
    eyJTdGF0ZW1lbnQiOilt7IlJlc291cmNlIjoiaHR0cDovL2QxMTExMTFhYmNkZWY4LmNsb3VkZnJvbnQubmV0L2dhbWVfZG93b

2 Set-Cookie: Domain=d111111abcdef8.cloudfront.net; Path=/; Secure; HttpOnly; CloudFront-Signature
    =dtKhpJ3aUYxqDIwepczPiDb9NXQ_

3 Set-Cookie: Domain=d111111abcdef8.cloudfront.net; Path=/; Secure; HttpOnly; CloudFront-Key-Pair-
    Id=APKA9ONS7QCOWEXAMPLE
```

Example `Set-Cookie` headers for one signed cookie when you're using the alternate domain name example.org in the URLs for your objects:

```
1 Set-Cookie: Domain=example.org; Path=/; Secure; HttpOnly; CloudFront-Policy=
    eyJTdGF0ZW1lbnQiOilt7IlJlc291cmNlIjoiaHR0cDovL2QxMTExMTFhYmNkZWY4LmNsb3VkZnJvbnQubmV0L2dhbWVfZG93b

2 Set-Cookie: Domain=example.org; Path=/; Secure; HttpOnly; CloudFront-Signature=
    dtKhpJ3aUYxqDIwepczPiDb9NXQ_

3 Set-Cookie: Domain=example.org; Path=/; Secure; HttpOnly; CloudFront-Key-Pair-Id=
```

`APKA90NS7QCOWEXAMPLE`

If you want to use an alternate domain name such as example.com in URLs, you must add the alternate domain name to your distribution regardless of whether you specify the `Domain` attribute. For more information, see Alternate Domain Names (CNAMEs) in the topic Values That You Specify When You Create or Update a Web Distribution.

## Creating a Policy Statement for a Signed Cookie That Uses a Custom Policy

To create a policy statement for a custom policy, perform the following procedure. For several example policy statements that control access to objects in a variety of ways, see Example Policy Statements for a Signed Cookie That Uses a Custom Policy.

**To create the policy statement for a signed cookie that uses a custom policy**

1. Construct the policy statement using the following JSON format.

```
{
    "Statement": [
        {
            "Resource":"URL of the object",
            "Condition":{
                "DateLessThan":{"AWS:EpochTime":required ending date and time in Unix time
                    format and UTC},
                "DateGreaterThan":{"AWS:EpochTime":optional beginning date and time in Unix
                    time format and UTC},
                "IpAddress":{"AWS:SourceIp":"optional IP address"}
            }
        }
    ]
}
```

Note the following:

- You can include only one statement.
- Use UTF-8 character encoding.
- Include all punctuation and parameter names exactly as specified. Abbreviations for parameter names are not accepted.
- The order of the parameters in the `Condition` section doesn't matter.
- For information about the values for `Resource`, `DateLessThan`, `DateGreaterThan`, and `IpAddress`, see Values That You Specify in the Policy Statement for a Custom Policy for Signed Cookies.

2. Remove all whitespace (including tabs and newline characters) from the policy statement. You might have to include escape characters in the string in application code.

3. Base64-encode the policy statement using MIME base64 encoding. For more information, see Section 6.8, Base64 Content-Transfer-Encoding in *RFC 2045, MIME (Multipurpose Internet Mail Extensions) Part One: Format of Internet Message Bodies*.

4. Replace characters that are invalid in a URL query string with characters that are valid. The following table lists invalid and valid characters.

---

[See the AWS documentation website for more details]

1. Include the resulting value in your `Set-Cookie` header after `CloudFront-Policy=`.

316

2. Create a signature for the `Set-Cookie` header for `CloudFront-Signature` by hashing, signing, and base64-encoding the policy statement. For more information, see Creating a Signature for a Signed Cookie That Uses a Custom Policy.

**Values That You Specify in the Policy Statement for a Custom Policy for Signed Cookies**

When you create a policy statement for a custom policy, you specify the following values.

**Resource**
The base URL including your query strings, if any:
`http://d111111abcdef8.cloudfront.net/images/horizon.jpg?size=large&license=yes`
If you omit the `Resource` parameter, users can access all of the objects associated with any distribution that is associated with the key pair that you use to create the signed URL. You can specify only one value for `Resource`. Note the following:

- **Protocol** – The value must begin with `http://` or `https://`.

- **Query string parameters** – If you have no query string parameters, omit the question mark.

- **Wildcards** – You can use the wildcard character that matches zero or more characters (*) or the wild-card character that matches exactly one character (?) anywhere in the string. For example, the value:

  `http://d111111abcdef8.cloudfront.net/*game_download.zip*`

  would include (for example) the following objects:

    - `http://d111111abcdef8.cloudfront.net/game_download.zip`
    - `http://d111111abcdef8.cloudfront.net/example_game_download.zip?license=yes`
    - `http://d111111abcdef8.cloudfront.net/test_game_download.zip?license=temp`

- **Alternate domain names** – If you specify an alternate domain name (CNAME) in the URL, you must specify the alternate domain name when referencing the object in your web page or application. Do not specify the Amazon S3 URL for the object.

**DateLessThan**
The expiration date and time for the URL in Unix time format (in seconds) and Coordinated Universal Time (UTC). Do not enclose the value in quotation marks.
For example, March 16, 2015 10:00 am UTC converts to 1426500000 in Unix time format.
For more information, see When Does CloudFront Check the Expiration Date and Time in a Signed Cookie?.

**DateGreaterThan (Optional)**
An optional start date and time for the URL in Unix time format (in seconds) and Coordinated Universal Time (UTC). Users are not allowed to access the object before the specified date and time. Do not enclose the value in quotation marks.

**IpAddress (Optional)**
The IP address of the client making the GET request. Note the following:

- To allow any IP address to access the object, omit the `IpAddress` parameter.

- You can specify either one IP address or one IP address range. For example, you can't set the policy to allow access if the client's IP address is in one of two separate ranges.

- To allow access from a single IP address, you specify:

  "*IPv4 IP address*/32"

- You must specify IP address ranges in standard IPv4 CIDR format (for example, 192.0.2.0/24). For more information, go to *RFC 4632, Classless Inter-domain Routing (CIDR): The Internet Address Assignment and Aggregation Plan*, http://tools.ietf.org/html/rfc4632. **Important**
  IP addresses in IPv6 format, such as 2001:0db8:85a3:0000:0000:8a2e:0370:7334, are not supported.

If you're using a custom policy that includes `IpAddress`, do not enable IPv6 for the distribution. If you want to restrict access to some content by IP address and support IPv6 requests for other content, you can create two distributions. For more information, see Enable IPv6 in the topic Values That You Specify When You Create or Update a Web Distribution.

## Example Policy Statements for a Signed Cookie That Uses a Custom Policy

The following example policy statements show how to control access to a specific object, all of the objects in a directory, or all of the objects associated with a key pair ID. The examples also show how to control access from an individual IP address or a range of IP addresses, and how to prevent users from using the signed cookie after a specified date and time.

If you copy and paste any of these examples, remove any whitespace (including tabs and newline characters), replace the applicable values with your own values, and include a newline character after the closing brace ( } ).

For more information, see Values That You Specify in the Policy Statement for a Custom Policy for Signed Cookies.

**Topics**

- Example Policy Statement: Accessing One Object from a Range of IP Addresses
- Example Policy Statement: Accessing All Objects in a Directory from a Range of IP Addresses
- Example Policy Statement: Accessing All Objects Associated with a Key Pair ID from One IP Address

### Example Policy Statement: Accessing One Object from a Range of IP Addresses

The following example custom policy in a signed cookie specifies that a user can access the object `http://d111111abcdef8.cloudfront.net/game_download.zip` from IP addresses in the range `192.0.2.0/24` until January 1, 2013 10:00 am UTC:

```
1 {
2     "Statement": [
3         {
4             "Resource":"http://d111111abcdef8.cloudfront.net/game_download.zip",
5             "Condition":{
6                 "IpAddress":{"AWS:SourceIp":"192.0.2.0/24"},
7                 "DateLessThan":{"AWS:EpochTime":1357034400}
8             }
9         }
10    ]
11 }
```

### Example Policy Statement: Accessing All Objects in a Directory from a Range of IP Addresses

The following example custom policy allows you to create signed cookies for any object in the `training` directory, as indicated by the * wildcard character in the `Resource` parameter. Users can access the object from an IP address in the range `192.0.2.0/24` until January 1, 2013 10:00 am UTC:

```
1 {
2     "Statement": [
3         {
4             "Resource":"http://d111111abcdef8.cloudfront.net/training/*",
5             "Condition":{
6                 "IpAddress":{"AWS:SourceIp":"192.0.2.0/24"},
7                 "DateLessThan":{"AWS:EpochTime":1357034400}
```

```
8          }
9        }
10     ]
11 }
```

Each signed cookie in which you use this policy includes a base URL that identifies a specific object, for example:

```
http://d111111abcdef8.cloudfront.net/training/orientation.pdf
```

**Example Policy Statement: Accessing All Objects Associated with a Key Pair ID from One IP Address**

The following sample custom policy allows you to set signed cookies for any object associated with any distribution, as indicated by the * wildcard character in the `Resource` parameter. The user must use the IP address 192.0.2.10/32. (The value 192.0.2.10/32 in CIDR notation refers to a single IP address, 192.0.2.10.) The objects are available only from January 1, 2013 10:00 am UTC until January 2, 2013 10:00 am UTC:

```
1 {
2    "Statement": [
3      {
4        "Resource":"http://*",
5        "Condition":{
6          "IpAddress":{"AWS:SourceIp":"192.0.2.10/32"},
7          "DateGreaterThan":{"AWS:EpochTime":1357034400},
8          "DateLessThan":{"AWS:EpochTime":1357120800}
9        }
10     }
11   ]
12 }
```

Each signed cookie in which you use this policy includes a base URL that identifies a specific object in a specific CloudFront distribution, for example:

```
http://d111111abcdef8.cloudfront.net/training/orientation.pdf
```

The signed cookie also includes a key pair ID, which must be associated with a trusted signer in the distribution (d111111abcdef8.cloudfront.net) that you specify in the base URL.

# Creating a Signature for a Signed Cookie That Uses a Custom Policy

The signature for a signed cookie that uses a custom policy is a hashed, signed, and base64-encoded version of the policy statement.

For additional information and examples of how to hash, sign, and encode the policy statement, see:

- Using a Linux Command and OpenSSL for Base64-Encoding and Encryption
- Code Examples for Creating a Signature for a Signed URL
- Tools and Code Examples for Configuring Private Content

**To create a signature for a signed cookie by using a custom policy**

1. Use the SHA-1 hash function and RSA to hash and sign the JSON policy statement that you created in the procedure To create the policy statement for a signed URL that uses a custom policy. Use the version of the policy statement that no longer includes whitespace but that has not yet been base64-encoded.

   For the private key that is required by the hash function, use the private key that is associated with the applicable active trusted signer. **Note**

The method that you use to hash and sign the policy statement depends on your programming language and platform. For sample code, see Code Examples for Creating a Signature for a Signed URL.

2. Remove whitespace (including tabs and newline characters) from the hashed and signed string.

3. Base64-encode the string using MIME base64 encoding. For more information, see Section 6.8, Base64 Content-Transfer-Encoding in *RFC 2045, MIME (Multipurpose Internet Mail Extensions) Part One: Format of Internet Message Bodies*.

4. Replace characters that are invalid in a URL query string with characters that are valid. The following table lists invalid and valid characters.

---

[See the AWS documentation website for more details]

1. Include the resulting value in the `Set-Cookie` header for the `CloudFront-Signature=` name-value pair, and return to To set a signed cookie using a custom policy to add the `Set-Cookie` header for `CloudFront-Key-Pair-Id`.

# Using a Linux Command and OpenSSL for Base64-Encoding and Encryption

You can use the following Linux command-line command and OpenSSL to hash and sign the policy statement, base64-encode the signature, and replace characters that are not valid in URL query string parameters with characters that are valid.

For information about OpenSSL, go to http://www.openssl.org.

```
![\[1\]](http://docs.aws.amazon.com/AmazonCloudFront/latest/DeveloperGuide/images/
callouts/1.png)cat policy | ![\[3\]](http://docs.aws.amazon.com/AmazonCloudFront/latest
/DeveloperGuide/images/callouts/2.png)tr -d "\n" | ![\[3\]](http://docs.aws.amazon.com/
AmazonCloudFront/latest/DeveloperGuide/images/callouts/3.png)openssl sha1 -sign private-key
.pem | ![\[4\]](http://docs.aws.amazon.com/AmazonCloudFront/latest/DeveloperGuide/images/
callouts/4.png)openssl base64 | ![\[5\]](http://docs.aws.amazon.com/AmazonCloudFront/latest/
DeveloperGuide/images/callouts/5.png)tr -- '+=/' '-_~'
```

where:

**1** cat reads the policy file.

**2** tr -d "\n" removes a newline character that was added by cat.

**3** OpenSSL hashes the file using SHA-1 and signs it using RSA and the private key file private-key.pem.

**4** OpenSSL base64-encodes the hashed and signed policy statement.

**5** tr replaces characters that are not valid in URL query string parameters with characters that are valid.

For code examples that demonstrate creating a signature in several programming languages see Code Examples for Creating a Signature for a Signed URL.

# Code Examples for Creating a Signature for a Signed URL

This section includes downloadable application examples that demonstrate how to create signatures for signed URLs. Examples are available in Perl, PHP, C#, and Java. You can use any of the examples to create signed URLs. The Perl script runs on Linux/Mac platforms. The PHP example will work on any server that runs PHP. The C# example uses the .NET Framework.

For an example of how to use cookies with Ruby on Rails, see Tools and Code Examples for Configuring Private Content in the topic Amazon CloudFront Resources.

You can find example code for signed URLs and for signed cookies in a variety of programming languages. Perform an internet search on `sample app` *language* `cloudfront signed URLs` or on `sample app` *language* `cloudfront signed cookies`.

**Topics**

- Create a URL Signature Using Perl
- Create a URL Signature Using PHP
- Create a URL Signature Using C# and the .NET Framework
- Create a URL Signature Using Java

# Create a URL Signature Using Perl

This section includes a Perl script for Linux/Mac platforms that you can use to create the signature for private content. To create the signature, run the script with command line arguments that specify the CloudFront URL, the path to the private key of the signer, the key ID, and an expiration date for the URL. The tool can also decode signed URLs.

**Note**
Creating a URL signature is just one part of the process of serving private content using a signed URL. For more information about the end-to-end process, see Using Signed URLs.

**Topics**

- Example of Using a Perl Script to Create a Signed URL
- Source for the Perl Script to Create a Signed URL

## Example of Using a Perl Script to Create a Signed URL

The following example shows how you can use the Perl script provided in this topic to create an RTMP distribution signature. To start, save the script as a file called cfsign.pl. Then run the script using the following command line arguments:

```
1 $ cfsign.pl --action encode --stream example/video.mp4 --private-key
2    /path/to/my-private-key.pem --key-pair-id PK12345EXAMPLE --expires 1265838202
```

This script generates the policy statement from the command line arguments. The signature that it generates is an SHA1 hash of the policy statement.

The following is an example base64-encoded stream name:

```
1 mp4:example/video.mp4%3FPolicy%3DewogICJTdGF0ZW1lbnQiOlt7CiAgICAgICJSZXNvdXJjZSI
2 6ImRyciIsCiAgICAgICJDb25kaXRpb24iOnsKICAgICAgICAiSXBBBZGRyZXNzIjp7IkFXUzpTb3VyY2V
3 JcCI6IjAuMC4wLjAvMCJ9LAogICAgICAgICJEYXRlTGVzc1RoYW4iOnsiQVdTOkVwb2NoVGltZSI6MjE
4 ONTkxNjgwMH0KICAgICAgfQogICAgfQogICAgEXAMPLE_%26Signature%3DewtHqEXK~68tsZt-eOFnZKGwTf2a
5 JlbKhXkK5SSiVqcG9pieCRV3xTEPtc29OzeXlsDvRycOM2WK0cXzcyYZhpl9tv2796ihHiCTAwIHQ8yP
6 17Af4nWtOLIZHoH6wkR3tU1cQHs8R1d-g-SlZGjNBXr~J2MbaJzm8i6EXAMPLE_%26Key-Pair-Id%3
7 DPK12345EXAMPLE
```

This signature authenticates the request to stream the private content example/video.mp4.

If you're using Adobe Flash Player and the stream name is passed in from a web page using JavaScript, you must base64-encode the signature and replace characters that are invalid in a URL request parameter (+, =, /) with characters that are valid (-, _, and ~, respectively).

If the stream name is not passed in from a web page, you don't need to base64-encode the signature. For example, you would not base64-encode the signature if you write your own player and the stream names are fetched from within the Adobe Flash .swf file.

The following example uses jwplayer with CloudFront.

```
1 <script type='text/javascript'>
2   var so1 = new SWFObject
3     ('http://d84l721fxaaqy9.cloudfront.net/player/player.swf',
4     'mpl', '640', '360', '9');
5   so1.addParam('allowfullscreen','true');
6   so1.addParam('allowscriptaccess','always');
7   so1.addParam('wmode','opaque');
8   so1.addVariable('streamer','rtmp://s33r3xe4ayhhis.cloudfront.net/cfx/st');
```

```
 9   so1.addVariable("file","mp4:example/video.mp4%3FPolicy%3DewogICJTdGF0ZW1lbnQi
10       Olt7CiAgICAgICJSZXNvdXJjZSI6ImRyciIsCiAgICAgICJDb25kaXRpb24iOnsKICAgICAgICA
11       iSXBBZGRyZXNzIjp7IkFXUzpTb3VyY2VJcCI6IjAuMC4wLjAvMCJ9LAogICAgICAgICJEYXRlTG
12       Vzc1RoYW4iOnsiQVdTOkVwb2NoVGltZSI6MjEONTkxNjgwMHOKICAgICAgfQogICAgfQogICAgXAMPLE_%
13       26Signature%3DewtHqEXK~68tsZt-eOFnZKGwTf2aJlbKhXkK5SSiVqcG9pieCRV3xTEPtc29O
14       zeXlsDvRycOM2WKOcXzcyYZhpl9tv2796ihHiCTAwIHQ8yP17Af4nWtOLIZHoH6wkR3tU1cQHs8
15       R1d-g-SlZGjNBXr~J2MbaJzm8i6EXAMPLE_%26Key-Pair-Id%3DPK12345EXAMPLE
16   so1.write('flv');
17 </script>
```

When you retrieve a stream to play from within an Adobe Flash .swf file, do not URL-encode the stream name. For example:

```
1 mp4:example/video.mp4?Policy=ewogICJTdGF0ZW1lbnQiOlt7CiAgICAgICJSZXNvdXJjZSI6ImR
2 yciIsCiAgICAgICJDb25kaXRpb24iOnsKICAgICAgICAiSXBBZGRyZXNzIjp7IkFXUzpTb3VyY2VJcCI
3 6IjAuMC4wLjAvMCJ9LAogICAgICAgICJEYXRlTGVzc1RoYW4iOnsiQVdTOkVwb2NoVGltZSI6MjEONTk
4 xNjgwMHOKICAgICAgfQogICAgfQogICAgXAMPLE_&Signature=ewtHqEXK~68tsZt-eOFnZKGwTf2aJlbKhXkK
5 5SSiVqcG9pieCRV3xTEPtc29OzeXlsDvRycOM2WKOcXzcyYZhpl9tv2796ihHiCTAwIHQ8yP17Af4nWt
6 OLIZHoH6wkR3tU1cQHs8R1d-g-SlZGjNBXr~J2MbaJzm8i6EXAMPLE_&Key-Pair-Id=PK12345
7 EXAMPLE
```

For more information about the command line switches and features of this toolee the comments in the Perl source code, which is included in the next section.

See also

- Create a URL Signature Using PHP
- Create a URL Signature Using C# and the .NET Framework
- Create a URL Signature Using Java
- Tools and Code Examples for Configuring Private Content

## Source for the Perl Script to Create a Signed URL

The following Perl source code can be used to create a signed URL for CloudFront. Comments in the code include information about the command line switches and the features of the tool.

```perl
 1 #!/usr/bin/perl -w
 2
 3 # Copyright 2008 Amazon Technologies, Inc.  Licensed under the Apache License, Version 2.0 (the
       "License");
 4 # you may not use this file except in compliance with the License. You may obtain a copy of the
       License at:
 5 #
 6 # http://aws.amazon.com/apache2.0
 7 #
 8 # This file is distributed on an "AS IS" BASIS, WITHOUT WARRANTIES OR CONDITIONS OF ANY KIND,
       either express or implied.
 9 # See the License for the specific language governing permissions and limitations under the
       License.
10
11 =head1 cfsign.pl
12
13 cfsign.pl - A tool to generate and verify AWS CloudFront signed URLs
14
15 =head1 SYNOPSIS
16
```

```
17 This script uses an existing RSA key pair to sign and verify AWS CloudFront signed URLs

18

19 View the script source for details as to which CPAN packages are required beforehand.

20

21 For help, try:

22

23 cfsign.pl --help

24

25 URL signing examples:

26

27 cfsign.pl --action encode --url http://images.my-website.com/gallery1.zip --policy sample_policy
      .json --private-key privkey.pem --key-pair-id mykey

28

29 cfsign.pl --action encode --url http://images.my-website.com/gallery1.zip --expires 1257439868
      --private-key privkey.pem --key-pair-id mykey

30

31 Stream signing example:

32

33 cfsign.pl --action encode --stream videos/myvideo.mp4 --expires 1257439868 --private-key privkey
      .pem --key-pair-id mykey

34

35 URL decode example:

36

37 cfsign.pl --action decode --url "http//mydist.cloudfront.net/?Signature=AGO-
      PgxkYo99MkJFHvjfGXjG1QDEXeaDb4Qtzmy85wqyJjK7eKojQWa4BCRcow__&Policy=
      eyJTdGF0ZW1lbnQiOlt7IlJlc291cmNlIjoiaHR0cDovLypicmFkbS5qcGciLCJDb25kaXRpb24iOnsiSXBBBZGRyZXNzIjp7I
      &Key-Pair-Id=mykey"

38

39

40 To generate an RSA key pair, you can use openssl and the following commands:

41

42 # Generate a 1024bit key pair

43 openssl genrsa -out private-key.pem 1024

44 openssl rsa -in private-key.pem -pubout -out public-key.pem

45

46

47 =head1 OPTIONS

48

49 =over 8

50

51 =item B<--help>

52

53 Print a help message and exits.

54

55 =item B<--action> [action]

56

57 The action to execute.   action can be one of:

58

59   encode - Generate a signed URL (using a canned policy or a user policy)

60   decode - Decode a signed URL

61

62 =item B<--url>

63

64 The URL to en/decode
```

```perl
65
66 =item B<--stream>
67
68 The stream to en/decode
69
70 =item B<--private-key>
71
72 The path to your private key.
73
74 =item B<--key-pair-id>
75
76 The AWS Portal assigned key pair identifier.
77
78 =item B<--policy>
79
80 The CloudFront policy document.
81
82 =item B<--expires>
83
84 The Unix epoch time when the URL is to expire. If both this option and
85 the --policy option are specified, --policy will be used. Otherwise, this
86 option alone will use a canned policy.
87
88 =back
89
90 =cut
91
92 use strict;
93 use warnings;
94
95 # you might need to use CPAN to get these modules.
96 # run perl -MCPAN -e "install <module>" to get them.
97 # The openssl command line will also need to be in your $PATH.
98 use File::Temp qw/tempfile/;
99 use Getopt::Long;
100 use IPC::Open2;
101 use MIME::Base64 qw(encode_base64 decode_base64);
102 use Pod::Usage;
103 use URI;
104
105 my $CANNED_POLICY
106     = '{"Statement":[{"Resource":"<RESOURCE>","Condition":{"DateLessThan":{"AWS:EpochTime":<
          EXPIRES>}}}]}';
107
108 my $POLICY_PARAM      = "Policy";
109 my $EXPIRES_PARAM     = "Expires";
110 my $SIGNATURE_PARAM   = "Signature";
111 my $KEY_PAIR_ID_PARAM = "Key-Pair-Id";
112
113 my $verbose = 0;
114 my $policy_filename = "";
115 my $expires_epoch = 0;
116 my $action = "";
117 my $help = 0;
```

```perl
118 my $key_pair_id = "";
119 my $url = "";
120 my $stream = "";
121 my $private_key_filename = "";
122
123 my $result = GetOptions("action=s"      => \$action,
124                         "policy=s"      => \$policy_filename,
125                         "expires=i"     => \$expires_epoch,
126                         "private-key=s" => \$private_key_filename,
127                         "key-pair-id=s" => \$key_pair_id,
128                         "verbose"       => \$verbose,
129                         "help"          => \$help,
130                         "url=s"         => \$url,
131                         "stream=s"      => \$stream,
132                     );
133
134 if ($help or !$result) {
135     pod2usage(1);
136     exit;
137 }
138
139 if ($url eq "" and $stream eq "") {
140     print STDERR "Must include a stream or a URL to encode or decode with the --stream or --url
            option\n";
141     exit;
142 }
143
144 if ($url ne "" and $stream ne "") {
145     print STDERR "Only one of --url and --stream may be specified\n";
146     exit;
147 }
148
149 if ($url ne "" and !is_url_valid($url)) {
150     exit;
151 }
152
153 if ($stream ne "") {
154     exit unless is_stream_valid($stream);
155
156     # The signing mechanism is identical, so from here on just pretend we're
157     # dealing with a URL
158     $url = $stream;
159 }
160
161 if ($action eq "encode") {
162     # The encode action will generate a private content URL given a base URL,
163     # a policy file (or an expires timestamp) and a key pair id parameter
164     my $private_key;
165     my $public_key;
166     my $public_key_file;
167
168     my $policy;
169     if ($policy_filename eq "") {
170         if ($expires_epoch == 0) {
```

```
171         print STDERR "Must include policy filename with --policy argument or an expires" .
172                         "time using --expires\n";
173         }
174
175         $policy = $CANNED_POLICY;
176         $policy =~ s/<EXPIRES>/$expires_epoch/g;
177         $policy =~ s/<RESOURCE>/$url/g;
178     } else {
179         if (! -e $policy_filename) {
180             print STDERR "Policy file $policy_filename does not exist\n";
181             exit;
182         }
183         $expires_epoch = 0; # ignore if set
184         $policy = read_file($policy_filename);
185     }
186
187     if ($private_key_filename eq "") {
188         print STDERR "You must specific the path to your private key file with --private-key\n";
189         exit;
190     }
191
192     if (! -e $private_key_filename) {
193         print STDERR "Private key file $private_key_filename does not exist\n";
194         exit;
195     }
196
197     if ($key_pair_id eq "") {
198         print STDERR "You must specify an AWS portal key pair id with --key-pair-id\n";
199         exit;
200     }
201
202     my $encoded_policy = url_safe_base64_encode($policy);
203     my $signature = rsa_sha1_sign($policy, $private_key_filename);
204     my $encoded_signature = url_safe_base64_encode($signature);
205
206     my $generated_url = create_url($url, $encoded_policy, $encoded_signature, $key_pair_id,
             $expires_epoch);
207
208
209     if ($stream ne "") {
210         print "Encoded stream (for use within a swf):\n" . $generated_url . "\n";
211         print "Encoded and escaped stream (for use on a webpage):\n" .  escape_url_for_webpage(
                 $generated_url) . "\n";
212     } else {
213         print "Encoded URL:\n" . $generated_url . "\n";
214     }
215 } elsif ($action eq "decode") {
216     my $decoded = decode_url($url);
217     if (!$decoded) {
218         print STDERR "Improperly formed URL\n";
219         exit;
220     }
221
222     print_decoded_url($decoded);
```

```perl
223 } else {
224     # No action specified, print help.  But only if this is run as a program (caller will be
            empty)
225     pod2usage(1) unless caller();
226 }
227
228 # Decode a private content URL into its component parts
229 sub decode_url {
230     my $url = shift;
231
232     if ($url =~ /(.*)\?(.*)/) {
233         my $base_url = $1;
234         my $params = $2;
235
236         my @unparsed_params = split(/&/, $params);
237         my %params = ();
238         foreach my $param (@unparsed_params) {
239             my ($key, $val) = split(/=/, $param);
240             $params{$key} = $val;
241         }
242
243         my $encoded_signature = "";
244         if (exists $params{$SIGNATURE_PARAM}) {
245             $encoded_signature = $params{"Signature"};
246         } else {
247             print STDERR "Missing Signature URL parameter\n";
248             return 0;
249         }
250
251         my $encoded_policy = "";
252         if (exists $params{$POLICY_PARAM}) {
253             $encoded_policy = $params{$POLICY_PARAM};
254         } else {
255             if (!exists $params{$EXPIRES_PARAM}) {
256                 print STDERR "Either the Policy or Expires URL parameter needs to be specified\n
                    ";
257                 return 0;
258             }
259
260             my $expires = $params{$EXPIRES_PARAM};
261
262             my $policy = $CANNED_POLICY;
263             $policy =~ s/<EXPIRES>/$expires/g;
264
265             my $url_without_cf_params = $url;
266             $url_without_cf_params =~ s/$SIGNATURE_PARAM=[^&]*&?//g;
267             $url_without_cf_params =~ s/$POLICY_PARAM=[^&]*&?//g;
268             $url_without_cf_params =~ s/$EXPIRES_PARAM=[^&]*&?//g;
269             $url_without_cf_params =~ s/$KEY_PAIR_ID_PARAM=[^&]*&?//g;
270
271             if ($url_without_cf_params =~ /(.*)\?$/) {
272                 $url_without_cf_params = $1;
273             }
274
```

```perl
275          $policy =~ s/<RESOURCE>/$url_without_cf_params/g;
276
277          $encoded_policy = url_safe_base64_encode($policy);
278      }
279
280      my $key = "";
281      if (exists $params{$KEY_PAIR_ID_PARAM}) {
282          $key = $params{$KEY_PAIR_ID_PARAM};
283      } else {
284          print STDERR "Missing $KEY_PAIR_ID_PARAM parameter\n";
285          return 0;
286      }
287
288      my $policy = url_safe_base64_decode($encoded_policy);
289
290      my %ret = ();
291      $ret{"base_url"} = $base_url;
292      $ret{"policy"} = $policy;
293      $ret{"key"} = $key;
294
295      return \%ret;
296  } else {
297      return 0;
298  }
299 }
300
301 # Print a decoded URL out
302 sub print_decoded_url {
303      my $decoded = shift;
304
305      print "Base URL: \n" . $decoded->{"base_url"} . "\n";
306      print "Policy: \n" . $decoded->{"policy"} . "\n";
307      print "Key: \n" . $decoded->{"key"} . "\n";
308 }
309
310 # Encode a string with base 64 encoding and replace some invalid URL characters
311 sub url_safe_base64_encode {
312      my ($value) = @_;
313
314      my $result = encode_base64($value);
315      $result =~ tr|+=/|-_~|;
316
317      return $result;
318 }
319
320 # Decode a string with base 64 encoding.  URL-decode the string first
321 # followed by reversing any special character ("+=/") translation.
322 sub url_safe_base64_decode {
323      my ($value) = @_;
324
325      $value =~ s/%([0-9A-Fa-f]{2})/chr(hex($1))/eg;
326      $value =~ tr|-_~|+=/|;
327
328      my $result = decode_base64($value);
```

```perl
329
330     return $result;
331 }
332
333 # Create a private content URL
334 sub create_url {
335     my ($path, $policy, $signature, $key_pair_id, $expires) = @_;
336
337     my $result;
338     my $separator = $path =~ /\?/ ? '&' : '?';
339     if ($expires) {
340         $result = "$path$separator$EXPIRES_PARAM=$expires&$SIGNATURE_PARAM=$signature&
341             $KEY_PAIR_ID_PARAM=$key_pair_id";
342     } else {
                $result = "$path$separator$POLICY_PARAM=$policy&$SIGNATURE_PARAM=$signature&
                    $KEY_PAIR_ID_PARAM=$key_pair_id";
343     }
344     $result =~ s/\n//g;
345
346     return $result;
347 }
348
349 # Sign a document with given private key file.
350 # The first argument is the document to sign
351 # The second argument is the name of the private key file
352 sub rsa_sha1_sign {
353     my ($to_sign, $pvkFile) = @_;
354
355     return write_to_program("openssl sha1 -sign $pvkFile", $to_sign);
356 }
357
358 # Helper function to write data to a program
359 sub write_to_program {
360     my ($prog, $data) = @_;
361
362     my $pid = open2(*README, *WRITEME, $prog);
363     print WRITEME $data;
364     close WRITEME;
365
366     # slurp entire contents of output into scalar
367     my $output;
368     local $/ = undef;
369     $output = <README>;
370     close README;
371
372     waitpid($pid, 0);
373
374     return $output;
375 }
376
377 # Read a file into a string and return the string
378 sub read_file {
379     my ($file) = @_;
380
```

```perl
381     open(INFILE, "<$file") or die("Failed to open $file: $!");
382     my $str = join('', <INFILE>);
383     close INFILE;
384
385     return $str;
386 }
387
388 sub is_url_valid {
389     my ($url) = @_;
390
391     # HTTP distributions start with http[s]:// and are the correct thing to sign
392     if ($url =~ /^https?:\/\//) {
393         return 1;
394     } else {
395         print STDERR "CloudFront requires absolute URLs for HTTP distributions\n";
396         return 0;
397     }
398 }
399
400 sub is_stream_valid {
401     my ($stream) = @_;
402
403     if ($stream =~ /^rtmp:\/\// or $stream =~ /^\/?cfx\/st/) {
404         print STDERR "Streaming distributions require that only the stream name is signed.\n";
405         print STDERR "The stream name is everything after, but not including, cfx/st/\n";
406         return 0;
407     } else {
408         return 1;
409     }
410 }
411
412 # flash requires that the query parameters in the stream name are url
413 # encoded when passed in through javascript, etc.  This sub handles the minimal
414 # required url encoding.
415 sub escape_url_for_webpage {
416     my ($url) = @_;
417
418     $url =~ s/\?/%3F/g;
419     $url =~ s/=/%3D/g;
420     $url =~ s/&/%26/g;
421
422     return $url;
423 }
424
425 1;
```

# Create a URL Signature Using PHP

Any web server that runs PHP can use the PHP demo code to create policy statements and signatures for private CloudFront RTMP distributions. The example creates a functioning web page with signed URL links that play a video stream using CloudFront streaming. To get the example, download Signature Code for Video Streaming in PHP.

You can also create signed URLs by using the `UrlSigner` class in the AWS SDK for PHP. For more information, see Class UrlSigner in the *AWS SDK for PHP API Reference*.

**Note**
Creating a URL signature is just one part of the process of serving private content using a signed URL. For more information about the entire process, see Using Signed URLs.

In the following code segment, the function `rsa_sha1_sign` hashes and signs the policy statement. The arguments required are a policy statement, an out parameter to contain the signature, and the private key for your AWS account or for a trusted AWS account that you specify. Next, the `url_safe_base64_encode` function creates a URL-safe version of the signature.

### Example RSA SHA1 Hashing in PHP

```
1  function rsa_sha1_sign($policy, $private_key_filename) {
2      $signature = "";
3
4      // load the private key
5      $fp = fopen($private_key_filename, "r");
6      $priv_key = fread($fp, 8192);
7      fclose($fp);
8      $pkeyid = openssl_get_privatekey($priv_key);
9
10     // compute signature
11     openssl_sign($policy, $signature, $pkeyid);
12
13     // free the key from memory
14     openssl_free_key($pkeyid);
15
16     return $signature;
17  }
18
19  function url_safe_base64_encode($value) {
20      $encoded = base64_encode($value);
21      // replace unsafe characters +, = and / with
22      // the safe characters -, _ and ~
23      return str_replace(
24          array('+', '=', '/'),
25          array('-', '_', '~'),
26          $encoded);
27  }
```

The following code constructs a *canned* policy statement needed for creating the signature. For more information about canned policies, see Creating a Signed URL Using a Canned Policy.

### Example Canned Signing Function in PHP

```
1  function get_canned_policy_stream_name($video_path, $private_key_filename, $key_pair_id,
       $expires) {
2      // this policy is well known by CloudFront, but you still need to sign it,
3      // since it contains your parameters
```

```
4    $canned_policy = '{"Statement":[{"Resource":"' . $video_path . '","Condition":{"DateLessThan
        ":{"AWS:EpochTime":'. $expires . '}}}]}';
5
6    // sign the canned policy
7    $signature = rsa_sha1_sign($canned_policy, $private_key_filename);
8    // make the signature safe to be included in a url
9    $encoded_signature = url_safe_base64_encode($signature);
10
11   // combine the above into a stream name
12   $stream_name = create_stream_name($video_path, null, $encoded_signature, $key_pair_id,
        $expires);
13   // url-encode the query string characters to work around a flash player bug
14   return encode_query_params($stream_name);
15   }
```

The following code constructs a *custom* policy statement needed for creating the signature. For more information about custom policies, see Creating a Signed URL Using a Custom Policy.

**Note**

The $expires variable is a date/time stamp that must be an integer, not a string.

**Example Custom Signing Function in PHP**

```
1  function get_custom_policy_stream_name($video_path, $private_key_filename, $key_pair_id, $policy
       ) {
2      // sign the policy
3      $signature = rsa_sha1_sign($policy, $private_key_filename);
4      // make the signature safe to be included in a url
5      $encoded_signature = url_safe_base64_encode($signature);
6
7      // combine the above into a stream name
8      $stream_name = create_stream_name($video_path, $encoded_policy, $encoded_signature,
           $key_pair_id, null);
9      // url-encode the query string characters to work around a flash player bug
10     return encode_query_params($stream_name);
11     }
```

For more information about the OpenSSL implementation of SHA-1, see The Open Source Toolkit for SSL/TLS.

See also

- Create a URL Signature Using Perl
- Create a URL Signature Using C# and the .NET Framework
- Create a URL Signature Using Java
- Tools and Code Examples for Configuring Private Content

# Create a URL Signature Using C# and the .NET Framework

The C# examples in this section implement an example application that demonstrates how to create the signatures for CloudFront private distributions using canned and custom policy statements. The examples includes utility functions based on the AWS .NET SDK that can be useful in .NET applications.

You can also create signed URLs and signed cookies by using the AWS SDK for .NET. In the AWS SDK for .NET API Reference, see the following topics:

- **Signed URLs** – Amazon.CloudFront > AmazonCloudFrontUrlSigner
- **Signed cookies** – Amazon.CloudFront > AmazonCloudFrontCookieSigner

**Note**
Creating a URL signature is just one part of the process of serving private content using a signed URL. For more information about the entire process, see Using Signed URLs.

To download the code, go to Signature Code in C#.

To use the RSA keys provided by AWS Account/Security in the .NET framework, you must convert the AWS-supplied .pem files to the XML format that the .NET framework uses.

After conversion, the RSA private key file is in the following format:

**Example RSA Private Key in the XML .NET Framework Format**

```
1  <RSAKeyValue>
2    <Modulus>
3      wO5IvYCP5UcoCKDo1dcspoMehWBZcyfs9QEzGi6Oe5y+ewGr1oW+vB2GPB
4      ANBiVPcUHTFWhwaIBd3oglmFOlGQljP/jOfmXHUK2kUUnI.nJp+oOBL2NiuFtqcW6h/L5lIpD8Yq+NRHg
5      Ty4zDsyr2880MvXv88yEFURCkqEXAMPLE=
6    </Modulus>
7    <Exponent>AQAB</Exponent>
8    <P>
9      5bmKDaTz
10     npENGVqz4Cea8XPH+sxt+2VaAwYnsarVUoSBeVt8WLloVuZGG9IZYmH5KteXEu7fZveYd9UEXAMPLE==
11   </P>
12   <Q>
13     1v9l/WN1a1N3rOK4VGoCokx7kR2SyTMSbZgF9IWJNOugR/WZw7HTnjipO3c9dy1Ms9pUKwUF4
14     6d7049EXAMPLE==
15   </Q>
16   <DP>
17     RgrSKuLWXMyBH+/l1Dx/I4tXuAJIrlPyo+VmiOc7b5NzHptkSHEPfR9s1
18     OKOVqjknclqCJ3Ig86OMEtEXAMPLE==
19   </DP>
20   <DQ>
21     pjPjvSFw+RoaTuOpgCA/jwW/FGyfN6iim1RFbkT4
22     z49DZb2IM885f3vf35eLTaEYRYUHQgZtChNEVOTEXAMPLE==
23   </DQ>
24   <InverseQ>
25     nkvOJTg5QtGNgWb9i
26     cVtzrL/1pFEOHbJXwEJdU99N+7sMK+1066DL/HSBUCD63qD4USpnfOmyc24inOEXAMPLE==</InverseQ>
27   <D>
28       Bc7mp7XYHynuPZxChjWNJZIq+A73gmOASDv6At7F8Vi9rOxUlQe/vOAQS3ycN8QlyR4XMbzMLYk
29       3yjxFDXo4ZKQtOGzLGteCU2srANiLv26/imXA8FVidZftTAtLviWQZBVPTeYIA69ATUYPEqOa5u5wjGy
30       UOij9OWyuEXAMPLE=
31   </D>
32  </RSAKeyValue>
```

335

The following C# code creates a signed URL that uses a canned policy by performing the following steps:

- Creates a policy statement.
- Hashes the policy statement using SHA1, and signs the result using RSA and the private key for your AWS account or for a trusted AWS account that you specify.
- Base64-encodes the hashed and signed policy statement and replaces special characters to make the string safe to use as a URL request parameter.
- Concatenates the applicable values.

For the complete implementation, see the example at Signature Code in C#.

### Example Canned Policy Signing Method in C#

```
1 public static string ToUrlSafeBase64String(byte[] bytes)
2 {
3     return System.Convert.ToBase64String(bytes)
4         .Replace('+', '-')
5         .Replace('=', '_')
6         .Replace('/', '~');
7 }
8
9 public static string CreateCannedPrivateURL(string urlString,
10     string durationUnits, string durationNumber, string pathToPolicyStmnt,
11     string pathToPrivateKey, string privateKeyId)
12 {
13     // args[] 0-thisMethod, 1-resourceUrl, 2-seconds-minutes-hours-days
14     // to expiration, 3-numberOfPreviousUnits, 4-pathToPolicyStmnt,
15     // 5-pathToPrivateKey, 6-PrivateKeyId
16
17     TimeSpan timeSpanInterval = GetDuration(durationUnits, durationNumber);
18
19     // Create the policy statement.
20     string strPolicy = CreatePolicyStatement(pathToPolicyStmnt,
21         urlString,
22         DateTime.Now,
23         DateTime.Now.Add(timeSpanInterval),
24         "0.0.0.0/0");
25     if ("Error!" == strPolicy) return "Invalid time frame." +
26         "Start time cannot be greater than end time.";
27
28     // Copy the expiration time defined by policy statement.
29     string strExpiration = CopyExpirationTimeFromPolicy(strPolicy);
30
31     // Read the policy into a byte buffer.
32     byte[] bufferPolicy = Encoding.ASCII.GetBytes(strPolicy);
33
34     // Initialize the SHA1CryptoServiceProvider object and hash the policy data.
35     using (SHA1CryptoServiceProvider
36         cryptoSHA1 = new SHA1CryptoServiceProvider())
37     {
38         bufferPolicy = cryptoSHA1.ComputeHash(bufferPolicy);
39
40         // Initialize the RSACryptoServiceProvider object.
41         RSACryptoServiceProvider providerRSA = new RSACryptoServiceProvider();
42         XmlDocument xmlPrivateKey = new XmlDocument();
43
44         // Load PrivateKey.xml, which you created by converting your
```

```
45        // .pem file to the XML format that the .NET framework uses.
46        // Several tools are available.
47        xmlPrivateKey.Load(pathToPrivateKey);
48
49        // Format the RSACryptoServiceProvider providerRSA and
50        // create the signature.
51        providerRSA.FromXmlString(xmlPrivateKey.InnerXml);
52        RSAPKCS1SignatureFormatter rsaFormatter =
53            new RSAPKCS1SignatureFormatter(providerRSA);
54        rsaFormatter.SetHashAlgorithm("SHA1");
55        byte[] signedPolicyHash = rsaFormatter.CreateSignature(bufferPolicy);
56
57        // Convert the signed policy to URL-safe base64 encoding and
58        // replace unsafe characters + = / with the safe characters - _ ~
59        string strSignedPolicy = ToUrlSafeBase64String(signedPolicyHash);
60
61        // Concatenate the URL, the timestamp, the signature,
62        // and the key pair ID to form the signed URL.
63        return urlString +
64            "?Expires=" +
65            strExpiration +
66            "&Signature=" +
67            strSignedPolicy +
68            "&Key-Pair-Id=" +
69            privateKeyId;
70    }
71 }
```

The following C# code creates a signed URL that uses a custom policy by performing the following steps:

1. Creates a policy statement.

2. Base64-encodes the policy statement and replaces special characters to make the string safe to use as a URL request parameter.

3. Hashes the policy statement using SHA1, and encrypts the result using RSA and the private key for your AWS account or for a trusted AWS account that you specify.

4. Base64-encodes the hashed policy statement and replacing special characters to make the string safe to use as a URL request parameter.

5. Concatenates the applicable values.

For the complete implementation, see the example at Signature Code in C#.

## Example Custom Policy Signing Method in C#

```
1 public static string ToUrlSafeBase64String(byte[] bytes)
2 {
3     return System.Convert.ToBase64String(bytes)
4         .Replace('+', '-')
5         .Replace('=', '_')
6         .Replace('/', '~');
7 }
8
9 public static string CreateCustomPrivateURL(string urlString,
10     string durationUnits, string durationNumber, string startIntervalFromNow,
11     string ipaddress, string pathToPolicyStmnt, string pathToPrivateKey,
12     string PrivateKeyId)
```

```csharp
13  {
14      // args[] 0-thisMethod, 1-resourceUrl, 2-seconds-minutes-hours-days
15      // to expiration, 3-numberOfPreviousUnits, 4-starttimeFromNow,
16      // 5-ip_address, 6-pathToPolicyStmt, 7-pathToPrivateKey, 8-privateKeyId
17
18      TimeSpan timeSpanInterval = GetDuration(durationUnits, durationNumber);
19      TimeSpan timeSpanToStart = GetDurationByUnits(durationUnits,
20          startIntervalFromNow);
21      if (null == timeSpanToStart)
22          return "Invalid duration units." +
23              "Valid options: seconds, minutes, hours, or days";
24
25      string strPolicy = CreatePolicyStatement(
26          pathToPolicyStmnt, urlString, DateTime.Now.Add(timeSpanToStart),
27          DateTime.Now.Add(timeSpanInterval), ipaddress);
28
29      // Read the policy into a byte buffer.
30      byte[] bufferPolicy = Encoding.ASCII.GetBytes(strPolicy);
31
32      // Convert the policy statement to URL-safe base64 encoding and
33      // replace unsafe characters + = / with the safe characters - _ ~
34
35      string urlSafePolicy = ToUrlSafeBase64String(bufferPolicy);
36
37      // Initialize the SHA1CryptoServiceProvider object and hash the policy data.
38      byte[] bufferPolicyHash;
39      using (SHA1CryptoServiceProvider cryptoSHA1 =
40          new SHA1CryptoServiceProvider())
41      {
42          bufferPolicyHash = cryptoSHA1.ComputeHash(bufferPolicy);
43
44          // Initialize the RSACryptoServiceProvider object.
45          RSACryptoServiceProvider providerRSA = new RSACryptoServiceProvider();
46          XmlDocument xmlPrivateKey = new XmlDocument();
47
48          // Load PrivateKey.xml, which you created by converting your
49          // .pem file to the XML format that the .NET framework uses.
50          // Several tools are available.
51          xmlPrivateKey.Load("PrivateKey.xml");
52
53          // Format the RSACryptoServiceProvider providerRSA
54          // and create the signature.
55          providerRSA.FromXmlString(xmlPrivateKey.InnerXml);
56          RSAPKCS1SignatureFormatter RSAFormatter =
57              new RSAPKCS1SignatureFormatter(providerRSA);
58          RSAFormatter.SetHashAlgorithm("SHA1");
59          byte[] signedHash = RSAFormatter.CreateSignature(bufferPolicyHash);
60
61          // Convert the signed policy to URL-safe base64 encoding and
62          // replace unsafe characters + = / with the safe characters - _ ~
63          string strSignedPolicy = ToUrlSafeBase64String(signedHash);
64
65          return urlString +
66              "?Policy=" +
```

```
67          urlSafePolicy +
68          "&Signature=" +
69          strSignedPolicy +
70          "&Key-Pair-Id=" +
71          PrivateKeyId;
72      }
73  }
```

**Example Utility Methods for Signature Generation** The following methods get the policy statement from a file and parse time intervals for signature generation.

```
1  public static string CreatePolicyStatement(string policyStmnt,
2      string resourceUrl,
3      DateTime startTime,
4      DateTime endTime,
5      string ipAddress)
6
7  {
8      // Create the policy statement.
9      FileStream streamPolicy = new FileStream(policyStmnt, FileMode.Open, FileAccess.Read);
10     using (StreamReader reader = new StreamReader(streamPolicy))
11     {
12         string strPolicy = reader.ReadToEnd();
13
14         TimeSpan startTimeSpanFromNow = (startTime - DateTime.Now);
15         TimeSpan endTimeSpanFromNow = (endTime - DateTime.Now);
16         TimeSpan intervalStart =
17             (DateTime.UtcNow.Add(startTimeSpanFromNow)) -
18             new DateTime(1970, 1, 1, 0, 0, 0, DateTimeKind.Utc);
19         TimeSpan intervalEnd =
20             (DateTime.UtcNow.Add(endTimeSpanFromNow)) -
21             new DateTime(1970, 1, 1, 0, 0, 0, DateTimeKind.Utc);
22
23         int startTimestamp = (int)intervalStart.TotalSeconds; // START_TIME
24         int endTimestamp = (int)intervalEnd.TotalSeconds;   // END_TIME
25
26         if (startTimestamp > endTimestamp)
27             return "Error!";
28
29         // Replace variables in the policy statement.
30         strPolicy = strPolicy.Replace("RESOURCE", resourceUrl);
31         strPolicy = strPolicy.Replace("START_TIME", startTimestamp.ToString());
32         strPolicy = strPolicy.Replace("END_TIME", endTimestamp.ToString());
33         strPolicy = strPolicy.Replace("IP_ADDRESS", ipAddress);
34         strPolicy = strPolicy.Replace("EXPIRES", endTimestamp.ToString());
35         return strPolicy;
36     }
37 }
38
39 public static TimeSpan GetDuration(string units, string numUnits)
40 {
41     TimeSpan timeSpanInterval = new TimeSpan();
42     switch (units)
43     {
44         case "seconds":
```

```
45          timeSpanInterval = new TimeSpan(0, 0, 0, int.Parse(numUnits));
46          break;
47       case "minutes":
48          timeSpanInterval = new TimeSpan(0, 0, int.Parse(numUnits), 0);
49          break;
50       case "hours":
51          timeSpanInterval = new TimeSpan(0, int.Parse(numUnits), 0 ,0);
52          break;
53       case "days":
54          timeSpanInterval = new TimeSpan(int.Parse(numUnits),0 ,0 ,0);
55          break;
56       default:
57          Console.WriteLine("Invalid time units;" +
58              "use seconds, minutes, hours, or days");
59          break;
60    }
61    return timeSpanInterval;
62 }
63
64 private static TimeSpan GetDurationByUnits(string durationUnits,
65    string startIntervalFromNow)
66 {
67    switch (durationUnits)
68    {
69       case "seconds":
70          return new TimeSpan(0, 0, int.Parse(startIntervalFromNow));
71       case "minutes":
72          return new TimeSpan(0, int.Parse(startIntervalFromNow), 0);
73       case "hours":
74          return new TimeSpan(int.Parse(startIntervalFromNow), 0, 0);
75       case "days":
76          return new TimeSpan(int.Parse(startIntervalFromNow), 0, 0, 0);
77       default:
78          return new TimeSpan(0, 0, 0, 0);
79    }
80 }
81
82 public static string CopyExpirationTimeFromPolicy(string policyStatement)
83 {
84    int startExpiration = policyStatement.IndexOf("EpochTime");
85    string strExpirationRough = policyStatement.Substring(startExpiration +
86       "EpochTime".Length);
87    char[] digits = { '0', '1', '2', '3', '4', '5', '6', '7', '8', '9' };
88
89    List<char> listDigits = new List<char>(digits);
90    StringBuilder buildExpiration = new StringBuilder(20);
91
92    foreach (char c in strExpirationRough)
93    {
94       if (listDigits.Contains(c))
95          buildExpiration.Append(c);
96    }
97    return buildExpiration.ToString();
98 }
```

See also

- Create a URL Signature Using Perl
- Create a URL Signature Using PHP
- Create a URL Signature Using Java
- Tools and Code Examples for Configuring Private Content

# Create a URL Signature Using Java

The Open source Java toolkit for Amazon S3 and CloudFront provides example code and information about CloudFront development in Java. For information about private distributions, go to Private Distributions at Programmer Guide: Code Samples.

You can also create signed URLs by using the `CloudFrontUrlSigner` class in the AWS SDK for Java. For more information, see Class UrlSigner in the *AWS SDK for Java API Reference*.

**Note**
Creating a URL signature is just one part of the process of serving private content using a signed URL. For more information about the entire process, see Using Signed URLs.

The following methods are from the Java open source toolkit for Amazon S3 and CloudFront. You must convert the private key from PEM to DER format for Java implementations to use it.

**Example Java Policy and Signature Encryption Methods**

```
1  // Signed URLs for a private distribution
2  // Note that Java only supports SSL certificates in DER format,
3  // so you will need to convert your PEM-formatted file to DER format.
4  // To do this, you can use openssl:
5  // openssl pkcs8 -topk8 -nocrypt -in origin.pem -inform PEM -out new.der
6  //    -outform DER
7  // So the encoder works correctly, you should also add the bouncy castle jar
8  // to your project and then add the provider.
9
10 Security.addProvider(new org.bouncycastle.jce.provider.BouncyCastleProvider());
11
12 String distributionDomain = "a1b2c3d4e5f6g7.cloudfront.net";
13 String privateKeyFilePath = "/path/to/rsa-private-key.der";
14 String s3ObjectKey = "s3/object/key.txt";
15 String policyResourcePath = "http://" + distributionDomain + "/" + s3ObjectKey;
16
17 // Convert your DER file into a byte array.
18
19 byte[] derPrivateKey = ServiceUtils.readInputStreamToBytes(new
20     FileInputStream(privateKeyFilePath));
21
22 // Generate a "canned" signed URL to allow access to a
23 // specific distribution and object
24
25 String signedUrlCanned = CloudFrontService.signUrlCanned(
26     "http://" + distributionDomain + "/" + s3ObjectKey, // Resource URL or Path
27     keyPairId,      // Certificate identifier,
28                     // an active trusted signer for the distribution
29     derPrivateKey, // DER Private key data
30     ServiceUtils.parseIso8601Date("2011-11-14T22:20:00.000Z") // DateLessThan
31     );
32 System.out.println(signedUrlCanned);
33
34 // Build a policy document to define custom restrictions for a signed URL.
35
36 String policy = CloudFrontService.buildPolicyForSignedUrl(
37     // Resource path (optional, can include '*' and '?' wildcards)
38     policyResourcePath,
```

```
39      // DateLessThan
40      ServiceUtils.parseIso8601Date("2011-11-14T22:20:00.000Z"),
41      // CIDR IP address restriction (optional, 0.0.0.0/0 means everyone)
42      "0.0.0.0/0",
43      // DateGreaterThan (optional)
44      ServiceUtils.parseIso8601Date("2011-10-16T06:31:56.000Z")
45      );
46
47  // Generate a signed URL using a custom policy document.
48
49  String signedUrl = CloudFrontService.signUrl(
50      // Resource URL or Path
51      "http://" + distributionDomain + "/" + s3ObjectKey,
52      // Certificate identifier, an active trusted signer for the distribution
53      keyPairId,
54      // DER Private key data
55      derPrivateKey,
56      // Access control policy
57      policy
58      );
59  System.out.println(signedUrl);
```

See also

- Create a URL Signature Using Perl
- Create a URL Signature Using PHP
- Create a URL Signature Using C# and the .NET Framework
- Tools and Code Examples for Configuring Private Content

# Using HTTPS with CloudFront

For web distributions, you can configure CloudFront to require that viewers use HTTPS to request your objects, so connections are encrypted when CloudFront communicates with viewers. You also can configure CloudFront to use HTTPS to get objects from your origin, so connections are encrypted when CloudFront communicates with your origin.

If you configure CloudFront to require HTTPS both to communicate with viewers and to communicate with your origin, here's what happens when CloudFront receives a request for an object. The process works basically the same way whether your origin is an Amazon S3 bucket or a custom origin such as an HTTP/S server:

1. A viewer submits an HTTPS request to CloudFront. There's some SSL/TLS negotiation here between the viewer and CloudFront. In the end, the viewer submits the request in an encrypted format.

2. If the object is in the CloudFront edge cache, CloudFront encrypts the response and returns it to the viewer, and the viewer decrypts it.

3. If the object is not in the CloudFront cache, CloudFront performs SSL/TLS negotiation with your origin and, when the negotiation is complete, forwards the request to your origin in an encrypted format.

4. Your origin decrypts the request, encrypts the requested object, and returns the object to CloudFront.

5. CloudFront decrypts the response, re-encrypts it, and forwards the object to the viewer. CloudFront also saves the object in the edge cache so that the object is available the next time it's requested.

6. The viewer decrypts the response.

For information about how to require HTTPS between viewers and CloudFront, and between CloudFront and your origin, see the following topics.

**Topics**

- Requiring HTTPS for Communication Between Viewers and CloudFront
- Requiring HTTPS for Communication Between CloudFront and Your Custom Origin
- Requiring HTTPS for Communication Between CloudFront and Your Amazon S3 Origin
- Using Alternate Domain Names and HTTPS
- Supported Protocols and Ciphers
- Charges for HTTPS Connections

# Requiring HTTPS for Communication Between Viewers and Cloud-Front

You can configure one or more cache behaviors in your CloudFront distribution to require HTTPS for communication between viewers and CloudFront. You also can configure one or more cache behaviors to allow both HTTP and HTTPS, so that CloudFront requires HTTPS for some objects but not for others. The configuration steps depend on which domain name you're using in object URLs:

- If you're using the domain name that CloudFront assigned to your distribution, such as d111111abcdef8.cloudfront.net, you change the **Viewer Protocol Policy** setting for one or more cache behaviors to require HTTPS communication. In that configuration, CloudFront provides the SSL/TLS certificate.

  To change the value of **Viewer Protocol Policy** by using the CloudFront console, see the procedure later in this section.

  For information about how to use the CloudFront API to change the value of the `ViewerProtocolPolicy` element, see UpdateDistribution in the *Amazon CloudFront API Reference*.

- If you're using your own domain name, such as example.com, you need to change several CloudFront settings. You also need to use an SSL/TLS certificate provided by AWS Certificate Manager (ACM), import a certificate from a third-party certificate authority into ACM or the IAM certificate store, or create and import a self-signed certificate. For more information, see Using Alternate Domain Names and HTTPS.

**Note**
If you want to ensure that the objects that viewers get from CloudFront were encrypted when CloudFront got them from your origin, always use HTTPS between CloudFront and your origin. If you recently changed from HTTP to HTTPS between CloudFront and your origin, we recommend that you invalidate objects in CloudFront edge locations. CloudFront will return an object to a viewer regardless of whether the protocol used by the viewer (HTTP or HTTPS) matches the protocol that CloudFront used to get the object. For more information about removing or replacing objects in a distribution, see Adding, Removing, or Replacing Objects in a Distribution.

To require HTTPS between viewers and CloudFront for one or more cache behaviors, perform the following procedure.

**To configure CloudFront to require HTTPS between viewers and CloudFront**

1. Sign in to the AWS Management Console and open the CloudFront console at https://console.aws.amazon.com/cloudfront/.

2. In the top pane of the CloudFront console, choose the ID for the distribution that you want to update.

3. On the **Behaviors** tab, choose the cache behavior that you want to update, and then choose **Edit**.

4. Specify one of the following values for **Viewer Protocol Policy**:
   **Redirect HTTP to HTTPS**
   Viewers can use both protocols. HTTP `GET` and `HEAD` requests are automatically redirected to HTTPS requests. CloudFront returns HTTP status code 301 (Moved Permanently) along with the new HTTPS URL. The viewer then resubmits the request to CloudFront using the HTTPS URL.
   If you send `POST`, `PUT`, `DELETE`, `OPTIONS`, or `PATCH` over HTTP with an HTTP to HTTPS cache behavior and a request protocol version of HTTP 1.1 or above, CloudFront redirects the request to a HTTPS location with a HTTP status code 307 (Temporary Redirect). This guarantees that the request is sent again to the new location using the same method and body payload.
   If you send `POST`, `PUT`, `DELETE`, `OPTIONS`, or `PATCH` requests over HTTP to HTTPS cache behavior with a request protocol version below HTTP 1.1, CloudFront returns a HTTP status code 403 (Forbidden). When a viewer makes an HTTP request that is redirected to an HTTPS request, CloudFront charges for both requests. For the HTTP request, the charge is only for the request and for the headers that CloudFront returns to the viewer. For the HTTPS request, the charge is for the request, and for the headers and the

object that are returned by your origin.

**HTTPS Only**

Viewers can access your content only if they're using HTTPS. If a viewer sends an HTTP request instead of an HTTPS request, CloudFront returns HTTP status code 403 (Forbidden) and does not return the object.

5. Choose **Yes, Edit**.

6. Repeat steps 3 through 5 for each additional cache behavior that you want to require HTTPS for between viewers and CloudFront.

7. Confirm the following before you use the updated configuration in a production environment:

   - The path pattern in each cache behavior applies only to the requests that you want viewers to use HTTPS for.
   - The cache behaviors are listed in the order that you want CloudFront to evaluate them in. For more information, see Path Pattern.
   - The cache behaviors are routing requests to the correct origins.

# Requiring HTTPS for Communication Between CloudFront and Your Custom Origin

If you want to require HTTPS for communication between CloudFront and your custom origin, *and* you're using the domain name that CloudFront assigned to your distribution in the URLs for your objects (for example, https://d111111abcdef8/.cloudfront/.net/logo/.jpg/), follow the procedures in this topic to do the following:

- Change the **Origin Protocol Policy** setting for the applicable origins in your distribution
- Install an SSL/TLS certificate on your custom origin server (this isn't required when you use an Amazon S3 origin)

If you're using an Amazon S3 bucket as your origin, see Requiring HTTPS for Communication Between CloudFront and Your Amazon S3 Origin.

If you're using an alternate domain instead of the domain that CloudFront assigned to your distribution, see Using Alternate Domain Names and HTTPS.

### Topics

- Changing CloudFront Settings
- Installing an SSL/TLS Certificate on Your Custom Origin Server
- About RSA and ECDSA Ciphers

## Changing CloudFront Settings

The following procedure explains how to configure CloudFront to use HTTPS to communicate with an Elastic Load Balancing load balancer, an Amazon EC2 instance, or another custom origin. For information about using the CloudFront API to update a web distribution, see UpdateDistribution in the *Amazon CloudFront API Reference*.

**To configure CloudFront to require HTTPS between CloudFront and your custom origin**

1. Sign in to the AWS Management Console and open the CloudFront console at https://console.aws.amazon.com/cloudfront/.

2. In the top pane of the CloudFront console, choose the ID for the distribution that you want to update.

3. On the **Origins** tab, choose the origin that you want to update, and then choose **Edit**.

4. Update the following settings:
   **Origin Protocol Policy**
   Change the **Origin Protocol Policy** for the applicable origins in your distribution:

   - **HTTPS Only** – CloudFront uses only HTTPS to communicate with your custom origin.

   - **Match Viewer** – CloudFront communicates with your custom origin using HTTP or HTTPS, depending on the protocol of the viewer request. For example, if you choose **Match Viewer** for **Origin Protocol Policy** and the viewer uses HTTPS to request an object from CloudFront, CloudFront also uses HTTPS to forward the request to your origin.

     Choose **Match Viewer** only if you specify **Redirect HTTP to HTTPS** or **HTTPS Only** for **Viewer Protocol Policy**.

     CloudFront caches the object only once even if viewers make requests using both HTTP and HTTPS protocols.
     **Origin SSL Protocols**
     Choose the **Origin SSL Protocols** for the applicable origins in your distribution. The SSLv3 protocol is less secure, so we recommend that you choose SSLv3 only if your origin doesn't support TLSv1 or later.

The TLSv1 handshake is both backwards and forwards compatible with SSLv3, but TLSv1.1 and TLSv1.2 are not. In this case, the openssl only sends a SSLv3 handshake.

5. Choose **Yes, Edit**.

6. Repeat steps 3 through 5 for each additional origin that you want to require HTTPS for between CloudFront and your custom origin.

7. Confirm the following before you use the updated configuration in a production environment:

   - The path pattern in each cache behavior applies only to the requests that you want viewers to use HTTPS for.
   - The cache behaviors are listed in the order that you want CloudFront to evaluate them in. For more information, see Path Pattern.
   - The cache behaviors are routing requests to the origins that you changed the **Origin Protocol Policy** for.

## Installing an SSL/TLS Certificate on Your Custom Origin Server

You can use an SSL/TLS certificate from the following sources on your custom origin:

- If your origin is an Elastic Load Balancing load balancer, you can use a certificate provided by AWS Certificate Manager (ACM). You also can use a certificate that is signed by a trusted third-party certificate authority and imported into ACM.
- For origins other than ELB load balancers, you must use a certificate that is signed by a trusted third-party certificate authority (CA), for example, Comodo, DigiCert, or Symantec.

When CloudFront uses HTTPS to communicate with your origin, CloudFront verifies that the certificate was issued by a trusted certificate authority. CloudFront supports the same certificate authorities that Mozilla does. For the current list, see Mozilla Included CA Certificate List. You can't use a self-signed certificate for HTTPS communication between CloudFront and your origin.

**Important**
If the origin server returns an expired certificate, an invalid certificate, or a self-signed certificate, or if the origin server returns the certificate chain in the wrong order, CloudFront drops the TCP connection, returns HTTP status code 502 (Bad Gateway), and sets the `X-Cache` header to `Error from cloudfront`. Also, if the full chain of certificates, including the intermediate certificate, is not present, CloudFront drops the TCP connection.

One of the domain names in the certificate must match one or both of the following values:

- The value that you specified for **Origin Domain Name** for the applicable origin in your distribution.
- If you configured CloudFront to forward the `Host` header to your origin, the value of the `Host` header. For more information about forwarding headers to your origin, see Configuring CloudFront to Cache Objects Based on Request Headers.

## About RSA and ECDSA Ciphers

The encryption strength of a communications connection depends on the key size and strength of the algorithm that you choose for your origin server's certificate. The two options that CloudFront supports for connections with a custom origin are RSA and Elliptic Curve Digital Signature Algorithm (ECDSA).

For lists of the RSA and ECDSA ciphers supported by CloudFront, see Supported SSL/TLS Protocols and Ciphers for Communication Between CloudFront and Your Origin.

## How RSA Ciphers Work

CloudFront and origin servers typically use RSA 2048-bit asymmetric keys for SSL/TLS termination. RSA algorithms use the product of two large prime numbers, with another number added to it to create a public key. The private key is a related number. The strength of RSA relies on the presumed difficulty of breaking a key that requires factoring the product of two large prime numbers. However, improvements in computer technology have weakened RSA algorithms because faster computer calculations mean that it's now easier to break the encryption.

If you want to maintain encryption strength while continuing to use RSA, one option would be to increase the size of your RSA keys. However, this approach isn't easily scalable because using larger keys increases the compute cost for cryptography.

## How ECDSA Ciphers Work

Alternatively, you could use an ECDSA certificate. ECDSA bases its security on a more complex mathematical problem than RSA that is harder to solve, which means that it takes more computer processing time to break ECDSA encryption. ECDSA is built on the principle that it is difficult to solve for the discrete logarithm of a random elliptic curve when its base is known, also known as the Elliptic Curve Discrete Logarithm Problem (ECDLP). This means that you can use shorter key lengths to achieve the equivalent security of using RSA with much larger key sizes.

In addition to providing better security, using ECDSA's smaller keys enables faster computing of algorithms, smaller digital certificates, and fewer bits to transmit during the SSL/TLS handshake. As a result, the smaller keys reduce the time that it takes for you to create and sign digital certificates for SSL/TLS termination on origin servers. Using a smaller key size therefore can increase throughput by reducing the compute cycles needed for cryptography, freeing up server resources to process other work.

## Choosing Between RSA and ECDSA Ciphers

Sample tests that we have run to compare, for example, 2048-bit RSA to 256-bit ECDSA (nistp256) have indicated that the nistp256 option was 95% faster than 2048-bit RSA while providing the same security strength as 3072-bit RSA.

CloudFront continues to support RSA for SSL/TLS connections. However, if you have concerns about the strength of your current encryption for SSL/TLS authentication for your origin servers, ECDSA could be a better option. The effort to enable ECDSA digital certificates compared to the security benefit that ECDSA brings is a trade-off that you will have to weigh in making your decision. In addition to enabling stronger encryption, the reduction in computational cost of cryptography while using ECDSA at your origin servers is an added advantage.

## Using ECDSA Ciphers

To use ECDSA for communications between CloudFront and your origin, do the following:

1. Generate a private key by using either of the supported curves (prime256v1 or secp384r1).

2. Generate an ECDSA Digital Certificate in the X.509 PEM format with a trusted certificate authority.

3. Set up your origin to prefer the ECDSA certificate.

Using ECDSA doesn't require any settings changes in the CloudFront console or APIs, and there is no additional fee.

# Requiring HTTPS for Communication Between CloudFront and Your Amazon S3 Origin

When your origin is an Amazon S3 bucket, CloudFront always forwards requests to S3 by using the protocol that viewers used to submit the requests. The default setting for the Origin Protocol Policy (Amazon EC2, Elastic Load Balancing, and Other Custom Origins Only) setting is **Match Viewer** and can't be changed.

If you want to require HTTPS for communication between CloudFront and Amazon S3, you must change the value of **Viewer Protocol Policy** to **Redirect HTTP to HTTPS** or **HTTPS Only**. The procedure later in this section explains how to use the CloudFront console to change **Viewer Protocol Policy**. For information about using the CloudFront API to update the `ViewerProtocolPolicy` element for a web distribution, see UpdateDistribution in the *Amazon CloudFront API Reference*.

Note the following about using HTTPS when the origin is an Amazon S3 bucket:

- If your Amazon S3 bucket is configured as a website endpoint, you can't configure CloudFront to use HTTPS to communicate with your origin because Amazon S3 doesn't support HTTPS connections in that configuration.
- Amazon S3 provides the SSL/TLS certificate, so you don't have to.

**To configure CloudFront to require HTTPS between CloudFront and your Amazon S3 origin**

1. Sign in to the AWS Management Console and open the CloudFront console at https://console.aws.amazon.com/cloudfront/.

2. In the top pane of the CloudFront console, choose the ID for the distribution that you want to update.

3. On the **Behaviors** tab, choose the cache behavior that you want to update, and then choose **Edit**.

4. Specify one of the following values for **Viewer Protocol Policy**:
   **Redirect HTTP to HTTPS**
   Viewers can use both protocols, but HTTP requests are automatically redirected to HTTPS requests. CloudFront returns HTTP status code 301 (Moved Permanently) along with the new HTTPS URL. The viewer then resubmits the request to CloudFront using the HTTPS URL.
   CloudFront doesn't redirect `DELETE`, `OPTIONS`, `PATCH`, `POST`, or `PUT` requests from HTTP to HTTPS. If you configure a cache behavior to redirect to HTTPS, CloudFront responds to HTTP `DELETE`, `OPTIONS`, `PATCH`, `POST`, or `PUT` requests for that cache behavior with HTTP status code 403 (Forbidden). When a viewer makes an HTTP request that is redirected to an HTTPS request, CloudFront charges for both requests. For the HTTP request, the charge is only for the request and for the headers that CloudFront returns to the viewer. For the HTTPS request, the charge is for the request, and for the headers and the object returned by your origin.
   **HTTPS Only**
   Viewers can access your content only if they're using HTTPS. If a viewer sends an HTTP request instead of an HTTPS request, CloudFront returns HTTP status code 403 (Forbidden) and does not return the object.

5. Choose **Yes, Edit**.

6. Repeat steps 3 through 5 for each additional cache behavior that you want to require HTTPS for between viewers and CloudFront, and between CloudFront and S3.

7. Confirm the following before you use the updated configuration in a production environment:
   - The path pattern in each cache behavior applies only to the requests that you want viewers to use HTTPS for.
   - The cache behaviors are listed in the order that you want CloudFront to evaluate them in. For more information, see Path Pattern.
   - The cache behaviors are routing requests to the correct origins.

# Using Alternate Domain Names and HTTPS

If you want your viewers to use HTTPS and you want to use your own domain name in the URLs for your objects (for example, `https://www.example.com/image.jpg`), you need to perform several additional steps, as explained in this topic. If you simply use your CloudFront distribution domain name in your URLs, for example, `https://d111111abcdef8.cloudfront.net/image.jpg`, follow the guidance in the following topic instead: Requiring HTTPS for Communication Between Viewers and CloudFront.

**Important**
When you add a certificate to your distribution, CloudFront immediately propagates the certificate to all of its edge locations. As new edge locations become available, CloudFront will propagate the certificate to those locations, too. You can't restrict the edge locations that CloudFront propagates the certificates to.

**Topics**

- Choosing How CloudFront Serves HTTPS Requests
- Requirements for Using SSL/TLS Certificates with CloudFront
- Limits on Using SSL/TLS Certificates with CloudFront (HTTPS Between Viewers and CloudFront Only)
- Configuring Alternate Domain Names and HTTPS
- Determining the Size of the Public Key in an SSL/TLS Certificate
- Increasing the Limit for SSL/TLS Certificates
- Rotating SSL/TLS Certificates
- Reverting from a Custom SSL/TLS Certificate to the Default CloudFront Certificate
- Switching from a Custom SSL/TLS Certificate with Dedicated IP Addresses to SNI

# Choosing How CloudFront Serves HTTPS Requests

If you want your viewers to use HTTPS and to use alternate domain names for your objects, you need to choose one of the following options for how CloudFront serves HTTPS requests:

- Use a dedicated IP address in each edge location
- Use Server Name Indication (SNI)

This section explains how each option works.

## Using a Dedicated IP Addresses to Serve HTTPS Requests (Works for All Clients)

If you configure CloudFront to serve HTTPS requests using dedicated IP addresses, CloudFront associates your alternate domain name with a dedicated IP address in each CloudFront edge location. When a viewer submits an HTTPS request for your content, here's what happens:

1. DNS routes the request to the IP address for your distribution in the applicable edge location.

2. CloudFront uses the IP address to identify your distribution and to determine which SSL/TLS certificate to return to the viewer.

3. The viewer and CloudFront perform SSL/TLS negotiation using your SSL/TLS certificate.

4. CloudFront returns the requested content to the viewer.

This method works for every HTTPS request, regardless of the browser or other viewer that the user is using.

**Important**
If you configure CloudFront to serve HTTPS requests using dedicated IP addresses, you incur an additional monthly charge. The charge begins when you associate your SSL/TLS certificate with a distribution and you enable the distribution. For more information about CloudFront pricing, see Amazon CloudFront Pricing. In addition, see Using the Same Certificate for Multiple CloudFront Distributions.

## Using SNI to Serve HTTPS Requests (Works for Most Clients)

If you configure CloudFront to serve HTTPS requests using Server Name Indication (SNI), CloudFront associates your alternate domain name with an IP address for each edge location, but the IP address is not dedicated to your distribution. When a viewer submits an HTTPS request for your content, DNS routes the request to the IP address for the applicable edge location. However, because the IP address isn't dedicated to your distribution, CloudFront can't determine, based on the IP address, which domain the request is for.

SSL/TLS negotiation occurs very early in the process of establishing an HTTPS connection. If CloudFront can't immediately determine which domain the request is for, it drops the connection. Using a dedicated IP address is one way to associate a request with a domain. The other is SNI, which is an extension to the TLS protocol that is supported by most modern browsers. When a viewer that supports SNI submits an HTTPS request for your content, here's what happens:

1. The viewer automatically gets the domain name from the request URL and adds it to a field in the request header.

2. When CloudFront receives the request, it finds the domain name in the request header and responds to the request with the applicable SSL/TLS certificate.

3. The viewer and CloudFront perform SSL/TLS negotiation.

4. CloudFront returns the requested content to the viewer.

For a current list of the browsers that support SNI, see the Wikipedia entry Server Name Indication.

If you want to use SNI but some of your users' browsers don't support SNI, you have several options:

- Configure CloudFront to serve HTTPS requests by using dedicated IP addresses instead of SNI.
- Use the CloudFront SSL/TLS certificate instead of a custom certificate. This requires that you use the CloudFront domain name for your distribution in the URLs for your objects, for example, `https://d111111abcdef8.cloudfront.net/logo.png`.

  If you use the default CloudFront certificate, viewers must support the SSL protocol TLSv1 or later. CloudFront doesn't support SSLv3 with the default CloudFront certificate.

  You also need to change the SSL/TLS certificate that CloudFront is using from a custom certificate to the default CloudFront certificate:

    - If you haven't used your distribution to distribute your content, you can just change the configuration. For more information, see Viewing and Updating CloudFront Distributions.
    - If you have used your distribution to distribute your content, you need to create a new CloudFront distribution and change the URLs for your objects to reduce or eliminate the amount of time that your content is unavailable. For more information, see Reverting from a Custom SSL/TLS Certificate to the Default CloudFront Certificate.

- If you can control which browser your users use, have them upgrade their browser to one that supports SNI.
- Use HTTP instead of HTTPS.

# Requirements for Using SSL/TLS Certificates with CloudFront

The requirements for SSL/TLS certificates are described in this topic. They apply, except as noted, to both of the following:

- Certificates for using HTTPS between viewers and CloudFront
- Certificates for using HTTPS between CloudFront and your origin

**Topics**

- Certificate Issuer
- AWS Region that You Request a Certificate In (for AWS Certificate Manager)
- Certificate Format
- Intermediate Certificates
- Key Type
- Private Key
- Permissions
- Size of the Public Key
- Supported Types of Certificates
- Certificate Expiration Date and Renewal
- Domain Names in the CloudFront Distribution and in the Certificate
- Minimum SSL Protocol Version
- Supported HTTP Versions

## Certificate Issuer

The certificate issuer you must use depends on whether you want to require HTTPS between viewers and CloudFront or between CloudFront and your origin:

- **HTTPS between viewers and CloudFront** – You can use a certificate that was issued by a trusted certificate authority (CA) such as Comodo, DigiCert, or Symantec; you can use a certificate provided by AWS Certificate Manager (ACM); or you can use a self-signed certificate.

- **HTTPS between CloudFront and a custom origin** – If the origin is *not* an ELB load balancer, such as Amazon EC2, the certificate must be issued by a trusted CA such as Comodo, DigiCert, or Symantec. If your origin is an ELB load balancer, you can also use a certificate provided by ACM. **Important** When CloudFront uses HTTPS to communicate with your origin, CloudFront verifies that the certificate was issued by a trusted CA. CloudFront supports the same certificate authorities as Mozilla; for the current list, see Mozilla Included CA Certificate List. You cannot use a self-signed certificate for HTTPS communication between CloudFront and your origin.

  For more information about getting and installing an SSL/TLS certificate, refer to the documentation for your HTTP server software and to the documentation for the certificate authority. For information about ACM, see the AWS Certificate Manager User Guide.

## AWS Region that You Request a Certificate In (for AWS Certificate Manager)

If you want to require HTTPS between viewers and CloudFront, you must change the AWS region to US East (N. Virginia) in the AWS Certificate Manager console before you request or import a certificate.

If you want to require HTTPS between CloudFront and your origin, and you're using an ELB load balancer as your origin, you can request or import a certificate in any region.

## Certificate Format

The certificate must be in X.509 PEM format. This is the default format if you're using AWS Certificate Manager.

## Intermediate Certificates

If you're using a third-party certificate authority (CA), in the .pem file, list all of the intermediate certificates in the certificate chain, beginning with one for the CA that signed the certificate for your domain. Typically, you'll find a file on the CA website that lists intermediate and root certificates in the proper chained order.

**Important**
Do not include the following: the root certificate, intermediate certificates that are not in the trust path, or your CA's public key certificate.

Here's an example:

```
1  -----BEGIN CERTIFICATE-----
2  Intermediate certificate 2
3  -----END CERTIFICATE-----
4  -----BEGIN CERTIFICATE-----
5  Intermediate certificate 1
6  -----END CERTIFICATE-----
```

## Key Type

CloudFront supports only RSA public/private key pairs.

## Private Key

If you're using a certificate from a third-party certificate authority (CA), note the following:

- The private key must match the public key that is in the certificate.
- The private key also must be an RSA private key in PEM format, where the PEM header is `BEGIN RSA PRIVATE KEY` and the footer is `END RSA PRIVATE KEY`.
- The private key cannot be encrypted with a password.

If AWS Certificate Manager (ACM) provided the certificate, ACM doesn't release the private key. The private key is stored in ACM for use by AWS services that are integrated with ACM.

## Permissions

You must have permission to use and import the SSL/TLS certificate, including permission from the certificate authority (CA) that issued the certificate to import it to a content delivery network (CDN).

If you're using AWS Certificate Manager (ACM), we recommend that you use AWS Identity and Access Management permissions to restrict access to the certificates. For more information, see Permissions and Policies in the *AWS Certificate Manager User Guide*.

## Size of the Public Key

The length of the public key for a certificate depends on where you're storing it.

- Importing a certificate into AWS Certificate Manager (ACM): public key length must be 1024 or 2048 bits. The limit for a certificate that you use with CloudFront is 2048 bits, even though ACM supports larger keys.
- Uploading a certificate to the AWS Identity and Access Management (IAM) certificate store: maximum size of the public key is 2048 bits.

We recommend using 2048 bits.

For information about the public keys for certificates provided by ACM, see ACM Certificate Characteristics in the *AWS Certificate Manager User Guide*.

For information about how to determine the size of the public key, see Determining the Size of the Public Key in an SSL/TLS Certificate.

## Supported Types of Certificates

CloudFront supports all types of certificates, including the following:

- Domain-validated certificates
- Extended validation (EV) certificates
- High-assurance certificates
- Wildcard certificates (`*.example.com`)
- Subject alternative name (SAN) certificates (`example.com` and `example.net`)

## Certificate Expiration Date and Renewal

If you're using certificates that you get from a third-party certificate authority (CA), you are responsible for monitoring certificate expiration dates and for renewing SSL/TLS certificates that you import into AWS Certificate Manager (ACM) or upload to the AWS Identity and Access Management certificate store.

If you're using ACM-provided certificates, ACM manages certificate renewals for you. For more information, see Managed Renewal in the *AWS Certificate Manager User Guide*.

## Domain Names in the CloudFront Distribution and in the Certificate

When you're using a custom origin, the SSL/TLS certificate on your origin includes a domain name in the Common Name field, and possibly several more in the Subject Alternative Names field. (CloudFront supports wildcard characters in certificate domain names.)

One of the domain names in the certificate must match the domain name that you specify for Origin Domain Name. If no domain name matches, CloudFront returns HTTP status code 502 (Bad Gateway) to the viewer.

## Minimum SSL Protocol Version

If you're using dedicated IP addresses, you can choose the minimum SSL protocol version for the connection between viewers and CloudFront by choosing a security policy.

For more information, see Security Policy in the topic Values That You Specify When You Create or Update a Web Distribution.

# Supported HTTP Versions

If you associate one certificate with more than one CloudFront distribution, all the distributions associated with the certificate must use the same option for Supported HTTP Versions. You specify this option when you create or update a CloudFront distribution.

# Limits on Using SSL/TLS Certificates with CloudFront (HTTPS Between Viewers and CloudFront Only)

Note the following limits on using SSL/TLS certificates with CloudFront. These limits apply only to the SSL/TLS certificates that you provision by using AWS Certificate Manager (ACM), or that you import into ACM or upload to the IAM certificate store for HTTPS communication between viewers and CloudFront.

**Maximum Number of Certificates per CloudFront Distribution**
You can associate a maximum of one SSL/TLS certificate with each CloudFront distribution.

**Maximum Number of Certificates that You Can Import into ACM or Upload to the IAM Certificate Store**
If you obtained your SSL/TLS certificates from a third-party CA, you need to store the certificates in one of the following locations:

- **AWS Certificate Manager** – For the current limit on the number of ACM certificates, see Limits in the *AWS Certificate Manager User Guide*. The listed limit is a total that includes certificates that you provision by using ACM and certificates that you import into ACM.
- **IAM certificate store** – For the current limit on the number of certificates that you can upload to the IAM certificate store for an AWS account, see Limitations on IAM Entities and Objects in the *IAM User Guide*. To request a higher limit, see Request IAM limit increase.

**Maximum Number of Certificates per AWS Account (Dedicated IP Addresses Only)**
If you want to serve HTTPS requests by using dedicated IP addresses, note the following:

- By default, CloudFront gives you permission to use two certificates with your AWS account, one for everyday use and one for when you need to rotate certificates for multiple distributions.
- If you're already using this feature but you need to increase the number of custom SSL/TLS certificates that you can use with your AWS account, go to the Support Center and create a case. Indicate how many certificates that you need permission to use, and describe the circumstances in your request. We'll update your account as soon as possible.

**Using the Same Certificate for CloudFront Distributions that Were Created by Using Different AWS Accounts**
If you're using a third-party CA and if you want to use the same certificate with multiple CloudFront distributions that were created by using different AWS accounts, you must import the certificate into ACM or upload it to the IAM certificate store once for each AWS account.
If you're using certificates provided by ACM, you can't configure CloudFront to use certificates that were created by a different AWS account.

**Using the Same Certificate for CloudFront and for Other AWS Services (IAM Certificate Store Only)** **
If you bought a certificate from a trusted certificate authority such as Comodo, DigiCert, or Symantec, you can use the same certificate for CloudFront and for other AWS services. If you're importing the certificate into ACM, you need to import it only once to use it for multiple AWS services.
If you're using certificates provided by ACM, the certificates are stored in ACM.

**Using the Same Certificate for Multiple CloudFront Distributions**
You can use the same certificate for any or all of the CloudFront distributions that you're using to serve HTTPS requests. Note the following:

- You can use the same certificate both for serving requests using dedicated IP addresses and for serving requests using SNI.

- You can associate only one certificate with each distribution.

- Each distribution must include one or more alternate domain names that also appear in the Common Name field or the Subject Alternative Names field in the certificate.

- If you're serving HTTPS requests using dedicated IP addresses and you created all of your distributions by using the same AWS account, you can significantly reduce your cost by using the same certificate for all distributions. CloudFront charges for each certificate, not for each distribution.

For example, suppose you create three distributions by using the same AWS account, and you use the same certificate for all three distributions. You would be charged only one fee for using dedicated IP addresses.

However, if you're serving HTTPS requests using dedicated IP addresses and using the same certificate to create CloudFront distributions in different AWS accounts, each account will be charged the fee for using dedicated IP addresses. For example, if you create three distributions by using three different AWS accounts and you use the same certificate for all three distributions, each account will be charged the full fee for using dedicated IP addresses.

# Configuring Alternate Domain Names and HTTPS

To use alternate domain names in the URLs for your objects and to use HTTPS between viewers and CloudFront, perform the applicable procedures.

**Topics**

- Requesting Permission to Use Three or More SSL/TLS Certificates
- Getting an SSL/TLS Certificate
- Importing an SSL/TLS Certificate
- Updating Your CloudFront Distribution

## Requesting Permission to Use Three or More SSL/TLS Certificates

If you need permission to permanently associate three or more SSL/TLS Dedicated IP certificates with CloudFront, perform the following procedure. For more details about HTTPS requests, see Choosing How CloudFront Serves HTTPS Requests

**Note**
This procedure is for using 3 or more DedicatedIP certificates across your CloudFront distributions. The default value is 2. Keep in mind you cannot bind more than 1 SSL certificate to a distribution.
You can only associate a single SSL/TLS certificate to a CloudFront distribution at a time. This number is for the total number of Dedicated IP SSL certificates you can use across all of your CloudFront distributions.

**To request permission to use three or more certificates with a CloudFront distribution**

1. Go to the Support Center and create a case.

2. Indicate how many certificates you need permission to use, and describe the circumstances in your request. We'll update your account as soon as possible.

3. Continue with the next procedure.

## Getting an SSL/TLS Certificate

Get an SSL/TLS certificate if you don't already have one. For more information, see the applicable documentation:

- To use a certificate provided by AWS Certificate Manager (ACM), see the AWS Certificate Manager User Guide. Then skip to Updating Your CloudFront Distribution. **Note**
  We recommend that you use ACM to provision, manage, and deploy SSL/TLS certificates on AWS managed resources.
- To get a certificate from a third-party certificate authority (CA), see the documentation provided by the certificate authority. When you have the certificate, continue with the next procedure.
- To create a self-signed certificate, see the documentation for the application that you're using to create and sign the certificate. Then continue with the next procedure.

## Importing an SSL/TLS Certificate

If you got your certificate from a third-party CA, import the certificate into ACM or upload it to the IAM certificate store:

**ACM (Recommended)**
ACM lets you import third-party certificates from the ACM console, as well as programmatically. For information about importing a certificate to ACM, see Importing Certificates into AWS Certificate Manager in the *AWS Certificate Manager User Guide.*

## IAM certificate store

If ACM is not available in your region, use the following AWS CLI command to upload your third-party certificate to the IAM certificate store. (For a list of the regions where ACM is available, see AWS Certificate Manager in the "AWS Regions and Endpoints" chapter of the *Amazon Web Services General Reference*.)

```
1 aws iam upload-server-certificate --server-certificate-name CertificateName --certificate-body
    file://public_key_certificate_file --private-key file://privatekey.pem --certificate-chain
    file://certificate_chain_file --path /cloudfront/path/
```

Note the following:

- **AWS Account** – You must upload the certificate to the IAM certificate store using the same AWS account that you used to create your CloudFront distribution.
- **--path Parameter** – When you upload the certificate to IAM, the value of the `-path` parameter (certificate path) must start with `/cloudfront/`, for example, `/cloudfront/production/` or `/cloudfront/test/`. The path must end with a `/`.
- **Existing certificates** – You must specify values for the `--server-certificate-name` and `--path` parameters that are different from the values that are associated with existing certificates.
- **Using the CloudFront Console** The value that you specify for the `--server-certificate-name` parameter in the AWS CLI, for example, `myServerCertificate`, appears in the **SSL Certificate** list in the CloudFront console.
- **Using the CloudFront API** – Make note of the alphanumeric string that the AWS CLI returns, for example, `AS1A2M3P4L5E67SIIXR3J`. This is the value that you will specify in the `IAMCertificateId` element. You don't need the IAM ARN, which is also returned by the CLI. For more information about the AWS CLI, see the AWS Command Line Interface User Guide and the AWS CLI Command Reference.

# Updating Your CloudFront Distribution

To update settings for your distribution, perform the following procedure:

**To configure your CloudFront distribution for alternate domain names**

1. Sign in to the AWS Management Console and open the CloudFront console at https://console.aws.amazon.com/cloudfront/.

2. Choose the ID for the distribution that you want to update.

3. On the **General** tab, choose **Edit**.

4. Update the following values:
   **Alternate Domain Names (CNAMEs)**
   Add the applicable alternate domain names. Separate domain names with commas, or type each domain name on a new line.
   **SSL Certificate (Web Distributions Only)**
   Choose **Custom SSL Certificate**, and choose a certificate from the list.
   Up to 100 certificates are listed here. If you have more than 100 certificates and you don't see the certificate that you want to add, you can type a certificate ARN in the field to choose it.
   If you uploaded a certificate to the IAM certificate store but it's not listed, and you can't choose it by typing the name in the field, review the procedure Importing an SSL/TLS Certificate to confirm that you correctly uploaded the certificate.
   After you associate your SSL/TLS certificate with your CloudFront distribution, do not delete the certificate from ACM or the IAM certificate store until you remove the certificate from all distributions and until the status of the distributions has changed to **Deployed**.
   **Clients Supported (Web Distributions Only)**
   Choose the applicable option:

- **All Clients**: CloudFront serves your HTTPS content using dedicated IP addresses. If you select this option, you incur additional charges when you associate your SSL/TLS certificate with a distribution that is enabled. For more information, see Amazon CloudFront Pricing.
- **Only Clients that Support Server Name Indication (SNI)**: Older browsers or other clients that don't support SNI must use another method to access your content. For more information, see Choosing How CloudFront Serves HTTPS Requests.

5. Choose **Yes, Edit**.

6. Configure CloudFront to require HTTPS between viewers and CloudFront:

   1. On the **Behaviors** tab, choose the cache behavior that you want to update, and choose **Edit**.

   2. Specify one of the following values for **Viewer Protocol Policy**:
      **Redirect HTTP to HTTPS**
      Viewers can use both protocols, but HTTP requests are automatically redirected to HTTPS requests. CloudFront returns HTTP status code 301 (Moved Permanently) along with the new HTTPS URL. The viewer then resubmits the request to CloudFront using the HTTPS URL.
      CloudFront doesn't redirect `DELETE`, `OPTIONS`, `PATCH`, `POST`, or `PUT` requests from HTTP to HTTPS. If you configure a cache behavior to redirect to HTTPS, CloudFront responds to HTTP `DELETE`, `OPTIONS`, `PATCH`, `POST`, or `PUT` requests for that cache behavior with HTTP status code 403 (Forbidden). When a viewer makes an HTTP request that is redirected to an HTTPS request, CloudFront charges for both requests. For the HTTP request, the charge is only for the request and for the headers that CloudFront returns to the viewer. For the HTTPS request, the charge is for the request, and for the headers and the object returned by your origin.
      **HTTPS Only**
      Viewers can access your content only if they're using HTTPS. If a viewer sends an HTTP request instead of an HTTPS request, CloudFront returns HTTP status code 403 (Forbidden) and does not return the object.

   3. Choose **Yes, Edit**.

   4. Repeat steps a through c for each additional cache behavior that you want to require HTTPS for between viewers and CloudFront.

7. Confirm the following before you use the updated configuration in a production environment:
   - The path pattern in each cache behavior applies only to the requests that you want viewers to use HTTPS for.
   - The cache behaviors are listed in the order that you want CloudFront to evaluate them in. For more information, see Path Pattern.
   - The cache behaviors are routing requests to the correct origins.

# Determining the Size of the Public Key in an SSL/TLS Certificate

When you're using CloudFront alternate domain names and HTTPS, the maximum size of the public key in an SSL/TLS certificate is 2048 bits. (This is the key size, not the number of characters in the public key.) If you use AWS Certificate Manager for your certificates, note that although ACM supports larger keys, you cannot use the larger keys with CloudFront.

You can determine the size of the public key by running the following OpenSSL command:

```
1 openssl x509 -in path and filename of SSL/TLS certificate -text -noout
```

where:

- `-in` specifies the path and filename of your SSL/TLS certificate.
- `-text` causes OpenSSL to display the length of the public key in bits.
- `-noout` prevents OpenSSL from displaying the public key.

Example output:

```
1 Public-Key: (2048 bit)
```

# Increasing the Limit for SSL/TLS Certificates

There are limits on the number of SSL/TLS certificates that you can import into AWS Certificate Manager or upload to AWS Identity and Access Management. There also is a limit on the number of SSL/TLS certificates that you can use with an AWS account when you configure CloudFront to serve HTTPS requests by using dedicated IP addresses. However, you can request higher limits.

**Topics**

- Certificates That You Can Import into ACM
- Certificates That You Can Upload to IAM
- Certificates That You Can Use with Dedicated IP Addresses

## Certificates That You Can Import into ACM

For the limit on the number of certificates that you can import into ACM, see ACM Limits in the *Amazon Web Services General Reference*.

To request a higher limit, create a case with the AWS Support Center. Specify the following values:

- **Regarding** – Accept the default value of **Service Limit Increase**
- **Limit Type** – Choose **Certificate Manager**
- **Region** – Specify the AWS Region where you want to import certificates
- **Limit** – Choose **(ACM) Number of ACM Certificates**

Then fill out the rest of the form.

## Certificates That You Can Upload to IAM

For the limit on the number of certificates that you can upload to IAM, see IAM Limits in the *Amazon Web Services General Reference*.

To request a higher limit, create a case with the AWS Support Center. Specify the following values:

- **Regarding** – Accept the default value of **Service Limit Increase**
- **Limit Type** – Choose **Certificate Manager**
- **Region** – Specify the AWS Region where you want to import certificates
- **Limit** – Choose **(IAM) Server Certificate Limit**

Then fill out the rest of the form.

## Certificates That You Can Use with Dedicated IP Addresses

For the limit on the number of SSL certificates that you can use for each AWS account when serving HTTPS requests using dedicated IP addresses, see CloudFront Limits in the *Amazon Web Services General Reference*.

To request a higher limit, create a case with the AWS Support Center. Specify the following values:

- **Regarding** – Accept the default value of **Service Limit Increase**
- **Limit Type** – Accept the default value of **CloudFront Distributions**
- **Limit** – Choose **Dedicated IP SSL Certificate Limit per Account**

Then fill out the rest of the form.

# Rotating SSL/TLS Certificates

If you're using certificates provided by AWS Certificate Manager (ACM), you don't need to rotate SSL/TLS certificates. ACM manages certificate renewals for you. For more information, see Managed Renewal in the *AWS Certificate Manager User Guide.*

**Note**
ACM does not manage certificate renewals for certificates that you acquire from third-party certificate authorities and import into ACM.

If you're using a third-party certificate authority and you imported certificates into ACM (recommended) or uploaded them to the IAM certificate store, you'll occasionally need to replace one certificate with another. For example, you need to replace a certificate when the expiration date on the certificate approaches.

**Important**
If you configured CloudFront to serve HTTPS requests by using dedicated IP addresses, you might incur an additional, pro-rated charge for using one or more additional certificates while you're rotating certificates. We recommend that you update your distributions promptly to minimize the additional charge.

To rotate certificates, perform the following procedure. Viewers can continue to access your content while you rotate certificates as well as after the process is complete.

**To rotate SSL/TLS certificates**

1. Increasing the Limit for SSL/TLS Certificates to determine whether you need permission to use more SSL certificates. If so, request permission and wait until permission is granted before you continue with step 2.

2. Import the new certificate into ACM or upload it to IAM. For more information, see Importing an SSL/TLS Certificate in the *Amazon CloudFront Developer Guide*

3. Update your distributions one at a time to use the new certificate. For more information, see Listing, Viewing, and Updating CloudFront Distributions in the *Amazon CloudFront Developer Guide.*

4. (Optional) After you have updated all of your CloudFront distributions, you can delete the old certificate from ACM or from IAM. **Important**
Do not delete an SSL/TLS certificate until you remove it from all distributions and until the status of the distributions that you have updated has changed to `Deployed`.

# Reverting from a Custom SSL/TLS Certificate to the Default Cloud-Front Certificate

If you configured CloudFront to use HTTPS between viewers and CloudFront, and you configured CloudFront to use a custom SSL/TLS certificate, you can change your configuration to use the default CloudFront SSL/TLS certificate. The process depends on whether you've used your distribution to distribute your content:

- If you have not used your distribution to distribute your content, you can just change the configuration. For more information, see Viewing and Updating CloudFront Distributions.
- If you have used your distribution to distribute your content, you need to create a new CloudFront distribution and change the URLs for your objects to reduce or eliminate the amount of time that your content is unavailable. To do that, perform the following procedure.

**To revert to the default CloudFront certificate**

1. Create a new CloudFront distribution with the desired configuration. For **SSL Certificate**, choose **Default CloudFront Certificate (*.cloudfront.net)**.

   For more information, see Task List for Creating a Web Distribution.

2. For objects that you're distributing using CloudFront, update the URLs in your application to use the domain name that CloudFront assigned to the new distribution. For example, change `https://www.example.com/images/logo.png` to `https://d111111abcdef8.cloudfront.net/images/logo.png`.

3. Either delete the distribution that is associated with a custom SSL/TLS certificate, or update the distribution to change the value of **SSL Certificate** to **Default CloudFront Certificate (*.cloudfront.net)**. For more information, see Viewing and Updating CloudFront Distributions. **Important**
   Until you complete this step, AWS continues to charge you for using a custom SSL/TLS certificate.

4. (Optional) Delete your custom SSL/TLS certificate.

   1. Run the AWS CLI command `list-server-certificates` to get the certificate ID of the certificate that you want to delete. For more information, see list-server-certificates in the *AWS CLI Command Reference*.

   2. Run the AWS CLI command `delete-signing-certificate` to delete the certificate. For more information, see delete-signing-certificate in the *AWS CLI Command Reference*.

# Switching from a Custom SSL/TLS Certificate with Dedicated IP Addresses to SNI

If you configured CloudFront to use a custom SSL/TLS certificate with dedicated IP addresses, you can switch to using a custom SSL/TLS certificate with SNI instead and eliminate the charge that is associated with dedicated IP addresses. The following procedure shows you how.

**Important**

This update to your CloudFront configuration has no effect on viewers that support SNI; they can access your content before and after the change, as well as while the change is propagating to CloudFront edge locations. Viewers that don't support SNI cannot access your content after the change. For more information, see Choosing How CloudFront Serves HTTPS Requests.

**To switch from a custom SSL/TLS certificate with dedicated IP addresses to SNI**

1. Sign in to the AWS Management Console and open the CloudFront console at https://console.aws.amazon.com/cloudfront/.

2. Choose the ID of the distribution that you want to view or update.

3. Choose **Distribution Settings**.

4. On the **General** tab, choose **Edit**.

5. Change the setting of **Custom SSL Client Support** to **Only Clients that Support Server Name Indication (SNI)**.

6. Choose **Yes, Edit**.

# Supported Protocols and Ciphers

You can choose HTTPS settings both for communication between viewers and CloudFront, and between CloudFront and your origin:

- **Between viewers and CloudFront** – If you require HTTPS between viewers and CloudFront, you also choose a security policy, which determines the protocols that viewers and CloudFront can use to communicate. In addition, a security policy determines which ciphers CloudFront can use to encrypt the content that it returns to viewers.
- **Between CloudFront and your origin** – If you require HTTPS between CloudFront and your origin, you also choose the protocols that CloudFront and your origin use to communicate. The protocols that you choose determine which ciphers your origin can use to encrypt content that it returns to CloudFront.

**Topics**

- Supported SSL/TLS Protocols and Ciphers for Communication Between Viewers and CloudFront
- Supported SSL/TLS Protocols and Ciphers for Communication Between CloudFront and Your Origin

## Supported SSL/TLS Protocols and Ciphers for Communication Between Viewers and CloudFront

To choose whether to require HTTPS between viewers and CloudFront, specify the applicable value for Viewer Protocol Policy.

If you choose to require HTTPS, you also choose the security policy that you want CloudFront to use for HTTPS connections. A security policy determines two settings:

- The SSL/TLS protocol that CloudFront uses to communicate with viewers
- The cipher that CloudFront uses to encrypt the content that it returns to viewers

We recommend that you specify **TLSv1.1_2016** unless your users are using browsers or devices that don't support TLSv1.1 or later. When you use a custom SSL certificate and SNI, you must use TLSv1 or later.

To choose a security policy, specify the applicable value for Security Policy. The following table lists the protocols and ciphers that CloudFront can use for each security policy.

A viewer must support at least one of the supported ciphers to establish an HTTPS connection with CloudFront. If you're using an SSL/TLS certificate in AWS Certificate Manager, a viewer must support one of the *-RSA-* ciphers. CloudFront chooses a cipher in the listed order from among the ciphers that the viewer supports. See also OpenSSL and RFC Cipher Names.

| | Security Policy | SSLv3 | TLSv1.0 | TLSv1_201 | TLSv1.1_2 | TLSv1.2_2 | SSL/TLS Protocols Supported |
|---|---|---|---|---|---|---|---|
| TLSv1.2 | | | | | | | |
| TLSv1.1 | | | | | | | |
| TLSv1 | | | | | | | |
| SSLv3 | | | | | | | |
| Ciphers Supported | | | | | | | |

368

| Security Policy | SSLv3 | TLSv1.0 | TLSv1_201 | TLSv1.1_2 | TLSv1.2_2 | SSL/TLS Protocols Supported |
|---|---|---|---|---|---|---|
| ECDHE-RSA-AES128-GC SHA256 | | | | | | |
| ECDHE-RSA-AES128-SH | | | | | | |
| ECDHE-RSA-AES128-SH | | | | | | |
| ECDHE-RSA-AES256-GC SHA384 | | | | | | |
| ECDHE-RSA-AES256-SH | | | | | | |
| ECDHE-RSA-AES256-SH | | | | | | |
| AES128-GC SHA256 | | | | | | |
| AES256-GC SHA384 | | | | | | |
| AES128-SH | | | | | | |
| AES256-SH | | | | | | |
| AES128-SH | | | | | | |
| DES-CBC3-SHA | | | | | | |
| RC4-MD5 | | | | | | |

## OpenSSL and RFC Cipher Names

OpenSSL and IETF RFC 5246, The Transport Layer Security (TLS) Protocol Version 1.2, use different names for the same ciphers. The following table maps the OpenSSL name to the RFC name for each cipher.

| OpenSSL Cipher Name | RFC Cipher Name |
|---|---|
| ECDHE-RSA-AES128-GCM-SHA256 | TLS_ECDHE_RSA_WITH_AES_128_GCM_SHA256 |
| ECDHE-RSA-AES128-SHA256 | TLS_ECDHE_RSA_WITH_AES_128_CBC_SHA256 |
| ECDHE-RSA-AES128-SHA | TLS_ECDHE_RSA_WITH_AES_128_CBC_SHA |
| ECDHE-RSA-AES256-GCM-SHA384 | TLS_ECDHE_RSA_WITH_AES_256_GCM_SHA384 |
| ECDHE-RSA-AES256-SHA384 | TLS_ECDHE_RSA_WITH_AES_256_CBC_SHA384 |
| ECDHE-RSA-AES256-SHA | TLS_ECDHE_RSA_WITH_AES_256_CBC_SHA |
| AES128-GCM-SHA256 | TLS_RSA_WITH_AES_128_GCM_SHA256 |
| AES256-GCM-SHA384 | TLS_RSA_WITH_AES_256_GCM_SHA384 |
| AES128-SHA256 | TLS_RSA_WITH_AES_128_CBC_SHA256 |
| AES256-SHA | TLS_RSA_WITH_AES_256_CBC_SHA |

| OpenSSL Cipher Name | RFC Cipher Name |
| --- | --- |
| AES128-SHA | TLS_RSA_WITH_AES_128_CBC_SHA |
| DES-CBC3-SHA | TLS_RSA_WITH_3DES_EDE_CBC_SHA |
| RC4-MD5 | TLS_RSA_WITH_RC4_128_MD5 |

## Supported SSL/TLS Protocols and Ciphers for Communication Between CloudFront and Your Origin

If you choose to require HTTPS between CloudFront and your origin, you can decided which SSL/TLS protocol to allow for the secure connection, and then pick any supported cipher for CloudFront (see the following tables) to establish an HTTPS connection to your origin.

CloudFront can forward HTTPS requests to the origin server by using the ECDSA or RSA ciphers listed in this section. Your origin server must support at least one of these ciphers for CloudFront to establish an HTTPS connection to your origin. To learn more about the two types of ciphers that CloudFront supports, see About RSA and ECDSA Ciphers.

**Note**
The following curves are supported for elliptic-curve-based ciphers:
prime256v1 secp384r1

OpenSSL and IETF RFC 5246, The Transport Layer Security (TLS) Protocol Version 1.2, use different names for the same ciphers. The following tables map the OpenSSL name to the RFC name for each cipher.

**Supported RSA Ciphers**

CloudFront supports the following RSA ciphers for connections with an origin:

| OpenSSL Cipher Name | RFC Cipher Name |
| --- | --- |
| ECDHE-RSA-AES128-SHA256 | TLS_ECDHE_RSA_WITH_AES_128_CBC_SHA256 |
| ECDHE-RSA-AES256-SHA384 | TLS_ECDHE_RSA_WITH_AES_256_CBC_SHA384 |
| AES256-SHA | TLS_RSA_WITH_AES_256_CBC_SHA |
| AES128-SHA | TLS_RSA_WITH_AES_128_CBC_SHA |
| DES-CBC3-SHA | TLS_RSA_WITH_3DES_EDE_CBC_SHA |
| RC4-MD5 | TLS_RSA_WITH_RC4_128_MD5 |

**Supported ECDSA Ciphers**

CloudFront supports the following ECDSA ciphers for connections with an origin:

| OpenSSL Cipher Name | RFC Cipher Name |
| --- | --- |
| ECDHE-ECDSA-AES256-GCM-SHA384 | TLS_ECDHE_ECDSA_WITH_AES_256_GCM_SHA384 |
| ECDHE-ECDSA-AES256-SHA384 | TLS_ECDHE_ECDSA_WITH_AES_256_CBC_SHA384 |
| ECDHE-ECDSA-AES256-SHA | TLS_ECDHE_ECDSA_WITH_AES_256_CBC_SHA |
| ECDHE-ECDSA-AES128-GCM-SHA256 | TLS_ECDHE_ECDSA_WITH_AES_128_GCM_SHA256 |
| ECDHE-ECDSA-AES128-SHA256 | TLS_ECDHE_ECDSA_WITH_AES_128_CBC_SHA256 |
| ECDHE-ECDSA-AES128-SHA | TLS_ECDHE_ECDSA_WITH_AES_128_CBC_SHA |

# Charges for HTTPS Connections

You always incur a surcharge for HTTPS requests. For more information, see Amazon CloudFront Pricing.

# Authentication and Access Control for CloudFront

To perform any operation on CloudFront resources, such as creating a web distribution or an invalidation, AWS Identity and Access Management (IAM) requires you to authenticate that you're an approved AWS user. If you're using the CloudFront console, you authenticate your identity by providing your AWS user name and a password. If you're accessing CloudFront programmatically, your application authenticates your identity for you by using access keys or by signing requests.

After you authenticate your identity, IAM controls your access to AWS by verifying that you have permissions to perform operations and access resources. If you are an account administrator, you can use IAM to control the access of other users to the resources that are associated with your account.

This chapter explains how to use AWS Identity and Access Management (IAM) and CloudFront to help secure your resources.

**Topics**

- Authentication
- Access Control

## Authentication

You can access AWS as any of the following types of identities:

- **AWS account root user** – When you first create an AWS account, you begin with a single sign-in identity that has complete access to all AWS services and resources in the account. This identity is called the AWS account *root user* and is accessed by signing in with the email address and password that you used to create the account. We strongly recommend that you do not use the root user for your everyday tasks, even the administrative ones. Instead, adhere to the best practice of using the root user only to create your first IAM user. Then securely lock away the root user credentials and use them to perform only a few account and service management tasks.

- **IAM user** – An IAM user is an identity within your AWS account that has specific custom permissions (for example, permissions to create a web distribution in CloudFront). You can use an IAM user name and password to sign in to secure AWS webpages like the AWS Management Console, AWS Discussion Forums, or the AWS Support Center.

  In addition to a user name and password, you can also generate access keys for each user. You can use these keys when you access AWS services programmatically, either through one of the several SDKs or by using the AWS Command Line Interface (CLI). The SDK and CLI tools use the access keys to cryptographically sign your request. If you don't use AWS tools, you must sign the request yourself. CloudFront supports *Signature Version 4*, a protocol for authenticating inbound API requests. For more information about authenticating requests, see Signature Version 4 Signing Process in the *AWS General Reference*.

- **IAM role** – An IAM role is an IAM identity that you can create in your account that has specific permissions. It is similar to an *IAM user*, but it is not associated with a specific person. An IAM role enables you to obtain temporary access keys that can be used to access AWS services and resources. IAM roles with temporary credentials are useful in the following situations:

  - **Federated user access** – Instead of creating an IAM user, you can use existing user identities from AWS Directory Service, your enterprise user directory, or a web identity provider. These are known as *federated users*. AWS assigns a role to a federated user when access is requested through an identity

372

provider. For more information about federated users, see Federated Users and Roles in the *IAM User Guide*.

- **AWS service access** – You can use an IAM role in your account to grant an AWS service permissions to access your account's resources. For example, you can create a role that allows Amazon Redshift to access an Amazon S3 bucket on your behalf and then load data from that bucket into an Amazon Redshift cluster. For more information, see Creating a Role to Delegate Permissions to an AWS Service in the *IAM User Guide*.

- **Applications running on Amazon EC2** – You can use an IAM role to manage temporary credentials for applications that are running on an EC2 instance and making AWS API requests. This is preferable to storing access keys within the EC2 instance. To assign an AWS role to an EC2 instance and make it available to all of its applications, you create an instance profile that is attached to the instance. An instance profile contains the role and enables programs that are running on the EC2 instance to get temporary credentials. For more information, see Using an IAM Role to Grant Permissions to Applications Running on Amazon EC2 Instances in the *IAM User Guide*.

## Access Control

To create, update, delete, or list CloudFront resources, you need permissions to perform the operation, and you need permissions to access the corresponding resources. In addition, to perform the operation programmatically, you need valid access keys.

The following sections describe how to manage permissions for CloudFront:

- Overview of Managing Access Permissions to Your CloudFront Resources
- Using Identity-Based Policies (IAM Policies) for CloudFront
- CloudFront API Permissions: Actions, Resources, and Conditions Reference

# Overview of Managing Access Permissions to Your CloudFront Resources

Every AWS resource is owned by an AWS account, and permissions to create or access a resource are governed by permissions policies.

**Note**

An *account administrator* (or administrator user) is a user that has administrator privileges. For more information about administrators, see IAM Best Practices in the *IAM User Guide.*

When you grant permissions, you decide who gets the permissions, the resources they get permissions for, and the actions that they get permission to perform.

**Topics**

- ARNs for CloudFront Resources
- Understanding Resource Ownership
- Managing Access to Resources
- Specifying Policy Elements: Resources, Actions, Effects, and Principals
- Specifying Conditions in a Policy

## ARNs for CloudFront Resources

All CloudFront resources—web and RTMP distributions, invalidations, and origin access identities—use the same format for Amazon Resource Names (ARNs):

```
arn:aws:cloudfront::optional-account-id:*
```

CloudFront provides API actions to work with each of these types of resources. For more information, see the Amazon CloudFront API Reference. For a list of actions and the ARN that you specify to grant or deny permission to use each action, see CloudFront API Permissions: Actions, Resources, and Conditions Reference.

## Understanding Resource Ownership

An AWS account owns the resources that are created in the account, regardless of who created the resources. Specifically, the resource owner is the AWS account of the principal entity (that is, the root account, an IAM user, or an IAM role) that authenticates the resource creation request.

The following examples illustrate how this works:

- If you use the root account credentials of your AWS account to create a web distribution, your AWS account is the owner of the distribution.
- If you create an IAM user in your AWS account and grant permissions to create a web distribution to that user, the user can create a web distribution. The AWS account that created the user owns the distribution.
- If you create an IAM role in your AWS account with permissions to create a web distribution, anyone who can assume the role can create a web distribution. Your AWS account, to which the role belongs, owns the distribution.

## Managing Access to Resources

A *permissions policy* specifies who has access to what. This section explains the options for creating permissions policies for CloudFront. For general information about IAM policy syntax and descriptions, see the AWS IAM Policy Reference in the *IAM User Guide.*

Policies attached to an IAM identity are referred to as identity-based policies (IAM policies), and policies attached to a resource are referred to as resource-based policies. CloudFront supports only identity-based policies (IAM policies).

**Topics**

- Identity-Based Policies (IAM Policies)
- Resource-Based Policies

## Identity-Based Policies (IAM Policies)

You can attach policies to IAM identities. For example, you can do the following:

- **Attach a permissions policy to a user or a group in your account** – An account administrator can use a permissions policy that is associated with a particular user to grant permissions for that user to create a web distribution.

- **Attach a permissions policy to a role (grant cross-account permissions)** – You can grant permissions to perform CloudFront actions to a user that was created in another AWS account. To do so, you attach a permissions policy to an IAM role, and then you allow the user in the other account to assume the role. The following example explains how this works for two AWS accounts, account A and account B:

  1. Account A administrator creates an IAM role and attaches to the role a permissions policy that grants permissions to create or access resources that are owned by account A.

  2. Account A administrator attaches a trust policy to the role. The trust policy identifies account B as the principal that can assume the role.

  3. Account B administrator can then delegate permissions to assume the role to users or groups in account B. This allows users in account B to create or access resources in account A.

  For more information about how to delegate permissions to users in another AWS account, see Access Management in the *IAM User Guide*.

The following example policy allows a user to perform the `CreateDistribution` action to programmatically create a web distribution for your AWS account:

```
1  {
2      "Version": "2012-10-17",
3      "Statement": [
4          {
5              "Effect": "Allow",
6              "Action": [
7                  "cloudfront:CreateDistribution"
8              ],
9              "Resource":"*"
10         }
11     ]
12 }
```

For information about the permissions required to perform operations by using the CloudFront console, see Permissions Required to Use the CloudFront Console. For more information about attaching policies to identities for CloudFront, see Using Identity-Based Policies (IAM Policies) for CloudFront. For more information about users, groups, roles, and permissions, see Identities (Users, Groups, and Roles) in the *IAM User Guide*.

## Resource-Based Policies

Other services, such as Amazon S3, support attaching permissions policies to resources. For example, you can attach a policy to an S3 bucket to manage access permissions to that bucket. CloudFront doesn't support attaching policies to resources.

## Specifying Policy Elements: Resources, Actions, Effects, and Principals

CloudFront includes API actions (see Amazon CloudFront API Reference) that you can use on each CloudFront resource (see ARNs for CloudFront Resources). You can grant a user or a federated user permission to perform any or all of these actions.

The following are the basic policy elements:

- **Resource** – You use an Amazon Resource Name (ARN) to identify the resource that the policy applies to. For more information, see ARNs for CloudFront Resources.
- **Action** – You use action keywords to identify resource operations that you want to allow or deny. For example, depending on the specified `Effect`, the `cloudfront:CreateDistribution` permission allows or denies the user permissions to perform the CloudFront `CreateDistribution` action.
- **Effect** – You specify the effect, either allow or deny, when a user tries to perform the action on the specified resource. If you don't explicitly grant access to an action, access is implicitly denied. You can also explicitly deny access to a resource, which you might do to make sure that a user cannot access it, even if a different policy grants access.
- **Principal** – In identity-based policies (IAM policies), the user that the policy is attached to is the implicit principal. For resource-based policies, you specify the user, account, service, or other entity that you want to receive permissions (applies to resource-based policies only). CloudFront doesn't support resource-based policies.

For more information about IAM policy syntax and descriptions, see the AWS IAM Policy Reference in the *IAM User Guide*.

For a showing all of the CloudFront API operations and the resources that they apply to, see CloudFront API Permissions: Actions, Resources, and Conditions Reference.

## Specifying Conditions in a Policy

When you grant permissions, you can use the IAM policy language to specify when a policy should take effect. For example, you might want a policy to be applied only after a specific date. For more information about specifying conditions in a policy language, see Condition in the *IAM User Guide*.

To express conditions, you use predefined condition keys. There are no condition keys specific to CloudFront. However, there are AWS-wide condition keys that you can use as appropriate. For a complete list of AWS-wide keys, see Available Keys for Conditions in the *IAM User Guide*.

# Using Identity-Based Policies (IAM Policies) for CloudFront

This topic provides examples of identity-based policies that demonstrate how an account administrator can attach permissions policies to IAM identities (that is, users, groups, and roles) and thereby grant permissions to perform operations on CloudFront resources.

**Important**
We recommend that you first review the introductory topics that explain the basic concepts and options to manage access to your CloudFront resources. For more information, see Overview of Managing Access Permissions to Your CloudFront Resources.

**Topics**

- Permissions Required to Use the CloudFront Console
- AWS Managed (Predefined) Policies for CloudFront
- Customer Managed Policy Examples

The following shows a permissions policy. The `Sid`, or statement ID, is optional:

```
{
    "Version": "2012-10-17",
    "Statement": [
        {
            "Sid": "AllowAllCloudFrontPermissions",
            "Effect": "Allow",
            "Action": ["cloudfront:*"],
            "Resource": "*"
        }
    ]
}
```

The policy grants permissions to perform all CloudFront operations, which is sufficient to access CloudFront programmatically. If you're using the console to access CloudFront, see Permissions Required to Use the CloudFront Console.

For a list of actions and the ARN that you specify to grant or deny permission to use each action, see CloudFront API Permissions: Actions, Resources, and Conditions Reference.

## Permissions Required to Use the CloudFront Console

To grant full access to the CloudFront console, you grant the permissions in the following permissions policy:

```
{
    "Version": "2012-10-17",
    "Statement":[
        {
            "Effect":"Allow",
            "Action":[
                "acm:ListCertificates",
                "cloudfront:*",
                "cloudwatch:DescribeAlarms",
                "cloudwatch:PutMetricAlarm",
                "cloudwatch:GetMetricStatistics",
                "elasticloadbalancing:DescribeLoadBalancers",
                "iam:ListServerCertificates",
                "sns:ListSubscriptionsByTopic",
                "sns:ListTopics",
```

```
16          "waf:GetWebACL",
17          "waf:ListWebACLs"
18        ],
19        "Resource":"*"
20      },
21      {
22        "Effect":"Allow",
23        "Action":[
24          "s3:ListAllMyBuckets",
25          "s3:PutBucketPolicy"
26        ],
27        "Resource":"arn:aws:s3:::*"
28      }
29    ]
30 }
```

Here's why the permissions are required:

### acm:ListCertificates

When you're creating and updating web distributions by using the CloudFront console and you want to configure CloudFront to require HTTPS between the viewer and CloudFront or between CloudFront and the origin, lets you view a list of ACM certificates.

This permission isn't required if you aren't using the CloudFront console.

### cloudfront:*

Lets you perform all CloudFront actions.

### cloudwatch:DescribeAlarms and cloudwatch:PutMetricAlarm

Let you create and view CloudWatch alarms in the CloudFront console. See also sns:ListSubscriptionsByTopic and sns:ListTopics.

These permissions aren't required if you aren't using the CloudFront console.

### cloudwatch:GetMetricStatistics

Lets CloudFront render CloudWatch metrics in the CloudFront console.

This permission isn't required if you aren't using the CloudFront console.

### elasticloadbalancing:DescribeLoadBalancers

When creating and updating web distributions, lets you view a list of Elastic Load Balancing load balancers in the list of available origins.

This permission isn't required if you aren't using the CloudFront console.

### iam:ListServerCertificates

When you're creating and updating web distributions by using the CloudFront console and you want to configure CloudFront to require HTTPS between the viewer and CloudFront or between CloudFront and the origin, lets you view a list of certificates in the IAM certificate store.

This permission isn't required if you aren't using the CloudFront console.

### s3:ListAllMyBuckets

When you're creating and updating web and RTMP distributions, lets you perform the following operations:

- View a list of S3 buckets in the list of available origins
- View a list of S3 buckets that you can save access logs in This permission isn't required if you aren't using the CloudFront console.

### S3:PutBucketPolicy

When you're creating or updating distributions that restrict access to S3 buckets, lets a user update the bucket policy to grant access to the CloudFront origin access identity. For more information, see Using an Origin Access Identity to Restrict Access to Your Amazon S3 Content.

This permission isn't required if you aren't using the CloudFront console.

`sns:ListSubscriptionsByTopic` and `sns:ListTopics`
When you create CloudWatch alarms in the CloudFront console, lets you choose an SNS topic for notifications.
These permissions aren't required if you aren't using the CloudFront console.

`waf:GetWebACL` and `waf:ListWebACLs`
Lets you view a list of AWS WAF web ACLs in the CloudFront console.
These permissions aren't required if you aren't using the CloudFront console.

## AWS Managed (Predefined) Policies for CloudFront

AWS addresses many common use cases by providing standalone IAM policies that are created and administered by AWS. These AWS managed policies grant necessary permissions for common use cases so that you can avoid having to investigate what permissions are needed. For more information, see AWS Managed Policies in the *IAM User Guide*. For CloudFront, IAM provides two managed policies:

- **CloudFrontFullAccess** – Grants full access to CloudFront resources. **Important**
  If you want CloudFront to create and save access logs, you need to grant additional permissions. For more information, see Permissions Required to Configure Logging and to Access Your Log Files.
- **CloudFrontReadOnlyAccess** – Grants read-only access to CloudFront resources.

### Note
You can review these permissions policies by signing in to the IAM console and searching for specific policies there. You can also create your own custom IAM policies to allow permissions for CloudFront API operations. You can attach these custom policies to the IAM users or groups that require those permissions.

## Customer Managed Policy Examples

You can create your own custom IAM policies to allow permissions for CloudFront API actions. You can attach these custom policies to the IAM users or groups that require the specified permissions. These policies work when you are using the CloudFront API, the AWS SDKs, or the AWS CLI. The following examples show permissions for a few common use cases. For the policy that grants a user full access to CloudFront, see Permissions Required to Use the CloudFront Console.

### Topics

- Example 1: Allow Read Access to All Web Distributions
- Example 2: Allow Creation, Updating, and Deletion of Web Distributions
- Example 3: Allow Creation and Listing of Invalidations

### Example 1: Allow Read Access to All Web Distributions

The following permissions policy grants the user permissions to view all web distributions in the CloudFront console:

```
1  {
2      "Version": "2012-10-17",
3      "Statement":[
4          {
5              "Effect":"Allow",
6              "Action":[
7                  "acm:ListCertificates",
8                  "cloudfront:GetDistribution",
9                  "cloudfront:GetDistributionConfig",
10                 "cloudfront:ListDistributions",
11                 "cloudfront:ListCloudFrontOriginAccessIdentities",
```

```
12          "elasticloadbalancing:DescribeLoadBalancers",
13          "iam:ListServerCertificates",
14          "sns:ListSubscriptionsByTopic",
15          "sns:ListTopics",
16          "waf:GetWebACL",
17          "waf:ListWebACLs"
18        ],
19        "Resource":"*"
20      },
21      {
22        "Effect":"Allow",
23        "Action":[
24          "s3:ListAllMyBuckets"
25        ],
26        "Resource":"arn:aws:s3:::*"
27      }
28    ]
29  }
```

## Example 2: Allow Creation, Updating, and Deletion of Web Distributions

The following permissions policy allows users to create, update, and delete web distributions by using the CloudFront console:

```
1  {
2    "Version": "2012-10-17",
3    "Statement":[
4      {
5        "Effect":"Allow",
6        "Action":[
7          "acm:ListCertificates",
8          "cloudfront:CreateDistribution",
9          "cloudfront:DeleteDistribution",
10         "cloudfront:GetDistribution",
11         "cloudfront:GetDistributionConfig",
12         "cloudfront:ListDistributions",
13         "cloudfront:UpdateDistribution",
14         "cloudfront:ListCloudFrontOriginAccessIdentities",
15         "elasticloadbalancing:DescribeLoadBalancers",
16         "iam:ListServerCertificates",
17         "sns:ListSubscriptionsByTopic",
18         "sns:ListTopics",
19         "waf:GetWebACL",
20         "waf:ListWebACLs"
21       ],
22       "Resource":"*"
23     },
24     {
25       "Effect":"Allow",
26       "Action":[
27         "s3:ListAllMyBuckets",
28         "s3:PutBucketPolicy"
29       ],
30       "Resource":"arn:aws:s3:::*"
```

```
31        }
32    ]
33 }
```

The `cloudfront:ListCloudFrontOriginAccessIdentities` permission allows users to automatically grant to an existing origin access identity the permission to access objects in an Amazon S3 bucket. If you also want users to be able to create origin access identities, you also need to allow the `cloudfront:CreateCloudFrontOriginAccessIdentity` permission.

## Example 3: Allow Creation and Listing of Invalidations

The following permissions policy allows users to create and list invalidations. It includes read access to CloudFront distributions because you create and view invalidations by first displaying settings for a distribution:

```
1  {
2      "Version": "2012-10-17",
3      "Statement":[
4          {
5              "Effect":"Allow",
6              "Action":[
7                  "acm:ListCertificates",
8                  "cloudfront:GetDistribution",
9                  "cloudfront:GetDistributionConfig",
10                 "cloudfront:ListDistributions",
11                 "cloudfront:ListCloudFrontOriginAccessIdentities",
12                 "cloudfront:CreateInvalidation",
13                 "cloudfront:GetInvalidation",
14                 "cloudfront:ListInvalidations",
15                 "elasticloadbalancing:DescribeLoadBalancers",
16                 "iam:ListServerCertificates",
17                 "sns:ListSubscriptionsByTopic",
18                 "sns:ListTopics",
19                 "waf:GetWebACL",
20                 "waf:ListWebACLs"
21             ],
22             "Resource":"*"
23         },
24         {
25             "Effect":"Allow",
26             "Action":[
27                 "s3:ListAllMyBuckets"
28             ],
29             "Resource":"arn:aws:s3:::*"
30         }
31     ]
32 }
```

# CloudFront API Permissions: Actions, Resources, and Conditions Reference

When you are setting up Access Control and writing a permissions policy that you can attach to an IAM identity (identity-based policies), you can use the following as a reference. The each CloudFront API operation, the corresponding actions for which you can grant permissions to perform the action, and the AWS resource for which you can grant the permissions. You specify the actions in the policy's `Action` field, and you specify the resource value in the policy's `Resource` field.

You can use AWS-wide condition keys in your CloudFront policies to express conditions. For a complete list of AWS-wide keys, see Available Keys in the *IAM User Guide*.

**Topics**

- Required Permissions for Actions on Web Distributions
- Required Permissions for Actions on RTMP Distributions
- Required Permissions for Actions on Invalidations
- Required Permissions for Actions on Origin Access Identities
- Required Permissions for CloudFront Actions Related to Lambda@Edge
- Required Permissions for Actions on Tags

## Required Permissions for Actions on Web Distributions

CreateDistribution
**Required Permissions (API Action):**

- `cloudfront:CreateDistribution`
- `acm:ListCertificates` (CloudFront console only)
- Only if you configure CloudFront to save access logs:
    - `s3:GetBucketAcl`
    - `s3:PutBucketAcl`
    - The S3 ACL for the bucket must grant you `FULL_CONTROL` **Resources:**
- CloudFront: *
- ACM: *
- Amazon S3: If you configure CloudFront to save access logs, you can optionally restrict access to a specified bucket.

CreateDistributionWithTags
**Required Permissions (API Action):**

- `cloudfront:CreateDistribution, cloudfront:TagResource`
- `acm:ListCertificates` (CloudFront console only)
- Only if you configure CloudFront to save access logs:
    - `s3:GetBucketAcl`
    - `s3:PutBucketAcl`
    - The S3 ACL for the bucket must grant you `FULL_CONTROL` **Resources:**
- CloudFront: *
- ACM: *
- Amazon S3: If you configure CloudFront to save access logs, you can optionally restrict access to a specified bucket.

GetDistribution
**Required Permissions (API Action):** `cloudfront:GetDistribution, acm:ListCertificates` (CloudFront console only)
**Resources:** *

GetDistributionConfig
**Required Permissions (API Action):** `cloudfront:GetDistributionConfig, acm:ListCertificates` (CloudFront console only)
**Resources:** *

ListDistributions
**Required Permissions (API Action):** `cloudfront:ListDistributions`
**Resources:** *

UpdateDistribution
**Required Permissions (API Action):**

- `cloudfront:UpdateDistribution`
- `acm:ListCertificates` (CloudFront console only)
- Only if you configure CloudFront to save access logs:
  - `s3:GetBucketAcl`
  - `s3:PutBucketAcl`
  - The S3 ACL for the bucket must grant you `FULL_CONTROL` **Resources:**
- CloudFront: *
- ACM: *
- Amazon S3: If you configure CloudFront to save access logs, you can optionally restrict access to a specified bucket.

DeleteDistribution
**Required Permissions (API Action):** `cloudfront:DeleteDistribution`
**Resources:** *


# Required Permissions for Actions on RTMP Distributions

CreateStreamingDistribution
**Required Permissions (API Action):** `cloudfront:CreateStreamingDistribution`
Only if you configure CloudFront to save access logs:

- `s3:GetBucketAcl`
- `s3:PutBucketAcl`
- The S3 ACL for the bucket must grant you `FULL_CONTROL` **Resources:** *
  If you configure CloudFront to save access logs, you can optionally restrict access to a specified bucket.

CreateStreamingDistributionWithTags
**Required Permissions (API Action):** `cloudfront:CreateStreamingDistribution, cloudfront:TagResource`
Only if you configure CloudFront to save access logs:

- `s3:GetBucketAcl`
- `s3:PutBucketAcl`
- The S3 ACL for the bucket must grant you `FULL_CONTROL` **Resources:** *
  If you configure CloudFront to save access logs, you can optionally restrict access to a specified bucket.

GetStreamingDistribution
**Required Permissions (API Action):** `cloudfront:GetStreamingDistribution`
**Resources:** *

GetStreamingDistributionConfig
**Required Permissions (API Action):** `cloudfront:GetStreamingDistributionConfig`
**Resources:** *

ListStreamingDistributions
**Required Permissions (API Action):** `cloudfront:ListStreamingDistributions`
**Resources:** *

UpdateStreamingDistribution
**Required Permissions (API Action):** `cloudfront:UpdateStreamingDistribution`
Only if you configure CloudFront to save access logs:

- `s3:GetBucketAcl`
- `s3:PutBucketAcl`
- The S3 ACL for the bucket must grant you `FULL_CONTROL` **Resources:** *
  If you configure CloudFront to save access logs, you can optionally restrict access to a specified bucket.

DeleteStreamingDistribution
**Required Permissions (API Action):** `cloudfront:DeleteDistribution`
**Resources:** *


## Required Permissions for Actions on Invalidations

CreateInvalidation
**Required Permissions (API Action):** `cloudfront:CreateInvalidation`
**Resources:** *

GetInvalidation
**Required Permissions (API Action):** `cloudfront:GetInvalidation`
**Resources:** *

ListInvalidations
**Required Permissions (API Action):** `cloudfront:ListInvalidations`
**Resources:** *


## Required Permissions for Actions on Origin Access Identities

CreateCloudFrontOriginAccessIdentity
**Required Permissions (API Action):** `cloudfront:CreateCloudFrontOriginAccessIdentity`
**Resources:** *

GetCloudFrontOriginAccessIdentity
**Required Permissions (API Action):** `cloudfront:GetCloudFrontOriginAccessIdentity`
**Resources:** *

GetCloudFrontOriginAccessIdentityConfig
**Required Permissions (API Action):** `cloudfront:GetCloudFrontOriginAccessIdentityConfig`
**Resources:** *

ListCloudFrontOriginAccessIdentities
**Required Permissions (API Action):** `cloudfront:ListDistributions`
**Resources:** *

UpdateCloudFrontOriginAccessIdentity
**Required Permissions (API Action):** `cloudfront:UpdateCloudFrontOriginAccessIdentity`
**Resources:** *

DeleteCloudFrontOriginAccessIdentity
**Required Permissions (API Action):** `cloudfront:DeleteCloudFrontOriginAccessIdentity`
**Resources:** *


## Required Permissions for CloudFront Actions Related to Lambda@Edge

To use Lambda@Edge, you need the following CloudFront permissions so you can create or update a distribution that includes triggers for Lambda functions. For information about the Lambda permissions that you need, see

Setting IAM Permissions in the "AWS Lambda@Edge" chapter in the *AWS Lambda Developer Guide*.

CreateDistribution
**Required Permissions (API Action):**

- `cloudfront:CreateDistribution`
- `acm:ListCertificates` (CloudFront console only)
- Only if you configure CloudFront to save access logs:
    - `s3:GetBucketAcl`
    - `s3:PutBucketAcl`
    - The S3 ACL for the bucket must grant you `FULL_CONTROL` **Resources:**
- CloudFront: *
- ACM: *
- Amazon S3: If you configure CloudFront to save access logs, you can optionally restrict access to a specified bucket.

CreateDistributionWithTags
**Required Permissions (API Action):**

- `cloudfront:CreateDistribution, cloudfront:TagResource`
- `acm:ListCertificates` (CloudFront console only)
- Only if you configure CloudFront to save access logs:
    - `s3:GetBucketAcl`
    - `s3:PutBucketAcl`
    - The S3 ACL for the bucket must grant you `FULL_CONTROL` **Resources:**
- CloudFront: *
- ACM: *
- Amazon S3: If you configure CloudFront to save access logs, you can optionally restrict access to a specified bucket.

UpdateDistribution
**Required Permissions (API Action):**

- `cloudfront:UpdateDistribution`
- `acm:ListCertificates` (CloudFront console only)
- Only if you configure CloudFront to save access logs:
    - `s3:GetBucketAcl`
    - `s3:PutBucketAcl`
    - The S3 ACL for the bucket must grant you `FULL_CONTROL` **Resources:**
- CloudFront: *
- ACM: *
- Amazon S3: If you configure CloudFront to save access logs, you can optionally restrict access to a specified bucket.

## Required Permissions for Actions on Tags

TagResource
**Required Permissions (API Action):** `cloudfront:TagResource`
**Resources:** *

UntagResource
**Required Permissions (API Action):** `cloudfront:UntagResource`
**Resources:** *

ListTagsForResource
**Required Permissions (API Action):** `cloudfront:ListTagsForResource`
**Resources:** *

# Access Logs

You can configure CloudFront to create log files that contain detailed information about every user request that CloudFront receives. These access logs are available for both web and RTMP distributions. If you enable logging, you can also specify the Amazon S3 bucket that you want CloudFront to save files in.

You can enable logging as an option that you specify when you're creating a distribution. For more information, see the Logging section of the **Values That You Specify When You Create or Update a Web Distribution ** topic.

**Topics**

- How Logging Works
- Choosing an Amazon S3 Bucket for Your Access Logs
- Permissions Required to Configure Logging and to Access Your Log Files
- File Name Format
- Timing of Log File Delivery
- Analyzing Access Logs
- Editing Your Logging Settings
- Deleting Log Files from an Amazon S3 Bucket
- Log File Format
- Charges for Access Logs

## How Logging Works

The following diagram shows how CloudFront logs information about requests for your objects.

The following explains how CloudFront logs information about requests for your objects, as illustrated in the previous graphic.

1. In this diagram, you have two websites, A and B, and two corresponding CloudFront distributions. Users request your objects using URLs that are associated with your distributions.

2. CloudFront routes each request to the appropriate edge location.

3. CloudFront writes data about each request to a log file specific to that distribution. In this example, information about requests related to Distribution A goes into a log file just for Distribution A, and information about requests related to Distribution B goes into a log file just for Distribution B.

4. CloudFront periodically saves the log file for a distribution in the Amazon S3 bucket that you specified when you enabled logging. CloudFront then starts saving information about subsequent requests in a new log file for the distribution.

Each entry in a log file gives details about a single request. For more information about log file format, see Log File Format.

## Choosing an Amazon S3 Bucket for Your Access Logs

When you enable logging for a distribution, you specify the Amazon S3 bucket that you want CloudFront to store log files in. If you're using Amazon S3 as your origin, we recommend that you do not use the same bucket for your log files; using a separate bucket simplifies maintenance.

You can store the log files for multiple distributions in the same bucket. When you enable logging, you can specify an optional prefix for the file names, so you can keep track of which log files are associated with which distributions.

If no users access your content during a given hour, you don't receive any log files for that hour.

## Permissions Required to Configure Logging and to Access Your Log Files

Your AWS account must have the following permissions for the bucket that you specify for log files:

- The S3 access control list (ACL) for the bucket must grant you `FULL_CONTROL`. If you're the bucket owner, your account has this permission by default. If you're not, the bucket owner must update the ACL for the bucket.
- `s3:GetBucketAcl`
- `s3:PutBucketAcl`

Note the following:

### ACL for the bucket

When you create or update a distribution and enable logging, CloudFront uses these permissions to update the ACL for the bucket to give the awsdatafeeds account `FULL_CONTROL` permission. The awsdatafeeds account writes log files to the bucket. If your account doesn't have the required permissions, creating or updating the distribution will fail.

In some circumstances, if you programmatically submit a request to create a bucket but a bucket with the specified name already exists, S3 resets permissions on the bucket to the default value. If you configured CloudFront to save access logs in an S3 bucket and you stop getting logs in that bucket, check permissions on the bucket to ensure that CloudFront has the necessary permissions.

### Restoring the ACL for the bucket

If you remove permissions for the awsdatafeeds account, CloudFront won't be able to save logs to the S3 bucket. To enable CloudFront to start again to save logs for your distribution, restore the ACL permission by doing one of the following:

1. Disable logging for your distribution in CloudFront, and then enable it again. For more information, see Logging in the **Values That You Specify When You Create or Update a Web Distribution** topic.

2. Add the ACL permission for awsdatafeeds manually by navigating to the S3 bucket in the Amazon S3 console and adding permission. To add the ACL for awsdatafeeds, you must provide the canonical name for the account, which is the following:

   `c4c1ede66af53448b93c283ce9448c4ba468c9432aa01d700d3878632f77d2d0`

   For more information about adding ACLs to S3 buckets, see Setting ACL Bucket Permissions in the **Amazon Simple Storage Service Console User Guide**.

### ACL for each log file

In addition to the ACL on the bucket, there's an ACL on each log file. The bucket owner has `FULL_CONTROL` permission on each log file, the distribution owner (if different from the bucket owner) has no permission, and the awsdatafeeds account has read and write permissions.

### Disabling logging

If you disable logging, CloudFront doesn't delete the ACLs for either the bucket or the log files. If you want, you can do that yourself.

## File Name Format

The name of each log file that CloudFront saves in your Amazon S3 bucket uses the following file name format:

`bucket-name.s3.amazonaws.com/optional-prefix/distribution-ID.YYYY-MM-DD-HH.unique-ID.gz`

The date and time are in Coordinated Universal time (UTC).

For example, if your bucket name is `mylogs`, your prefix is `myprefix/`, and your distribution ID is `EMLARXS9EXAMPLE`, your file names look similar to this:

```
mylogs.s3.amazonaws.com/myprefix/EMLARXS9EXAMPLE.2014-11-14-20.RT4KCN4SGK9.gz
```

When you enable logging for a distribution, you can specify an optional prefix for the file names, so you can keep track of which log files are associated with which distributions. If you include a value for the log file prefix and your prefix doesn't include a /, CloudFront adds one automatically. If your value does include a /, CloudFront doesn't add another one.

The .gz at the end of the file name indicates that CloudFront has compressed the log file using gzip.

## Timing of Log File Delivery

CloudFront delivers access logs for a distribution up to several times an hour. In general, a log file contains information about the requests that CloudFront received during a given time period. CloudFront usually delivers the log file for that time period to your Amazon S3 bucket within an hour of the events that appear in the log. Note, however, that some or all log file entries for a time period can sometimes be delayed by up to 24 hours. When log entries are delayed, CloudFront saves them in a log file for which the file name includes the date and time of the period in which the requests occurred, not the date and time when the file was delivered.

When creating a log file, CloudFront consolidates information for your distribution from all of the edge locations that received requests for your objects during the time period that the log file covers.

CloudFront can save more than one file for a time period depending on how many requests CloudFront receives for the objects associated with a distribution.

CloudFront begins to reliably deliver access logs about four hours after you enable logging. You might get a few access logs before that time.

**Note**
If no users request your objects during the time period, you don't receive any log files for that period.

## Analyzing Access Logs

Because you can receive multiple access logs per hour, we recommend that you combine all the log files you receive for a given period into one file. You can then analyze the data for that period more quickly and accurately.

One way to analyze your access logs is to use Amazon Athena. Athena is an interactive query service that can help you analyze data for AWS services, including CloudFront. To learn more, see Querying Amazon CloudFront Logs in the Amazon Athena User Guide.

In addition, the following AWS blog posts discuss some ways to analyze access logs.

AWS Blog: Amazon CloudFront Request Logging (for content delivered via HTTP)

AWS Blog: Amazon CloudFront Now Supports Streaming Access Logs (for content delivered via RTMP)

AWS Blog: Enhanced CloudFront Logs, Now With Query Strings

**Important**
We recommend that you use the logs to understand the nature of the requests for your content, not as a complete accounting of all requests. CloudFront delivers access logs on a best-effort basis. The log entry for a particular request might be delivered long after the request was actually processed and, in rare cases, a log entry might not be delivered at all. When a log entry is omitted from access logs, the number of entries in the access logs won't match the usage that appears in the AWS usage and billing reports.

## Editing Your Logging Settings

You can enable or disable logging, change the Amazon S3 bucket where your logs are stored, and change the prefix for log files by using the CloudFront console or the CloudFront API. Your changes to logging settings take effect within 12 hours.

For more information, see the following topics:

- Updating a web or an RTMP distribution using the CloudFront console: Viewing and Updating CloudFront Distributions.
- Updating a web distribution using the CloudFront API: UpdateDistribution in the *Amazon CloudFront API Reference*.
- Updating an RTMP distribution using the CloudFront API: UpdateStreamingDistribution in the *Amazon CloudFront API Reference*.

To use the CloudFront API to change access log settings for web distributions, you must use the 2009-04-02 or later version of the API. To use the CloudFront API to change access log settings for RTMP distributions, you must use the 2010-05-01 or later version of the API.

## Deleting Log Files from an Amazon S3 Bucket

CloudFront does not automatically delete log files from your Amazon S3 bucket. For information about deleting log files from an Amazon S3 bucket, see the following topics:

- Using the Amazon S3 console: Deleting an Object in the *Amazon Simple Storage Service Console User Guide*.
- Using the REST API: DELETE Object in the *Amazon Simple Storage Service API Reference*.
- Using the SOAP API: DeleteObject in the *Amazon Simple Storage Service API Reference*.

## Log File Format

### Topics

- Web Distribution Log File Format
- RTMP Distribution Log File Format

Each entry in a log file gives details about a single user request. The log files for web and for RTMP distributions are not identical, but they share the following characteristics:

- Use the W3C extended log file format. (For more information, go to http://www.w3.org/TR/WD-logfile.html.)

- Contain tab-separated values.

- Contain records that are not necessarily in chronological order.

- Contain two header lines: one with the file-format version, and another that lists the W3C fields included in each record.

- Substitute URL-encoded equivalents for spaces and non-standard characters in field values.

  These non-standard characters consist of all ASCII codes below 32 and above 127, plus the characters in the following table. The URL encoding standard is RFC 1738. For more information, go to http://www.ietf.org/rfc/rfc1738.txt.

| URL-Encoded Value | Character |
| --- | --- |
| %3C | < |

| URL-Encoded Value | Character |
|---|---|
| %3E | > |
| %2522 | " |
| %23 | # |
| %25 | % |
| %7B | { |
| %7D | } |
| %7C | \| |
| %255C | \ |
| %5E | ^ |
| %7E | ~ |
| %5B | [ |
| %5D | ] |
| %60 | ` |
| %27 | ' |
| %2520 | space |

## Web Distribution Log File Format

The log file for a web distribution includes the following fields in the listed order.

| Field Number | Field Name | Description |
|---|---|---|
| 1 | date | The date on which the event occurred in the format yyyy-mm-dd, for example, 2015-06-30. The date and time are in Coordinated Universal Time (UTC). |
| 2 | time | The time when the Cloud-Front server finished responding to the request (in UTC), for example, 01:42:39. |
| 3 | x-edge-location | The edge location that served the request. Each edge location is identified by a three-letter code and an arbitrarily assigned number, for example, DFW3. The three-letter code typically corresponds with the International Air Transport Association airport code for an airport near the edge location. (These abbreviations might change in the future.) For a list of edge locations, see the Amazon CloudFront detail page, http://aws.amazon.com/cloudfront. |

| Field Number | Field Name | Description |
|---|---|---|
| 4 | sc-bytes | The total number of bytes that CloudFront served to the viewer in response to the request, including headers, for example, 1045619. |
| 5 | c-ip | The IP address of the viewer that made the request, for example, `192.0.2.183` or `2001:0 db8:85a3:0000:0000:8a2e :0370:7334`. If the viewer used an HTTP proxy or a load balancer to send the request, the value of `c-ip` is the IP address of the proxy or load balancer. See also `X-Forwarded-For` in field 20. |
| 6 | cs-method | The HTTP access method: DELETE, GET, HEAD, OPTIONS, PATCH, POST, or PUT. |
| 7 | cs(Host) | The domain name of the CloudFront distribution, for example, d111111abcdef8.cloud-front.net. |
| 8 | cs-uri-stem | The portion of the URI that identifies the path and object, for example, /images/daily-ad.jpg. |
| 9 | sc-status | One of the following values: [See the AWS documentation website for more details] |
| 10 | cs(Referer) | The name of the domain that originated the request. Common referrers include search engines, other websites that link directly to your objects, and your own website. |
| 11 | cs(User-Agent) | The value of the User-Agent header in the request. The User-Agent header identifies the source of the request, such as the type of device and browser that submitted the request and, if the request came from a search engine, which search engine. For more information, see User-Agent Header. |

| Field Number | Field Name | Description |
|---|---|---|
| 12 | cs-uri-query | The query string portion of the URI, if any. When a URI doesn't contain a query string, the value of `cs-uri-query` is a hyphen (-). For more information, see Configuring CloudFront to Cache Based on Query String Parameters. |
| 13 | cs(Cookie) | The cookie header in the request, including name-value pairs and the associated attributes. If you enable cookie logging, CloudFront logs the cookies in all requests regardless of which cookies you choose to forward to the origin: none, all, or a whitelist of cookie names. When a request doesn't include a cookie header, the value of `cs(Cookie)` is a hyphen (-). For more information about cookies, see Configuring CloudFront to Cache Objects Based on Cookies. |
| 14 | x-edge-result-type | How CloudFront classifies the response after the last byte left the edge location. In some cases, the result type can change between the time that CloudFront is ready to send the response and the time that CloudFront has finished sending the response. For example, in HTTP streaming, suppose CloudFront finds a segment in the edge cache. The value of `x-edge-response-result-type`, the result type immediately before CloudFront begins to respond to the request, is `Hit`. However, if the user closes the viewer before CloudFront has delivered the entire segment, the final result type—the value of `x-edge-result-type`—changes to `Error`. Possible values include: [See the AWS documentation website for more details] |

| Field Number | Field Name | Description |
|---|---|---|
| 15 | x-edge-request-id | An encrypted string that uniquely identifies a request. |
| 16 | x-host-header | The value that the viewer included in the `Host` header for this request. This is the domain name in the request: [See the AWS documentation website for more details] |
| 17 | cs-protocol | The protocol that the viewer specified in the request, either http or https. |
| 18 | cs-bytes | The number of bytes of data that the viewer included in the request (client to server bytes), including headers. |
| 19 | time-taken | The number of seconds (to the thousandth of a second, for example, 0.002) between the time that a CloudFront edge server receives a viewer's request and the time that CloudFront writes the last byte of the response to the edge server's output queue as measured on the server. From the perspective of the viewer, the total time to get the full object will be longer than this value due to network latency and TCP buffering. |
| 20 | x-forwarded-for | If the viewer used an HTTP proxy or a load balancer to send the request, the value of `c-ip` in field 5 is the IP address of the proxy or load balancer. In that case, `x-forwarded-for` is the IP address of the viewer that originated the request. If the viewer did not use an HTTP proxy or a load balancer, the value of `x-forwarded-for` is a hyphen (-). The `X-Forwarded-For` header contains IPv4 addresses (such as 192.0.2.44) and IPv6 addresses (such as 2001:0db8:85a3:0000:0000:8a2e:0370:7334), as applicable. |

| Field Number | Field Name | Description |
| --- | --- | --- |
| 21 | ssl-protocol | When `cs-protocol` in field 17 is `https`, the SSL protocol that the client and CloudFront negotiated for transmitting the request and response. When `cs-protocol` is `http`, the value for `ssl-protocol` is a hyphen (-). Possible values include the following: [See the AWS documentation website for more details] |
| 22 | ssl-cipher | When `cs-protocol` in field 17 is `https`, the SSL cipher that the client and CloudFront negotiated for encrypting the request and response. When `cs-protocol` is `http`, the value for `ssl-cipher` is a hyphen (-). Possible values include the following: [See the AWS documentation website for more details] |
| 23 | x-edge-response-result-type | How CloudFront classified the response just before returning the response to the viewer. See also `x-edge-result-type` in field 14. Possible values include: [See the AWS documentation website for more details] |
| 24 | cs-protocol-version | The HTTP version that the viewer specified in the request. Possible values include HTTP/0.9, HTTP/1.0, HTTP/1.1, and HTTP/2.0. |

| Field Number | Field Name | Description |
|---|---|---|
| 25 | fle-status | When field-level encryption is configured for a distribution, a code that indicates whether the request body was successfully processed. If field-level encryption is not configured for the distribution, the value of `fle-status` is a hyphen (-). When CloudFront successfully processes the request body, encrypts values in the specified fields, and forwards the request to the origin, the value of the `fle-status` column is `Processed`. The value of `x-edge-result-type`, column 14, can still indicate a client-side or server-side error. If the request exceeds a field-level encryption limit, `fle-status` contains one of the following error codes, and CloudFront returns HTTP status code 400 to the viewer. For a list of the current limits on field-level encryption, see Limits on Field-Level Encryption. [See the AWS documentation website for more details] Other possible values for fle-status include the following: [See the AWS documentation website for more details] |
| 26 | fle-encrypted-fields | The number of fields that CloudFront encrypted and forwarded to the origin. CloudFront streams the processed request to the origin as it encrypts data, so `fle-encrypted-fields` can have a value even if the value of `fle-status` is an error. If field-level encryption is not configured for the distribution, the value of `fle-encrypted-fields` is a hyphen (-). |

**Note**

Question marks (?) in URLs and query strings are not included in the log.

The following is an example log file for a web distribution:

```
1  #Version: 1.0
```

2 #Fields: date time x-edge-location sc-bytes c-ip cs-method cs(Host) cs-uri-stem sc-status cs(
      Referer) cs(User-Agent) cs-uri-query cs(Cookie) x-edge-result-type x-edge-request-id x-host-
      header cs-protocol cs-bytes time-taken x-forwarded-for ssl-protocol ssl-cipher x-edge-
      response-result-type cs-protocol-version fle-status fle-encrypted-fields
3 2014-05-23 01:13:11 FRA2 182 192.0.2.10 GET d111111abcdef8.cloudfront.net /view/my/file.html 200
      www.displaymyfiles.com Mozilla/4.0%20(compatible;%20MSIE%205.0b1;%20Mac_PowerPC) - zip
      =98101 RefreshHit MRVMF7KydIvxMWfJIglgwHQwZsbG2IhRJ07sn9AkKUFSHS9EXAMPLE== d111111abcdef8.
      cloudfront.net http - 0.001 - - - RefreshHit HTTP/1.1 Processed 1
4 2014-05-23 01:13:12 LAX1 2390282 192.0.2.202 GET d111111abcdef8.cloudfront.net /soundtrack/happy
      .mp3 304 www.unknownsingers.com Mozilla/4.0%20(compatible;%20MSIE%207.0;%20Windows%20NT
      %205.1) a=b&c=d zip=50158 Hit xGN7KWpVEmB9Dp7ctcVFQC4E-nrcOcEKS3QyAez--06dV7TEXAMPLE==
      d111111abcdef8.cloudfront.net http - 0.002 - - - Hit HTTP/1.1 - -

### RTMP Distribution Log File Format

Each record in an RTMP access log represents a playback event, for example, connect, play, pause, stop, disconnect, and so on. As a result, CloudFront generates multiple log records each time a viewer watches a video. To relate log records that stem from the same stream ID, use the x-sid field.

**Note**

Some fields have values for all events, and some have values only for Play, Stop, Pause, Unpause, and Seek events. Usually, when the log file contains a hyphen (-) for a field, the field isn't relevant for the corresponding event.

The following table describes the fields that are present in each record in the RTMP distribution log file, regardless of the type of event. The fields appear in the log in the order listed.

| Field Number | Field Name | Description |
| --- | --- | --- |
| 1 | date | The date on which the event occurred in the format yyyy-mm-dd, for example, 2014-05-23. The date and time are in Coordinated Universal Time (UTC). |
| 2 | time | The time when the server received the request (in UTC), for example, 01:42:39. |
| 3 | x-edge-location | The edge location where the playback event occurred. Each edge location is identified by a three-letter code and an arbitrarily assigned number, for example, DFW3. The three-letter code typically corresponds with the International Air Transport Association airport code for an airport near the edge location. (These abbreviations might change in the future.) For a list of edge locations, see the Amazon CloudFront detail page, http://aws.amazon.com/cloudfront. |

| Field Number | Field Name | Description |
|---|---|---|
| 4 | c-ip | Client IP, for example, 192.0.2.183. |
| 5 | x-event | The event type. This is a Connect, Disconnect, Play, Stop, Pause, Unpause, or Seek event. |
| 6 | sc-bytes | The running total number of bytes sent from the server to the client, up to the time of the event. |
| 7 | x-cf-status | A code indicating the status of the event. Currently, "OK" is the only value for this field. New functionality in the future could require new status codes. |
| 8 | x-cf-client-id | An opaque string identifier that can be used to differentiate clients. This value is unique for each connection. |
| 9 | cs-uri-stem | The stem portion of the URI, including the application and the application instance. This is sometimes referred to as the FMS connect string. For example, rtmp://shqshne4jdp4b6.cloudfront.net/cfx/st. |
| 10 | cs-uri-query | The query string portion of the URI that is included on the connect string. |
| 11 | c-referrer | The URI of the referrer. |
| 12 | x-page-url | The URL of the page from which the SWF is linked. |
| 13 | c-user-agent | The value of the User-Agent header in the request. The User-Agent header identifies the type of device that submitted the request. For more information, see User-Agent Header. |

The following fields usually have values only for Play, Stop, Pause, Unpause, and Seek events. For other events, they contain a single hyphen (-). These fields appear in the log after the fields in the preceding table and in the order listed.

| Field | Description |
|---|---|
| x-sname | The stream name. |
| x-sname-query | The stream query string, if any. |
| x-file-ext | The stream type, for example, FLV. |

| Field | Description |
|-------|-------------|
| x-sid | The stream ID. This is a unique integer identifier for the connection. |

**Note**

Question marks (?) in URLs and query strings are not included in the log.

The following is an example of a log file for an RTMP distribution:

```
1 #Version: 1.0
2 #Fields: date time x-edge-location c-ip x-event sc-bytes x-cf-status x-cf-client-id cs-uri-stem
      cs-uri-query c-referrer x-page-url c-user-agent x-sname x-sname-query x-file-ext x-sid
3 2010-03-12   23:51:20   SEA4    192.0.2.147    connect     2014    OK
      bfd8a98bee0840d9b871b7f6ade9908f     rtmp://shqshne4jdp4b6.cloudfront.net/cfx/st   key=value
         http://player.longtailvideo.com/player.swf   http://www.longtailvideo.com/support/jw-
      player-setup-wizard?example=204    LNX%2010,0,32,18    -    -    -    -
4 2010-03-12   23:51:21   SEA4    192.0.2.222    play    3914    OK
      bfd8a98bee0840d9b871b7f6ade9908f     rtmp://shqshne4jdp4b6.cloudfront.net/cfx/st   key=value
         http://player.longtailvideo.com/player.swf   http://www.longtailvideo.com/support/jw-
      player-setup-wizard?example=204    LNX%2010,0,32,18    myvideo    p=2&q=4    flv    1
5 2010-03-12   23:53:44   SEA4    192.0.2.4    stop    323914   OK
      bfd8a98bee0840d9b871b7f6ade9908f     rtmp://shqshne4jdp4b6.cloudfront.net/cfx/st   key=value
         http://player.longtailvideo.com/player.swf   http://www.longtailvideo.com/support/jw-
      player-setup-wizard?example=204    LNX%2010,0,32,18    dir/other/myvideo    p=2&q=4    flv
         1
6 2010-03-12   23:53:44   SEA4    192.0.2.103    play    8783724    OK
      bfd8a98bee0840d9b871b7f6ade9908f     rtmp://shqshne4jdp4b6.cloudfront.net/cfx/st   key=value
         http://player.longtailvideo.com/player.swf   http://www.longtailvideo.com/support/jw-
      player-setup-wizard?example=204    LNX%2010,0,32,18    dir/favs/myothervideo    p=42&q=14
      mp4    2
7 2010-03-12   23:56:21   SEA4    192.0.2.199    stop    429822014    OK
      bfd8a98bee0840d9b871b7f6ade9908f     rtmp://shqshne4jdp4b6.cloudfront.net/cfx/st   key=value
         http://player.longtailvideo.com/player.swf   http://www.longtailvideo.com/support/jw-
      player-setup-wizard?example=204    LNX%2010,0,32,18    dir/favs/myothervideo    p=42&q=14
      mp4    2
8 2010-03-12   23:59:44   SEA4    192.0.2.14   disconnect   429824092    OK
      bfd8a98bee0840d9b871b7f6ade9908f     rtmp://shqshne4jdp4b6.cloudfront.net/cfx/st   key=value
         http://player.longtailvideo.com/player.swf   http://www.longtailvideo.com/support/jw-
      player-setup-wizard?example=204    LNX%2010,0,32,18    -    -    -    -
```

## Charges for Access Logs

Access logging is an optional feature of CloudFront. There is no extra charge for enabling access logging. However, you accrue the usual Amazon S3 charges for storing and accessing the files on Amazon S3 (you can delete them at any time). For more information about charges for CloudFront, see CloudFront Reports.

# Monitoring CloudFront Activity Using CloudWatch

Amazon CloudFront integrates with Amazon CloudWatch metrics so that you can monitor your website or application. CloudFront currently provides six free metrics, and these metrics don't count against CloudWatch limits. When viewing metrics, you can specify a time interval of as little as one minute for time periods in the previous two weeks.

## Viewing Metrics for a Distribution

**To view metrics for a distribution in the CloudWatch console**

1. Sign in to the AWS Management Console and open the CloudFront console at https://console.aws.amazon. com/cloudfront/.

2. In the navigation pane, click **Monitoring and Alarms**.

3. In the **CloudFront Metrics and Alarms From CloudWatch** pane, specify the following values:
   **From and To**
   Select the date and time range for which you want to display CloudWatch metrics.
   **Granularity**
   Specify the interval of the data points, for example, one per minute or one per hour. Note that the time period that you choose affects the available granularity. For example, if you choose to view data for two weeks, the finest granularity is one hour, and if you choose to view data for 24 hours, the finest granularity is one minute.
   **Web Distribution**
   Select the distribution that you want to display metrics for.

4. Click **Update Graph** to refresh the graph based on the settings that you specified.

## Receiving Notifications

**To receive an Amazon Simple Notification Service (Amazon SNS) notification based on a Cloud-Front metric**

1. On the **CloudFront Metrics and Alarms From CloudWatch** page, expand the list of existing alarms to confirm that the alarm that you want to create doesn't already exist.

2. Click **Create Alarm**.

3. In the **Create Alarm** dialog box, specify the following values:
   **Metric**
   Choose the metric for which you want to create the alarm.
   **Distribution**
   Choose the CloudFront distribution for which you want to create the alarm.
   **Name of alarm**
   Enter a name for the alarm.
   **Send notification to**
   Choose the existing Amazon SNS topic that you want to send notification to if the status of this metric triggers an alarm.
   **Whenever metric *operator value***
   Specify when CloudWatch should trigger an alarm and send a notification to the specified email list. For example, to receive notification when the 5xx error rate exceeds 1%, you'd specify the following:
   **Whenever Average of 5xxErrorRate > 1**
   Note the following about specifying values for *value*:
   - Enter only whole numbers without punctuation. For example, to specify one thousand, enter **1000**.

- For 4xx, 5xx, and total error rates, the value that you specify is a percentage.
- For requests, bytes downloaded, and bytes uploaded, the value you specify is in units, for example, 1000000000 bytes.

**For at least** $x$ **consecutive periods of** *time period*

Specify how many consecutive time periods of the specified duration the metric must meet the criteria before CloudWatch sends notification. When you choose a value, you need to find an appropriate balance between a value that produces frequent notifications for fleeting problems and delayed notifications for real problems.

4. If you created a new Amazon SNS topic, when you click **Create**, Amazon SNS sends you an email with information about the new topic. Follow the instructions in the email.

## Downloading Data in CSV Format

You can download the CloudWatch Metrics report in CSV format. This section explains how to download the report and describes the values in the report.

**To download the CloudWatch Metrics report in CSV format**

1. While viewing the CloudWatch metrics, click **CSV**.

2. In the **Opening** *file name* dialog box, choose whether to open or save the file.

### Information About the Report

The first few rows of the report include the following information:

**Version**
The CloudFront reporting version.

**Report**
The name of the report.

**DistributionID**
The ID of the distribution that you ran the report for.

**StartDateUTC**
The beginning of the date range for which you ran the report, in Coordinated Universal Time (UTC).

**EndDateUTC**
The end of the date range for which you ran the report, in Coordinated Universal Time (UTC).

**GeneratedTimeUTC**
The date and time on which you ran the report, in Coordinated Universal Time (UTC).

**Granularity**
The time period for each row in the report, for example, ONE_MINUTE.

### Data in the CloudWatch Metrics Report

The report includes the following values:

**DistributionID**
The ID of the distribution that you ran the report for.

**FriendlyName**
An alternate domain name (CNAME) for the distribution, if any. If a distribution has no alternate domain names, the list includes an origin domain name for the distribution.

**TimeBucket**

The hour or the day that data applies to, in Coordinated Universal Time (UTC).

**Requests**

The total number of requests for all HTTP status codes (for example, 200 or 404) and all methods (for example, GET, HEAD, or POST) during the time period.

**BytesDownloaded**

The number of bytes that viewers downloaded for the specified distribution during the time period.

**BytesUploaded**

The number of bytes that viewers uploaded to your origin for the specified distribution during the time period.

**TotalErrorRatePct**

Requests for which the HTTP status code was a 4xx or 5xx error for the specified distribution during the time period.

**4xxErrorRatePct**

Requests for which the HTTP status code was a 4xx error for the specified distribution during the time period.

**5xxErrorRatePct**

Requests for which the HTTP status code was a 5xx error for the specified distribution during the time period.

## Amazon CloudFront Metrics

The `AWS/CloudFront` namespace includes the following metrics.

**Note**

Only one statistic, Average or Sum, is applicable for each metric. However, all statistics are available through the console, API, and AWS Command Line Interface. In the following table, each metric specifies the statistic that is applicable to that metric.

| Metric | Description |
|---|---|
| Requests | The number of requests for all HTTP methods and for both HTTP and HTTPS requests. Valid Statistics: Sum Units: None |
| BytesDownloaded | The number of bytes downloaded by viewers for `GET`, `HEAD`, and `OPTIONS` requests. Valid Statistics: Sum Units: None |
| BytesUploaded | The number of bytes uploaded to your origin with CloudFront using `POST` and `PUT` requests. Valid Statistics: Sum Units: None |
| TotalErrorRate | The percentage of all requests for which the HTTP status code is 4xx or 5xx. Valid Statistics: Average Units: Percent |
| 4xxErrorRate | The percentage of all requests for which the HTTP status code is 4xx. Valid Statistics: Average Units: Percent |
| 5xxErrorRate | The percentage of all requests for which the HTTP status code is 5xx. Valid Statistics: Average Units: Percent |

## Dimensions for CloudFront Metrics

CloudFront metrics use the CloudFront namespace and provide metrics for two dimensions:

| Dimension | Description |
| --- | --- |
| DistributionId | The CloudFront ID of the distribution for which you want to display metrics. |
| Region | The region for which you want to display metrics. This value must be Global. The Region dimension is different from the region in which CloudFront metrics are stored, which is US East (N. Virginia). |

# Using AWS CloudTrail to Capture Requests Sent to the CloudFront API

CloudFront is integrated with CloudTrail, an AWS service that captures information about every request that is sent to the CloudFront API by your AWS account, including your IAM users. CloudTrail periodically saves log files of these requests to an Amazon S3 bucket that you specify. CloudTrail captures information about all requests, whether they were made using the CloudFront console, the CloudFront API, the AWS SDKs, the CloudFront CLI, or another service, for example, AWS CloudFormation.

You can use information in the CloudTrail log files to determine which requests were made to CloudFront, the source IP address from which each request was made, who made the request, when it was made, and so on. To learn more about CloudTrail, including how to configure and enable it, see the *AWS CloudTrail User Guide*.

**Note**
CloudFront is a global service. To view CloudFront requests in CloudTrail logs, you must update an existing trail to include global services. For more information, see Updating a Trail and About Global Service Events in the *AWS CloudTrail User Guide*.

**Topics**

- CloudFront Information in CloudTrail Log Files
- Understanding CloudFront Log File Entries

## CloudFront Information in CloudTrail Log Files

When you enable CloudTrail, CloudTrail captures every request that you make to every AWS service that CloudTrail supports. (For a list of supported services, see Supported Services in the *AWS CloudTrail User Guide*.) The log files aren't organized or sorted by service; each log file might contain records from more than one service. CloudTrail determines when to create a new log file.

**Note**
CloudTrail supports all CloudFront API actions.

Every log file entry contains information about who made the request. The user identity information in the log file helps you determine whether the request was made using root or IAM user credentials, using temporary security credentials for a role or federated user, or by another AWS service. For more information, see userIdentity Element in the *AWS CloudTrail User Guide*.

You can store log files for as long as you want. You can also define Amazon S3 lifecycle rules to archive or delete log files automatically.

By default, your log files are encrypted by using Amazon S3 server-side encryption (SSE).

You can choose to have CloudTrail publish Amazon SNS notifications when new log files are delivered if you want to take quick action upon log file delivery. For more information, see Configuring Amazon SNS Notifications in the *AWS CloudTrail User Guide*.

You can also aggregate log files from multiple AWS regions and multiple AWS accounts into a single Amazon S3 bucket. For more information, see Aggregating CloudTrail Log Files to a Single Amazon S3 Bucket in the *AWS CloudTrail User Guide*.

## Understanding CloudFront Log File Entries

Each JSON-formatted CloudTrail log file can contain one or more log entries. A log entry represents a single request from any source and includes information about the requested action, including any parameters, the date and time of the action, and so on. The log entries are not guaranteed to be in any particular order; they are not an ordered stack trace of API calls.

The `eventName` element identifies the action that occurred and the API version that was used to perform that action. For example, the following `eventName` value indicates that a web distribution was updated, and the 2014-01-31 API version was used to perform the action:

`UpdateDistribution2014_01_31`

The following example shows a CloudTrail log entry that demonstrates five actions:

- Updating a web distribution configuration. The value of `eventName` is `UpdateDistribution`.
- Listing web distributions that are associated with the current account. The value of `eventName` is `ListDistributions`.
- Getting the configuration for a specific web distribution. The value of `eventName` is `GetDistribution`.
- Creating an invalidation batch request. The value of `eventName` is `CreateInvalidation`.
- Listing origin access identities that are associated with the current account. The value of `eventName` is `ListCloudFrontOriginAccessIdentities`.

```
1  {
2      "Records": [{
3          "eventVersion": "1.01",
4          "userIdentity": {
5              "type": "IAMUser",
6              "principalId": "A1B2C3D4E5F6G7EXAMPLE",
7              "arn": "arn:aws:iam::111122223333:user/smithj",
8              "accountId": "111122223333",
9              "accessKeyId": "AKIAIOSFODNN7EXAMPLE",
10             "userName": "smithj"
11         },
12         "eventTime": "2014-05-06T18:00:32Z",
13         "eventName": "UpdateDistribution2014_01_31",
14         "sourceIPAddress": "192.0.2.17",
15         "userAgent": "aws-sdk-ruby/1.39.0 ruby/1.9.3 x86_64-linux",
16         "requestParameters": {
17             "id": "EDFDVBD6EXAMPLE",
18             "ifMatch": "E9LHASXEXAMPLE",
19             "distributionConfig": {
20                 "restrictions": {
21                     "geoRestriction": {
22                         "quantity": 0,
23                         "restrictionType": "none"
24                     }
25                 },
26                 "customErrorResponses": {
27                     "quantity": 0
28                 },
29                 "defaultRootObject": "index.html",
30                 "aliases": {
31                     "quantity": 1,
32                     "items": ["example.com"]
33                 },
34                 "logging": {
35                     "bucket": "",
36                     "enabled": false,
37                     "prefix": "",
38                     "includeCookies": false
39                 },
40                 "viewerCertificate": {
41                     "iAMCertificateId": "A1B2C3D4E5F6G7EXAMPLE",
```

```
42        "sSLSupportMethod": "sni-only"
43      },
44      "callerReference": "2014-05-06 64832",
45      "defaultCacheBehavior": {
46          "targetOriginId": "Images",
47          "allowedMethods": {
48              "items": ["GET",
49              "HEAD"],
50              "quantity": 2
51          },
52          "forwardedValues": {
53              "cookies": {
54                  "forward": "none"
55              },
56              "queryString": false
57          },
58          "minTTL": 300,
59          "trustedSigners": {
60              "enabled": false,
61              "quantity": 0
62          },
63          "viewerProtocolPolicy": "redirect-to-https",
64          "smoothStreaming": false
65      },
66      "origins": {
67          "items": [{
68              "customOriginConfig": {
69                  "hTTPSPort": 443,
70                  "originProtocolPolicy": "http-only",
71                  "hTTPPort": 80
72              },
73              "domainName": "myawsbucket.s3-website-us-east-2.amazonaws.com",
74              "id": "Web page origin"
75          },
76          {
77              "customOriginConfig": {
78                  "hTTPSPort": 443,
79                  "originProtocolPolicy": "http-only",
80                  "hTTPPort": 80
81              },
82              "domainName": "myotherawsbucket.s3-website-us-west-2.amazonaws.com",
83              "id": "Images"
84          }],
85          "quantity": 2
86      },
87      "enabled": true,
88      "cacheBehaviors": {
89          "allowedMethods": {
90              "items": ["GET",
91              "HEAD"],
92              "quantity": 2
93          },
94          "trustedSigners": {
95              "enabled": false,
```

405

```
96                    "quantity": 0
97                  },
98                  "targetOriginId": "Web page origin",
99                  "smoothStreaming": false,
100                 "viewerProtocolPolicy": "redirect-to-https",
101                 "minTTL": 300,
102                 "forwardedValues": {
103                   "cookies": {
104                     "forward": "none"
105                   },
106                   "queryString": false
107                 },
108                 "pathPattern": "*.html"
109               }],
110               "quantity": 1
111             },
112             "priceClass": "PriceClass_All",
113             "comment": "Added an origin and a cache behavior"
114           }
115         },
116         "responseElements": {
117           "eTag": "E2QWRUHEXAMPLE",
118           "distribution": {
119             "domainName": "d111111abcdef8.cloudfront.net",
120             "status": "InProgress",
121             "distributionConfig": {
122             distributionConfig response omitted
123             },
124             "id": "EDFDVBD6EXAMPLE",
125             "lastModifiedTime": "May 6, 2014 6:00:32 PM",
126             "activeTrustedSigners": {
127               "quantity": 0,
128               "enabled": false
129             },
130             "inProgressInvalidationBatches": 0
131           }
132         },
133         "requestID": "4e6b66f9-d548-11e3-a8a9-73e33example",
134         "eventID": "5ab02562-0fc5-43d0-b7b6-90293example"
135       },
136       {
137         "eventVersion": "1.01",
138         "userIdentity": {
139           "type": "IAMUser",
140           "principalId": "A1B2C3D4E5F6G7EXAMPLE",
141           "arn": "arn:aws:iam::111122223333:user/smithj",
142           "accountId": "111122223333",
143           "accessKeyId": "AKIAIOSFODNN7EXAMPLE",
144           "userName": "smithj"
145         },
146         "eventTime": "2014-05-06T18:01:35Z",
147         "eventName": "ListDistributions2014_01_31",
148         "sourceIPAddress": "192.0.2.17",
149         "userAgent": "aws-sdk-ruby/1.39.0 ruby/1.9.3 x86_64-linux",
```

```
150        "requestParameters": null,
151        "responseElements": null,
152        "requestID": "52de9f97-d548-11e3-8fb9-4dad0example",
153        "eventID": "eb91f423-6dd3-4bb0-a148-3cdfbexample"
154    },
155    {
156        "eventVersion": "1.01",
157        "userIdentity": {
158            "type": "IAMUser",
159            "principalId": "A1B2C3D4E5F6G7EXAMPLE",
160            "arn": "arn:aws:iam::111122223333:user/smithj",
161            "accountId": "111122223333",
162            "accessKeyId": "AKIAIOSFODNN7EXAMPLE",
163            "userName": "smithj"
164        },
165        "eventTime": "2014-05-06T18:01:59Z",
166        "eventName": "GetDistribution2014_01_31",
167        "sourceIPAddress": "192.0.2.17",
168        "userAgent": "aws-sdk-ruby/1.39.0 ruby/1.9.3 x86_64-linux",
169        "requestParameters": {
170            "id": "EDFDVBD6EXAMPLE"
171        },
172        "responseElements": null,
173        "requestID": "497b3622-d548-11e3-8fb9-4dad0example",
174        "eventID": "c32289c7-005a-46f7-9801-cba41example"
175    },
176    {
177        "eventVersion": "1.01",
178        "userIdentity": {
179            "type": "IAMUser",
180            "principalId": "A1B2C3D4E5F6G7EXAMPLE",
181            "arn": "arn:aws:iam::111122223333:user/smithj",
182            "accountId": "111122223333",
183            "accessKeyId": "AKIAIOSFODNN7EXAMPLE",
184            "userName": "smithj"
185        },
186        "eventTime": "2014-05-06T18:02:27Z",
187        "eventName": "CreateInvalidation2014_01_31",
188        "sourceIPAddress": "192.0.2.17",
189        "userAgent": "aws-sdk-ruby/1.39.0 ruby/1.9.3 x86_64-linux",
190        "requestParameters": {
191            "invalidationBatch": {
192                "callerReference": "2014-05-06 64947",
193                "paths": {
194                    "quantity": 3,
195                    "items": ["/images/new.jpg",
196                    "/images/logo.jpg",
197                    "/images/banner.jpg"]
198                }
199            },
200            "distributionId": "EDFDVBD6EXAMPLE"
201        },
202        "responseElements": {
203            "invalidation": {
```

```
204            "createTime": "May 6, 2014 6:02:27 PM",
205            "invalidationBatch": {
206                "callerReference": "2014-05-06 64947",
207                "paths": {
208                    "quantity": 3,
209                    "items": ["/images/banner.jpg",
210                    "/images/logo.jpg",
211                    "/images/new.jpg"]
212                }
213            },
214            "status": "InProgress",
215            "id": "ISRZ85EXAMPLE"
216        },
217        "location": "https://cloudfront.amazonaws.com/2014-01-31/distribution/EDFDVBD6EXAMPLE/
                invalidation/ISRZ85EXAMPLE"
218        },
219        "requestID": "4e200613-d548-11e3-a8a9-73e33example",
220        "eventID": "191ebb93-66b7-4517-a741-92b0eexample"
221    },
222    {
223        "eventVersion": "1.01",
224        "userIdentity": {
225            "type": "IAMUser",
226            "principalId": "A1B2C3D4E5F6G7EXAMPLE",
227            "arn": "arn:aws:iam::111122223333:user/smithj",
228            "accountId": "111122223333",
229            "accessKeyId": "AKIAIOSFODNN7EXAMPLE",
230            "userName": "smithj"
231        },
232        "eventTime": "2014-05-06T18:03:08Z",
233        "eventName": "ListCloudFrontOriginAccessIdentities2014_01_31",
234        "sourceIPAddress": "192.0.2.17",
235        "userAgent": "aws-sdk-ruby/1.39.0 ruby/1.9.3 x86_64-linux",
236        "requestParameters": null,
237        "responseElements": null,
238        "requestID": "42ca4299-d548-11e3-8fb9-4dad0example",
239        "eventID": "7aeb434f-eb55-4e2a-82d8-417d5example"
240    }]
241 }
```

# Tagging Amazon CloudFront Distributions

Tags are words or phrases that you can use to identify and organize your AWS resources. You can add multiple tags to each resource, and each tag includes a key and a value that you define. For example, the key might be "domain" and the value might be "example.com". You can search and filter your resources based on the tags you add.

When you apply tags to CloudFront distributions or other AWS resources (such as Amazon EC2 instances or Amazon S3 buckets) and activate the tags, AWS generates a cost allocation report as a comma-separated value (CSV file) with your usage and costs aggregated by your active tags. You can apply tags that represent business categories (such as cost centers, application names, or owners) to organize your costs across multiple services. For more information about using tags for cost allocation, see Use Cost Allocation Tags in the AWS Billing and Cost Management User Guide.

For the current limit on the number of tags that you can add to a distribution, see Limits. To request a higher limit, create a case with the AWS Support Center.

Note the following:

- You can tag web and RTMP distributions, but you can't tag origin access identities or invalidations.
- Tag Editor and Resource Groups are currently not supported for CloudFront.

You can also apply tags to resources by using the CloudFront API, AWS CLI, SDKs, and AWS Tools for Windows PowerShell. For more information, see the following documentation:

- CloudFront API – See the following operations in the *Amazon CloudFront API Reference*:
  - ListTagsForResource
  - TagResource
  - UntagResource
- AWS CLI – See cloudfront in the *AWS CLI Command Reference*
- SDKs – See the applicable SDK documentation on the AWS Documentation page
- Tools for Windows PowerShell – See Amazon CloudFront in the AWS Tools for PowerShell Cmdlet Reference

**Topics**

- Tag Restrictions
- Adding, Editing, and Deleting Tags for Distributions

## Tag Restrictions

The following basic restrictions apply to tags:

- Maximum number of tags per resource – 10
- Maximum key length – 128 Unicode characters
- Maximum value length – 256 Unicode characters
- Valid values for key and value – a-z, A-Z, 0-9, space, and the following characters: _ . : / = + - and @
- Tag keys and values are case sensitive
- Don't use `aws:` as a prefix for keys; it's reserved for AWS use

## Adding, Editing, and Deleting Tags for Distributions

The following procedure explains how to add, edit, and delete tags for your distributions in the CloudFront console.

**To add tags, edit, or delete tags for a distribution**

1. Sign in to the AWS Management Console and open the CloudFront console at https://console.aws.amazon.com/cloudfront/.

2. Choose the ID for the distribution that you want to update.

3. Choose the **Tags** tab.

4. Choose **Add or edit tags**.

5. On the Add or edit tags page, you can do the following:
   **Add a tag**
   Enter a key and, optionally, a value for the tag.
   **Edit a tag**
   Change the key, the value, or both. You can also delete the value for a tag, but the key is required.
   **Delete a tag**
   Choose the **X** on the right side of the value field.

6. Choose Save.

# Troubleshooting

Troubleshoot common problems you might encounter with Amazon CloudFront and find possible solutions.

**Topics**

- Troubleshooting Distribution Issues
- Troubleshooting Error Responses from Your Origin

# Troubleshooting Distribution Issues

Use the information here to help you diagnose and fix access-denied issues or other common issues that you might encounter when working with Amazon CloudFront distributions.

## I Can't View the Files in My Web Distribution

If you can't view the files in your CloudFront web distribution, see the following topics for some common solutions.

### Did You Sign Up for Both CloudFront and Amazon S3?

To use Amazon CloudFront with an Amazon S3 origin, you must sign up for both CloudFront and Amazon S3, separately. For more information about signing up for CloudFront and Amazon S3, see Getting Started with CloudFront.

### Are Your Amazon S3 Bucket and Object Permissions Set Correctly?

If you are using CloudFront with an Amazon S3 origin, the original versions of your content are stored in an Amazon S3 bucket. The easiest way to use CloudFront with Amazon S3 is to make all your objects publicly readable in Amazon S3. To do this, you must explicitly enable public read privileges for each object that you upload to Amazon S3.

If your content is not publicly readable, you must create a CloudFront origin access identity so that CloudFront can access it. For more information about CloudFront origin access identities, see Using an Origin Access Identity to Restrict Access to Your Amazon S3 Content.

Object properties and bucket properties are independent. You must explicitly grant privileges to each object in Amazon S3. Objects do not inherit properties from buckets, and object properties must be set independently of the bucket.

### Is Your Alternate Domain Name (CNAME) Correctly Configured?

If you already have an existing CNAME record for your domain name, update that record or replace it with a new one that points to your distribution's domain name.

Also, make sure that your CNAME record points to your distribution's domain name, not your Amazon S3 bucket. You can confirm that the CNAME record in your DNS system points to your distribution's domain name. To do so, use a DNS tool like dig. For information about dig, see http://www.kloth.net/services/dig.php.

The following example shows a dig request for a domain name called `images.example.com` and the relevant part of the response. Under `ANSWER SECTION`, see the line that contains `CNAME`. The CNAME record for your domain name is set up correctly if the value on the right side of CNAME is your CloudFront distribution's domain name. If it's your Amazon S3 origin server bucket or some other domain name, then the CNAME record is set up incorrectly.

```
1  1.     [prompt]>
2  2.  dig images.example.com
3  3.
4  4.     ; <<>> DiG 9.3.3rc2 <<>> images.example.com
5  5.     ;; global options:  printcmd
6  6.     ;; Got answer:
7  7.     ;; ->>HEADER<<- opcode: QUERY, status: NOERROR, id: 15917
```

```
 8  8.        ;; flags: qr rd ra; QUERY: 1, ANSWER: 9, AUTHORITY: 2, ADDITIONAL: 0
 9  9.        ;; QUESTION SECTION:
10 10.        ;images.example.com.           IN     A
11 11.        ;; ANSWER SECTION:
12 12.        images.example.com. 10800 IN    CNAME    d111111abcdef8.cloudfront.net.
13 13.        ...
14 14.        ...
```

For more information about CNAMEs, see Adding and Moving Alternate Domain Names (CNAMEs).

**Are You Referencing the Correct URL for Your CloudFront Distribution?**

Make sure that the URL that you're referencing uses the domain name (or CNAME) of your CloudFront distribution, not your Amazon S3 bucket or custom origin.

**Do You Need Help Troubleshooting a Custom Origin?**

If you need AWS to help you troubleshoot a custom origin, we probably will need to inspect the `X-Amz-Cf-Id` header entries from your requests. If you are not already logging these entries, you might want to consider it for the future. For more information, see Using Amazon EC2 or Other Custom Origins. For further help, see the AWS Support Center.

## I Can't View the Files in My RTMP Distribution

If you can't view the files in your RTMP distribution, are your URL and your playback client correctly configured? RTMP distributions require you to use an RTMP protocol instead of HTTP, and you must make a few minor configuration changes to your playback client. For information about creating RTMP distributions, see Task List for Streaming Media Files Using RTMP.

## Error Message: Certificate: <certificate-id> Is Being Used by CloudFront

**Problem:** You're trying to delete an SSL/TLS certificate from the IAM certificate store, and you're getting the message "Certificate: <certificate-id> is being used by CloudFront."

**Solution:** Every CloudFront web distribution must be associated either with the default CloudFront certificate or with a custom SSL/TLS certificate. Before you can delete an SSL/TLS certificate, you must either rotate the certificate (replace the current custom SSL/TLS certificate with another custom SSL/TLS certificate) or revert from using a custom SSL/TLS certificate to using the default CloudFront certificate. To do that, perform the procedure in the applicable section:

- Rotating SSL/TLS Certificates
- Reverting from a Custom SSL/TLS Certificate to the Default CloudFront Certificate

# Troubleshooting Error Responses from Your Origin

If CloudFront requests an object from your Amazon S3 bucket or custom origin server and your origin returns an HTTP 4xx or 5xx status code, there's a problem with communication between CloudFront and your origin. The following sections describe common causes for selected HTTP status codes and provides some possible solutions.

**Topics**

- HTTP 502 Status Code (Bad Gateway)
- HTTP 503 Status Code (Service Unavailable)
- HTTP 504 Status Code (Gateway Timeout)

# HTTP 502 Status Code (Bad Gateway)

An HTTP 502 status code (Bad Gateway) indicates that CloudFront wasn't able to serve the requested object because it couldn't connect to the origin server.

**Topics**

- SSL/TLS Negotiation Failure Between CloudFront and a Custom Origin Server
- Origin Is Not Responding with Supported Ciphers/Protocols
- SSL/TLS Certificate on the Origin Is Expired, Invalid, Self-signed, or the Certificate Chain Is in the Wrong Order
- Origin Is Not Responding on Specified Ports in Origin Settings

## SSL/TLS Negotiation Failure Between CloudFront and a Custom Origin Server

If you use a custom origin and you configured CloudFront to require HTTPS between CloudFront and your origin, the problem might be mismatched domain names. The SSL/TLS certificate that is installed on your origin includes a domain name in the **Common Name** field and possibly several more in the **Subject Alternative Names** field. (CloudFront supports wildcard characters in certificate domain names.) One of the domain names in the certificate must match one or both of the following values:

- The value that you specified for **Origin Domain Name** for the applicable origin in your distribution.
- The value of the `Host` header if you configured CloudFront to forward the `Host` header to your origin. For more information about forwarding the `Host` header to your origin, see Configuring CloudFront to Cache Objects Based on Request Headers.

If the domain names don't match, the SSL/TLS handshake fails, and CloudFront returns an HTTP status code 502 (Bad Gateway) and sets the `X-Cache` header to `Error from cloudfront`.

To determine whether domain names in the certificate match the **Origin Domain Name** in the distribution or the `Host` header, you can use an online SSL checker or OpenSSL. If the domain names don't match, you have two options:

- Get a new SSL/TLS certificate that includes the applicable domain names.

  If you use AWS Certificate Manager (ACM), see Request a Certificate in the *AWS Certificate Manager User Guide* to request a new certificate.

- Change the distribution configuration so CloudFront no longer tries to use SSL to connect with your origin.

### Online SSL Checker

To find an SSL test tool, search the Internet for "online ssl checker." Typically, you specify the name of your domain, and the tool returns a variety of information about your SSL/TLS certificate. Confirm that the certificate contains your domain name in the **Common Names** or **Subject Alternative Names** fields.

### OpenSSL

To determine whether CloudFront is able to establish a connection with your origin, you can use OpenSSL to try to make an SSL/TLS connection to your origin and to verify that the certificate on your origin is correctly configured. If OpenSSL is able to make a connection, it returns information about the certificate on the origin server.

The command that you use depends on whether you use a client that supports SNI (Server Name Indication).

**Client supports SNI**

```
openssl s_client connect domainname:443 servername domainname
```

**Client doesn't support SNI**
```
openssl s_client connect domainname:443
```

Replace *domainname* with the applicable value:

- **If you aren't forwarding the Host header to the origin** – Replace *domainname* with your origin's domain name.
- **If you are forwarding the Host header to the origin** – Replace *domainname* with the CNAME that you're using with your CloudFront distribution.

## Origin Is Not Responding with Supported Ciphers/Protocols

CloudFront connects to origin servers using ciphers and protocols. For a list of the ciphers and protocols that CloudFront supports, see Supported Ciphers and Protocols. If your origin does not respond with one of these ciphers or protocols in the SSL/TLS exchange, CloudFront fails to connect. You can validate that your origin supports the ciphers and protocols by using SSL Labs:

- SSL Labs

  Type the domain name of your origin in the **Hostname** field, and then choose **Submit**. Review the **Common names** and **Alternative names** fields from the test to see if they match your origin's domain name.

  After the test is finished, find the **Protocols** and **Cipher Suites** sections in the test results to see which ciphers or protocols are supported by your origin. Compare them with the list of Supported Ciphers and Protocols.

**Note**
If you're using Elastic Load Balancing, see SSL Security Policies for Elastic Load Balancing in the *Elastic Load Balancing User Guide* to learn how to set the ciphers and protocols. Using the Predefined Security Policy *ELBSecurityPolicy-2016-08* gives CloudFrontaccess to your elastic load balancer. If you want to restrict it further using a custom policy, you must allow the ciphers that CloudFront supports.

## SSL/TLS Certificate on the Origin Is Expired, Invalid, Self-signed, or the Certificate Chain Is in the Wrong Order

If the origin server returns the following, CloudFront drops the TCP connection, returns HTTP status code 502 (Bad Gateway), and sets the X-Cache header to Error from cloudfront:

- An expired certificate
- Invalid certificate
- Self-signed certificate
- Certificate chain in the wrong order

**Note**
If the full chain of certificates, including the intermediate certificate, is not present, CloudFront drops the TCP connection.

For information about installing an SSL/TLS certificate on your custom origin server, see Requiring HTTPS for Communication Between CloudFront and Your Custom Origin.

## Origin Is Not Responding on Specified Ports in Origin Settings

When you create an origin on your CloudFront distribution, you can set the ports that CloudFront connects to the origin with for HTTP and HTTPS traffic. By default, these are TCP 80/443. You have the option to modify these ports. If your origin is rejecting traffic on these ports for any reason, or if your backend server isn't responding on the ports, CloudFront will fail to connect.

To troubleshoot these issues, check any firewalls running in your infrastructure and validate that they are not blocking the supported IP ranges. For more information, see AWS IP Address Ranges in the *Amazon Web Services General Reference*. Additionally, verify whether your web server is running on the origin.

# HTTP 503 Status Code (Service Unavailable)

An HTTP 503 status code (Service Unavailable) typically indicates a performance issue on the origin server. In rare cases, it indicates that CloudFront temporarily can't satisfy a request because of limited resources at an edge location.

**Topics**

- Origin Server Does Not Have Enough Capacity to Support the Request Rate
- CloudFront Was Not Able to Resolve Your Origin Domain Due to DNS Issues
- CloudFront Caused the Error Due to Limited Resources at the Edge Location
- Lambda Function Associated with Your Distribution is Invalid

## Origin Server Does Not Have Enough Capacity to Support the Request Rate

CloudFront generates this error when the origin server is overwhelmed with incoming requests. CloudFront then relays the error back to the user. To resolve this issue, try the following solutions:

- If you use Amazon S3 as your origin server, optimize the performance of Amazon S3 by following the best practices for key naming. For more information, see Request Rate and Performance Considerations in the *Amazon Simple Storage Service Developer Guide.*
- If you use Elastic Load Balancing as your origin server, see 503 Error Classic.
- If you use a custom origin, examine the application logs to ensure that your origin has sufficient resources, such as memory, CPU, and disk size. If you use Amazon EC2 as the backend, make sure that the instance type has the appropriate resources to fulfill the incoming requests. For more information, see Instance Types in the *Amazon EC2 User Guide for Linux Instances.*

## CloudFront Was Not Able to Resolve Your Origin Domain Due to DNS Issues

When CloudFront receives a request for an object that is expired or is not stored in its cache, it makes a request to the origin to get the updated object. To make a successful request to the origin, CloudFront performs a DNS resolution on the origin domain name. However, when the DNS service that hosts your domain is experiencing issues, CloudFront cannot resolve the domain name to get the IP address, resulting in a 503 error. To fix this issue, contact your DNS provider, or, if you are using Amazon Route 53, see Amazon Route 53 DNS.

To further troubleshoot this issue, ensure that the authoritative name servers of your origin's root domain or zone apex (such as `example.com`) are functioning correctly. Your authoritative name servers then receive the request and return the IP address that is associated with the domain, and are the same as the DNS servers that you used to set up your CloudFront distribution. Use the following commands to find the name servers for your apex origin:

```
1 dig OriginAPEXDomainName NS +short
2 nslookup -query=NS OriginAPEXDomainName
```

When you have the names of your name servers, use the following commands to query the domain name of your origin against them to make sure that each responds with an answer:

```
1 dig OriginDomainName @NameServerFromAbove
2 nslookup OriginDomainName NameServerFromAbove
```

## CloudFront Caused the Error Due to Limited Resources at the Edge Location

You will receive this error in the rare situation that CloudFront can't route requests to the next best available edge location, and so can't satisfy a request. This error is common when you perform load testing on your

CloudFront distribution. To help prevent this, follow the Load Testing CloudFront guidelines for avoiding 503 (Capacity Exceeded) errors.

If this happens in your production environment, contact AWS Support.

## Lambda Function Associated with Your Distribution is Invalid

CloudFront returns this error when a Lambda@Edge function that is configured on a cache behavior for your distribution returns an error during runtime and exits before the CloudFront request is fulfilled.

To troubleshoot this issue, examine the execution logs for your Lambda function. Make sure you look at the log files in the region where the function executed. For more information, see CloudWatch Metrics and CloudWatch Logs for Lambda Functions.

# HTTP 504 Status Code (Gateway Timeout)

An HTTP 504 status code (Gateway Timeout) indicates that when CloudFront forwarded a request to the origin (because the requested object wasn't in the edge cache), one of the following happened:

- The origin returned an HTTP 504 status code to CloudFront.
- The origin didn't respond before the request expired.

An origin will return an HTTP 504 status code if CloudFront traffic is blocked to the origin by a firewall or security group, or if the origin isn't accessible on the internet. Check for those issues first. Then, if access isn't the problem, explore application delays and server timeouts to help you identify and fix the issues.

**Topics**

- Configure the Firewall on Your Origin Server to Allow CloudFront Traffic
- Configure the Security Groups on Your Origin Server to Allow CloudFront Traffic
- Make Your Custom Origin Server Accessible on the Internet
- Find and Fix Delayed Responses from Applications on Your Origin Server

## Configure the Firewall on Your Origin Server to Allow CloudFront Traffic

If the firewall on your origin server blocks CloudFront traffic, CloudFront returns an HTTP 504 status code, so it's good to make sure that isn't the issue before checking for other problems.

The method that you use to determine if this is an issue with your firewall depends on what system your origin server uses:

- If you use an IPTable firewall on a Linux server, you can search for tools and information to help you work with IPTables.
- If you use Windows Firewall on a Windows server, see Add or Edit Firewall Rule on Microsoft Technet.

When you evaluate the firewall configuration on your origin server, look for any firewalls or security rules that block traffic from CloudFront edge locations, based on the published IP address range.

If the CloudFront IP address range is whitelisted on your origin server, make sure to update your server's security rules to incorporate changes. You can subscribe to an Amazon Simple Notification Service (SNS) topic and receive notifications when the IP address range file is updated. After you receive the notification, you can use code to retrieve the file, parse it, and make adjustments for your local environment." For more information, see Subscribe to AWS Public IP Address Changes via Amazon SNS.

## Configure the Security Groups on Your Origin Server to Allow CloudFront Traffic

If your origin uses Elastic Load Balancing, review the ELB security groups and make sure that the security groups allow inbound traffic from CloudFront.

You can also use AWS Lambda to automatically update your security groups to allow inbound traffic from CloudFront.

## Make Your Custom Origin Server Accessible on the Internet

If CloudFront can't access your custom origin server because it isn't publicly available on the internet, CloudFront returns an HTTP 504 error.

CloudFront edge locations connect to origin servers through the internet. If your custom origin is on a private network, CloudFront can't reach it. Because of this, you can't use private servers, including internal Classic Load Balancers, as origin servers with CloudFront.

To check that internet traffic can connect to your origin server, run the following commands (where OriginDomainName is the domain name for your server):

For HTTPS traffic:

- nc -zv OriginDomainName 443
- telnet OriginDomainName 443

For HTTP traffic:

- nc -zv OriginDomainName 80
- telnet OriginDomainName 80

## Find and Fix Delayed Responses from Applications on Your Origin Server

Server timeouts are often the result of either an application taking a very long time to respond, or a timeout value that is set too low.

A quick fix to help avoid HTTP 504 errors is to simply set a higher CloudFront timeout value for your distribution. But we recommend that you first make sure that you address any performance and latency issues with the application and origin server. Then you can set a reasonable timeout value that helps prevent HTTP 504 errors and provides good responsiveness to users.

Here's an overview of the steps you can take to find performance issues and correct them:

1. Measure the typical and high-load latency (responsiveness) of your web application.

2. Add additional resources, such as CPU or memory, if needed. Take other steps to address issues, such as tuning database queries to accommodate high-load scenarios.

3. If needed, adjust the timeout value for your CloudFront web distribution.

Following are details about each step.

### Measure typical and high-load latency

To determine if one or more backend web application servers are experiencing high latency, run the following Linux curl command on each server:

```
curl -w "Connect time: %{time_connect} Time to first byte: %{time_starttransfer} Total time:
 %{time_total} \n" -o /dev/null https://www.example.com/yourobject
```

**Note**
If you run Windows on your servers, you can search for and download curl for Windows to run a similar command.

As you measure and evaluate the latency of an application that runs on your server, keep in mind the following:

- Latency values are relative to each application. However, a Time to First Byte in milliseconds rather than seconds or more, is reasonable.

- If you measure the application latency under normal load and it's fine, be aware that viewers might still experience timeouts under high load. When there is high demand, servers can have delayed responses or not respond at all. To help prevent high-load latency issues, check your server's resources such as CPU, memory, and disk reads and writes to make sure that your servers have the capacity to scale for high load.

  You can run the following Linux command to check the memory that is used by Apache processes:

  ```
  watch -n 1 "echo -n 'Apache Processes: ' && ps -C apache2 --no-headers | wc -l && free
  -m"
  ```

- High CPU utilization on the server can significantly reduce an application's performance. If you use an Amazon EC2 instance for your backend server, review the CloudWatch metrics for the server to check the CPU utilization. For more information, see the Amazon CloudWatch User Guide. Or if you're using your own server, refer to the server Help documentation for instructions on how to check CPU utilization.

- Check for other potential issues under high loads, such as database queries that run slowly when there's a high volume of requests.

### Add resources, and tune servers and databases

After you evaluate the responsiveness of your applications and servers, make sure that you have sufficient resources in place for typical traffic and high load situations:

- If you have your own server, make sure it has enough CPU, memory, and disk space to handle viewer requests, based on your evaluation.
- If you use an Amazon EC2 instance as your backend server, make sure that the instance type has the appropriate resources to fulfill incoming requests. For more information, see Instance Types in the Amazon EC2 User Guide.

In addition, consider the following tuning steps to help avoid timeouts:

- If the Time to First Byte value that is returned by the curl command seems high, take steps to improve the performance of your application. Improving application responsiveness will in turn help reduce timeout errors.
- Tune database queries to make sure that they can handle high request volumes without slow performance.
- Set up keep-alive (persistent) connections on your backend server. This option helps to avoid latencies that occur when connections must be re-established for subsequent requests or users.
- If you use ELB as your origin, learn how you can reduce latency by reviewing the suggestions in the following Knowledge Center article: How to troubleshoot ELB high latency.

### If needed, adjust the CloudFront timeout value

If you have evaluated and addressed slow application performance, origin server capacity, and other issues, but viewers are still experiencing HTTP 504 errors, then you should consider changing the time that is specified in your web distribution for origin response timeout. To learn more, see Origin Response Timeout.

# Load Testing CloudFront

Traditional load testing methods don't work well with CloudFront because CloudFront uses DNS to balance loads across geographically dispersed edge locations and within each edge location. When a client requests content from CloudFront, the client receives a DNS response that includes a set of IP addresses. If you test by sending requests to just one of the IP addresses that DNS returns, you're testing only a small subset of the resources in one CloudFront edge location, which doesn't accurately represent actual traffic patterns. Depending on the volume of data requested, testing in this way may overload and degrade the performance of that small subset of CloudFront servers.

CloudFront is designed to scale for viewers that have different client IP addresses and different DNS resolvers across multiple geographic regions. To perform load testing that accurately assesses CloudFront performance, we recommend that you do all of the following:

- Send client requests from multiple geographic regions.
- Configure your test so each client makes an independent DNS request; each client will then receive a different set of IP addresses from DNS.
- For each client that is making requests, spread your client requests across the set of IP addresses that are returned by DNS, which ensures that the load is distributed across multiple servers in a CloudFront edge location.

# CloudFront Streaming Tutorials

For information about using CloudFront for live streaming and on-demand streaming, see Configuring Video Streaming Web Distributions.

## RTMP Streaming

- On-Demand Video Streaming Using CloudFront and JW Player

# On-Demand Video Streaming Using CloudFront and JW Player

When you stream media files using CloudFront, you provide both your media file and the media player with which you want end users to play the media file. To use the JW Player media player to stream media files with CloudFront, perform the procedures in the following topics:

1. Uploading Media and JW Player Files to an Amazon S3 Bucket

2. Creating CloudFront Web and RTMP Distributions

3. Embedding Video in a Web Page

4. Uploading the HTML File and Playing the Video

This tutorial is based on the free edition of JW Player version 7.3. For more information about JW Player, go to the JW Player website.

For more information about streaming media using CloudFront, see Working with RTMP Distributions.

## Uploading Media and JW Player Files to an Amazon S3 Bucket

You can upload your media files and your media player files to the same Amazon S3 bucket or to separate buckets. For this tutorial, you'll upload an .mp4 or .flv media file and the JW Player media player files to the same bucket.

**To upload media and JW Player files to an Amazon S3 bucket**

1. If you don't already have the files for the JW Player media player, download the player (JW Player 7) from the Downloads page on the JW Player website. Then extract the contents of the .zip file.

2. Sign in to the AWS Management Console and open the Amazon S3 console at https://console.aws.amazon.com/s3/.

3. In the Amazon S3 console, choose **Create Bucket**.

4. In the **Create Bucket** dialog, enter a bucket name. **Important**
   For your bucket to work with CloudFront, the name must conform to DNS naming requirements. For more information, go to Bucket Restrictions and Limitations in the *Amazon Simple Storage Service Developer Guide*.

5. Select a region for your bucket. By default, Amazon S3 creates buckets in the US Standard region. We recommend that you choose a region close to you to optimize latency, minimize costs, or to address regulatory requirements.

6. Choose **Create**.

7. Select your bucket in the **Buckets** pane, and choose **Upload**.

8. On the **Upload - Select Files** page, choose **Add Files**, and add the following files:

   - jwplayer.flash.swf
   - jwplayer.js
   - Your .mp4 or .flv media file.

9. Grant public read permissions for the files that you added in the previous step.

   1. Choose **Set Details**.

   2. On the **Set Details** page, choose **Set Permissions**.

   3. On the **Set Permissions** page, choose **Make everything public**.

10. Choose **Start Upload**.

## Creating CloudFront Web and RTMP Distributions

To configure CloudFront to stream a media file, you need a CloudFront web distribution for the JW Player files and an HTML file, and an RTMP distribution for the media file. Perform the following two procedures to create a web distribution and an RTMP distribution.

**To create a CloudFront web distribution for your JW Player files**

1. Open the CloudFront console at https://console.aws.amazon.com/cloudfront/.

2. Choose **Create Distribution**.

3. On the first page of the **Create Distribution Wizard**, in the **Web** section, choose **Get Started**.

4. On the second page of the wizard, choose in the **Origin Domain Name** field, and select the Amazon S3 bucket that you created in the procedure To upload media and JW Player files to an Amazon S3 bucket. If you have a lot of Amazon S3 buckets, you can type the first few characters of the bucket name to filter the list.

5. Accept the default values for the remaining fields, and choose **Create Distribution**.

6. After CloudFront creates your distribution, the value of the **Status** column for your distribution will change from **InProgress** to **Deployed**. This should take less than 15 minutes.

   The domain name that CloudFront assigns to your distribution appears in the list of distributions. The domain name also appears on the Distribution Settings page for a selected distribution.)

**To create a CloudFront RTMP distribution for your media file**

1. In the CloudFront console, choose **Create Distribution**.

2. In the **Create Distribution Wizard**, in the **RTMP** section, choose **Get Started**.

3. On the second page of the wizard, choose in the **Origin Domain Name** field, and select the Amazon S3 bucket that you created in the procedure To upload media and JW Player files to an Amazon S3 bucket. If you have a lot of Amazon S3 buckets, you can type the first few characters of the bucket name to filter the list.

4. Accept the default values for the remaining fields on the **Create Distribution** page, and choose **Create Distribution**.

5. After CloudFront creates your distribution, the value of the **Status** column for your distribution will change from **InProgress** to **Deployed**. This should take less than 15 minutes.

   The domain name that CloudFront assigns to your distribution appears in the list of distributions. The domain name also appears on the Distribution Settings page for a selected distribution.

## Embedding Video in a Web Page

The following example shows you how to embed a video in a web page using the web and RTMP distributions that you created in Creating CloudFront Web and RTMP Distributions.

Perform the following steps:

1. Sign in to the JW Player website. If you don't already have a JW Player account, create one.

2. On the Downloads page, get the license key for the player that you downloaded earlier in this tutorial.

3. Copy the HTML code below, and paste it into a text editor.

4. Review the comments in the HTML file, and replace the following placeholders with the applicable values:

- WEB-DISTRIBUTION-DOMAIN-NAME
- RTMP-DISTRIBUTION-DOMAIN-NAME
- VIDEO-FILE-NAME
- LICENSE-KEY

5. Save the file with a .html filename extension, for example, jwplayer-example.html.

```html
1  <HTML>
2  <HEAD>
3  <TITLE>Amazon CloudFront Streaming with JW Player 7</TITLE>
4
5  <!-- Call the JW Player JavaScript file, jwplayer.js.
6  Replace WEB-DISTRIBUTION-DOMAIN-NAME with the domain name of your
7  CloudFront web distribution, for example, d1234.cloudfront.net
8  (begins with "d"). This causes a browser to download the JW Player file
9  before streaming begins.
10
11 Replace LICENSE-KEY with your personal license key from JW Player.
12 -->
13
14 <script type='text/javascript' src='WEB-DISTRIBUTION-NAME/jwplayer.js'></script>
15 <script type='text/javascript' src='WEB-DISTRIBUTION-NAME/jwplayer.flash.swf'></script>
16 <script>jwplayer.key="LICENSE-KEY";</script>
17
18 </HEAD>
19
20 <BODY>
21 <H1>This video is streamed by CloudFront and played by JW Player 7.</H1>
22
23 <!-- Replace RTMP-DISTRIBUTION-DOMAIN-NAME with the domain name of your
24 RTMP distribution, for example, s5678.cloudfront.net (begins with "s").
25
26 Replace VIDEO-FILE-NAME with the name of your .mp4 or .flv video file,
27 including the .mp4 or .flv filename extension. For example, if you uploaded
28 my-vacation.mp4, enter my-vacation.mp4. You might need to prepend "mp4:" to the
29 name of your video file, for example, mp4:my-vacation.mp4.
30
31 If the file is in a subdirectory, include the subdirectory name just before
32 the file name, for example:
33
34 "rtmp://RTMP-DISTRIBUTION-DOMAIN-NAME/cfx/st/sample-directory/VIDEO-FILE-NAME"
35 -->
36
37
38 <div id="my-video"></div>
39 <script type="text/javascript">
40 jwplayer("my-video").setup({
41  'file': 'rtmp://RTMP-DISTRIBUTION-DOMAIN-NAME/cfx/st/VIDEO-FILE-NAME',
42  'width': '720',
43  'height': '480',
44  'primary': 'flash',
45  'autostart': 'true'
46 });
47 </script>
```

```
48
49 </BODY>
50 </HTML>
```

## Uploading the HTML File and Playing the Video

To play the video using the HTML file that you created in Embedding Video in a Web Page, upload the file to your Amazon S3 bucket, and use the URL for your CloudFront distribution.

**To upload the HTML file and play the video**

1. Open the Amazon S3 console at https://console.aws.amazon.com/s3/.

2. Select your bucket, and choose **Upload**.

3. On the **Upload - Select Files** page, choose **Add Files**, and add your HTML file.

4. Grant public read permissions for the HTML file that you added in the previous step.

    1. Choose **Set Details**.

    2. On the **Set Details** page, choose **Set Permissions**.

    3. On the **Set Permissions** page, choose **Make everything public**.

5. Choose **Start Upload**.

6. To play the video, enter the following URL in a web browser:

    ```
    http://domain name of your CloudFront web distribution/your HTML file name
    ```

# Limits

CloudFront entities have the following limits. Note that Lambda@Edge has specific limits as well, that are in addition to the default CloudFront limits.

**Topics**

- General Limits
- General Limits on Web Distributions
- Limits on Whitelisted Cookies (Web Distributions Only)
- Limits on Whitelisted Query Strings (Web Distributions Only)
- Limits on Custom Headers (Web Distributions Only)
- Limits on SSL Certificates (Web Distributions Only)
- Limits on Invalidations
- Limits on Field-Level Encryption
- Limits on Lambda@Edge
- Limits on RTMP Distributions

## General Limits

| Entity | Limit |
| --- | --- |
| Data transfer rate per distribution | 40 Gbps Request a higher limit |
| Requests per second per distribution | 100,000 Request a higher limit |
| Tags that can be added to a CloudFront web or RTMP distribution | 50 |
| Objects that you can serve per distribution | Unlimited |
| Maximum length of a request, including headers and query strings | 20,480 bytes |
| Maximum length of a URL | 8,192 bytes |
| Active CloudFront key pairs for trusted signers For more information, see Specifying the AWS Accounts That Can Create Signed URLs and Signed Cookies (Trusted Signers). | 2 |

## General Limits on Web Distributions

| Entity | Limit |
| --- | --- |
| Web distributions per AWS account For more information, see Working with Web Distributions. | 200 Request a higher limit |
| Maximum file size for HTTP GET, POST, and PUT requests | 20 GB |
| Response timeout per origin For more information, see Origin Response Timeout (Amazon EC2, Elastic Load Balancing, and Other Custom Origins Only). | 4-60 seconds Request a higher limit |

| Entity | Limit |
|---|---|
| File compression: range of file sizes that CloudFront compresses For more information, see Serving Compressed Files. | 1,000 to 10,000,000 bytes |
| Alternate domain names (CNAMEs) per distribution For more information, see Adding and Moving Alternate Domain Names (CNAMEs). | 100 Request a higher limit |
| Origins per distribution | 25 Request a higher limit |
| Cache behaviors per distribution | 25 Request a higher limit |

## Limits on Whitelisted Cookies (Web Distributions Only)

| Entity | Limit |
|---|---|
| Whitelisted cookies per cache behavior For more information, see Configuring Cloud- Front to Cache Objects Based on Cookies. | 10 Request a higher limit |
| Total number of bytes in whitelisted cookie names (doesn't apply if you configure Cloud- Front to forward all cookies to the origin) | 512 minus the number of whitelisted cookies |

## Limits on Whitelisted Query Strings (Web Distributions Only)

| Entity | Limit |
|---|---|
| Maximum number of characters in a whitelisted query string | 128 characters |
| Maximum number of characters total for all whitelisted query strings in the same parame- ter | 512 characters |
| Whitelisted query strings per cache behav- ior For more information, see Configuring CloudFront to Cache Based on Query String Parameters. | 10 Request a higher limit |

## Limits on Custom Headers (Web Distributions Only)

| Entity | Limit |
|---|---|
| Whitelisted headers per cache behavior For more information, see Configuring Cloud- Front to Cache Objects Based on Request Headers. | 10 Request a higher limit |

| Entity | Limit |
|---|---|
| Custom headers: maximum number of custom headers that you can configure CloudFront to forward to the origin For more information, see Forwarding Custom Headers to Your Origin (Web Distributions Only). | 10 name/value pairs Request a higher limit |
| Custom headers: maximum length of a header name | 256 characters |
| Custom headers: maximum length of a header value | 1,783 characters |
| Custom headers: maximum length of all header values and names combined | 10,240 characters |

## Limits on SSL Certificates (Web Distributions Only)

| Entity | Limit |
|---|---|
| SSL certificates per AWS account when serving HTTPS requests using dedicated IP addresses (no limit when serving HTTPS requests using SNI) For more information, see Using HTTPS with CloudFront. | 2 Request a higher limit |
| SSL certificates that can be associated with a CloudFront web distribution | 1 |

## Limits on Invalidations

| Entity | Limit |
|---|---|
| Object invalidation: maximum number of objects allowed in active invalidation requests, excluding wildcard invalidations For more information, see Invalidating Objects (Web Distributions Only). | 3,000 |
| Object invalidation: maximum number of active wildcard invalidations allowed | 15 |
| Object invalidation: maximum number of objects that one wildcard invalidation can process | Unlimited |

## Limits on Field-Level Encryption

| Entity | Limit |
| --- | --- |
| Maximum length of a field to encrypt For more information, see Using Field-Level Encryption to Help Protect Sensitive Data. | 16 KB |
| Maximum number of fields in a request body when field-level encryption encryption is configured | 10 |
| Maximum length of a request body when field-level encryption is configured | 1 MB |
| Maximum number of field-level encryption configurations that can be associated with one AWS account | 10 |
| Maximum number of field-level encryption profiles that can be associated with one AWS account | 10 |
| Maximum number of public keys that can be added to one AWS account | 10 |
| Maximum number of fields to encrypt that can be specified in one profile | 10 |
| Maximum number of CloudFront distributions that can be associated with a field-level encryption configuration | 20 |
| Maximum number of query argument profile mappings that can be included in a field-level encryption configuration | 5 |

## Limits on Lambda@Edge

The limits in this section apply to Lambda@Edge. These limits are in addition to the default CloudFront and Lambda limits, which also apply. See the default Lambda limits in the Limits section of the *AWS Lambda Developer Guide.*

**Note**
Lambda dynamically scales capacity in response to increased traffic, within your account's limits. For more information, see the Scaling section of the *AWS Lambda Developer Guide.*

In addition, be aware that there are some other restrictions when using Lambda@Edge functions. For more information, see Requirements and Restrictions on Lambda Functions.

**Limits that differ by event-type**

| Entity | Origin request and response event limits | Viewer request and response event limits |
| --- | --- | --- |
| Function resource allocation | Same as Lambda limits | 128 MB |
| Function timeout. The function can make network calls to resources such as Amazon S3 buckets, DynamoDB tables, or Amazon EC2 instances in AWS Regions. | 30 seconds | 5 seconds |
| Size of a response that is generated by a Lambda function, including headers and body | 1 MB | 40 KB |

| Entity | Origin request and response event limits | Viewer request and response event limits |
|---|---|---|
| Maximum compressed size of a Lambda function and any included libraries | 50 MB | 1 MB |

## Other limits

| Entity | Limit |
|---|---|
| Distributions per AWS account that you can create triggers for | 25 Request a higher limit |
| Triggers per distribution | 25 Request a higher limit |
| Requests per second | 10,000 (in each region) Request a higher limit |
| Concurrent executions For more information, see Lambda Function Concurrent Executions in the *AWS Lambda Developer Guide*. | 1000 (in each region) Request a higher limit |

## Limits on RTMP Distributions

| Entity | Limit |
|---|---|
| RTMP distributions per AWS account For more information, see Working with RTMP Distributions. | 100 Request a higher limit |

# Amazon CloudFront Resources

Although fairly simple to use, CloudFront is rich in functionality. The resources listed here can help you learn more about CloudFront.

**Topics**

- Additional Amazon CloudFront Documentation
- Getting Support
- CloudFront Developer Tools and SDKs
- Tips from the Amazon Web Services Blog
- Invalidating Objects
- Tools and Code Examples for Configuring Private Content

## Additional Amazon CloudFront Documentation

The following related resources can help you as you work with this service.

- Amazon CloudFront API Reference – Gives complete descriptions of the API actions, parameters, and data types, and a list of errors that the service returns.
- CloudFront What's New – Announcements of new CloudFront features and recently added edge locations.
- Technical documentation for the Amazon Simple Storage Service (S3) – A detailed discussion of the Amazon S3 service, including the basics of getting started, an overview of the service, a programming reference, and an API reference.
- Amazon CloudFront product information – The primary web page for information about CloudFront, including features and pricing information.
- Terms of Use – Detailed information about our copyright and trademark; your account, license, and site access; and other topics.

## Getting Support

Support for CloudFront is available in a number of forms.

- Discussion forums – A community-based forum for developers to discuss technical questions related to CloudFront.
- AWS Support Center – This site brings together information about your recent support cases and results from AWS Trusted Advisor and health checks, as well as providing links to discussion forums, technical FAQs, the service health dashboard, and information about AWS support plans.
- AWS Premium Support Information – The primary web page for information about AWS Premium Support, a one-on-one, fast-response support channel to help you build and run applications on AWS Infrastructure Services.
- Contact Us – Links for inquiring about your billing or account. For technical questions, use the discussion forums or support links above.

## CloudFront Developer Tools and SDKs

See the Developer Tools page for links to developer resources that provide documentation, code samples, release notes, and other information to help you build innovative applications with AWS.

In addition, Amazon Web Services provides software development kits for accessing CloudFront programmatically. The SDK libraries automate a number of common tasks, including cryptographically signing your service requests, retrying requests, and handling error responses.

- AWS SDK for Java – Setup and other documentation

- AWS SDK for .NET – Setup and other documentation
- AWS SDK for PHP – Setup and other documentation
- AWS SDK for Ruby – Setup and other documentation

## Tips from the Amazon Web Services Blog

The AWS Blog has a number of posts to help you use CloudFront. For example, see the following blog posts about using Drupal and WordPress with CloudFront.

- Accelerating your Drupal Content with Amazon CloudFront
- How to accelerate your WordPress site with Amazon CloudFront

## Invalidating Objects

In addition to the invalidation methods provided by CloudFront, you can use the following third-party tools to invalidate objects.

**Note**
These tools were developed by third-party vendors who are not associated with Amazon Web Services. For information on how to use these tools, please refer to the vendor's documentation or contact the vendor.

- CloudBerry Explorer – http://cloudberrylab.com
- Ylastic – http://ylastic.com
- Cyberduck – http://cyberduck.io
- CloudFront Invalidator – https://github.com/swook/jQuery-CloudFront-Invalidator
- CDN Planet CloudFront Purge Tool – http://www.cdnplanet.com/tools/cloudfront-purge-tool/

You can also search for code samples on Github, https://github.com. Search for the phrase *CloudFront invalidation*.

## Tools and Code Examples for Configuring Private Content

In addition to the methods provided by CloudFront, the following third-party tools provide web forms for configuring your distribution for private content. Some of the tools also provide web forms for creating signed URLs.

- **CloudBerry** – Supports configuring a distribution for private content and supports creating signed URLs.

  For information about using CloudBerry for CloudFront private content, go to How to Configure Private Content for CloudFront Streaming with CloudBerry.

  For information on setting a default root object, see How to set CloudFront Default Object with CloudBerry S3 Explorer.

For more information about private content, see the blog post New Amazon CloudFront Feature: Private Content on the AWS blog.

For an example of how to use signed cookies, use your domain name in object URLs, and still use the SSL certificate for the cloudfront.net domain, see the Space Vatican blog post Using CloudFront Signed Cookies. This allows you to use an alternate domain name with HTTPS without incurring the expense of dedicated IP addresses or the limitations of SNI, as documented in Using Alternate Domain Names and HTTPS.

# Document History

The following table describes the latest important changes to the CloudFront documentation.

- **API Version:** 2017-10-30
- **Latest documentation update:** March 20, 2018

| Change | Description | Date Changed |
|---|---|---|
| New Feature | Lambda@Edge now enables you to further customize the delivery of content stored in an Amazon S3 bucket, by allowing you to access additional whitelisted headers, including custom headers, within origin-facing events. For more information, see these examples showing personalization of content based on viewer location and viewer device type. | March 20, 2018 |
| New Feature | You can now use Amazon CloudFront to negotiate HTTPS connections to origins using Elliptic Curve Digital Signature Algorithm (ECDSA). ECDSA uses smaller keys that are faster, yet, just as secure, as the older RSA algorithm. For more information, see Supported SSL/TLS Protocols and Ciphers for Communication Between CloudFront and Your Origin and About RSA and ECDSA Ciphers. | March 15, 2018 |
| New Feature | Lambda@Edge enables you to customize error responses from your origin, by allowing you to execute Lambda functions in response to HTTP errors that Amazon CloudFront receives from your origin. For more information, see these examples showing redirects to another location and response generation with 200 status code (OK). | December 21, 2017 |

| Change | Description | Date Changed |
|---|---|---|
| New Feature | A new CloudFront capability, field-level encryption, helps you to further enhance the security of sensitive data, like credit card numbers or personally identifiable information (PII) like social security numbers. For more information, see Using Field-Level Encryption to Help Protect Sensitive Data. | December 14, 2017 |
| Doc history archived | Older doc history was archived. | December, 2017 |

# AWS Glossary

For the latest AWS terminology, see the AWS Glossary in the *AWS General Reference*.